The Bloodybacks

The Bloodybacks

The British Serviceman in North America
and the Caribbean 1655-1783

Reginald Hargreaves

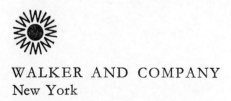

WALKER AND COMPANY
New York

For
Major JOHN CAMPBELL ALGER
United States Army (Ret)
Amicus vitæ solatium

Acknowledgments

I AM UNDER the very greatest obligation to Miss Kathleen M. Withy, B.A., for her invaluable help in preparing the manuscript, bibliography and index. I am also most grateful to Mr D. W. King, O.B.E., F.L.A., for his ever-ready counsel and practical assistance; to David Erskine, Naval Archivist, and the members of the Library Staff of the Royal United Service Institution, as to the Staff of the Public Record Office. A special word of thanks is due to Mr G. E. White, F.L.A., North Regional Librarian, Hampshire County Library, as to Vice-Admiral Sir Aubrey Mansergh, K.B.E., C.B., D.S.C., R.N., Brigadier John Stephenson, O.B.E., and Mr T. H. McGuffie, M.A., F.R.Hist. S.

For permission to quote from the respective works cited I am greatly indebted to the following authors and publishers: to Professor John W. Shy and the Princeton University Press for an extract from *Toward Lexington*; to Arthur Bernon Tourtellot, Doubleday and Company and Hutchinson and Company for comments in *William Diamond's Drum*; to J. Clarence Webster, and the Ryerson Press, Toronto, for the *Journal of Jeffrey Amhurst*, to Macmillan and Company for my citations from the late Sir John Fortescue's monumental *History of the British Army*; to the Kennikat Press of Port Washington, New York, for *Letters of German Troops* (originally published in 1924 and released in 1964 by the Kennikat Press); to Jonathan Cape and Company for the *Journal of Nicholas Creswell*; to the Harvard University Press, of Cambridge,

Massachusetts, for the *Diary of Frederick Mackenzie*; and to the Manchester University Press for *Letters from America*.

To my numerous kindly hosts in the United States, whose ready cooperation enabled me to view for myself many of the localities with which my narrative is concerned, my indebtedness is beyond adequate expression.

'It is with His Majesty's Navies, Ships of War, and forces by sea, under the good Providence and Protection of God, that the Wealth, Safety and Strength of this Kingdom is so much concerned.'

Articles of War, 1661

'Nothing has ever been made until the soldier has made safe the field where the building shall be built, and the soldier is the scaffolding until it has been built; and the soldier gets no reward but honour.'

Eric Linklater, *Crisis in Heaven*

Contents

Introduction

'The blood of English shall manure the ground.'
Richard II, Act iv, Scene 1

THERE ARE FEW quarters of the globe, few seas, however distant, that the British Serviceman has not penetrated at one time or another in the faithful fulfilment of his duty. The sweltering plains of India, the whip-lash of an Atlantic gale, the dreary heights before Sevastopol, the smiling sunshine of the Mediterranean, Lisbon's great harbour, the dusty highways of the Iberian peninsula, and, time and time again, the war-worn cockpit of Europe and the guardian Channel waters – in their turn he has known them all.

Cromwell's quarrel with Spain took the first orthodox British expeditionary force across the Atlantic; and for the succeeding hundred and fifty-nine years the Officers and men of the two Fighting Services made increasingly intimate acquaintance with the North American mainland, as with the Caribbean and its islands.

It is with the activities of the successive generations of redcoats and bluejackets serving in this particular latitude that the following pages are concerned; and whenever possible, and appropriate, the testimony of actual participants in the events described has been resorted to. In this particular, although in the period under review literacy was any-thing but widespread, diligent search will unearth quite a fair number of personal memoirs and letters attributable to the military. But similar material from the pen of the seafarer has been singularly hard to trace. The explanation for this curious imbalance in the literary output of the two Services can, I think, be accounted for if proper allowance be made for the widely differing circumstances in which the soldier and the sailor wrought out their days, and the nature of their respective task schedules. The late Major Guy du Maurier once observed that the soldier's life on active service consisted of 'long periods of utter boredom interspersed with moments of intense fright'. In other words, when not on the line of march or in actual contact with the enemy, he has ample time on his hands in which, if he be that way inclined, to put pen to paper. The sailor, on the other hand, has always been kept busy — more especially in the days of sail. Moreover, in the period with which this narrative is concerned, the watch below pigged it in cramped, overcrowded quarters where personal privacy, let alone reasonable quiet, were out of the question. To this dissimilarity in their respective environments and modes of daily life must be attributed the marked discrepancy in the soldier's and the sailor's literary output.

Early in the autumn of 1914 Kaiser Wilhelm II promulgated an Order of the Day addressed to his troops, in which he referred to General French's *verächtlich kleines Heer* — 'General French's contemptibly small force'. Misinterpreted as General French's *verächtliches kleines Heer* — 'contemptible little army' — it endowed the men of the original B.E.F. with that sobriquet of 'Old Contemptibles' in which their wry sense of humour took so genuine a pride.

In much the same way the men of the British Regiments left in North America after the expulsion of the French from Canada found a perverse satisfaction in referring to themselves as 'the Bloodybacks' — the somewhat opprobrious term with which they had been dubbed by the New Englanders in general and the Bostonians in particular. It was not long before the mariners serving in H.M. ships — equally well acquainted with the excoriating effect of the lash — also claimed to share in a *cognomen* which, originating as a term of contempt, had been adopted by those at whom the jeer had been directed with something little short of sardonic relish. (The sailor also responded to the nickname of 'Limey', in reference to his regular consumption of lime juice as a prophylactic against scurvy; but he undoubtedly qualified as a genuine 'Bloodyback'.)

The British Serviceman has always held by his own scale of values and cultivated his own dour but imperturbable sense of humour; both of which have served him well in more tight corners than there are fine days in an English summer.

What follows is the story of his activities in a land, and its adjacent waters, from which he took his professional departure—save for one brief but infinitely regrettable interlude in 1812–1814—a little over a century and three-quarters ago. This involves taking into consideration the whole story of the War of Independence; ground upon which it behoves the historian, like Agag, to 'walk delicately'.

My own interest in the subject was first aroused when, in the Spring of 1918, I was privileged to undertake a certain amount of liaison work with a United States infantry formation, newly arrived in France and headed by an up-and-coming young Officer, Douglas MacArthur. Since then my interest in this particular period of American history has never waned: it has indeed remained a subject of constant study. As the outcome of that study I firmly proclaim myself—as a certain distinguished American President once professed himself in an entirely different context—a 'darned neutral'. If criticism is indulged in during the course of my exposition, it is entirely without bias: double-barrelled would perhaps be the best term for it, since it is discharged with complete impartiality. For, most emphatically, I refuse to take sides.

If this leaves me open to be sniped at by *both* sides, so be it. Time's perspective shall be my justification.

Nowadays, the Bloodybacks' presence on the other side of the Atlantic, either as friend or foe, is little remembered. Indeed, there are few passers-by, even among his own itinerant fellow-countrymen, to pause and ponder the inscription on the grave of those of his kind who fell at Concord Bridge.

> They came three thousand miles, and died
> To keep the past upon the Throne;
> Unheard, beyond the ocean tide,
> The English mother made her moan.

American hands have tended these Bloodybacks' last resting-place, watching over it with increasing solicitude and care as old enmities burnt themselves out and the spirit of kinship—cemented in two world conflicts—arose from the scattered embers.

Were they alive today, the Bloodybacks of Concord would be the first to welcome the metamorphosis with a grunt of unqualified approval.

Reginald Hargreaves.

Part One

Outposts of Empire

'It is the sinfullest thing in the world to forsake
or destitute a Plantation once in forwardness: for
besides the dishonour, it is the guiltiness of blood
of many commiserable persons.'

Francis Bacon (Of Plantations)

I

Early Days

> 'And consequently it is a precept or generall rule of Reason, that every man ought to endeavour Peace, as far as he has hope of obtaining it; and when he cannot obtain it, that he may seek and use all helps and advantages of Warre.'
>
> *Thomas Hobbes*

THE COUNTRY which fails to expand rarely remains static; almost invariably it contracts, diminishing steadily in consequence and prosperity. The traditional method of expansion was, of course, to found overseas settlements in some sparsely populated and hitherto unexploited land.

With venturers going forth to establish such settlements, the question arose of the degree of responsibility the Motherland should assume for the protection of those selfsame colonies, at least throughout their early formative years.

Whatever the abstract judgement on the matter, in practical terms, so far as the pristine North American Plantations were concerned, England was too distracted by political upheaval and civil war on her own soil to afford that protective guardianship of which her voluntary expatriates so often stood in need. In Virginia and New England there were no standing regular forces to stave off the forays of hostile Redskins, no permanent Fighting Marine to cope with raids on water-borne commerce staged in turn by Spanish and Dutch privateers, as by piratical sea-rovers 'sailing on the account'.

Where the Red Indians were concerned, the settlers could look for no better protection than could be afforded by the armed bands got together by Captain John Smith for the defence of the settlements on the James river and the Chesapeake, and those similar bodies raised in New England by Miles Standish, who had seen service in the

19

Netherlands, Daniel Patrick and Captain John Underhill, who had fought in Ireland, Spain and the Low Countries.

In the wild new land in which he had made his home, practically every man owned a firearm, and necessity had taught him the use of it. And thus was born the image of the 'embattled farmer' so dear to the trans-Atlantic heart; whose ideal has always been the sturdy Cincinnatus, ready at any moment to exchange the plough for the musket, in preference to that costly incubus upon the body politic and potential 'instrument of tyranny', the Regular soldier. One of the most deep-rooted of American prejudices, this blind distrust of the professional fighting man, was epitomized by Governor Winthrop's unconsciously self-revelatory comment, 'To erect a standing authority of military men might even overthrow the civil power'—and in the process considerably circumscribe the arbitrary authority wielded with such enormous self-satisfaction by Governor John Winthrop![1]

But even in its most elementary form warfare is a corporate activity, demanding for its effective prosecution both discipline and training. In due course, therefore, organized bodies of militia were formed in all vulnerable areas, with a muster for instruction every Sunday, at the outset, and much recourse to such counsel as could be derived from study of Feuquières' military treatise in translation. It was, perhaps, the Ancient and Honourable Artillery Company of Boston which first demonstrated the value of steady training and proper integration. Established in 1638 by Ronald Cady and Robert Keayne, an erstwhile householder of Windsor and member of the City of London's venerable volunteer formation of similar title, it was probably the most efficient body of citizen soldiers in North America.

But enthusiasm for regular instruction soon waned, until compulsory parades were reduced to three a year; and in general 'training was of the most meagre character. Officers were political appointees, or else they were elected by their own men on a popularity basis; most of them being entirely unfitted for any military task.'[2]

With civil war raging in the Mother-country, the attitude of the New England and the more southerly Plantations towards the respective parties to the contest differed widely. While the Puritan settlements fully sympathized with Parliament's anti-monarchism, it as strongly dis-

---

[1] John Winthrop (1588–1649), Governor of Massachusetts Bay Colony from 1629 to 1649.

[2] *A Compact History of the United States Army*, Colonel R. Ernest Dupuy.

approved of the military autocracy which was rapidly replacing it. In the circumstances the temptation to sever all ties with the homeland was not to be resisted, and the Massachusetts Assembly lost no time in declaring the absolute independence of the New England Plantations, basing their fiat, ironically enough, on the somewhat ambiguous terms of a Royal Charter whose validity at other times they had never hesitated to call into question.

But to aspire to independence before means of self-protection have been perfected is to court disaster; as the massacre of seven hundred settlers by the Indians on the Maundy Thursday of 1644 had only too starkly demonstrated. Moreover, only deliberate myopia could have ignored the increasing hold on Manhattan and the Hudson by the Dutch; the island having been purchased from the Indians in 1626 for sixty guilders' worth of trade goods.[1]

Virginia and Maryland, on the other hand, like the West Indian islands of Antigua, Bermuda, St Kitts, Nevis and Barbados, had remained predominantly Royalist in sympathy; although the last-named had been reduced to sullen acceptance of the Cromwellian regime by an expedition under the command of the Parliamentary General-at-Sea, Sir George Ayscue.

In effect, only a combination of cajolery, covert threat and economic pressure sufficed to persuade the Colonists to pay at least lip service to the overriding suzerainty of the English Commonwealth and subsequent Protectorate.

Then in 1655,

> Venables and Penn,
> Two bloody-minded men,
> In an evil hour
> The seas did explore,
> And blund'ring about
> A cursed hole found out.[2]

In effect, Cromwell's quarrel with Spain had brought an expedition to the West Indies intent on the capture of San Domingo as a stepping-stone for further conquests on the mainland. Should the venture prove successful it would be far easier to furnish armed protection for the Chesapeake tobacco fleet in its passage across the Atlantic, as also for the burgeoning trade carried on by Newfoundland and New England

---

[1] Approximately the equivalent of twenty-four dollars.
[2] A rhyme concocted by one of the crew serving under Admiral William Penn.

with the British possessions in the West Indies. Furthermore, the transport of Massachusetts' and New Hampshire's invaluable naval stores—
masting, ship's timber, turpentine and tar[1]—to England's dockyards
would be under far more reliable guardianship.

The organization of the enterprise, however, had demanded very
considerable effort. For to fit out two fleets of forty and of twenty-five
vessels for an expedition to tropic waters three thousand miles distant
was to strain available dockyard resources almost to the point of exhaustion. Moreover, the medley of '3,000 land souldiers in six regiments and
100 Horse' scarcely represented the 'New Model' Army at its best.[2]

Recruited and trained in 1645 by Fairfax, Cromwell and dour,
tobacco-chewing George Monck, the 'New Model' had been put on a
sound organizational footing by the experienced Philip Skippon,
veteran of the Hispano-Dutch wars in the Netherlands. Expertly drilled,
strictly disciplined, 'they had new red coats given them, for the terrible
name thereof';[3] and although it had been necessary to resort to con-
scription to maintain the ranks up to full strength, the hard core of the
force were 'men who made some conscience of what they did; men
who knew what they fought for, and loved what they knew'.

For the expedition to San Domingo, however, Cromwell had committed the egregious error of withholding complete regiments, under
their own Officers, and substituting hastily improvised corps made up
in part of 'a sad miscellany of broken Royalists, unruly Levellers, and
the like'[4]—many of whom had preferred service in the ranks to imprisonment—with some thousand raw recruits enlisted at Barbados.
Of these last Venables sourly commented that they were 'bold to do
mischief, not to be commanded as souldiers, nor to be kept in any civil
order; being the most profane debauched persons that ever we saw,
scorners of religion, indeed men so loose as not to be kept under discipline and so cowardly as not to be made to fight'.[5] A lawless rabble
such as this placed a heavy burden on the expedition's ration strength
while in no way adding to its military efficiency.

The distribution of command was equally faulty. The military Com-

---

[1] These stores were a valuable source of income to New England. In 1553, for example,
the Parliamentary Council of State placed an order with certain traders for 10,000 barrels
of tar and £5,000 worth of ship's timber.

[2] Henry Whistler, *Journal of the West Indian Expedition*, B.M. Sloane MS. 3926.

[3] James Heath, *Chronicles*. Here may be found the origin of the term 'Redcoat' to describe
the British soldier.

[4] Thomas Carlyle, *Cromwell*.   [5] *Narrative of General Venables*, edited C. H. Firth.

mander-in-Chief was Robert Venables, whose ability to hunt down
Tories in Ireland constituted his only claim to martial fame. Admiral
William Penn, on the other hand, had rendered outstanding service in
the recent war against the Dutch and could be regarded as thoroughly
reliable. Matters were further complicated, however, by the presence of
a trio of Civil Commissioners, whose responsibility it was to ensure
that the State should have its due share of such profits, in the way of
booty, as the venture might yield. Lastly, Venables was accompanied
by his wife, Elizabeth, a virago whose ability to set everyone at loggerheads amounted to perverted genius.

Gladly turning its back on its assembly area in Barbados—tersely
described by Henry Whistler as 'the dunghill whereon England doth
cast forth its rubbish'—in due course the expedition arrived off San
Domingo, with everyone 'big with expectation of gold told up in
bags'.[1] In the general excitement, the fact was lost sight of that since
leaving Barbados the fleet had become separated from its victualling
hulks, and that food was fast running short. In any case the provisions
furnished by General Desborough were of the poorest quality and
almost inedible; while at Barbados the only replenishments had come
from stocks which had been rejected in England and sent out hopefully
by the victuallers to seek a less fastidious market in the West Indies.
On passage from Barbados, half rations had been the order of the day,
of which the bread or biscuit was 'most beastly rotten', so that on
making their landfall the men were already badly undernourished.

Then, on the eve of attempting a forced landing, a bitter dispute arose
over the plunder which it was expected the city would yield. The Civil
Commissioners insisted that 'all preys and booties got by sea or land'
should 'be employed for the public service'. Venables protested, vehem-
ently supported by his wife. 'Ships and large quantities of treasure captured in towns or forts might be so disposed of,' he argued, 'but to
attempt to reserve captured property of every kind, or all sorts of
pillage, for that purpose would disgust both soldiers and Officers, and
cause a mutiny. For this was so contrary to what had been practised in
England', the leader further pointed out, 'that I doubted it would be
impossible to satisfy them.'[2]

In this contention Venables was fully supported by precedent. The
Cromwellian soldier, whatever his other concessions to Puritan austerity,
held tenaciously to the medieval tradition regarding the man-at-arms'

---

[1] Letter of Colonel Thomas Modyford. [2] *The Narrative of General Venables.*

right to 'lawful plunder'. After the battle of Naseby in June 1645, for example, the *Moderate Intelligencer*[1] reported that, 'We hear that Cromwell's regiment have grown wise, for having helped to beat the enemy out of the field, they did not, as at Marston Moor, leave them that fought least to get most, but fell on the good booty as well as others; some had jewels, others diamond rings, some were content with silver, good apparel, horses, or what else they could get.' Again, at the storming of Dundee, in 1651, the troops 'had the plunder of the town for all that day and night'; while the ships in the harbour had been reserved for sale for the benefit of the officers; George Monck waxing highly indignant when the Commissioners with the Army sought to dispose of the vessels for the benefit of the State. As for the seamen, the hope of prize money of one sort or another had always been regarded as a rightful compensation for their meagre wage, and the harsh, disease-ridden conditions they were called upon to endure on shipboard.

Ultimately, therefore, the Commissioners were forced to agree that 'lawful plunder' should be permitted so long as they, in the name of the State, had first call on such major booty as might fall into the conquerors' possession. This was better than nothing, although a great deal less than the man in the ranks and before the mast had been looking forward to so eagerly.

It followed that neither the sailor nor the soldiery were in particularly enthusiastic mood by the time a landing had been effected 'at Punto de Nazao, about seven leagues westward of San Domingo'. Once ashore, instead of pushing forward rapidly, with an advance guard and flankers out to afford maximum protection against surprise, 'the souldiers brought forth a large statue of the Virgin Mary, well accoutred, and pelted her to death with oranges. Heere they also found a black Virgin Mary to inveigle the blackes to worship.'[2]

Persuaded ultimately to take the line of march, the troops speedily found themselves entangled in a virtually trackless forest, thick with hampering undergrowth. Since Venables had omitted to equip the troops with 'blackjacks' (water bottles) everyone was soon suffering from raging thirst. 'Thus wee lay without water', recorded Adjutant-General Jackson, 'ready to perish, and worn with hunger and lack of sleep, till about midnight [when] wee drew off.' In the outcome, the leading body of troops under Jackson's immediate command fell into

---

[1] The issue for 19th to 26th June, 1945.
[2] Rawlinson MS., D. 1208, I, 62 (Bodleian library).

an ambush. Spanish lances speedily proved their superiority over the top-heavy English pike; and the survivors of the advance party fled in panic — the Adjutant-General well in the lead — throwing the main body into inextricable confusion.

With that, operations came to an end, in a welter of dispute and mutual recrimination. The soldiery had been unsuccessful in securing their objective, and by their failure had deprived the seamen of their expected plunder. The public disgrace of the peccant Adjutant-General — who had his sword broken over his head and was degraded to the lowly standing of 'an abject pioneer' — did nothing to distract attention from the inescapable fact that the whole muddled venture had been a pitiable fiasco; with Mistress Venables's burden of complaint so shrill and all-embracing that one of the Commissioners wrote hastily to Cromwell begging him never again to permit a General's wife to accompany her husband on active service.[1]

With tropical fever taking an increasing toll of the disgruntled men, so that the death-roll swiftly mounted to two hundred a day,[2] it was obvious that nothing more of any value could be attempted in San Domingo. So in sour defeat and blistering humiliation what was left of the expedition took to its ships and set sail for Jamaica. Here the bold front assumed by an unhampered Admiral Penn led to the island's easy capture. A small garrison was left in occupation — to sicken and die of endemic fever within a very few weeks — while the main armament trailed gloomily homewards to face the wrath of an outraged Lord Protector. The incarceration of Penn and Venables in the Tower of London led nowhere, since the Civil Commissioners very uncivilly attributed the failure of the enterprise to the constant criticism and unending stream of misguided counsel forthcoming from the self-opinionated Mistress Venables.

In plain truth, from the outset the organization of the expedition was as negligent and defective as the subsequent leadership was fumbling and spiritless, while fomenting extremely bad blood between the Army and the Navy. Altogether, Britain's first attempt to furnish protection for her North American settlements could scarcely be ranked as anything but a humiliating failure.

When 'the King came into his own again' as Charles II rode through

---

[1] Lillington's *Narrative*.
[2] *Journal of the English Army in the West Indies*, Marl. Miscell. VI.

the streets of London on that sparkling May morning of 1660, neither
the joyful ringing of the bells nor the frenzied acclamations of the
crowd could obscure the uncompromising fact that England's Treasury
harboured no more than the derisory sum of £11 2s 10d.[1] Moreover,
the extravagance and economic ineptitude which had characterized the
Commonwealth and Protectorate had left the country saddled with outstanding liabilities totalling £1,888,352, of which the Navy debt accounted for no less than £1,250,000; wages alone being in arrear to the
tune of £354,000. The cost of the upkeep of Cromwell's useless trophy
of Dunkirk stood at £130,000 *per annum*;[2] while the late Lord Protector's many unsettled obligations included the sum of £19,303 for his
wantonly grandiose State funeral.

A steady expansion of the country's industry and overseas commerce
was clearly essential; although this would inevitably clash with the
Dutch, still resentful of the restrictions imposed by the Cromwellian
Navigation Act, but stubbornly determined to create a monopoly in
the spice market, while securing the lion's share of the world's highly
lucrative maritime carrying trade.

In the general plans for building up the country's home and overseas
commerce the Commissioners of Customs were quick to point out that,
'the Plantations are His Majesty's Indies, without charge to him raised
and supported by his English subjects, who employ above two hundred
sail of good ships every year, and begin to grow into commodities of
great value and esteem'.[3]

In any case the King was determined that the North American Plantations—loyal Virginia in particular—should not be overlooked in the
general design to create 'a marine empire, the different members of
which should stand to each other as do Yorkshire and Lancashire'.

Where Virginia was concerned, even when the Lord Protector had
sent a powerful fleet into the Chesapeake to 'bring the people of the
Plantation to a proper sense of their duty', so strong had been royalist
sentiment that the show of resistance the settlers had made under their
Governor, Sir William Berkeley, had been sufficiently resolute to win
them an 'agreement' by which, although nominally subject to Parliamentary control, 'the liberties of the Colonists were more fully secured

---

[1] cf. Sir Arthur Bryant, *King Charles II*.

[2] Without the support of Calais, Dunkirk was valueless as a war-time port and in any
case its waters were too shallow to harbour vessels of any but the lightest draught.

[3] Acts of the Privy Council, Colonial Series (1613–1680).

than they had ever been. Indeed, they were allowed all the rights which the Declaration of Independence a century and a quarter later charged the King of Great Britain with violating.'[1] With 'Tumble-down Dick's' bankrupt regime reeling towards ruin and oblivion, 'Berkeley proclaimed the exiled Monarch, and issued writs for an Assembly in the name of the King'.[2] With due formality Charles II had been hailed as Sovereign of England, Scotland, Ireland, *and Virginia*; in acknowledgment of which the still expatriated Monarch had given orders for the armorial bearings of the Old Dominion to be quartered with those of the other three countries in the national flag. In response, the Assembly had despatched an embassy to Breda to invite the royal exile to cross the seas to become in actual fact King of Virginia. Indeed, Charles had been on the point of sailing for America when the summons had come which restored him to the throne of his forefathers.

Despite his casual manner and deceptive air of indolence, Charles had a remarkably long memory — both for injuries inflicted and benefits conferred. If he felt less warmly for disapproving puritan New England than for loyal Virginia, he was far too shrewd not to recognize that, where their well-being and progress were concerned, all the Plantations were interdependent.

But the Old Dominion was separated from the New England settlements by the alien enclave of the New Netherlands, with New Amsterdam, perched on the tip of Manhattan Island, serving as a port of entry to territory which extended up the River Hudson to Fort Orange (Albany) in a domain famous for its beaver meadows. Founded by the Dutch West Indies Company, the neighbouring Swedish Colony on the Delaware had been forcibly incorporated in the Corporation's territory in 1655.

Although the New Englanders had regarded the region to their south-west as theirs to exploit in due course, they sought to make the best of their 'Butterbox' neighbours established in the Hudson and Manhattan Island. But the Hollanders' reprehensible habit of exchanging weapons and powder for the Indian's skins, their unscrupulous trading methods, their incurable tendency to afford sanctuary to refugees from New England justice, and their arbitrary seizure of the Swedish settlements on the Delaware, combined to foster an attitude of wary hostility on the part of the inhabitants of Massachusetts and

[1] B. J. Lossing, *Field Book of the Revolution.*
[2] *ibid.*

Connecticut, which the unaccommodating posture adopted by Petrus Stuyvesant, Governor of New Amsterdam, did nothing to conciliate.

In 1664, with hostilities clearly impending with the Dutch, the King wisely took time by the forelock and authorized two strokes against them; the first, an expedition, under Sir Robert Holmes, against the Hollander possessions on the Guinea Coast; the second an attempt to seize New Amsterdam. If and when acquired, administration of the territory between the Connecticut river and the Delaware was to be entrusted to the King's brother, James, Duke of York and Albany.

It was only fitting, therefore, that command of the enterprise against New Amsterdam should be entrusted to the Duke's Groom of the Bed-chamber, Colonel Richard Nicolls, who was endowed with a warrant to raise the number of troops necessary to ensure the mission's success.

At the Restoration such few armed forces as were still in being were lacking in anything approaching a centralized organization.

The Fleet, consisting of 135 warships of all rates, totalling some 25,000 tons, was in urgent need of re-fitting. But dearth of money hampered the work of rehabilitation in every department. For such was the lack of funds that 'the credit of the Navy office', as the young Samuel Pepys glumly recorded, 'was brought so low that none will sell anything without our personal security given for same'. When the Queen Mother crossed the Channel to visit her son there was not enough powder in the warships' magazine even to fire a Royal Salute. But with the capable James, Duke of York, as Lord High Admiral and head of a newly constituted and thoroughly efficient Navy Board, the very best use was made of such money as a parsimonious House of Commons could be persuaded to part with; and gradually the Royal Navy, as it had become, was restored to something like the combat efficiency it had known on the outbreak of the first Anglo-Dutch war in 1652.

So far as the land forces were concerned, it behoved the King to 'walk delicately'. The prejudice against the maintenance of any standing military force, entertained by a large section of the population, had been strongly reinforced by the employment of the redcoats—under the Cromwellian 'rule of the Major Generals'—as vigilantes. Empowered to enforce puritan legislation against travelling or cooking a meal on the Sabbath, or even 'walking abroad for pleasure', the ill repute they had acquired as law-enforcement minions was not easy to live down. In the main, such elements of the 'New Model' Army as survived were only awaiting disbursement of their arrears of pay to undergo demobilization; although George Monck's Coldstream Regiment solemnly mustered on Tower Hill to lay down its arms as a Commonwealth formation – and as solemnly picked them up again, amidst great rejoicing, as the Lord General's Regiment of Foot Guards.[1] Certain Cavaliers, who had constituted themselves the King's personal bodyguard during his years of exile, joined with the officers and men withdrawn from the garrisoning of Dunkirk to form the 1st of Grenadier Foot Guards; while two Regiments of Life Guards and one of Horse Guards – Lord Oxford's 'Blues' – completed the establishment of the Household Troops. Their duties were to hold the Tower of London, Windsor and Portsmouth, and guard the King's person; while they could be 'employed as police or thief-takers, patrolling the high roads, suppressing conventicles, and at the London playhouses keeping the peace'.[2]

The dowry brought to the King by his Consort, Catherine of Braganza, included the lonely outpost of Tangier. Surrounded by warlike Moors, the city obviously needed a garrison. So a request was made to Louis XIV to restore the Regiment of Douglas, the representatives of the Scots Brigade of Gustavus Adolphus, more recently hired in the French service. Thus in due course 'Pontius Pilate's Bodyguard' – as the Regiment was somewhat ironically termed in reference to its claim to antiquity – took its place as the 1st Foot, or Royal Scots. To enable the Scots to be retained on the Home Establishment two further formations were raised, for garrisoning Tangier. These were the 1st or Royal Dragoons and the 2nd or Queen's Regiment of Foot.

Since experience in the first Anglo-Dutch war had demonstrated the value of controlled musketry on shipboard when rival fleets became embroiled in a general *mêlée*, in 1664 authority was given for the formation of the Duke of York and Albany's Maritime Regiment of Foot. Originally dubbed 'Neptune's Bodyguard' and sometimes referred to as the Yellow Regiment on the score of its yellow uniform jacket, in these days it is better known as the Royal Marines – or more familiarly as the 'Jollies', or the 'Leathernecks'.

In 1666, on the entry of the French into the Anglo-Dutch war, the Privy Council commissioned Sir Tobias Bridge to raise and command a garrison battalion of 800 men for the defence of Barbados, the Motherland's most valuable possession in the Caribbean. But this formation received no permanent designation.

[1] At the Restoration Monck had been ennobled as the Duke of Albemarle.
[2] Public Record Office Warrant Books

With hostilities pending against the Dutch which might easily include the attempted invasion of British soil,[1] the total of troops available, even allowing for a certain amount of support from a reorganized militia, made no provision for such forces as would be needed for an expedition overseas.

In the circumstances Nicolls was empowered to raise three detachments to supplement the crews of the trio of warships earmarked for the venture. There was little difficulty in enrolling the necessary men, despite the recent legislation permitting ex-soldiers to follow a guild-protected craft without first having undergone apprenticeship to it.[2] There were plenty of veterans of the civil war only too ready to take up arms again. So on 25th February Colonel Legg, Lieutenant of the Ordnance, was authorized to issue '500 firelocks, 500 matchlocks, 50 carabines, with pikes, pistols, a mortar, powder, match and ball, spades, shovels and harness'. Four days later the Clerk of the Signet was directed to disburse £4,000 to the Treasurer of the Navy on Nicoll's behalf, by way of meeting immediate expenses.

On 23rd April Nicolls—already appointed Deputy Governor of the settlement he was yet to capture—received his final orders. These included instructions 'to discourse [with the New England leaders] on the best means to reduce the Dutch on Long Island', and 'to see that the Act of Navigation be punctually observed'.

After ten weeks at sea the expedition arrived at its destination; and Nicolls hastened to take counsel of Winthrop, Governor of Connecticut, and some of Massachusetts' leading citizens, as to the best plan to be pursued.

New Amsterdam was furnished with a fort and enclosed by a stout palisade.[3] But it was useless for Stuyvesant to bluster that he 'had a commission to fight against such as shall disturb our settlement'. The inhabitants' reluctance to meet the cost of their upkeep had reduced the militia to a mere handful; half the members of which had long since traded the muskets issued to them for the furs brought in by the local Indians. Moreover, Nicolls's expeditionary force had been readily reinforced by a body of volunteers from Connecticut and a further two hundred from Massachusetts. Against a combined force of close on

---

[1] In July 1667 an actual attempt was made by the Dutch to seize Landguard Fort, in the Harwich estuary, as a *point d'appui* for a full-scale invasion. It was beaten off with heavy loss to the would-be invaders.

[2] By the terms of 12 Car. II, cap. 16.

[3] Wall Street commemorates the siting of his palisade.

two thousand, Stuyvesant could muster no more than one hundred men, plus two hundred and fifty citizens capable of bearing arms, but of doubtful loyalty and scant enthusiasm for hazarding their skins. Above all, there was an entire want of any communal spirit of resistance. With Hollander, Swede, Jew, and Quaker, and Anabaptist English, there was no unity of race, religion, language or common purpose. Moreover, the report the Governor received from his master-gunner that, 'were I to commence firing in the morning, I should have used up all by noon', was a sufficiently stark indication that an effective defence was out of the question. The humiliation the Dutch had wrought on New Sweden was about to be done unto them.

It was useless for Stuyvesant to bluster to his unresponsive Council that he would sooner be carried out dead than surrender; for their part they were far more minded to surrender than to risk the slightest chance of being carried out injured, let alone dead. All too alluring was Governor Winthrop's advice to his friends amongst the township's inhabitants, to 'seek peace rather than to court destruction'.

With the British warships menacing the township from their moorings in Gravesend Bay, and the New England militia strongly encamped near Breukelen (Brooklyn), Nicolls informed the deputation that waited on him that his demand was for the immediate acknowledgement of English sovereignty, and the surrender of 'all forts, towns or places of strength'. In return he would 'confirm and secure every man in his estate, life and liberty'. Refusal of the offer would entail 'all the miseryes of warr, which they bring upon themselves'.

With this, Stuyvesant, to prevent 'the effusion of Christian blood', agreed to capitulate on the terms nominated; and the next day the garrison — such as it was — marched out of the works 'with drums beating, Colours flying, and with lighted matches'.

With no more than a parade of strength and determination New Amsterdam had been metamorphosed into New York; the seaboard of New England had been linked with that of Maryland and Virginia; while the predominance of the English stock throughout the burgeoning Plantations had been assured.

By the Treaty of Breda, of July 1667, which brought the Second Dutch War to a close, Holland was compensated for the loss of the New Netherlands by her retention of tropical Surinam in Guiana. In 1673, during the course of the Third Anglo-Dutch War, the Hollanders again briefly occupied New York. But with the Peace of Nymeguen of 1678 the township and surrounding territory reverted to the English Crown to remain under its suzerainty for the succeeding century.

King Charles's design to create a 'marine empire' through the steady increase in the country's merchant fleet inevitably involved the retention of a Navigation Act originally conceived in the days of Richard II and more recently strengthened under the Commonwealth.[1] In expanding the measure, the trade of the Plantations was undoubtedly placed under such irksome restriction that the Colonists were very apt to lose sight of the fact that, although they might be circumscribed as to the markets in which they were free to trade, on the other hand they enjoyed a complete monopoly and assured sales in those to which they did have access.

Another and perhaps more legitimate ground for complaint was the high-handed manner in which some of the Royal Governors carried out their duties in their respective domains. In this respect Sir William Berkeley, for many years the representative of the home Government in Virginia, was certainly the target for a considerable measure of regional criticism. Accused of admitting to his intimacy only those few men of wealth and substance resident in the Colony, he was regarded with jealous suspicion by the ordinary run of the people whose confidence he had failed to retain through his later years of office. In any case they were extremely difficult folk to govern.

> A love of freedom inclining to anarchy pervaded the whole countryside. Among the people loyalty was a feebler passion than the love of liberty. Existence without government seemed to promise to the general mass a greater degree of happiness than the tyranny of the European governments. Men feared injustice more than they did disorder. It was among such a people, which till the Restoration had found the wilderness a safe protection against tyranny, that the pressure of increasing grievances began to excite open discontent.[2]

Into this tense and potentially combustible community a dangerously volatile element was introduced with the arrival in the Colony in 1674 of a certain Nathaniel Bacon. The son of a well-to-do landowner of Suffolk, Bacon was described by his tutor at Cambridge[3] as 'a young

[1] See Appendix A.
[2] George Bancroft, *A History of the United States of America*.
[3] John Ray.

gentleman of good parts and quick wit', but as one who 'could not contain himself within bounds'. After leaving University, Bacon had read for the Bar just long enough to acquire legal glibness without any compensating forensic profundity. It was consequent on his involvement in a dubious complot to defraud an acquaintance out of a substantial slice of his patrimony that Bacon's father had endowed his enterprising offspring with £1,800 by way of capital, and hastily shipped him off in one of the tobacco fleet homeward bound for Virginia. Acquiring a 1,230 acre plantation at Curles Neck, Bacon was speedily honoured by appointment to the Council of State by favour of the Governor himself, whom Bacon could claim as a cousin by marriage.

For Virginia, 1675 was a year of widespread trade depression and straitened means. Legitimate trade with the Indian tribes was nearly at a standstill; and with the tobacco crop a failure, the settlers' concentration on the leaf's cultivation to the exclusion of any other product reduced many of the smaller landowners to a state of temporary poverty; in which a heavy rate of taxation, mostly for the upkeep of the militia, was an almost intolerable burden. Yet with the strife against the local Indians in New England liable to spread to the Virginian frontier, Berkeley would have been failing in his duty had he omitted to legislate for trouble on his own borders; hopeful as he might be that certain friendly tribes, such as the Pamunkeys, might exert a quietening influence on the more tempestuous of their neighbours. Conciliation was Berkeley's aim, but both his policy and the unprovocative measures of defence he had put in train came under violent abuse from the settlers on the borderlands. With Bacon as their vociferous spokesman, they demanded authority to organize themselves as vigilantes; and when a roving band of Susquehannas wantonly killed the overseer on the Bacon Plantation, the owner put himself at the head of three hundred armed men, and set off to punish the marauding 'Tawnies'.

By taking the law into his own hands, without any sort of commission from the Governor, Bacon had put himself entirely out of court; and Berkeley was left with no option but to denounce him as a rebel. Worse was to follow when it emerged that Bacon and his followers had not slain or wounded a single hostile Indian but 'had contented themselves with frightening away, killing, or enslaving most of the friendly neighbouring Indians, and taking their beaver skins and land as spoils'.[1] As the contemporary chronicler Philip Ludwell duly noted, 'wee have

[1] Wilcomb E. Washburn, *The Governor and the Rebel.*

not now that wee know of 100 Freind Indians on all our Borders, but at least 1500 more enemies than wee needed to have'.[1]

At the outset, however, the Governor's efforts to call the defiant Bacon to account were hamstrung by the lack of armed force to support his authority. The militia were in limited strength, with the majority of those available scattered at strategic points to ensure the frontier defence. Bacon, on the other hand, was at the head of a numerous armed mob aroused to such a pitch by their self-elected champion's strident demagogy that they not only returned him a burgess for Henrico County, but demanded that he be commissioned as nothing less than General-in-Command of all operations against the Indians.

For the moment the harassed Berkeley could do no more than temporize. The virus of insubordination had become epidemic, and popular resentment at the concentration of power in an oligarchy of the older and more responsible members of the Colony, and in the limitation of the franchise to freeholders, found widespread expression in unbridled tumult and open defiance of law and order.

Until support could be organized locally or be sent to him from England, the Governor had no option but to make a show of yielding. 'The Long Assembly was dissolved and a new one elected; new laws were granted; universal suffrage was endorsed; arbitrary taxation was abolished; and Bacon was appointed Commander-in-Chief';[2] although the Governor evinced a curious tardiness in appending his signature to the Commission which would accord official sanction to the Assembly's choice of military leader.

Fearing that he might yet be outwitted, Bacon assembled five hundred of his staunchest supporters, and with them at his heels marched off to Jamestown to demand that his Commission, duly endorsed, be handed over to him forthwith. Still playing for time, Berkeley presented him with the signed parchment. With this Bacon set off, ostensibly to deal with another marauding band of the Susquehannah.

With the prime fomenter of popular unrest temporarily out of the way, Berkeley boldly took the step of publishing a proclamation reversing all the recent enactments of the burgesses; once more declaring Bacon a traitor, and calling on all subjects loyal to the throne to rally to the defence of its duly appointed representatives. Upon this intel-

[1] Ludwell to Sir Henry Coventry, Secretary of State.
[2] B. J. Lossing, *Field Book of the Revolution*. An attempt was also made to introduce prohibition, but this was received with distinctly tempered enthusiasm.

ligence reaching him, an infuriated Bacon wheeled in his tracks and headed again for Jamestown, intent on the complete overthrow of the existent apparatus of government.

The resources at Berkeley's disposal were meagre. Less than a hundred men of the Virginia militia were available for his support; and such few Regulars as made up the Independent Company left behind by the Duke of York, after the loss and subsequent recovery of the township named after him, were unavailable, being split up between the metropolis on the Hudson and the frontier town of Albany. Temporarily the Governor removed himself to the relative safety of Accomac County, on the eastern shore of the Chesapeake. Writing to the Court of St James's to inform the authorities of the current state of affairs in Virginia, the aged and wearied veteran begged to be relieved of his post as soon as a successor could arrive to take over.

With the news that he had again been denounced as a rebel, a ranting, roaring Bacon had hurriedly turned back from the frontier and reached the Middle Plantation[1] on July 29th; his followers eagerly plundering the estates of Berkeley and his loyalist supporters in and about neighbouring Green Spring. On July 30th Bacon issued a bellicose counter-proclamation in which Berkeley and a number of his henchmen were commanded to surrender themselves and suffer the confiscation of their properties, on the score that they had shown themselves 'traytors to the People'. The Governor himself was accused of fomenting civil war by opposing Bacon's policy of extermination with regard to the Indians; and popular clamour urged the firebrand himself to set up his own civil government. It was further proposed that all householders should pledge themselves under oath to resist whatever force might be sent from England for Berkeley's support. Four ships in the James river were then seized and armed with ordnance from Jamestown fort; although one vessel subsequently contrived to escape and bring the Governor intelligence of all that had transpired at Jamestown, and of Bacon's renewed but entirely unwarranted onslaught against the inoffensive Pamunkeys.

For his part Berkeley, by authorizing the sharing of booty and promising to relieve volunteers of certain fiscal dues, had got together a sufficient number of loyalists and militia to encourage him into taking active steps for the rebellion's suppression. The first move was to re-capture the ships in the James river; the vessels gladly going over to the loyalists' side. Thereafter, a rabble of five hundred insurgents, under

[1] The site of Williamsburg.

Thomas Hansford, one of Bacon's lieutenants, was driven from Jamestown; which, on September 7th, was occupied and put in a state of defence by the Governor and three hundred armed loyalist supporters.

In England meanwhile preparations had promptly been put in hand to send Berkeley the armed support of which he was so patently in need. To this force the Foot Guards between them furnished a nucleus totalling 425 officers and men. The balance of the 1,130 troops assigned to the mission was made up of contingents from the Lord Admiral's Regiment (Marines), the 3rd Foot (the Buffs), the 8th Foot (King's Liverpool Regiment) and from certain unattached Garrison Companies. In command was Colonel Herbert Jeffreys; and since there was considerable uncertainty as to whether Berkeley were alive or dead, he was armed with a Commission to act, if necessary, as Lieutenant-Governor. He was supported by Sir John Berry, in control of the Naval escort, and by the agent for the Colony, Colonel Francis Moryson; the three of them being empowered to act as a Commission to enquire into all the circumstances of the rebellion. Preparations were hurried forward as expeditiously as possible, but it was not until December 3rd that three sloops of war, the *Bristol*, the *Rose* and the *Dartmouth*, left Deal harbour in company with the eight transports, after a delay of ten days attributable to the unfavourable but prevailing south-westerly wind. The *Rose*, running aground and damaging her rudder, was further delayed, and only caught up with her consorts as they were clearing the Channel's western approaches. Ahead of the convoy the 30-gun sloop *Concord*, commanded by Captain Thomas Grantham, was on steady passage across the Atlantic, bearing the news that succour was on its way.

Meanwhile Bacon and the more reckless of his followers had hurried to Jamestown, where they promptly laid the Governor and his garrison under close siege. Supplies were secured by raiding Berkeley's Green Spring plantation and the properties of his neighbours. The insurgent leader also seized the wives of several of the more prominent loyalists to serve as hostages, callously placing them on the earthwork ramparts, in full view of Jamestown's defenders, as his men laboured on the ditch they were digging to circumvallate the town's stockade.

It may have been with some idea of rescuing the helpless hostages that Berkeley ordered a sally against Bacon's lines of investment. But the stroke was as feebly delivered as it was ill organized; the loyalists, 'like scholers going to schoole, going out with heavie harts, but returned home with light heeles'.

With comprehensible distrust in his extemporized troops' fighting quality, Berkeley thereupon evacuated the capital, which was immediately occupied by Bacon and his followers. That night the rebel leader deliberately put the whole town to the torch — 'to prevent a future siege' — burning down the State House and the oldest church in the whole of the northern Colonies. From the ships in which they had taken refuge, Berkeley and his men watched in silence the lurid flames leap into the sky.

It was at this precarious juncture that the Governor was usefully reinforced by the arrival in the James river of the *Young Prince* of London, commanded by Captain Robert Morris; which, with Captain Nicholas Prynne's *Richard and Elizabeth*, added appreciably both to Berkeley's strength and his mobility. Indeed, the substantial aid afforded them by the captains and crews of these merchant craft was subsequently recognized by a memorandum of the Privy Council which warmly affirmed that 'the main service for reducing the rebels to their obedience was done by the seamen and commanders of ships then riding in the rivers', and recommended that they be suitably rewarded.[1]

Looting and sabotage had progressively dissipated such little discipline as Bacon had been able to impose on his followers; and such efforts as he made to hold them in check dwindled to vanishing point when the rebel leader, installed in the house of Major Thomas Pale on Portopotank Creek, was stricken with 'a Bloody Flux, a Lousy Disease, so that the swarmes of Vermyn that had bred in his Body he could not destroy but by throwing his Shirts into the Fire as often as he shifted himself'.[2]

On 26th October Bacon breathed his last curse and was hurried into an obscure grave which could never thereafter be identified.

With Bacon's death the flames of insurrection steadily subsided, although here and there the embers glowed ominously. In many instances they were firmly stamped out by Captain Grantham and his bluejackets, who had sailed into the York river on 21st November; although Berkeley's militia still encountered fierce resistance from certain scattered rebel bands.

Jeffreys and Berry, with the first contingent of troops, dropped anchor in the James river on 29th January, 1677; the balance of the force putting in an appearance on 11th February. Since they had arrived

[1] C.S.P. Col. 1674–1676, 1035.
[2] Charles McLean Andrews, *Narrative of the Insurrections*, 1675–1690.

too late actively to participate in the rebellion's suppression, there was little welcome for them even from the most law-abiding. For despite the fact that at the outset the redcoats found themselves 'quite destitute of quarters; no place fit to receive them',[1] and were forced to bivouac at the Governor's ruined plantation of Green Spring, the fear persisted that they would be billeted on the people and subsisted at the community's expense. Even when it became known that the Crown was prepared to compensate all those who furnished the troops with rations, the inhabitants' attitude of distrust and disfavour underwent little change for the better. Hostility to the professional fighting man — not the enemy of peace, but its ever-watchful guardian — had become instinctive, and was to harden into an inexpugnable tradition.

In all the controversy which speedily developed between the Governor and the members of the Commission of Enquiry as to who was responsible for what, who was to be penalized, who pardoned, and who rewarded, the members of the armed forces took no part. 'Theirs not to reason why', especially about matters that were outside their knowledge. Having no particular task to fulfil other than by their presence to serve as a reminder that rightful authority had been restored, they carried out their routine duties and made such comfort for themselves as they could.

In the May of 1677 an order arrived from Whitehall to send back all but a hundred men to act as a token force, and 'any others who of their own free will desire to stay as planters or servants'. There were not many to take advantage of this opportunity to settle in a new land. Save for a few 'details' despatched to replace casualties at St Kitts and Jamaica, the bulk of the troops boarded their transports, homeward bound, and very well content that matters had so fallen out.

Yet it is impossible not to reflect that had the mother country's military resources permitted the early stationing of a small body of British troops along the Virginia border, the whole unhappy business of the Bacon insurrection would almost certainly have been avoided. As it was, with Dutch hostility and Gallic duplicity to deal with, the authorities had been hard put to it to raise the necessary naval and military forces even for the homeland's own defence.

But at least Virginia's hour of distress and turmoil had not found the home government indifferent to her plight.

[1] Sir John Berry and Colonel Francis Moryson to Sir Joseph Williamson, Secretary of State.

2

His Majesty's Servants

'They are England's best answer of defence and weapon of offence.
If we may have peace, they have purchased it; if we must have war,
they will manage it.'

Robert Devereux, Earl of Essex

THE FIRST ATTEMPT to put England's Fighting Marine on a sound
organizational and administrative footing had come in 1653, when
Robert Blake, George Monck and William Penn had put their heads
together to draw up the *Instructions for the Better Ordering of the Fleet in
Fighting*, and those *Articles of War* by which the lives and activities of
the men serving afloat were in future to be governed. On paper, the
Instructions were as inflexible and peremptory as the *Articles* were
draconic; for of the latter's thirty-nine clauses one third carried the
death penalty, without alternative, for those found guilty of their
infringement; while another third included it as a permissible award.
For all that, the delinquent stood a better chance of obtaining justice
at the hands of one of the new Courts of War than if he had remained
at the mercy of the old traditional 'laws and customs of the sea'. It is
not without significance, however, that the promulgation of the *Articles*
was very shortly followed by the first recorded instance of a 'flogging
round the fleet', when William Hancock, carpenter's mate of the *Hound*,
was tried and found guilty of 'drunkenness, swearing and uncleanliness'. The verdict decreed that he should 'be cashiered, and receive ten
lashes of the whip by the side of each flagship present, with a paper in
his hat stating his crime; a drum beating at the boat's head'. And when
the Bo'sun's mate set about his grim work it was anything but a case
of 'brushing flies off a sleeping Venus'. Thus the sailor made grim

39

acquaintance with that Cromwellian instrument of punishment—already painfully familiar to the soldier—known as 'the whip with nine tails', or 'the cat'; whose constant application was in due course to earn for the men of both Services the opprobrious nickname of 'the Bloodybacks'.

With Charles II safely installed in Whitehall, the state of insolvency into which the country had been plunged during the latter days of the Commonwealth was reflected in the neglect of what at one period had been a powerful and well-organized Fighting Marine. It took some time, therefore, for the Restoration period to earn the right to be termed 'the golden age of the Royal Navy'. For the burden of debt carried over from the previous regime and the reluctance of Parliament to furnish the necessary funds for the Service's upkeep grievously slowed down the Navy Board's unwearying effort to consolidate the excellent inaugural work carried out by Blake and his fellow Commissioners.

Yet with James Duke of York at the head of an experienced administration, which included the indefatigable Samuel Pepys as Clerk of the Acts,[1] in due course the Royal Navy once more achieved a strength and cohesion which rendered it far too formidable to be successfully challenged—as the Dutch discovered in the conflict of 1664–1667 and again in that of 1672–1674. Only in the June of 1667 had Parliamentary neglect to pay the seamen's long outstanding wage claims, plus the effect on available man-power of the Great Plague, combined so materially to weaken the Navy that De Ruyter had been enabled to thread his way past the Gunfleet Sand at the head of sixty-six warships. To the House of Commons's eternal shame, they were piloted by renegade British seamen who openly declared, 'We did heretofore fight for tickets; now we fight for dollars'.[2] With the half-completed defence works at Sheerness blown up and the chain across the Medway cleared out of the way, the Dutchman's subordinate, Van Ghent, had succeeded in seizing and setting fire to no less than two score English vessels, lying at their moorings, including the warships *Royal James*, *Loyal London* and *Royal Oak*. Most humiliating of all had been the capture of the stately *Royal Charles*, with a 'Butterbox' trumpeter mounted on the poop to sound off the derisory ditty 'Joan's Placket is Torn'.

[1] He became Secretary to the Navy Board in 1686.
[2] 'Tickets' were issued to the hands in lieu of money, and were only encashable at a heavy discount.

British Parliaments have rarely been capable of grasping the fact that it is idle to talk of national prosperity until they have first made sure of national security. So it was not until the King, out of the subsidy of £84,700 he received from Louis XIV, had paid £76,000 straight into the Navy Board's coffers, that the country's first line of defence had been put on a really sound footing.

Not only was an adequate fleet maintained in home waters, but throughout the Anglo-Dutch conflict of 1672–1674 it had been possible to station two men-o'-war as guardships in the Chesapeake; and the tobacco fleet could be met as far south-west as the Azores and given full protection until it made port in England. Furthermore, escorts could be provided for the fishing fleet, of up to 500 craft, outward bound in the spring for the Grand Banks of Newfoundland, and home-ward bound in the autumn with their holds crammed with salted cod for all the Catholic countries of Europe.

As the guardians of commercial enterprise it can fairly be said that the men of the Royal Navy fully earned their meagre wage of 19s a month for an Ordinary Seaman, and 24s for a fully qualified A.B.; a rate of pay which compared very unfavourably with that obtaining in the vessels of the Honourable East India Company and most other mercantile shipowners.

For its Officers the Royal Navy looked to certain aristocratic families with a seafaring tradition, to the manor house, and to the parsonage. There was no lack of capable leaders; although some of the 'young gentlemen Captains' speedily earned Mr Pepys's displeasure by blandly endowing themselves with leave of absence from their ships whenever the mood took them. The lure of London was hard to resist; with 'pretty, witty Nellie Gwynn' displaying her charms at the playhouse in Drury Lane; the delights of the French cuisine at Chatelin's fashionable eating-house in Covent Garden; and those enticing establishments hard by, where Mother Temple's and Madame Bennett's sprightly *protégées* were as conveniently frail as they were unquestionably fair. These 'gentleman captains' were, of course, a variant of the Elizabethan 'gentleman venturer', of whom veterans such as George Monck 'cried out against most mightily', while longing for 'the old plain sea-captains that served with him formerly'.

Not that there were any dearth of such rugged, rough-hewed, 'tar-paulin captains', many of whom had 'come up through the hawsehole', having originally served before the mast and made their way through

2*

Warrant Rank,[1] as Bo'sun, Gunner, or Carpenter, to the ultimate
dignity of the quarter-deck.

In the upper echelons of command the active rank of Admiral had
taken the place of the designation General-at-Sea borne by Robert Blake
and others among his contemporaries. Hitherto, officials with the appel-
lation of Admiral had confined their activities to presiding over the
shore-based Admiralty Courts; although many Mayors of ports such
as London, Southampton and Dartmouth also bore the title. The Mayor
of Kingston-upon-Hull, for example, was also Admiral of the Humber;
the Mayor of Boston, Admiral of the Wash, while another civic
dignitary was known as Admiral of the Firth of Forth. There was even
a dignitary known as the Admiral of the Herrings.

For operational purposes the Fleet was divided into Red, White and
Blue squadrons, in that order of precedence; the Admiral of the Red
commanding the centre, he of the White the van, or leading formation,
while he of the Blue commanded the rear.

A major proportion of the prize money awarded for the capture of an
enemy vessel, together with freight money, the fee for carrying bullion
or coin to its destination, supplemented the pay of senior Officers, which
for the highest rank stood at £3 rising to £4 a day.

Jobbery was not unknown where senior appointments were concerned, although it was far less flagrant under the Restoration Navy
Board than it was to become in times subsequent to the 'glorious'
revolution of 1688. Influence certainly played its part in procuring
nomination as a 'King's Letter Boy', whereby youths of good family,
of not more than sixteen years of age, went to sea literally to 'learn the
ropes', and much else of which the embryo Officer was required to
make himself the master. After continuing afloat until the age of twenty
in his capacity of Midshipman, the aspirant for Commissioned rank
proceeded to the Tower of London to undergo oral examination as to
his fitness for appointment to a Lieutenancy. Other maritime tyros were
entered on the ship's books nominally as 'Captain's servants', and there
was a small category which came under the heading of 'Volunteer';
both classes undergoing similar training, and enjoying similar prospects
to those of the 'King's Letter Boy'.

Life in the gunroom, which was the hub of the Midshipman's existence, was certainly no bed of roses. Discipline was strict, with punishments which ranged from 'starting' — brisk work with a rope's end or

[1] The equivalent of Warrant Rank had been instituted by Henry VIII.

a rattan cane—and 'facing paintwork',[1] up to mast-heading and 'kissing the gunner's daughter', a procedure whereby the delinquent was bent over the cascabel of a gun and soundly birched.

So far as the lower deck was concerned, almost from the very earliest days the task of manning ship had presented a continuing and vexatious problem. As early as the reign of Edward III (1327–1377) the authority vested in the three Admirals appointed by the King endowed them with the power of 'chusing, either within the liberties or otherwise, as many men as they might think necessary to manning the fleet, and seizing and impressing them, if they were unwilling to go aboard'; while in 1378 Richard II had given legal sanction to a countrywide system of impressment.[2]

Both Edward VI and Elizabeth I had sponsored extra 'fish days', additional to those already on the weekly calendar, when no flesh might be consumed, under penalty of a heavy fine.[3] These measures had been imposed 'to encourage the breed of fishermen', from whose experienced ranks both the Mercantile and the Fighting Marine greatly preferred to replenish their ships' companies. Even with this stimulant to the increase of the coastal population, demand far exceeded the supply of qualified seamen, and resort had to be made to the imposition of definite quotas to be furnished by specific localities. But again expectation exceeded fulfilment. A return rendered during the Anglo-Dutch conflict of 1652–1654 revealed that in response to the order to furnish a hundred men for drafting into the Fleet, the Mayor of Southampton had produced a beggarly array of twenty-one. They were accompanied by the specious explanation that owing to lack of trade and the dearth of vessels in port, seafarers were not to be had. At the same time Sandwich's warrant for forty able-bodied seamen had brought in eighty protesting landsmen, while no more than half of Ramsgate's quota of eighty A.B.s had been finally handed over.

In Restoration days the payment of the mariner's hard-earned wage was so often in arrears that service in the Royal Navy was the last thing to which a 'blue water man' aspired. For Mr Pepys's modest aim to settle up with the foremast hand 'once a year at furthest' was rarely achieved. Indeed, a Royal Navy Captain was more than usually

---

[1] The equivalent of the schoolboy's punishment of being 'stood in the corner'.
[2] Rich. II, Stat. I, cap. 4.
[3] See 2–3 Edw. VI, Stat. I, cap. 19; 5 Eliz. Stat. I, cap 5; 27 Eliz. Stat. I, cap. 11; 35 Eliz. Stat. I, cap. 7.

fortunate if over thirty per cent of his ship's company was made up of experienced seafarers.

For the balance there was nothing for it but to resort to the press; which in times of acute shortage did not scruple to haul in men already serving in colliers, usually exempt from impressment, as were youths bound in apprenticeship. Another course of virtually involuntary supply consisted of what was known as 'the Lord Mayor's men'. These were young men of respectable family caught riotously drunk in the streets or in bawdy houses or other questionable premises within the confines of the City. Given the option of disgracing their relatives by appearing before a Bench of Magistrates, or joining the Royal Navy, many of them took to the sea as the only way out of the dilemma they had contrived for themselves. Magistrates were also empowered to hand over to the naval authorities such civic undesirables as convicted criminals, debtors, smugglers, paupers, and men who had deserted their families.

Hustled off to the frowsty, verminous hulks moored in the Thames for the reception and ultimate distribution of the press gang's nightly haul, they joined the disgruntled huddle of artisans, labourers, ship assistants, petty thieves, louse-bitten footpads, pest-ridden loafers and 'poor masterless men', who were responsible for the widespread incidence of 'ship's fever'[1] with which the Fleet was so consistently afflicted.

Distributed over the various vessels in the Fleet, the newcomers were known as 'waisters', their station being in the ship's waist until they had learned something of the tasks which could only be entrusted to a practised seaman. They were, of course, immediately posted either to the port or starboard watches[2], and subjected to the strict disciplinary code by which the whole ship's company was bound; with a scale of punishments which ranged from a ceremonial application of the 'cat', to running the gauntlet — the penalty awaiting a convicted thief. After this it was almost a matter of ribaldry to witness the treatment meted out to a drunkard, when the delinquent was roused up in the fore rigging and 'salt water poured down his throat by the aid of a funnel until the water passed right through him'.

---

[1] 'Ship's fever', like gaol fever and camp fever, was a louse-borne form of typhus, encouraged on shipboard by overcrowding, verminous clothing and physical uncleanliness.

[2] It was not until the days of Captain Reginald Hall, R.N., under the Fisher regime, that the three watch system was introduced.

Hard work such as was demanded of the sailor on shipboard demands ample sustenance. But although Pepys worked out a reasonably generous scale of subsistence,[1] it was anything but usual for the foremast hand to get the full benefit of it.

To begin with, there was the innate rascality of the contractor who, working in collusion with an equally grasping Purser, furnished supplies in short measure — while charging for them in full — and of such atrocious quality as to be virtually inedible. Of his own day Monson recorded of one revictualling that 'there appeared a certain proportion of beef and pork able with its scent to have poisoned the whole company';[2] while of the biscuit it was said that 'only the old hands knew just how to rap it against some solid substance to eject the larger of the bitter red eel-like weevils and the "bargemen", or maggots, by which it was inhabited. The really knowing ones consumed it only after dark.' Both the beer and the water were speedily polluted, the former becoming sour and the latter turning putrid, largely through being stored in unscoured wooden casks.[3]

Fundamentally, however, the real trouble with the sailor's dietary was its imbalance, its lack of proteins and vitamins. This absence of the necessary anti-scorbutic elements in his daily fare inevitably led to punctual appearance of scurvy — the mariner's scourge from the earliest days of protracted voyages under sail. In Elizabethan times John Hawkyns had put it on record that in twenty years' experience of the sea he had known ten thousand mariners to perish of this one complaint; and conditions had not appreciably improved with the turn of the seventeenth century. The Dutch had experimented with such palliatives as *sauerkraut* and 'a rob of sower oranges and lemons'; the curative value of the juice of citrus fruits having been endorsed by Felix Plater in 1608, by Thomas Willis in 1667, and again by Francis de la Boe of Leyden in 1674. But it had occurred to no one as yet that, if taken in time and in sufficient quantity, lime or lemon juice might serve not only as a cure, but as a prophylactic.

To ever-present scurvy, calenture, 'ship's fever', smallpox, the raging fevers endemic to such tropic latitudes as the West Indies, was added chronic constipation, attributable in part to ill-balanced rations and partly to the sedentary nature of the seaman's daily round. In a fumbling

---

[1] See Appendix B.
[2] Monson's *Naval Tracts*, IV, 147.
[3] Metal water containers were not introduced into the Royal Navy until 1815.

attempt to offset the hands' lack of normal bodily exercise the experienced commander, whenever possible, would give the order,
'Hands to dance and skylark'. This was the signal for the ship's fiddler
to scrape out a lively hornpipe, or for the hands to indulge in the
healthy rough-and-tumble of 'baiting the bear', or a wrestling bout, a
turn at leap frog, or even a friendly set-to with the bare 'maulies',
all in the hope of rectifying their unhealthy condition of internal
stasis.

In other respects the Sick and Hurt Commission, established under
the Commonwealth, did what it could for the ailing and the wounded;
the latter being eligible for certain 'awards', which varied in value
according to the nature of the injury suffered. Thus the loss of a leg or
an arm was compensated at the rate of £6 13s 4d 'as present relief, and
so much settled as an annual pension for his lifetime'; fatal injury to an
eye entitled the sufferer to an immediate payment of £4 and a like sum
annually. Greenwich Palace, turned into a Naval Hospital to commemorate the British victories of Barfleur and La Hogue, of 1692,
served to house the 'old geese' who had qualified for honourable
retirement; accommodation being eventually provided for 2,710 of
them. The Chatham Chest, established by Hawkyns in 1588 'for the
relief of the maimed and superannuated mariner', and to which every
seaman contributed 6d a month, also helped the mariner whose days
of active service had ended. But although the monthly coppers were
punctually deducted from the wages of all seamen — Royal Navy or
mercantile marine — as a contribution to the Sixpenny Chest, founded
for Greenwich Hospital's upkeep, only those mariners who had been
injured while on voluntary or impressed service with the Fighting
Marine qualified for admission to the establishment.

Although continuity of service was as yet unknown, and the hands
signed on anew for each fresh commission, since desertion imposed a
serious drain on Naval man-power, shore leave was virtually unknown
save for a few senior ratings. When the vessel made port she was kept
at her moorings.

In the course of an hour the ship was surrounded with shore boats.
First the married men had liberty to take their wives on board, and
then the young men had their girls come off and took them on
board; a curious sight to see boats crowded with blooming young
girls all for sale. Our crew were mostly young men and caused the

boatmen to have a quick despatch, or as we usually term it, a ready market.[1]

It was left to the womenfolk, who swarmed all over the vessel, to smuggle aboard the liquor which helped to create a positive bacchanalia 'tween decks, to which the Master-at-arms turned a temporarily blind eye. With the Blue Peter hoisted as a signal that the craft was on the point of sailing, 'orders came to send all the girls ashore except one woman to each mess, the married women certainly to have the preference'.[2]

Almost from the outset the presence of a certain number of women on shipboard had been unofficially countenanced. A sempstress 'to make and mend the Captain's clothes', a couple of women to help with the officers' laundering — somehow they contrived to accompany the craft on her 'lawful occasions'. Indeed, it was not uncommon — save in wartime — for senior Warrant Officers to take their offspring to sea with them; one such was the son of the Carpenter, Alfred Cox, of H.M.S. *Minerva*, a little lad not old enough even to be rated a 'ship's boy'. The Restoration divine, Bishop Williams, may not have been exaggerating when he averred that 'Providence made man to live ashore, and it is necessity alone which drives him to sea'; but nobody could outdo the British sailor in making the very best of necessity.

Thus the Royal Navy, with 105 vessels in commission in 1688 — exclusive of fire-ships — was fully prepared to play its part in the almost constant warfare in which Britain was to be embroiled from 1689 to 1713, and again in the even more gruelling conflicts which raged almost without intermission from 1739 to 1783.

Possibly because initially there were fewer calls on its services, the Army's growth was considerably slower than that of the Royal Navy. At the time of Charles II's death in 1685 the military establishment had increased by no more than the addition of the Buffs — the Holland Regiment, made up of expatriated Englishmen brought back from service with the Dutch — and the 4th Foot, raised in the West Country in 1680 and originally known as the 2nd Tangerines.

The attempt of 'Mr Crofts the King's bastard',[3] as the 'Protestant

[1] John Weatherall's *Memoirs*. He was writing of the mid-eighteenth century, but conditions were much the same earlier on.

[2] Weatherall, *op. cit.*

[3] Charles II's natural son, James, Duke of Monmouth.

Defender', to wrest the throne from James II led to the latter's hurried recruitment of the 5th to 18th Foot, the 1st to 6th Dragoons, and the two Regiments which, originally Dragoons, were destined to become the 3rd and 4th Hussars.

But in his son-in-law, William of Orange, James II had a far more deadly and unscrupulous enemy than the *insouciant* Duke of Monmouth. While hypocritically congratulating his father-in-law on the birth of a son by his second wife, William spurred on his English propaganda agents to emphasize the dangers inherent in what was now an assured Catholic succession. So effective were their efforts that a number of seamen burst in upon Sandwich's Town Major with a demand to put the place in a state of defence against 'the wild Irish'. Another band of seafarers seized Deal, Walmer and Dover castles 'to defend them against the damned Frenchies who are going to be called in by the King'.

With powerful Whig families prepared to put up with any puppet-king so long as they secured the political power and sweets of office so long denied them, the way was paved for one of the brashest 'take-over bids' in history. Thus it came about that with the sentry under the window of his Whitehall quarters absentmindedly whistling the jingling little anti-Jacobite ditty of *Lillibulero*, the last of the Stuart Kings took refuge in flight; leaving 'Orange Billy' to sidle on to a Throne to which he had no greater claim than that for twenty-one years he had been married to the Heiress Apparent.

The immediate and inevitable consequence was war with the French. More regiments were hastily recruited, while an attempt was made to reorganize – and reanimate – the Militia, in the rather wistful hope that from its ranks the Regular Army would be reinforced by substantial drafts.

While it is impossible to deny the political astuteness with which William contrived to bolster Dutch defiance of the French with the whole weight of Britain's resources, it is equally undeniable that his devious talents did not extend to command in the field. The British reverses at Stienkirk and Neerwinden (Landen) – the latter, apart from Malplaquet and Borodino, witnessing the most appalling slaughter in the span of two hundred years – were of such severity that the Whig Government was only too anxious to conclude the Peace of Ryswick and thus gain a breathing space – for which, incidentally, the French were equally thankful.

The resumption of hostilities when both sides had been given an opportunity to reorganize their resources was a moral certainty. For all that, the British Parliament was insistent that the strength of the Regular Army be reduced from 87,000 to a mere token force of 7,000 of all arms.

With the outbreak of the War of the Spanish Succession in 1702 all, of course, was to do again.

By this time the Army's organization had undergone certain significant modifications. Hitherto no legal powers existed for the punishment of military offences in time of peace, except by civil courts. In consequence mutiny and desertion frequently went unpenalized, rather than that the cumbersome machinery of civil justice should be invoked; and discipline had suffered accordingly. In 1689, therefore, a Bill, known as the Mutiny Act,[1] was passed legalizing the institution of military courts. The preamble of the Act also included the proviso, 'The raising of a standing army within the United Kingdom in time of peace, unless it be with the consent of Parliament, is against the law'. In effect, it depended entirely upon the whim of Parliament whether or no the country's land forces should continue in existence. If it deemed such a force needful, it annually determined its numbers and voted the necessary funds for their upkeep. But so long as the enticing opportunities for financial gain attached to the office of Paymaster-General to the Forces continued to excite the cupidity of politicians, there was little fear of the Army declining into oblivion. Henry Guy, who held the office under William III, acquired an enormous fortune by his manipulation of those public funds which passed through his prehensile hands.[2] Robert Walpole was only to exchange the post for the even more lucrative office of Chancellor of the Exchequer; while until his death in 1774 Henry Fox was enjoying an annual income of £25,000 from his unaudited balances, although he had resigned as Paymaster-General in 1765.

But although Parliament could 'vote the Army', its 'government, command and disposition' remained part of the Royal Prerogative.[3]

In effect, the man in the red coat still regarded himself as one of His

[1] I William and Mary, I, 5.

[2] Guy left his enormous fortune to William Pulteney (subsequently Earl of Bath), which enabled him to enter politics suitably 'breeched'.

[3] Such it was to remain until 1870, when it was settled that the Prerogative should be exercised on behalf of the Sovereign by a Secretary of State for War responsible to Parliament.

Majesty's servants; and many of the ideals which had inspired the King's forces in medieval days still lingered on.

To raise a regiment, the Sovereign awarded a Warrant to someone of acknowledged integrity and reasonable substance; men, as the Marlburian veteran, Humphrey Bland, expressed it, 'who had some stake in the established order of affairs, and the last in the world to bow their necks to a military dictatorship'.[1] Allocated a lump sum of money annually for the regiment's upkeep, the formation virtually became the Colonel's property, and at the outset was known by his name and carried Colours displaying his armorial bearings.

The Warrant-holder was, of course, responsible for clothing and equipping his men out of the annual grant he received from the Treasury. After paying all expenses, the balance went into the Colonel's own pocket; and with a conscientious individual intent on doing his best for the formation he had been entrusted to raise and administer, the balance left over as his personal profit amounted to no great sum.

With a man of less scruple, however, there were innumerable opportunities to line the pocket by cutting down on the quality of the uniforms and arms with which he furnished his rank and file, disposing of Commissions at 'over-regulation' rates, and many other devious ways and means. A contractor would be called in to garb a formation, and to recompense himself for the heavy bribe pouched by the Colonel-proprietor, he would substitute shoddier material for the uniforms and poorer quality leather for the equipment than would have been the case had he not been forced to 'pay through the nose' to secure the contract. The heavier the preliminary *douceur*, the lower the standard of the material furnished. There was one instance, indeed, of a Colonel clothing his regiment in the cast-off uniforms of another formation.

The regimental agent, who dealt with the sale of Commissions in the new unit, also expected his rake-off, both from the Colonel and the aspiring Officer with whom he negotiated. This put a premium on exacting more than the contemporary standard price the said Commission commanded.

This 'purchase' system was, of course, a method of procedure which evolved from the Elizabethan practice of buying shares in a company of gentlemen venturers. A Commission as Ensign in a sound 'marching regiment' cost on average four hundred pounds, that for a Cornet in a

[1] The same sentiment in similar words was later to be expressed both by Wellington and Palmerston.

crack cavalry formation, seven hundred guineas. These payments helped to reimburse the Colonel-proprietor for his outlay in equipping his unit; although the Crown reserved the right to dispose of the Commission of every Officer who had been promoted — say, for gallantry in the field — without having purchased his rank, or had fallen in action. Unofficially, over-regulation terms could also be exacted for a Commission in a particularly popular or fashionable formation; a transaction in which the agent's percentage accounted for a considerable proportion of the sum finally agreed.

The purchase of a Commission entitled its holder to half-pay when not actively employed with a formation, and was, in effect, a means of securing an annuity for life. Each step in promotion called for a further disbursement, and a Lieutenant-Colonel of Infantry who had purchased his promotion rank by rank had laid out something like £7,000; if his service had been with one of the Regiments of Household Cavalry, a sum in the region of £13,000.

Obviously the system was open to abuse, since the man with ample means but little military experience or aptitude would purchase promotion over the head of a war-trained veteran of limited means. Moreover, it was not unknown for the purchase price of a Commission to be laid down on behalf of a schoolboy, who of course made no appearance with the formation to which he had been accredited, although his parents or guardian drew the pay appropriate to his rank.

Since it was conveniently taken for granted that the individual aspiring to a Commission would be a man of some private means, pay rates — for which the State was responsible — scarcely erred on the side of generosity. That portion of the remuneration theoretically paid in advance was barely sufficient for his subsistence. The balance, known as 'arrears' or 'clearings', was — again theoretically — paid yearly, after deduction of poundage — a shilling in the pound to the Paymaster-General — and one day's full pay for the upkeep of Chelsea Hospital.[1] The Commissary-General of the Musters then stepped in with a demand for one day's pay, a tax which caused so much discontent that it was subsequently reduced to one third of a day's pay. There were other exactions, 'sanctioned by custom and antiquity', such as payments to the auditors, the clerks of the Treasury, the Exchequer, and the Pay

---

[1] It is open to debate whether the first suggestion for the establishment of 'an asylum for wounded and superannuated soldiers' originated with Sir Stephen Fox or, as tradition has it, with Nell Gwyn.

Warrant Office, all of which ate further into emoluments which in no sense can be termed extravagant. For even by mid-eighteenth century the daily pay of a Subaltern Officer had not risen beyond 4s 6d, that of a Captain 12s 6d, that of a Major 18s 6d, and that of a Lieutenant-Colonel £1 1s 6d. There were certain 'allowances on going into camp', and for 'parties sent on the recruiting service'; and all ranks qualified for certain disability payments; as did their widows and off-spring should they meet with fatal injury while on active service.

'Disbanded Officers, called Reformado's, or "reformed", sometimes carried arms as privates, till they could be reinstated.'[1] Or they might do duty as supernumerary Officers while drawing no more than their half-pay. There were also a certain number of 'gentleman volunteers' serving in the ranks and hopeful of being awarded a Commission without purchase as a reward for devoted service or conspicuous gallantry in the field.

The most fortunate individual was the bearer of victory despatches, who might be rewarded with a purchase-free step in rank, the gift of a handsome charger, or even a cash bounty of anything up to £500.

In effect, what the State relied upon was a steady supply of reasonably endowed men, deriving from the rural gentry, who were imbued with a real sense of service, and in addition 'were able to secure more willing obedience with less effort than others, born as they were into the habit of command and authority'.[2]

There were, of course, a certain number of swashbuckling *chevaliers d'epée* amongst the officers such as Ben Jonson epitomized in his Captain Bobadil and Farquhar in his Captain Brazen. They were men who supplemented their meagre pay and small private resources by means of the dice box, the 'devil's picture-boards', and by taking full advantage of the manifold opportunities for chicanery and malfeasance presented by the contemporary system of regimental finance. The procurement of pay for men who appeared only at musters—the *passe-volant*, 'faggot', or 'hautbois'—showing up on parade and then scrambling out of their borrowed uniforms and disappearing, was matched by the exploitation of 'widows' men', soldiers who had died shortly after one muster but whose names were kept on the books till the next —their pay being drawn and pocketed by the company commander. Nor were opportunities lacking for such men to add appreciably to

[1] Francis Grose. *Military Antiquities.*
[2] Hon. Sir John Fortescue, *The Raleigh Lecture on History.*

their pickings by sly little deals over the men's rations or their billeting money.

Fortunately, such unabashed soldiers of fortune were in a minority. The general success of the British in arms indicates that there were very many more to anticipate James Wolfe's sage advice, 'An Officer should never think he does too much. Officers should attend the looks of their men and, if they are thinner and paler than usual, the reason for their falling off should be enquired into, and proper means taken to restore them to their former vigour.' It was *care* of their men, not only their leadership in action, which was to endow the relationship between the Officers and other ranks with a quality of mutual trust and confidence not to be surpassed in any other army in the world.

One of the most expensive assignments to come the junior Officer's way was to be sent out with 'beating orders', to round up recruits 'by beat of drum' or any other methods of persuasion that a fertile imagination and not too scrupulous a regard for the law might suggest to him. For there were innumerable incidental expenses for which the trifling allowances deriving from the regimental 'Stock Purse' made no provision. Normally the bounty paid to a recruit stood at 42s. But in times of acute shortage the bait had very considerably to be increased; and the 'Stock Purse' was rarely in a position to meet the additional charge. It was a very well endowed individual who emerged from a recruiting mission without a load of personal debt to be cleared off by the best means that could be devised—which put another premium on yielding to bribery.

As Britain entered on the lengthy struggle over the Spanish succession, the rapid increase of the Army fighting under the Duke of Marlborough in Flanders involved a progressively urgent demand for recruits to replace casualties and keep the various formations up to strength.

What all Commanding Officers sought was 'respectable, docile country lads, brought up by careful thrifty parents in a decent cottage home'.[1] But the supply of such admirable raw material was not inexhaustible, and the recruiting party was condemned to fling its net far more widely and indiscriminately. To get a potential but hesitant recruit thoroughly fuddled with liquor and while in this condition slip into his pocket the 'Queen's shilling' which was visible testimony to the fact that he had consented to enlist, was an oft-practised device. Eager

[1] Hon. Sir John Fortescue, *The British Soldier and the Empire*.

youths, too young even to be entered as drummer boys, would sometimes be 'bound' to report on reaching acceptable age by being attested
and then sent home temporarily on furlough, to let the years catch up
with them. This happened in the case of the young John Wilson, for
example, who recorded that his future C.O. directed that 'I should go
home on ffurloe, and let him have three months pay advance, and his
ffurloe for a full year, both of which I had next morning, and committed to the charge of Ensigne Halliday's Brother to See me safe
home'. In due course the Recruiting Officer 'sent a Serjeant for me to
meet him the next day at Kircaldie, which I accordingly did, and then
he asked me again in the presence of the Provost of the Town, Sir
Robert Douglas and his Brother, if I continued Stedfast in my Resolution to go abroad. I replied that I did', and the following day, duly
attested, one more recruit set out to swell the ranks of the 15th
Foot.[1]

So long as the aspirant was of the necessary height—at one time reduced to five feet, three and a half inches—was not ruptured nor verminous, or palpably suffering from some contagious disease, the procedure on attestation was little more than perfunctory; as Kit Welsh[2]
discovered when she decided to follow her husband to the wars by
enlisting. 'Having ordered my affairs,' she recorded, 'I cut off my hair,
and dressed me in a suit of my husband's, having had the precaution to
quilt the waistcoat, to preserve my breasts from hurt, which were not
large enough to betray my sex, and putting on my wig and hat...I went
to the sign of the Golden Last, where Ensign Herbert Lawrence, who
was beating up for recruits, kept his rendezvous.' Hailed as 'a clever
brisk young fellow', Kit was promptly given 'a guinea enlisting money,
and a crown to drink the King's health', and ordered to be enrolled
without further ado. Obviously she underwent no medical examination,
or her sex would have been revealed there and then, instead of remaining
undisclosed until her relegation to hospital as the outcome of taking a
severe scalp wound at the battle of Ramillies, several years later.[3]

The casual manner in which recruitment was conducted is witnessed
by an advertisement in the *London Gazette* for 1688, offering the reward
of one guinea for the apprehension of a deserter distinguished by 'six

---

[1] *The Journal of Serjeant John Wilson*, 1701–1711.

[2] Subsequent marriages changed her name to Davis and then to Ross.

[3] See *The Life and Adventures of Mrs Christian Davies commonly called Mother Ross*, edited
by Hon. Sir John Fortescue.

toes on his left foot, on his hand two fingers growing together, and the little toe of his left foot sticking out of his shoe'.

It was the sense of adventure rather than any monetary inducement which persuaded most men to enlist. For the 'private centinal's' pay was a meagre 8d a day. Of this sum 'sixpence a day was set apart for his subsistence, and was nominally inviolable. The balance, £3 0s 10d a year, was called the "gross off-reckonings", which was subject of course to a deduction of five per cent for the Paymaster-General, and of one day's pay to Chelsea Hospital, whereby the "gross off-reckonings" were reduced to £2 8s. This last amount, dignified by the title of "net off-reckonings", was made over to the Colonel for the clothing of the regiment, an item which included not only the actual garments, but also the sword and belt, and, as time went on, the bayonet and cartridge box.'[1] Moreover, the pittance to which the soldier was entitled was more often than not, many months, even years, in arrears.

Active service brought the opportunity to qualify for certain additional emoluments, such as the 2s 6d paid to any man who volunteered to make one of the 'Forlorn Hope' organized to undertake some particularly desperate venture, and who was fortunate enough to survive. There were comparable payments for the 'ladder men', the individuals who dashed forward ahead of their comrades to place the scaling ladders in position against the enemy walls when a stronghold had to be taken by assault. Heavy work with spade and mattock, which every siege operation involved, brought in anything up to an additional 5s a week.

As the heavy fighting in Flanders demanded more and more replacements, so the general standard of recruits inevitably deteriorated, and conditions became much the same as those described by Barnaby Rich over a hundred years earlier. 'In England', he wrote in 1587, 'when service happeneth, we disburthen the prisons of thieves, we rob the taverns and ale-houses of tosspots and ruffians, we scour both town and country for rogues and vagabonds.' Certainly the Mutiny and Impressment Acts of 1703–1705 empowered justices of the peace 'to raise and levy such able-bodied men as have no lawful calling or employment, or visible means for their maintenance and livelihood, to serve as soldiers'; and the magistrates' efforts were more than enthusiastically supplemented by a whole swarm of crimps, only too eager to qualify for the bounty offered to anyone 'bringing in a man'. Nor were

[1] Hon. Sir John Fortescue, *History of the British Army*, (vol. I.)

they at all pernickety as to the suitability or otherwise of the recruits
they brought forward to 'pass muster'; presenting temporarily
smartened-up habitual drunkards or poor gormless youths of feeble
intellect with equal aplomb. One notorious London crimp of the name
of Tooley even resorted to kidnapping pure and simple.[1]

In some instances the payment of 'smart money' — a polite euphemism
for a bribe — would enable an unwilling recruit to back out of the
engagement he had entered into when under the influence of drink; a
clandestine transaction from which the Recruiting Serjeant was the
prime beneficiary.

Enlistment was nominally for life, or until discharged as no longer fit
for service as the outcome of wounds or increasing years. Men with
impaired health but still capable of limited service were relegated to
Invalid Companies, to be called upon in an emergency.

The haphazard recruiting system also offered almost endless opportunity to the unscrupulous bounty-snatcher, the type who would
enlist in — say Durham, draw the bounty paid over on attestation, do a
few days duty with his unit, then desert, to reappear in Winchester and
go through the whole process again, before making off once more, and
heading for yet another area in which to work a similar deceit yet a
third time. And so *ad infinitum*, until run to earth and penalized. Even
then the deserter, like nearly all classes of malefactor, could evade
punishment by accepting service in the deadly West Indies; where the
mortality rate was so appalling that one return revealed that, of 4,945
Officers and men sent to garrison the British possessions in these latitudes in the early Spring, the death roll by the middle of May had
come to 1,800.

Under peacetime conditions elsewhere the most common form of
disability was rupture, for which contemporary surgical skill furnished
an extremely dubious remedy. For the wounded and seriously ailing
Chelsea Hospital provided accommodation for 538 in-patients, with
double that number of out-patients making do as best they could on a
subsistence allowance of 1s a day. For the Irish Establishment the
hospital at Kilmainham, Dublin, had accommodation for 140 in-
patients, with a correspondingly smaller nominal roll of out-patients.
It is to be feared, however, that such leeches and chirurgeons as lent

---

[1] With James II in exile, Ireland ceased to be a recruiting ground for the Army. Indeed,
between 1691 and 1791 no less than 480,000 Hibernian 'Wild Geese' sought and obtained
military service in France, Austria and Spain.

their services to the Army or the Navy were scarcely amongst the most eminent in a calling whose general knowledge of the ills the flesh is heir to, and the injury it can sustain, was still dangerously elementary.

In the Cavalry, whose six or seven troops were made up of forty other ranks, the men were equipped with a sling carbine and cartouche box for ammunition, sword and pistols; although the tendency was progressively to discourage the wasteful and unrewarding practice of firing from the saddle, and to rely on shock action with the *arme blanche*. Dragoons, however, had something of the characteristics of mounted infantry, being armed with muskets and, after 1672, with bayonets.

The Artillery was not as yet a separate formation, but worked their battalion guns in close association with the Infantry. In the same way the Engineers were not yet organized as a corps; while the humble position occupied by the pioneer is sufficiently indicated by the fact that to be 'degraded to a common pioneer' was regarded as a remarkably unpleasant form of punishment.

With the Infantry, evolutions were few and simple; the Infantrymen confronted their enemies drawn up in three ranks, wreaked the maximum possible execution with a single blast of musketry, and then went in with the cold steel—those 'bayonets with slipones conform' (rings) which took the place of the original plug bayonets after the battle of Killiecrankie in 1689.

The firearm itself was the prototype of the 'Brown Bess'[1] which was faithfully to serve the British Army right up to the time of the Crimean War. The weapon had a barrel thirty-nine inches in length, which threw a spherical ball (fourteen to the pound) to an effective range of approximately two hundred yards, although anything like accuracy of aim was impossible at more than a hundred yards, and doubtful even at that. The flints which sparked off the priming powder wore out very quickly, and even in action had to be changed every twenty rounds or so; a nerve-racking process to perform under enemy fire. The short life of the flint in action added considerably to the burden of supplies. With Braddock's force of 2,100, in the campaign of 1755, for example, 142,000 spare musket flints were carried with the baggage, together with 1,800 of a smaller variety for pistols. The best black flints derived from Brandon in Suffolk, whose flint-knappers were particularly skilled craftsmen. Kentish flints came next highest in general estimation.

---

[1] The 'Brown Bess' was in general issue by 1690. (Charles ffoulkes, *Arms and Armament*).

'Brown Bess' stood up well to active service conditions, but was a cumbersome piece to handle, demanding thirty-seven words of command to complete the parade-ground process of loading and firing. But its hitting power was formidable. Well trained troops could get off four rounds a minute; although misfires were often as frequent as one in every twenty shots fired — attributable to faulty flints. Wet weather, however, tended to render both weapon and powder useless.

A device known as a pricker was employed to free the touch-hole from accumulating carbon, to avoid a flash in the pan; and it was not unknown for the soldier to urinate down the barrel of his fire-arm to clear it from 'fouling'.

A lighter weapon, the fuzil, was issued to the Fusiliers, who guarded and worked with the Artillery, occasionally helping to serve the guns under the more expert direction of the artillators and matrosses. Returning from a review of the troops on Hounslow Heath in 1678, John Evelyn made the diary entry, 'Now were brought into service a new sort of soldiers, called *Grenadiers*, who were dexterous in throwing grenades, everyone having a pouch full; they had furred caps with coped crowns like Janizaries, which made them look very fierce; and some had long hoods hanging down behind, as we picture fools. Their clothing being likewise piebald, yellow and red'.[1]

The Fusiliers also wore the mitre-shaped head-dress; while the Grenadiers were further distinguished by being armed with heavy hammer-hatchets for hewing down the palisades in the attack on a fortified place.

Where his subsistence was concerned, generally speaking the man in the ranks was better circumstanced when on active service than when stationed at home. With Marlborough's forces in Flanders, bread waggons and 'beef on the hoof' followed close on the Army's heels; while lesser wants were catered for by a swarm of sutlers, whose activities — like the prices they charged — were subject to control by the Provost Martial and the regimental Seconds-in-Command. If the diet very largely consisted of boiled beef, boiled potatoes, cheese and rye bread, that was because the transportable cooking utensils were not of a kind to deal with much else, save an occasional ration of boiled bacon.

At home there was limited barrack accommodation for the Life Guards and the 'Blues' at Somerset House and the Royal Mews — where

[1] John Evelyn's *Diary*. For a time three troops of Horse Grenadiers were attached to the Life Guards.

now stands the National Gallery—with stabling in Leicester Fields. The Foot Guards crammed in as best they could in the Savoy and the Tower. Such garrison posts as Dover, Southsea and Pendennis Castles served to house some of the Infantry of the Line; the rest had to be 'farmed out'.[1] Since billeting on private property without 'the free and voluntary consent of the owner'—rarely accorded—was contrary to the law,[2] the bulk of the troops had to be found accommodation in 'inns, livery stables, ale-houses, victualling houses, and all houses selling brandy, strong waters, cyder or metheglin by retaile'. For the sum of eightpence *per capita* mine host was under obligation to furnish his unbidden guests with sleeping quarters, 'victuals, fire and candles'. It was a payment which left little margin for profit, although some land-lords were not above cutting down shamelessly on provender the better to line their own pockets. In this particular, conditions had little improved even by the end of the century, when one chronicler recorded, 'My comrades, on quitting the house, evinced their dis-approbation of the treatment they had met with by writing with a lighted candle on the ceiling, "D——d bad quarters. —How are you off for pea soup? —Lead dumplings. —Lousy beds. —Dirty sheets." '[3]

In one particular, however, the soldiery were better circumstanced than their comrades of the sister Service—at least there was a recognized quota of women officially 'married on the strength'. Regulations made allowance for five wives per troop or company. Providing they under-took the laundering for their formation, and in war-time were prepared to do their best as nurses in the elementary field hospitals, they were recompensed at the rate of sixpence a day and half rations.[4]

There were as yet no such things as married quarters; a blanket-screened corner of the barrack room, or the ale-house attic, if on the line of march, was the best that the soldier's wife could devise in the way of privacy for herself and any children of the marriage. But 'the custom was not without its good points, as the women exercised a steadying influence over the men, while the latter seldom if ever forgot that a woman was in the room, and anyone who did forget was promptly brought to order by the others'.[5] For the unofficial 'kangaroo

---

[1] In 1702 there was barrack accommodation for approximately 5,000 officers and men.
[2] I William and Mary, II, iv (38).
[3] Memoirs of the Military Career of John Shipp.
[4] A quarter ration was allowed for each child of the marriage.
[5] Field-Marshal Sir William Robertson. Having enlisted as a trooper in the 16th (Queen's) Lancers, Robertson was speaking from personal experience.

courts' convened and operated by the men themselves had a very short way with anyone whose general manner of conducting himself threatened to disturb the general weal.

Apart from the 'regulated' wives, there was always a certain number of poor drabs who had chosen to follow the men of their choice, and who trailed along at the heels of the regiment. Lacking any sort of official standing, they failed to qualify either for pay or rations, and eked out the few coppers and scraps of food their men contrived to pass over to them by thankfully undertaking any casual work that came their way.

It was when a formation was on the move that both the wives and the doxies—particularly the latter—underwent the greatest hardship. 'It is notorious' wrote Charles James, 'that, during a march, these unfortunate women were at the mercy of every inn-keeper in the kingdom; obliged to every waggoner for occasional conveyance on the roads in the worst of weather; and when they arrived in camp or barracks, they and their husbands were left to provide for themselves without the least regard to common decency and good order.'[1]

Discipline was as draconic with the Army as with the Navy. Even so late as the Marlborough campaigns blasphemy could be punished by piercing the offender's tongue with a red-hot spike. The 'whip with nine tails' was resorted to as the punishment for a score of military offences; and its prevalence was accepted with stoical philosophy. After all, it was far from unknown to the delinquent civilian; while a soldier of the Border Regiment confided to his *Journal* that he did not feel he had become a man until he had been sentenced to the 'cat'. The minimum award was twenty-five lashes, the maximum—seldom imposed—was one thousand five hundred. The record was achieved in the reign of George II, when, at one time and another, a particularly insubordinate linesman, over a period of sixteen years, was awarded no less than 30,000 lashes. Yet it was reported of him that 'the man is hearty and well, and in no way concerned'. Moreover, it is not without significance that in some instances deputations of the more orderly elements in a formation waited on their Commanding Officer to petition him to 'impose the lash more freely', since, 'if the more turbulent among us are not kept in subjection, life for us will be a hell upon earth'.

Lesser forms of punishment included the wooden horse and the whirligig. The first named 'was formed of planks nailed together, so as

[1] Charles James's *Military Companion*.

to form a sharp ridge or angle about eight or nine feet long, this ridge represented the back of the horse. It was supported by four posts or legs, about six or seven feet long, placed on a stand made moveable by trucks; to complete the resemblance a head and tail were added. When a soldier was sentenced to ride this horse, he was placed on the back with his hands tied behind him, and frequently, to increase the punishment, had muskets tied to his legs, to prevent, as it was jocularly said, his horse kicking him off; this punishment being chiefly inflicted on the infantry, who were supposed unused to ride'.[1]

The Whirligig, for the punishment of 'petit sutlers, jews, brawling women, and such-like persons', was 'a kind of circular wooden cage, which turn'd on a pivot; and when set in motion, whirled round with amazing velocity, that the delinquent became extremely sick, and commonly emptied his or her body through every aperture'.[2]

Picketing was a punishment very largely confined to the Cavalry and Artillery, in which 'a long post being driven in the ground, the delinquent was ordered to mount a stool near it, when his right hand was fastened to a hook in the post by a noose round his waist, drawn up as tight as it could be stretched; a stump, the height of the stool, with its end cut to a round and blunt point, was then driven into the ground near the post before mentioned, and the stool being taken away, the bare heel of the sufferer was made to rest on this stump'. A quarter of an hour of this infliction was as much as most men could endure.

Occasionally the stocks were resorted to by some more compassionate Commanding Officer in the hope that public exposure to ridicule and contempt would shame the delinquent into repentance and future good behaviour. With the Braddock expedition to Fort Duquesne, of 1755, for example, a contemporary diary contains the entry:

> The General arriv'd after being expected three days. This day was put a Soldier in Stocks for getting drunk, to try what it would do, for whipping would not serve him.[3]

Yet for all the severity of the disciplinary system by which their lives were governed, the men of the rank and file remained remarkably cheerful and resilient; their rough voices raised on the line of march in such lilting ditties as *Lillibulero* and *Over the Hills and Far Away*; the

---

[1] Francis Grose, *op. cit.*
[2] *ibid.*
[3] Diary of Captain Cholmley's batman.

steady tramp of the column given rhythmic emphasis by the measured cadence of the fifes and drums. The drum—like the clash-pans, or cymbals—was Saracenic in origin; and as far back as the early days of the sixteenth century Henry VIII had sent all the way to Vienna for kettle-drums which could be played a-horse; for the kettle-drum and the trumpet were primarily reserved for the Cavalry.[1] With the Artillery train of 1705 the kettle-drums, and drummer, were distinguished by making their progress in 'an open chariot, richly ornamented, and drawn by no less than six long-tailed, richly-maned white horses'.

For his part, the 'footslogger' managed very well with fife, side-drum and horn. Tramping steadily through the murk and incessant rain which characterized Marlborough's epic march to the Danube, the red-coated ranks singing their favourite *British Grenadiers* epitomized their own *élan* and stout fighting quality when they roared out the challenging quatrain:

> When e'er we are commanded to storm the palisades,
> Our leaders march with fusees,[2] and we with hand-grenades;
> We throw them from the glacis, about the enemies' ears,
> Sing tow, row, row, row, row, row, for the British Grenadiers.

With the Earl of Peterborough's complementary campaign in the Iberian Peninsula, another ditty gained great popular favour which, over three-quarters of a century later, and with slightly altered words, was to be used by his political enemies to denigrate the King's second son, Frederick Duke of York, in command of the British contingent with the 'Coalition Army' in Flanders:

> The brave old King of Spain,
> He had ten thousand men;
> He marched them up a very high hill
> Then marched them down again.

It was the Marlborough campaigns, with the Schellenberg, Blenheim, Ramillies, Oudenarde and Malplaquet a carillon of victory, which served to consolidate the British Army and give it cohesion and that imperishable *esprit de corps* which has served to inspire it in good times

---

[1] Charles II's Life Guard had been fitted out with one kettle-drummer and four trumpeters per troop, in addition to the pair of kettle-drums and two trumpeters attached to the Colonel Commanding.

[2] i.e. fusils.

and in bad. For nothing serves to bind a body of men in comradeship as perils shared and privations endured in common.

No less worthy of record is the stout work of the Royal Navy in that Mediterranean Sea they virtually made their own. The bold seizure of Gibraltar by Sir George Rooke, victory in the sea-fight off Malaga, the capture of Barcelona, of Alicante, of Iviza and Majorca, and above all the establishment of a secure base in Minorca, constituted a magnificent counterpoint to Marlborough's triumphs in Europe's traditional cockpit. Further afield, the value of Commodore Martin's capture of Nova Scotia was only dimmed by the failure of combined operations against the French in Quebec.

Not that there was any great love lost between the two Services. There was a saying often to be heard on a warship's lower deck: 'A messmate before a shipmate, a shipmate before a stranger, a stranger before a dog, and a dog before a soldier.' To which the redcoat's retort was, 'A man only goes to sea when he can't get an honest job ashore; if there were more prisons, there'd be fewer sailors!'

Perhaps it was only in their defensive attitude towards the general public that the bluejacket and the redcoat felt a real sense of comradeship.

For the sailor ashore found scant welcome save from the harpies who battened on his open-hearted generosity. As for the 'common soldier', such was the distrust and contempt in which he was held that—like 'servants in livery'—he was forbidden access to all enclosed public parks; while the indigent veteran, thrown on the streets, if caught begging without the written permission of his former Commanding Officer or a magistrate, laid himself open to the hangman's noose. As Prince Rupert of the Rhine once grimly commented: 'A soldier's life is a life of honour, but a dog would not lead it.'

It has been written that a country gets the Government it deserves. If Britain had got no more than the Army and the Navy she *deserved*, she would long since have been conquered and trampled out of existence as a sovereign power.

3

Border War and Troubled Seas

'Good fences make good neighbours.'
Old Adage

WITH THE Peace of Nymeguen of 1678 and the reversion of New York
to English control, the authorities in Whitehall immediately took steps
to furnish a small body of troops – no more than a hundred Officers and
men – to garrison both Albany and New York itself. In due course a
detachment from the New York contingent was removed to distant
Esopus[1] and then to the 'furthest dorp'.

Once settled, these soldiers were dropped from the Duke's pay...
This scheme of settling Regular soldiers on small, contiguous
parcels of land in order to provide a defensive barrier is one that
recurs frequently in later memoranda on the Colonies. It never
seemed to work; the Governor of New York soon wrote that the
soldiers at Esopus 'are becoming more the nursery of Newgate,
than persons who have taken on them a settled and resolved life'.[2]

In addition to the New York company and a handful of troops in
Boston, there was what can only be termed a token garrison of twenty
men at New Castle, on the Delaware, and another of similar number at
Pemaquid.

The lowering threat of war with France called for the reconstitution
of the two companies at St Kitts, where the men had been without pay

[1] The original capital of New York Colony.
[2] John Shy, *Toward Lexington*; cf. N.Y.C.D. 426.

for three years, 'so that', as it was reported to the Privy Council, 'they are naked and have onely subsisted by the charity of the planters, and the care of their Colonell'. In 1678 two more companies of a hundred men apiece were sent to Jamaica; and by the end of the year a further two companies had been established in Virginia, drawn from the forces sent to quell Bacon's rebellion; although as yet nothing more substantiall than correspondence emerged from the discussion whether or no to install a garrison to watch over British interests in Newfoundland.

The pay of these overseas formations, together with the cost of the ordnance and the other stores they required, came to the not inconsiderable sum of £15,400 a year. Yet none of them could pretend to a permanent 'establishment'; while far too many of their rank and file came into the category of those who had 'left their country for their country's good'.

In general, where England's contemporary overseas military forces were concerned, the factious, narrow-minded Puritan element invariably gave preference to the local amateur — in the form of the militiaman — over the professional fighting man. Hence the necessity to hide away and give no permanent identity to those Colonial garrisons whose fundamental purpose was, after all, no more than the preservation of the inhabitants' life and liberty and the protection of those commercial interests in which the Puritan was anything but disinterested.

With James II confronting a populace as suspicious of his truckling to the French as the majority of it was resentful of his fidelity to the Roman faith, the Army, even more perhaps than the Navy, was violently riven in its sympathies. When the 12th Foot[1] were drawn up on Blackheath in the King's presence, and were informed that they must either sign a pledge to carry out the royal policy of indulgence towards Catholics as well as other sectarians, or leave his service forthwith, 'whole ranks without hesitation took him at his word, and grounded their arms; while two Officers and a few privates, all of them Catholics, alone consented to sign'.[2] Dismissal involved something more than exclusion from the Army. It meant the forfeiture of all arrears of pay and of the price of the Officers' Commissions. But on a matter of principle, there was no hesitation; the King's command of his servants' obedience did not extend to control of their spiritual beliefs. It is not without a strong element of irony that hundreds of the

[1] Subsequently known as the Suffolk Regiment.
[2] Fortescue, *History of the British Army*, (vol. I.)

3

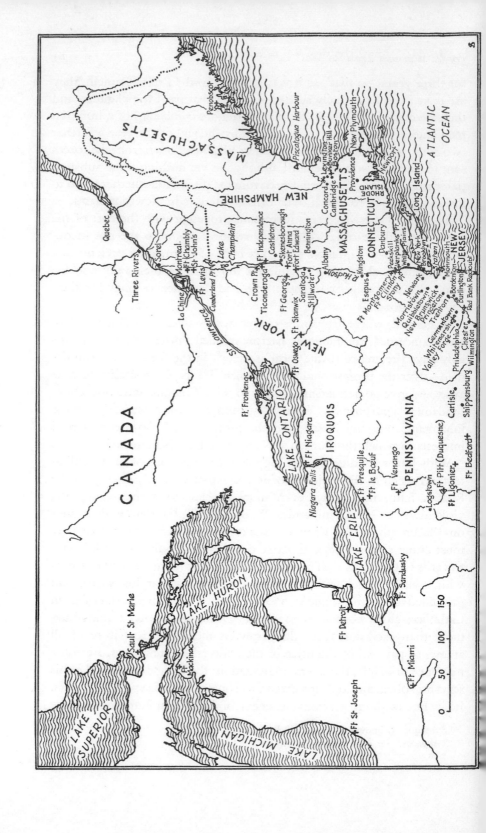

disbanded officers and men, seeking a refuge in Holland, subsequently came to furnish a considerable proportion of the troops supporting William of Orange's successful attempt to jockey himself on to England's throne.

So far as the Plantations were concerned, the man appointed by James II as Governor-General of the whole of the North American Colonies was Sir Edmund Andros. In the October of 1674 he had accepted the surrender of New York Colony from the Dutch and re-asserted the authority of the Proprietory; a procedure he had carried into execution—especially in Connecticut, Massachusetts, Rhode Island and New Jersey—with the minimum of tact and the maximum of over-bearing hauteur. In effect, James II's perfectly laudable design to unite the Plantations under a single centralized authority, the better to ensure their combined defence, had been hampered at every turn as much by Andros's maladroit handling of the project as by the settlers' obsession with the fetish of regional as well as personal liberty.

When the conscientious but obstinate King elected to forfeit his Kingdom for a rosary, the news of his deposition and flight, and of the instalment of 'Orange Billy' on England's throne, reached Boston on the fourth day of April 1689. The Governor-General being what he was, the bearer of such bodeful tidings was promptly clapped into gaol; but the intelligence he bore could not be suppressed; and 'the preachers had already matured the evil design of a revolution'.[1] 'There is a general buzzing among the people, great with expectation of their old Charter, or they know not what',[2] was Andros's message to Captain James, the garrison commander, accompanied by an order for the troops to be ready for action.

About nine o'clock in the morning Captain John George, R.N., commander of the British frigate moored in Boston roads, hurried ashore to ascertain what was going forward, and was promptly put under restraint by a crowd of local ship's carpenters. Everywhere tumult and wild excitement mounted as the crowds thronging the streets rapidly increased in number and boldness. Seeking to quiet the throng, the royalist Sheriff was made prisoner by the mob; while 'boys ran along the streets with clubs'; and from all quarters the drums beat to rally the militia. In vain Andros sought to win over a majority of the Council to his support. Resisted on all sides, he and a few of his immediate henchmen

[1] Nathaniel Byfield, *Account of the Late Revolution*. (P.R.O.)
[2] *ibid.*

withdrew to Fort Hill, where the exiguous garrison had been put under arms.

Once again Andros sought a conference with the leaders of what was obviously a well-concerted uprising, but his overtures were scorned. With the local militia swarming to join their Colours, the mere handful of royalist troops which constituted Andros's only hope of salvation would have had little chance of effecting anything but indiscriminate and useless slaughter. Standing sullenly in their ranks, they attempted no counter move when the militia, eagerly helped by the mob, 'turned the guns in the waterside sconce on the Fort'. And this despite the fact that their own cannon were 'all loden with small-shot'. The Governor-General's peremptory order to open up musketry fire on the milling crowd of militia and townsfolk was also totally ignored. Raving and cursing, Andros fell on the reluctant files, beating them with the flat of his sword and demanding that they take instant action, until an exasperated Dutchman in the ranks rounded on him to demand, ' "What the devil, should I fight a t'ousand men?", and so ran into the house.'[1] Thus there was virtually no resistance when the militia, at the direction of Captain Wait Winthrop, methodically set about stripping the apathetic huddle of Regulars of their arms.

With the arrest of Andros and certain of his closest supporters, the insurrectionary movement had achieved its purpose; and Boston happily set up a form of government which William eventually found it expedient to approve.

Where New York was concerned, heterogeneous as the population might be, it embodied a numerous Dutch element whose sympathies were all in favour of the fellow-countryman who had supported his wife's claim to the succession to such good purpose as to have usurped most of the powers which still resided in the royal prerogative. Since Sir Francis Nicholson, New York's Governor, showed extreme reluctance formally to proclaim the accession of William and Mary, unrest amongst the Hollanders mounted rapidly, and soon found a vociferous leader in Jacob Leisler, 'a man of headstrong temper, restless disposition, and very narrow capacity'.[2]

Inflated by the plaudits of the mob which had made him their champion, Leisler placed himself at the head of a number of armed men and marched on New York's Fort—where Nicholson and some of the more

[1] Samuel Prince, *Correspondence*.
[2] George Bancroft, *History of the Colonisation of the United States*.

responsible members of the community had taken refuge—and demanded the stronghold's surrender in the name of King William.

Once again the handful of Regulars in garrison showed no disposition to face up to a mob which greatly outnumbered them, and Leisler was allowed to take possession of the fort unimpeded.

At this juncture a letter arrived from England addressed in dangerously general terms 'to such as for the time take care for administering the laws of the province'. Without the slightest hesitation, Leisler regarded this missive as being addressed to himself and as endowing him with the authority to act as Lieutenant-Governor.

Nicholson had cravenly fled the country; but some of the stouterhearted of the Colony's élite had retired to the Fort at Albany, declaring their intention of holding it in the name of King William, and disavowing all connection with the self-elevated Leisler. This was more than the latter's rapidly acquired sense of power and consequence was prepared to tolerate; and James Milbourne, his prospective son-in-law, was sent at the head of a numerous armed force to take possession of the outpost. Once again the minuscule oddment of Regulars was in no position —and certainly in no mood—to take positive defensive action, and the stronghold was surrendered without demur; both the few men of the garrison and the refugees from New York seeking sanctuary in the neighbouring Colonies. This gave Leisler an admirable excuse to confiscate the estates of those substantial but fugitive New York citizens who were no longer in a position to protect their own property.

But Leisler's hour of trumpery glory was soon to end. The first check came with the arrival of the *Beaver* bearing Captain Ingoldsby, whose royal commission to take over New York's defences was backed by the substantial body of troops under his command. With a self-confidence little short of impudence, Leisler offered to procure him quarters in the town. 'Possession of His Majesty's fort is what I demand', was Ingoldsby's curt retort; but Leisler continued to protest that the newcomer had produced no order from the King nor even from Henry Sloughter, the newly appointed Governor, whose arrival was daily expected.

Quietly but resolutely, Ingoldsby marched his men into the town, where the more responsible citizens welcomed them warmly; although there was a good deal of rioting by the rowdier elements among Leisler's following, and some blood was spilt. With Sloughter's appearance on the scene Leisler made a brave show of keeping up appearances by sending to enquire what orders the new Governor bore for him. The rebel leader's communication was ignored and his messenger detained. 'Next morning, Leisler asked, by letter, to whom he should surrender the fort. The letter went unheeded; and Sloughter, giving no notice to the rebel, commanded Ingoldsby "to arrest Leisler, and the persons called his council".'[1]

Ingoldsby had sufficient force to carry the order unflurriedly into effect; and

the prisoners, eight in number, were promptly arraigned before a special court...Six of the inferior insurgents made their defence, were convicted of high treason, and were reprieved. Leisler and Milbourne denied to the Governor the power to institute a tribunal for judging his predecessor, and they appealed to the King. On their refusal to plead, they were condemned of high treason as mutes, and sentenced to death; Joseph Dudley, of New England, now chief justice in New York, giving the opinion that Leisler had no legal authority whatever. 'Certainly never greater villains lived', wrote Sloughter; but he 'resolved to wait for the royal pleasure, if by any other means than hanging he could keep the country quiet'.

It was the vote of the reconstituted Assembly, however, which finally persuaded the Governor to take individual action in the matter; and Leisler and his chief lieutenant were duly condemned to the gallows. It was a resolution which undoubtedly met with the full approval of a monarch whose authority was far too brittle to encourage even a hint of challenge.

It is clear that the troops which accompanied Captain Ingoldsby — two companies, each of a hundred men — were of a different quality from the scratch garrisons which had been left to moulder in Boston, New York and Albany. Ingoldsby's men had carried out their duties resolutely but with admirable restraint, calmly refusing to be provoked into hasty action by the hostile New York mob. They were, of course, little more than a token force. It followed that by 1693, with war raging against the French in the Netherlands and French military power steadily building up in Canada, reinforcements had somehow to be found for North America. In December, therefore, the King in Council gave orders that two companies, each of a hundred men, 'and sufficient recruits to make the existing companies in New York up to strength',

[1] Bancroft, *op. cit.*

be enlisted forthwith and sent overseas at the earliest possible moment; a ukase which was duly carried into effect.[1]

Less than four months later another Warrant was issued for the forming of four companies, together with 'a chaplain, surgeon, storekeeper, armourer, and two matrosses, to be maintained out of the surplusage due on the thirty *per centum* difference between English and New York money. Each company to consist of a Captain, 2 Lieutenants, 3 Serjeants, 3 Corporals, 2 drummers, and 100 men.'[2]

By August the troops had been embodied and fitted out, and were *en route* to their embarkation port. On the line of march they were temporarily quartered in Petersfield Parish Church; and considerable disagreement arose between the military and town authorities on the delicate question of defilement and a claim for damages.

But the Plantations were destined never to see this particular contingent of 'Bloodybacks'. For by November they were once more in England, after three months of unspeakable hardship. Battered by vile weather; assailed by a number of French privateers; herded together in overcrowded, pest-ridden, foully insanitary ship's quarters, not more than forty out of the whole muster had escaped illness or injury. For, as the victim of another freighter-turned-transport put it, life in such circumstances was 'continual destruction in the foretop, the pox above board, the plague between decks, hell in the forecastle, and the devil at the helm'.[3]

Reconstituted, however, the four companies finally reached New York, by way of Boston, in the June of 1695.

Such negligible contributions to the Colonies' defence amounted, of course, to little more than a gesture of goodwill. But since the flimsy Peace of Ryswick, of 1697, amounted to no more than a pause in a life-and-death struggle which was bound to be renewed as soon as the respective belligerents were once again in a fit state to take the field, to meet the demand for the four to six battalions required in the West Indies, and the troops looked for in North America, imposed a drain upon available resources it was far from easy to meet. Moreover, service in nearly all the overseas garrisons was extremely unpopular both with Officers and men. In North America the redcoat felt alien and unwelcome. In the West Indies so appalling was the mortality from fever and

---

[1] C.S.P. Col., 1693–1696, 754.
[2] C.S.P. Col., 1693–1696, 998.
[3] Guardsman John Marshall Deane, First Foot Guards.

other regional health hazards, that to be posted to any island in the Caribbean was tantamount to being sentenced to death.

> Once shipped off to the West Indies, the men seem to have been totally forgotten. No proper provision was made for paying them; Colonels who cared for their men were compelled to borrow money to save them from starvation; Colonels who did not care came home with many of their Officers, and left the men to shift for themselves.[1]

When the single company for the defence of Newfoundland left England in 1701, their destination had to be kept from them lest the men of the rank and file should desert *en masse*.[2]

Yet the North American settlements were clearly under growing threat. As early as 1636 the percipient Thomas Trelawny had warned that unless measures were taken to arrest French encroachment, 'there will bee butt small hopes in Continuing our plantations so neere them who daylye drawe towards us, whose neighbourhood (I much feare) will prove very prejudiciall unto us'. In at least some quarters in the homeland awareness of this threat was just as acute as in the Colonies themselves.

In 1493 the 'line' drawn by Pope Alexander VI had allocated virtually the whole of the American Continent to Portugal and Spain. A little over a century later a successor on the Papal Throne, Paul V, had blandly assented to Louis XIII's casual grant of all the territory from Florida to the St Lawrence to Jean de Biencourt, Seigneur de Poutraincourt; an endowment which completely disregarded England's claim to the extensive domain extending from the Allegheny and Appalachian mountain ranges eastwards to the sea; tenure of which was based upon Cabot's voyages of discovery in the service of the thrifty Henry VII, who had acquired a potential empire for a down payment of ten pounds and a pension of eighty pounds a year for the bold venturer who had lighted upon it.

It was to this land of promise that the Elizabethans had come to found Virginia; it was on the north-eastern seaboard of New England that an error in navigation had deposited the *Mayflower*'s Puritan pioneers.

---

[1] Fortescue, *op. cit.*

[9] After 1704 garrisons were also wanted for Gibraltar and Minorca.

At the outset the immigrants' greatest peril had arisen out of the hostility of the indigenous Indians to the interlopers on territory they naturally regarded as their own. In 1616 a great wave of plague had practically eliminated the Indians in the area of the first settlements. But as the tribes had gradually been restored to strength, the immigrants' honest attempts to purchase a foothold had all too often been nullified by unscrupulous encroachments on preserves which the indigenous inhabitants were determined to keep for themselves. In the early days the newcomers had often been hard put to it to hold their own. But as the immigrant population steadily increased, superior weapons and more effective organization had frequently resulted in the overthrow of the 'Tawnies' at the hands of the 'Palefaces'; defeats so sanguinary that in 1622 and again in 1637 and 1644 they had amounted to something little short of massacre. In general, the New England Colonies, with their clusters of small townships, had been in a better position to hold their own against the Indian menace than Virginia and Maryland, with their far more scattered homesteads. It was this consideration which had so strongly inclined Governor Berkeley towards conciliation in 1675; when the last delirious uprising of the Narragansetts and their allies in New England – 'King Philip's[1] war' – had threatened to spread to Virginia and Maryland. Relying on stealth and superior forest lore, the Indians had initially possessed the advantage, putting Lancaster, Groton and Medfield to the torch, forcing the abandonment of Simsbury, and inflicting heavy damage on Springfield, Marlboro and Rehobath. Constant assaults were delivered against Andover, Woburn, Sudbury, Bridgewater, Hatfield and Hadley, with heavily mounting casualties on both sides. Enduring for over a year, 'it was the storm in which the ancient inhabitants of the land were to vanish away. They rose without hope, therefore they fought without mercy. For them as a nation there was no tomorrow.' And with 'King Philip's' death the flames of revolt died down to sullenly smouldering embers.

The suppression of the uprising had been entirely the responsibility of the militia and such volunteers as had temporarily been added to their ranks. But successful as they had been in subduing the Redskin menace, a far greater danger was building up on their frontiers, which was destined not only to tax their own energies to the full, but ultimately to call for full scale intervention on the part of the motherland.

Up to the mid-seventeenth century French Canada had been no more

[1] Philip of Pokoneket, better known as 'King Philip'.

3*

than a rival competitor in the trade with the Indians in beaver skins and other peltry. It was a traffic out of which had arisen a tendency for the tribes not reconciled to the twelve to fifteen natives leagued together in the Five Nations,[1] to put themselves under French protection; for the members of the Iroquoian clans generally to favour the Colonists of English stock.

Then in 1665 Louis XIV's enterprising chief Minister, Colbert, had posted to Quebec one of the most promising members of his political *kindergarten* — Jean Baptiste Talon. It was the Minister's design that, under the new Intendant, Canada — already garrisoned by the veteran Régiment Carignan-Salières — should be transformed from a struggling foreign mission, run by a handful of fanatical Jesuits, into a province of France. The first need was to establish a well-peopled and prosperous dependency based upon the River St Lawrence. Within three years the population of three thousand[2] had doubled, very largely owing to the importation of assorted consignments of *filles du roi*, nubile but dowerless wenches willing to marry anyone in a position to provide them with a home. Although their distribution was reminiscent of nothing so much as the disposal of Christian slaves in an Oriental *Sok*, there were few to call the cold-blooded transaction into question. 'The Vestal Virgins', one of the garrison wrote home, 'were heaped up in three different Apartments, where the Bridegrooms singled out their Brides just as a Butcher do's an Ewe from amongst a Flock of Sheep. In the three Seraglios there was as much variety and change of Diet as could satisfie the most whimsical Appetite; for here were some big, some little, some fair, some brown, some fat, and some meagre.'

Under Talon's capable supervision a riparian community had come into being which added a hardy peasant stock to the breed of roving *coureur-de-bois*. Subsequent to the Treaty of Aix-la-Chapelle, of 1668, the secularization of the dependency had gone steadily forward.

Too impetuous in his eagerness to realize his dream of a great overseas empire, Talon had been recalled to France in 1670; the year which had witnessed Charles II's incorporation of the Hudson Bay Company, and the erection in that unwelcoming territory of a certain number of forts, complete with small garrisons, for its protection. Talon's succes-

---

[1] Six Nations up to the fratricidal strife of 1672, as they were again to become early in the eighteenth century.

[2] Less than the contemporary population of Rhode Island.

sor had been that tough old veteran of the Thirty Years' War, Louis de Baume, Comte de Frontenac and Pillau; no less a visionary than his aspiring predecessor. 'Quebec', he wrote exultantly to the Minister, 'could be no better situated as the future capital of a great empire. The colonies of foreign nations are trembling with fright. The measures we have taken to confine them within narrow limits do not permit them to extend themselves, except at the peril of having war declared against them as usurpers; and this, in fact, is what they seem greatly to fear.' The 'steps' referred to included the siting of a number of fortifications at strategic points — such as Niagara and on the *détroit* separating Lake Huron from Lake Erie. But Frontenac's unending differences with the inflexible Bishop Laval had led to the old warrior's recall to France by the time Robert Cavalier Sieur de la Salle, thrusting down the waters of the mighty Mississippi, had debouched into the Gulf of Mexico. As the outcome of this daring feat of exploration the whole of the territory through which La Salle had passed, the vast hinterland between the Alleghenies and the Rocky Mountains, from the Rio Grande and the Gulf of Mexico to the uppermost waters of the Missouri, had been brazenly annexed to the French Crown.

With the great bowstring of the Mississippi forming an arc enclosing the British settlers on their narrow Atlantic shelf, they were confined to a limited terrain from which it would be a matter of no great difficulty to expel them, bag and baggage, when the moment came to take possession of the whole of America, from Florida to the Arctic Circle, in the name of his Most Christian Majesty, Louis XIV.

The Colonists' only immediate riposte to these grandiose Gallic pretensions was to conclude a treaty with the Iroquoian confederacy which brought the Five Nations specifically under the protection of the English Crown;[1] a pact which incidentally reinforced the white men's territorial claims beyond the River Ohio. In Quebec the new Intendant, Jacques de Brissay, Marquis de Denonville, hastened to strengthen the French grip on the far West and build up a confederacy of the Western Indian tribes. He then busied himself in consolidating the defences on the *détroit* and drawing up plans for the erection of a proper fort just below Niagara, to bar approach to the Erie waterway from south and east. Then, mustering some three thousand French Regulars, Canadian

---

[1] The prime members of the confederacy were the Seneca, Onondaga, Cayuga, Oneida and Mohawks. Their original fighting strength had been some 3,500 braves. By 1700 this total had declined to approximately 1,100.

militia and friendly Indians, he fell on the Seneca, who suffered severe casualties and the loss of much of their livestock.

Thomas Dongan, Governor of New York, immediately protested that the Frenchmen had invaded 'the King my Master's territories in hostill manner'; and formally demanded the return of the English and Redskin prisoners in French hands. It was left to the Iroquois to take more positive action. In a blinding hailstorm, some fifteen hundred warriors fell on La Chine — just west of Montreal — fired the settlement, butchered two hundred of its inhabitants on the spot, and carried off another hundred to be tortured at leisure. With Denonville cowering helplessly behind Montreal's defences, Canada was prostrated by the most terrible disaster it had yet experienced.

Heavily preoccupied as he might be in Europe, Louis had no intention of letting his burgeoning province of New France slip through his fingers by default. The septuagenarian Frontenac was retrieved from unsought retirement and packed off, in the King's own words, 'to serve me as you did before'.

Arrived once more in Quebec, Frontenac speedily evolved a plan for the outright conquest of the New England settlements. A cross-country march, at the head of a thousand Regulars and six hundred militia, would bring him to Albany, hard by the River Hudson. A dash down the waterway would end in his junction with a couple of French warships awaiting his arrival off the tip of Manhattan Island. The township's reduction would present no difficulty; and with its two hundred wooden dwellings put to the torch, New York could be used as a base for the conquest of all the territory lying between the Hudson and the St Croix river, which bounded the mainland districts of French-held Acadia to the westward. It was a stroke which, if successful, would consummate the ruin of some eighteen thousand Colonists and the total subjugation of their catspaw Iroquois.

But, yielding to the contemporary temptation to put the capture of profitable 'prize' above all other considerations, the French fleet failed to put in an appearance on time. The elaboration of an alternative plan was abruptly halted by the dismaying intelligence that the nine Indian tribes of the interior — hitherto regarded as virtually under French suzerainty — had signed a treaty with the English Colonists and the Iroquois, and openly expressed their readiness to join in the extermination of the French. In the vital matter of trading policy, genuinely warming English 'strouds' and 'duffels' and sound Jamaica rum had finally triumphed over shoddy, threadbare Gallic blankets and liberally watered French brandy.

Frontenac's riposte was to raid Schenectady, the last outpost of New York. The two snowmen sentinels hopefully erected by the militia as guardians of the unbarred gates were contemptuously kicked aside, the garrison of one junior Officer and eight bemused militiamen knocked on the head, and the settlement sent up in flames. In the confused fighting which followed, sixty of the inhabitants were slaughtered; while of the refugees who struggled through the snow to the sanctuary of Albany twenty-five lost one or more limbs owing to frostbite. Salmon Falls, in New Hampshire, was the next victim, where the township was fired, thirty of the inhabitants tomahawked in their beds, and fifty-four women and children borne away into degrading captivity. A similar fate was visited on Port Royal, in Casco Bay;[1] where five hundred blood-crazed assailants fell on a hundred half-trained militia, who were wounded, slain, or marched away as prisoners, in shameless violation of the pledge to extend quarter and freedom to all who surrendered.

The naked brutality of Frontenac's campaign of musket, tomahawk and firebrand was the one thing capable of jolting the Colonists out of their preoccupation with their purely domestic issues and turning their minds to the formulation of counter-measures against a momentarily triumphant enemy. With sixteen more frontier posts overrun and the French-inspired massacre of Dover's helpless inhabitants by the Abenakis, a retaliatory plan was agreed upon by the respective Assemblies of the Colonies concerned. One expedition—fitted out mainly by New York and Connecticut, and under the leadership of Fitz John Winthrop —was to set out by way of the Richelieu river to attempt the seizure of Montreal, while a second armament of seven ships, two hundred and eighty seamen and five hundred drafted militiamen sallied forth for a descent on that sector of Acadia lying to the south-east of the bay of Fundy. This venture was to be under the leadership of Sir William Phips, former Boston apprentice shipwright, adventurer, and amateur gentleman, who had acquired no little fame through having retrieved £300,000 from a sunken Spanish galleon, quelled his mutinous crew with his bare fists, and received the accolade from Charles II in return for his tactful surrender of the 'King's share' of the treasure-trove.

With plenty of real vigour behind his bluster, Phips speedily hustled Port Royal into surrender; sparing such of the inhabitants as were

[1] Portland. Gulf of Maine.

prepared, with whatever mental reservation, to take the oath of loyalty to King William III. Phips then proceeded to commandeer all the local shipping and rifle the fort, where instinct guided him unerringly to the French Commandant's money chest, whose contents he lost no time in impounding. To this haul of specie he added a few trifles of negotiable property in the way of 'six silver spoons, six silver forks, one silver cup in the shape of a gondola, a pair of pistols, three new wigs', some useful kitchen utensils, and a number of articles of clothing which included 'one red waistcoat and four nightcaps with lace edging'. As a 'snapper up of unconsidered trifles', Autolycus could have learned a lesson from the eminently practical William Phips.

With so stimulating an example, Phips's followers proceeded to strip the town bare; their loot including so prodigious a store of brandy that, on the expedition's return to its home port, for a time the price of prime *eau-de-vie* underwent a sharp decline.

No such fortune, however, attended the enterprise against Montreal. A party of Mohawks, led by Peter Schuyler, pushing forward as far as the St Lawrence, had been bloodily repulsed. The balance of the force had scarcely advanced beyond Wood Creek, where they had been halted by shortage of provisions and a virulent outbreak of smallpox. 'The expedition had ended in mutual recriminations, which did but express and confirm the hereditary antipathy of Connecticut and New York.'[1]

Phips's success against Port Royal had been sufficiently encouraging to warrant a second venture, this time against Quebec itself.[2] By mid-October, therefore, an armament of thirty-four small vessels, bearing two thousand seamen, militia and volunteers, was threading its way through the uncharted waters of the St Lawrence, to deploy before Quebec's defences. Only four of the vessels were armed with light-weight ordnance; but with their appearance the populace momentarily yielded to panic, scurrying away to seek safety in the west; while the nuns of the Hotel Dieu, burying their silver and sacred vessels, sought to assemble enough carts to ensure their evacuation to Lorette, out of range of artillery fire. Confidence was very largely restored, however, when Frontenac came hurrying down from up-country at the head of a useful reinforcement of five hundred men.

---

[1] Bancroft, *op. cit.*

[2] Quebec had been in English possession in 1629, but had been handed back to the French by the terms of the Treaty of St Germain of 1654. Acadia had been conquered in 1632 but was restored by the Treaty of Breda in 1667.

Phips, who never hesitated to overcall his hand, promptly sent an emissary ashore to demand unconditional surrender and formal submission to the Crown of England.

Frontenac exploded in a retort which has become classic: 'I will answer your General', he roared, 'only by the mouth of my cannon, that he may learn that a man like me is not to be summoned after this fashion. Let him do his best, and I will do mine.'

In keeping with all this extravagant fanfaronade the ensuing warlike activities were more notable for a lavish expenditure of powder and shot than for anything particularly notable in the way of generalship. An amphibious attempt on Quebec by way of Beauport and the Charles river, to the east of the city, was spasmodically supported by a feeble bombardment from the vessels in the basin. But this sort of closely integrated combined operation calls for far more military skill and experience than Phips had at his disposal. With Frontenac giving as good as he got, the Rear-Admiral's flag worn by the Bostonian at his masthead shot away, gleefully retrieved by an aquatic Frenchman and borne in triumph to the Citadel, the battered New England armada put about and limped down the St Lawrence, hustled by a blustering wind. Winter storms, encountered on the passage home, added their inexorable toll to the total lost in action.

While Quebec chanted a *Te Deum* for its deliverance, and proudly displayed the captured flag in the choir, Boston sought to palliate the all-round failure of the enterprise by averring that its ambitious design had 'fallen under the awful frown of God'. The authorities then proceeded to commit the unpardonable enormity of paying off their tattered troops and seamen in barely negotiable paper money.

Inspired by the successful defence of Quebec, it was not long before loyally Francophile Canadians were seeping back to their abandoned homesteads in Acadia; while a belated descent on La Prairie, across the river from Montreal, led by Peter Schuyler at the head of some three hundred Iroquois, did little to disguise the lack of success achieved elsewhere.

Next the blond giant Iberville Le Moyne led a small but highly efficient force into Hudson's Bay, to fall on the inconsiderable garrison at Fort Hayes, which was ignominiously captured before the sleeping men could struggle into their breeches. Slumbering Fort Rupert also fell to surprise attack, together with an English ship lying at her moorings nearby. The exploit was rounded off by the seizure of Fort Albany,

on the eastern shore of James bay; the success of the whole enterprise
being attributable as much to the absence of adequate naval force in the
Hudson Bay area as to the firm, centralized direction which distinguished every contemporary venture embarked upon by the French in
Canada.

There was sound organization, too, behind the incessant Franco-
Indian raids which kept the borderlands and their embryo townships
in a perpetual state of alarm. During the February and March of 1697
mixed bands attacked and ravished Andover and Haverhill; frontier
hamlets, yet within twenty-five miles of Boston. Port Royal could not
be held, and the French contrived to capture the Massachusetts fort at
Pemaquid; the Boston authorities making no sustained effort to hold
their enemies at bay since 'it would be very grievous to take the people
from their labour', and there was 'likewise no money to support the
charge'.

In 1697 the political economist John Locke had reported to the
Board of Trade and Plantations that, 'There is force anough in the
Colonies to repel all the attempts made by the French and Indians, nor
can it be imagined that so great a number of English should think it
much to employ their own hands and purses in the defence of their
estates, lives and families'.

Unfortunately, to concert a combined effort against the French by
all the Provinces concerned seemed entirely beyond realization.

> The inability of all the English Colonies to subordinate their in-
> dividual concerns to a unified effort against the common enemy
> was a major weakness that persisted through the entire succession
> of colonial wars...Typically, the Colonies nearest the danger were
> most ardent for action; while Colonies not immediately threatened
> showed a marked reluctance to commit themselves.[1]

In effect, regional self-absorption proved even stronger than the longing for security, with the inevitably calamitous result.

Further humiliation came with the news of Iberville's successful encounter with three British warships in Hudson's Bay and his capture
of Fort Nelson, together with £20,000 worth of furs, which were
awaiting transhipment. From this exploit Iberville went on to seize
Newfoundland, an impudent *chevauchée* supinely assented to in the Peace
of Ryswick, of 1697—signed less than a year before the ubiquitous

[1] Douglas Edward Leach, *The Northern Colonial Frontier*.

Iberville went on to establish a French settlement at the mouth of the Mississippi. Thus not only were the New England fisherfolk denied access to the Newfoundland Banks, but the French were in firm possession of the two gateways giving access to the vast hinterland beyond the Appalachians.

From 1702 until 1712 all Britain's energies were concentrated upon frustrating Louis XIV's ambition to achieve the hegemony of Europe and further extend his realm to include the whole of North America. Stretched as their resources were, however, in the first year of the Spanish Succession conflict the British Government did at least contrive to organize an expedition for the reclamation of Newfoundland. Command of the enterprise was bestowed on Commodore John Leake, a man 'who took his bottle freely, but never was disguised by it'. Hoisting his pendant in the 60-gun *Exeter*, and accompanied by H.M.S. *Lichfield*, *Medway*, *Reserve*, *Montagu* and *Assistance*, he sailed briskly across the Atlantic to carry out his mission.

Arriving at his destination, and having 'ordered all the boats manned and armed,...he sent them ashore. Soon after landing their men, they drove the French from the place, burning and destroying all the houses together with all their stages for building ships, all their shallops and boats, some vessels that were already built, and others near finished, with everything belonging to them.'[1] The illicit fishing 'stages' at Trepassy, St Mary's and St Lawrence were also demolished, and the French fort at St Patrick totally dismantled. From beginning to end the 'Bloodybacks' concerned had carried out their task with exemplary efficiency and despatch; with no individual pillaging to mar the complete impersonality with which they executed their orders.

Only a little earlier an abortive French attempt to capture Charlestown,[2] South Carolina, had merely served to throw into high relief the success of a British expedition into the Indian territory between the Savannah and Alatamahaw rivers. 'The English flag having been carried in triumph through the wilderness, the savages were overawed; and Great Britain established a new claim to the central forests that were soon to be named Georgia.'[3]

The year 1704, however, witnessed a very different performance from

[1] Stephen Martin Leake, *Life of Sir John Martin Leake*.
[2] So termed up to the time of the Revolution.
[3] Bancroft, *op. cit.*

Admiral Graydon. Sent out with a squadron whose primary purpose was the protection of the West Indies trade, he was instructed to take the northern course with the object of capturing Placentia, on the deeply indented bay of that name, to the west of St John's, Newfoundland. Although in command of a powerful armament, Graydon had no stomach for the task with which he had been entrusted. An obliging council of war having come to the convenient conclusion that the enterprise was impractical and would 'tend to dishonour Her Majesty's arms', the Admiral altered course and headed for his ultimate destination. Thereafter, no one was more indignantly surprised than he to find himself dismissed the Service.

Fortunately, Sir George Rooke in the Mediterranean and the Duke of Marlborough on the Danube were offering ample proof that they were made of far sterner metal.

Europe, of course, called for the consistent concentration of British effort. Yet a squadron could always be found for the West Indies station; while the 48-gun *Southampton*—relieved in 1701 by the *Shoreham* —kept watch over the Chesapeake, to deal with any enemy privateer that might venture into the bay. But soon the increase from four to eight hundred in the quota of seamen allotted to the Chesapeake convoy proved insufficient to guarantee the tobacco fleet from loss from enemy privateers and vessels 'sailing on the account'. This was very largely attributable to the fact that there were far too many individual sailings and a good deal of slackness in getting the tobacco ships ready for sea in time to join the convoy, leaving home waters in May and returning in the following October. Not that Virginia, Maryland and New England were without their own daring and resourceful privateers. Richard Johnson, master of the Maryland brigantine *Betty*, was only one of many successful skippers sailing under Letters of Marque and Reprisal. Even the notorious Captain William Kidd had briefly enjoyed the trust and confidence of the New England authorities, having been sent out under a Letter of Marque to round up such infamous *filibustiers* as Thomas Tew of Rhode Island, and Thomas Wake and William Maze of New York. Interpreting his instructions with such latitude as to leave no doubt that he himself had indulged in piracy on a very considerable scale, Kidd's rash return to New York 'with his ship a-groan with her weight of booty', for which he found it very difficult legitimately to account, led to his summary arrest and his despatch in chains, aboard H.M.S. *Advice*, for trial in England. Charged with murder as well as piracy, Kidd was found guilty and met his end at Execution Dock, Wapping.

The New England authorities were, of course, quite capable of dealing with offenders caught in local waters. For John Quelch, who had tossed the master of the Marblehead brigantine *Charles* over the side before seizing the vessel and making off to 'sail on the account', was by no means the only malefactor to make grim acquaintance with the gibbet erected on Scarel's Wharf in Boston.

New England privateers had steadily driven the Acadian fisherfolk from their home waters and when Louis Hector Callières — Frontenac's successor as Governor[1] — sent Lieutenant Neuvillette to deal with the situation, a sanguinary encounter ensued in which the Frenchman was killed and his vessel captured.

Successful French aggression along the borderlands, however, continued unabated; Cotton Mather complaining with considerable warrant that the merciless enemy forays were 'the chief sources of New England's misery'. For despite the fact that several of its homesteads were stoutly stockaded to serve as 'garrison houses', in the mid-winter of 1704 the populous settlement of Deerfield, Massachusetts, was devastated by a Franco-Indian band three hundred and eighty strong, led by Hertel de Rouville and Pierre Boucher. Approaching silently on snowshoes under cover of darkness, the raiders were busy at their fell work of slaughter before the majority of their victims had aroused themselves from sleep. Forty-seven of those who tried to fight back were slain with every circumstance of barbarity; of the hundred and twelve men, women and children who were borne away in captivity only the hardiest survived to be paraded in front of Callières's successor, the ageing but formidable Marquis de Vaudreuil-Cavagnal.

Not that Deerfield was alone in the outrage and misery which had been inflicted upon it. Indeed, the foray against the peaceful little riverside settlement of Haverhill, on the Merrimac, met with so little organized resistance as to encourage Iberville to press for a full-scale expedition, advancing by way of Chaudière and Kennebec, whose objective would be nothing less than the capture of Boston itself.

It was in his capacity as Governor of New York that Lord Cornbury sought yet again to give substance to the somewhat shallow hope that the universal danger would serve to unite the respective Colonies in a confederation capable of evolving a common plan of defence which

---

[1] Frontenac had died in 1698, and been given sepulture in the church of the Recollets.

owed nothing to the support of the Iroquois; whom he stigmatized as 'a very uncertain people to trust, who do lie under very strong temptation from the French'. But mutual jealousies and incompatibilities proved stronger even than the common sense of danger; and such measures of defence as were put in hand were sporadic and entirely wanting in co-ordination.

The best that could be contrived was to designate sixteen townships, from Hadley, in Massachusetts, to Wells, in Maine, to serve as an outpost line. In this forward defence area the local militia was reinforced by especially recruited Colonial infantry and cavalry. In these countermeasures, however, the four Independent Companies of British Regulars stationed in North America were scheduled for no specific task other than that of forming a minuscule general reserve to the militia. Progressively dwindling in strength and grossly neglected by those at home responsible for their upkeep and well-being, their employment in the field in any case could have made little difference to the course taken by events. The suspicion is not to be suppressed, however, that the Royalist Governors were by no means averse to having a small but disciplined force available for the support of an authority openly challenged almost as often as it was privately condemned.

The best answer to hostile penetration is counter-penetration. With this consideration in mind, in 1704 the Indian fighter, Benjamin Church, headed a force of seven hundred militia and volunteers in an attempt to recapture Port Royal. At the outset Church was successful in luring Biron Custine from his defences to offer open battle. But the outcome of the indecisive encounter left the Frenchman still in possession of the guardian fortress, and Church in such a state of baffled irresolution as entirely to forfeit the confidence and support of his followers. No better fortune attended the 1709 expedition organized by the Newbury militia Colonel, John March; despite the support afforded the enterprise by H.M.S. *Deptford*, and the fact that the French garrison had become so demoralized that Subercase — who had succeeded Custine as Commandant — experienced considerable difficulty in averting a mutiny and a concerted move on the part of the garrison and inhabitants to sue for peace.

Since Port Royal's reduction remained an objective of primary importance, the Colonies finally agreed to petition the mother country for that solid aid to which their precarious position as fledgling extensions of the homeland fully entitled them. It was a request which was assured of immediate and careful attention. For there were many, both in Parliament and the City, to recall Lord Bellomont's searching comment[1] that, should the defence of their settlements be left solely to the Colonists, 'it would put an opportunity in their hands for setting up an independence of the Crown, which it must be feared all the Plantations on the whole of the Continent have too great a propensity to'. Since the bulk of the Colonial stock was still sturdily British in origin and outlook, this is perhaps less surprising than his Lordship appeared to find it.

In the event — with Malplaquet and the fall of Lille, Douai and Mons just over the horizon — Samuel Vetch, Massachusetts' representative in England, returned to Boston with the assurance that a Naval squadron and five veteran regiments would shortly be on their way to assist in the conquest of Acadia. If all went as planned, operations against Canada would follow on the reduction of Port Royal.

To further the general design, the Colonies were to furnish fifteen hundred men for a synchronized overland advance on Montreal, together with a contingent for the Port Royal expedition; the Iroquois confederation, apart from the Seneca, also agreeing to play their part in the enterprise. Despite the grumbling of the predominantly Dutch traders in Albany, perturbed at this threat to their clandestine traffic with Canada, the main Colonial force cheerfully assembled at Wood Creek under Colonel Francis Nicholson, former Lieutenant Governor of New York and an experienced Indian fighter.

Erecting his store houses and defences, Nicholson anxiously awaited the word which would set him on the road to confidently anticipated victory. But the weeks sped by and still no orders arrived. Instead, pestilence came to ravage the dispirited camp, and the death-roll mounted rapidly. It was not until 11th October that Nicholson received a despatch informing him that the whole enterprise would have to be postponed. An unfavourable turn of fortune had necessitated the diversion of the promised British troops to Portugal.

In the circumstances it is scarcely a matter for surprise that the Colonists' bitter disappointment should have been succeeded by a girding resentment and mounting suspicion of those authorities in the mother country who appeared so inconsequently to have falsified their pledged word, while plunging the Plantations deeply into debt. It is perfectly comprehensible that the settlers and their leaders should have

---

[1] Written during his Governorship of New York, 1698–1701

failed to make allowance for the fact that to the authorities in London
America was far distant; that troublesome events nearer home, in the
Low Countries, in Spain and in Portugal, should have been accorded
priority of attention.

In the outcome it was clear that America had been anything but
forgotten. For Peter Schuyler had added a note of well-calculated
personal appeal when he had persuaded five Mohawk chiefs to accompany him to London. Although, unfortunately, one of them had died
on passage across the Atlantic, the arrival of the remainder in the
metropolis had caused a sensation. Tricked out in sumptuous gold-
laced scarlet robes, they had been received in audience by the Queen,
monopolized a whole issue of Addison's *Spectator*, and so strikingly
epitomized the Colonies' urge to be relieved, once and for all, from the
French menace on the borderlands, that public support for an early
enterprise against Port Royal had been virtually without a dissentient
voice.

By early September of 1704 Commodore Martin in H.M.S. *Dragon*,
accompanied by H.M.S. *Lowestoft*, *Caesar*, *Feversham* and the *Star* bomb-
ketch, together with a substantial body of Marines, arrived in Boston
harbour. The convoy was completed by a hospital vessel, store ships
and transports. To supplement the British forces, four regiments of
volunteers had been recruited from Massachusetts, Rhode Island,
Connecticut and New Hampshire; brought in by 'encouragements'
which included 'a coat worth thirty shillings', and a pledge that all
survivors of the venture would be permitted to retain the 'Queen's
musket' with which they had been issued.[1] Thirty local vessels had also
been provided for the Provincials' transportation; while Nicholson,
with the local rank of General, was in command of the Colonial troops
and nominally of the Marine contingent; with the ubiquitous Samuel
Vetch acting as Adjutant-General.

By the end of the month the armament was at the river-mouth leading
to Port Royal; the loss of the *Caesar* on the rocks being more than made
good by the arrival of Captain Mathews in H.M.S. *Chester*.

Confronted by so formidable a force, Subercase was quickly brought
to realize that successful resistance was scarcely in question. It was all
of seven years since his troops had been re-equipped with new weapons,
and five since they had been issued with new uniforms. Their pay was

[1] This was the type of weapon referred to as the 'old Queen's arm' in James Russell
Lowell's poem *The Gun Over the Hearth*.

badly in arrears, and their morale had reached a pitch of defeatism almost on a par with that of the townsfolk.

In any case Nicholson was throwing away no chances. After careful reconnaissance the whole force was landed in a camp of investment set up well out of range of the fortress artillery. The Naval guns then opened up their bombardment, with excellent practice from the bomb-ketch; and although the troops' approach march met with a good deal of harassing fire, and any man who strayed from the ranks was immediately set upon by Redskins skulking in the thickets, casualties were not inordinate.

With his defence works under close investment, Subercase beat the *chamade* and sent a flag to request that the womenfolk of the garrison, headed by 'our Major's lady', might be permitted to leave the fort and seek the protection of the invaders' camp. Despite the proximity of barbarous savages on the prowl about the outskirts of the lines, the niceties of civilized warfare were observed with exquisite courtesy, and the French Commandant's petition was immediately granted. Twittering vivaciously, *ces dames* were hospitably received, dined and wined with the very best the camp's meagre resources could provide, and generally treated with every consideration; although Nicholson was not without his suspicions of the sharp-eyed officer sent along with the ladies 'to look after them'. However, since his reports to Subercase could be calculated rather to hasten than to delay the Frenchman's submission, his circulation between the besiegers' camp and the beleaguered fortress was in no way restricted or discouraged.

On 2nd October, having put up a sufficient show of resistance to comply with the prevailing standards of military 'honour', Subercase signed terms of capitulation which guaranteed him the customary 'honours of war' and the return of his garrison to France. Where the local inhabitants were concerned, it was ordained that so long as they took the oath of allegiance to Queen Anne they could remain undisturbed in the enjoyment of their property. Otherwise they must take their departure from the territory within two years.

The ceremony of surrender was performed with all possible *punctilio*; Nicholson carrying courtesy to the length of providing transport for yet another bevy of *ces dames*, who had taken refuge up-stream from Port Royal.[1]

[1] C.S.P. Colonial, America and West Indies, vol. XXV and XXVI; S.P. Domestic, 42, vol. LXVIII, Entry Books, Military, vol. 41.

With its occupation by the British-Colonial forces, Port Royal was re-named Annapolis[1] in honour of the Queen, the territory itself being known thereafter as Nova Scotia. With its possession, together with that of Newfoundland, the entrance to the St Lawrence was commanded from the south-west and north-east. Moreover, with the Bay of Fundy under British control, the whole of New England's seaboard, together with its extensive fishing interests and the overseas trade in naval stores and lumber, was rendered free from hostile interference.

With a secure base in Nova Scotia, the oft-mooted enterprise against Quebec could at last be given serious consideration; although the problem of staging the venture was anything but advantaged by the hostile attitude maintained by the native Acadians and the equally irreconcilable Indian tribe of Micmacs. Throughout the whole of the summer of 1711, from these and many other sources of intelligence, the Marquis de Vaudreuil-Cavagnal, in the Governor's chateau in Quebec, learned of Boston's growing expectation of the arrival of a British fleet. News also reached him that once again Nicholson was mustering a formidable array at Wood Creek. Day and night Quebec busied itself with preparations for defence, amidst a buzz of conflicting rumours which sent the Sieur de Valtrie hurrying down the St Lawrence in search of authentic news.

As de Vaudreuil incredulously scanned a despatch reporting that Nicholson had broken camp and withdrawn his men and stores to Albany, de Valtrie landed from his canoe on the Ile aux Oeufs. On the rocks at the Pointe aux Anglais—as it was later to be dubbed—the hulls of several wrecked vessels lay half submerged in the water, while others were to be made out along the lengthy granite slab of the Ile aux Oeufs itself. There were hundreds of bloated corpses rocking gently in the shoals, some of them of women; while many of them were garbed in the British soldier's familiar red coat. Amidst the dead sheep and horses, the huddle of tools, casks, sea-chests, table ware and personal possessions, was a scatter of papers, many of them in the form of a proclamation boldly affirming that the whole of North America belonged to Great Britain by 'just and undisputable right and title', and giving notice that only those would be spared who offered no resistance to the forces of Her Britannic Majesty, 'come to take possession'.

---

[1] Not to be confused with 'the Town Land of the Proctors', or 'Town Land at Severn', known as Anne Arundle Town, Maryland, until 1703, when it was also given the name of Annapolis in honour of the Queen.

These grisly relics served as the sole memorial to the ambitious enterprise sponsored by the Tory Government which had been swept into power by the General Election of November 1710. With the full support of the new Parliamentary leaders, Robert Harley and the brilliant but hopelessly unstable Henry St John, a formidable fleet had set out for Canadian waters under the command of Admiral Sir Hovenden Walker, who had served responsibly if without particular distinction at Barfleur and under Leake in the Mediterranean. Crammed in their fetid transports, between five and six thousand Bloodybacks had for their leader Brigadier John Hill, whose chief claim to public attention lay in the fact that he was the brother of the doe-eyed, softly-spoken but extremely wily Abigail Masham, who had replaced the Duchess of Marlborough as Queen Anne's Mistress of the Robes and *confidante*.

As events were only too tragically to demonstrate, neither Hovenden, Walker nor Hill possessed the competence and resolution to fulfil the trust reposed in them; although it is unquestionable that the Admiral was dogged by singularly ill fortune. Lacking charts or any personal knowledge of local waters, despite a thick fog Walker had risked putting in at the mouth of the St Lawrence; where 'not one of his pilots could say, as did Cook in 1759, that he was "satisfied with being acquainted with the channel" '.[1] Navigating with the aid of occasional glimpses of the coastline, in heavy swirling mist and a tearing gale, the fleet was rapidly driven on to a lee shore, with practically no warning of the dangers it was approaching. At the moment of crisis the Admiral had to be summoned from his slumber by an agitated officer, with the plea, 'For God's sake come on deck, or we shall certainly be lost!' On the second appeal Walker left his cabin, in dressing-gown and slippers; to see the combers breaking over saw-toothed rocks almost beneath his bows. Above the threatening boom of the waves could be heard the cries of drowning men and the screech of running gear as some of the vessels sought desperately to claw off the land. But before most of the craft could find sea room to manœuvre, eight transports had been cast away together with two invaluable store ships.

Walker had come to the St Lawrence obsessed with fears of 'adamantine frosts', 'mountains of snow', and other meteorological handicaps. Thus on the heels of the initial disaster, weather conditions occupied

---

[1] *The Walker Expedition to Quebec*. Edited by Gerald S. Graham (Navy Records Society), W.O. 325/23. Treasury Papers, T. i, 132–4 & 175.

the attention of the council of war to the virtual exclusion of the more relevant fact that the loss of the store ships had dangerously reduced the supply of provisions. Such rations as were still available could not be made to last more than a few weeks; there was little chance of being restocked from England under eight or nine months; and it was impossible to estimate how long the expedition might be held up before Quebec. But navigational considerations finally persuaded the council of war to postpone the venture to some later date. As the Admiral reported to Lord Dartmouth, 'The respective pilots on board the men-of-war having been severally examined in the presence of the aforesaid Rear-Admiral and Captains, wee are unanimously of opinion, that by reason of the ignorance of the said pilots, it is wholly impracticable to go up the river St Lawrence with the men-of-war and transports as far as Quebec, as also the uncertainty and rapidity of the currents as by fatall experience we have found'.[1]

With a powerful armament still in being, this was a pusillanimous resolve less characteristic of the Hovenden Walker of Barfleur and Cadiz than of the craven, shuffling 'Jacky' Hill of the political coffee-houses and the Whitehall back stairs.

None the less the fact was not to be gainsaid that so long as Cape Breton Island remained unfortified by the French, and British-Colonial forces retained their grip on Newfoundland and Nova Scotia, the approaches to the vital St Lawrence waterway were no longer under untrammelled French control.

[1] S.P.C.O. V, IX, 12.

4

The Loom of Conflict

'St George he was for England,
St Denis was for France:
Sing "Honi soit qui mal y pense".'

IN THE DECEMBER OF 1711 the Duke of Marlborough, as the outcome of political intrigue, was dismissed from all his public employments. His successor as Commander-in-Chief was the Duke of Ormonde, 'a slight unmeritable man, meet to be sent on errands', but scarcely of the calibre to fill the place left vacant by the dismissal of the superbly accomplished and successful 'Corporal John'.

By the instruction of a thoroughly spineless administration, Ormonde was to inaugurate no active operations against the French; which, in view of his singular lack of military talent, was perhaps just as well.

However, the fact was not to be gainsaid that the hereditary foe had been consistently outfought for over a decade. So even if the outcome of the peace negotiations leading to the Treaty of Utrecht left a good deal to be desired, at least the compact ensured the separation of the Crowns of France and Spain, and left Great Britain in possession of the Caribbean island of St Kitts, Acadia and Newfoundland; although by some oversight the French were allowed to retain the adjacent Cape Breton Island. In addition, there was formal recognition of British rights in Hudson's Bay. Spain sullenly yielded Gibraltar and Minorca, and in so doing acknowledged the supremacy of the Royal Navy in the Mediterranean; while Antwerp—that 'dagger pointing straight at England's heart'—was safely out of hostile clutches.

One further concession wrung from the Spaniards was the *Asiento* which assigned to the newly formed South Sea Company the exclusive right, for thirty years, to export 4,800 negroes annually to the Spanish Colonies; while one vessel a year was permitted to trade with the overseas Spanish dominions—a proviso destined to prove a fruitful source of trouble.

Fortunately for the Royal Navy there were too many salaried officials dependent upon it, too many vested interests concerned in profitably supplying the Fleet's many needs, for it to be completely forgotten and left entirely without funds. Even so, the Navy vote was progressively reduced; whilst such new vessels as left the stocks were so crude and slovenly in design that one Admiral caustically remarked that they must have been 'manufactured by the mile and cut off in chunks when required'. Vessels were slow, crank, cramped, over-gunned, and so deficient in bearing forward that their pitching in bad weather gravely endangered the masts. On the other hand, the introduction of such frigates as the 600-ton, 28-gun *Cerberus* and the 650-ton, 32-gun *Theseus* led in due course to the construction of 1,000-ton, 36-gun craft that were both powerful and speedy.

Since the cost of living had risen steadily over the years, while the Royal Navy seaman's wage had been pegged at its old rate—and more often than not was months in arrears—the task of manning H.M. ships presented an increasingly difficult problem. As heretofore, in times of peace the seafarer in the Mercantile Marine was far better renumerated; in times of war the Crown's recent surrender of its right to a share in Prize Money rendered service in a privateer an infinitely more attractive proposition than doing duty with the Royal Navy. These considerations had been clearly brought out as early as 1693 by Purser Henry Moydman in his pamphlet *England's Safety, or a Bridle on the French King*. Affirming that the Fleet could be fully manned without impressment were the hands properly and regularly paid, Moydman went on to recommend a system of registration for seamen by which the Royal Navy would be supplied by 'able and daring haulbolings instead of raw lads and persons who had never been to sea'. An attempt to maintain such a register was persisted in until 1710, when its proven failure to help in keeping even a diminished Royal Navy up to strength necessitated a reversion to the press.

All in all, however, with Holland, in a maritime sense, reduced to the rank of a second-class Power, and France at least temporarily out of the running, Britain could advance an entirely legitimate claim to be regarded both as a Mediterranean and an Atlantic Power, as well as sovereign of the seas in European waters.

The sailor has always enjoyed greater popularity with the general public than the soldier, possibly because the former contributes more obviously towards keeping the larder filled and commerce active than does the latter. Where defence is concerned, while profoundly thankful for the professionalism of the Royal Navy, the English bias in favour of amateurism has always favoured a rickety militia system in preference to a strong and thoroughly well-trained standing Army; while for such overseas campaigns as were unavoidable a hastily extemporized expeditionary force could be built up on the smallest possible cadre of Regulars. Immediate disbandment, of course, awaited such a force the moment its task had been accomplished. It occurred to no one that improvisation trebles the cost of war while gravely imperilling its outcome.

Thus in 1713 the echoes of the last shot had scarcely faded into silence before the wholesale demobilization of the forces under arms was incontinently hurried forward. By Christmas thirteen regiments of Dragoons and twenty-two of Foot, together with several companies of 'Invalids', had been disbanded. By early 1714 the British Establishment had sunk to less than 30,000 men, including all colonial garrisons. Of these last named, four independent companies were in Newfoundland and four in Nova Scotia.[1] During the course of the war the 38th Foot had been sent to the Leeward Islands; and the tradition having arisen that, once installed, a colonial garrison, even if formed by a regiment of the Line, was irremovable, the unfortunate South Staffordshires remained in the Caribbean, without relief, for well over half a century. The Bahamas and Bermuda required a company apiece; although it was not until 1720 that it was deemed advisable to send an additional company to Carolina. Fifteen years later the fear of a servile rising on the part of the Jamaican negroes led to a tremendous ferreting around to find the men to bring the garrison there up to eight companies; while in 1737–1738 Georgia was to be furnished with a whole regiment.[2] This was formed by the simple process of turning over the whole of the effective rank and file of the 25th Foot[3] to the Governor, General James Oglethorpe.

[1] In 1717 they were merged to form the 40th Foot, subsequently to be known as the 1st Battalion the Prince of Wales's Volunteers, South Lancashire Regiment.
[2] Secretary's Common Letter Book, 25th October, 1737.
[3] Subsequently known as the King's Own Scottish Borderers.

In 1713 it was sought to mitigate abrupt discharge from the ranks by the payment of a small bounty, while great inducements were held out to beguile the newly-disbanded into re-enlisting for service in the Colonies. But apart from the additional risk to health embodied in service in so many foreign stations, actual living conditions were often so appalling as to render memories of a billet in a frowzy English ale-house positively heartwarming. At this period the man in the ranks was without greatcoat or an issue of blankets.[1] It followed that at some stations conditions of service were almost unendurable. In New York, for example, men on the frontier guards marched to their posts knee-deep in snow, and, for want of bedding, lay down to sleep in their clothes; their Serjeant having to awaken them from time to time lest they should freeze to death. At Annapolis Royal and Placentia the so-called barracks were falling down in ruin; and in a single winter forty-nine men out of two weak companies perished for want of a blanket to keep the cold at bay.[2] Moreover, as the men's subsistence in stations such as Newfoundland and Nova Scotia was entrusted to rascally civilian contractors, they were often short of the barest necessities. On the other hand, despite the ever-present risk of dysentery, malaria, 'Yellow Jack' and smallpox, service in the Caribbean was undoubtedly less arduous and comfortless, very largely owing to the sympathetic attitude of the civil population. In Jamaica, for example, a local enactment granted an especial allowance of provisions for all ranks.[3] Antigua went even further, offering barracks, light, fuel and additional pay, with a bounty or a free passage home, and the equivalent of a Chelsea pension, to every man who completed ten years' service. In general, however, assignment to the West Indies was tantamount to courting early death or enduring perpetual exile.

The only alternative method of keeping the Colonial garrisons putatively up to strength—particularly in the Caribbean—was by the steady exportation of white 'servants' from the homeland; that is to say, 'of men, women and children saved from the gaol or the gallows, plucked naked and starving out of the gutter, trepanned by scoundrelly crimps, or kidnapped bodily in the streets and "spirited", as the phrase

[1] Some battalions possessed a certain number of 'watch coats', which were issued to the sentries in turn before they were marched off to their respective posts.

[2] Warrant Books (1723), vol. VIII, 339.

[3] The West Indian Islands imported virtually all their consumable stores, which added appreciably to the cost of living.

went, across the Atlantic'.[1] Bound as indentured servants, during their period of servitude they were under obligation to take their place in the ranks of the militia; and once manumitted their recruitment was eagerly sought by the corps which formed the Regular garrison — although this procedure was strenuously opposed by planters eager to retain the men's service in return for a reasonable wage.

Although the Treaty of Utrecht had enabled the government slightly to augment the garrisons in New York, Nova Scotia and Newfoundland, even so the number of Regular troops distributed over these three centres barely totalled nine hundred. And this at a time when the French were hard at work on the erection of an elaborate fortification — on plans prepared shortly before his death by the distinguished fortress-architect Sébastien le Prestre de Vauban — on the east coast of Cape Breton Island. When completed, the stronghold — with walls ten feet thick and thirty feet high — and the township it enclosed was given the name of Louisbourg, and was fondly referred to by the French as the 'Dunkirk of America'. Owing to climatic conditions, however, the defensive works were in constant need of repair; while without being supported by supremacy at sea, the garrison possessed little more than nuisance value.

Of far greater significance were the new forts erected at Niagara and at Chambly, to cover Montreal from any attack by way of Lake Champlain. To these outworks was presently to be added a massive stronghold of stout masonry at Crown Point, on the western shore of the selfsame lake. For despite his recent humiliating defeat in Europe, Louis XIV was in no mind either to abandon or even to abate his grandiose territorial claims in North America — as was obliquely witnessed by the fact that the vessel which brought Quebec news of the conclusion of the peace treaty was crammed with another consignment of *filles-du-roi*, whose appearance was greeted even more rapturously than the intelligence that hostilities had ended.

For although sullen acceptance of a suspension of strife might prevail in Europe, in North America, especially in the Kennebec–St Croix area, the highly combustible atmosphere put a premium on a continuing resort to arms. In this region the border between New France and New England had never been clearly defined; and with the British settlers constantly edging further into territory the Abenaki regarded as exclusively their own, the tribe could easily be spurred to 'take up

[1] Fortescue, *op. cit.*

the hatchet'; work peculiarly to the taste of the rabid Anglophobe Fra Sebastien Rasles. A fanatical Jesuit, his hatred of the heretic settlers over the border was as ruthless and sadistic as that of his infamous compatriot, the Abbé Joseph Louis le Loutre, whose scalp-money payment, in a single two-year period, totalled 1,100 livres.

Inflamed by Rasles's unceasing exhortations, the Abenaki hurled themselves at the settlement at Brunswick, where they burned many of the houses, slaughtered a number of the inhabitants and bore away numerous prisoners. As Pascal sorrowfully comments, 'Men never do evil so relentlessly as in the name of religion'.

For all of three years the savage alternation of raid and counter-raid pursued its blood-drenched, destructive course. At length, in the August of 1724, the British settlers struck back in strength, assailing Rasles's fortified mission house and killing a number of the Abenakis who had built their wigwams in close proximity to it. In the course of the fighting Rasles himself was slain; and with the death of this 'constant & Notorious Fomenter and Incendiary to the Indians to kill, burn and destroy', an exhausted peace descended on a region hitherto abandoned to ceaseless conflict.[1] As a precaution, however, a stronghold known as Fort Dummer was built on the western bank of the Connecticut river, eleven miles above the township of Northfield.

It was the Abenaki's preference for good quality English 'strouds' and 'duffels' as much as anything which served to reconcile them to the English 'Palefaces' on their borders; a similar longing to that which kept the local Delaware and Susquehannock on generally amicable terms with Pacifist-Quaker Pennsylvania. Such friction as arose was very largely attributable to the avarice and sharp practice characterizing a certain element among the traders, despite legislation to ensure that the Indians were accorded something approximating to a square deal.

The accession of George I in 1714 can hardly be said directly to have affected the North American Plantations, although the repercussions of Britain's acceptance of the Hanoverian dynasty were to set the Colonists' destiny on a course which even the most percipient could scarcely have foreseen.

With Hanover as an additional burden on Britain's exiguous apparatus of defence, and the alarming implications of the Jacobite uprisings

[1] The conflict was known as Dummer's War, after the Governor of the Bay Colony.

of 1715 and 1718 — when it had been necessary to embody twenty-five companies of Chelsea Pensioners and hire six thousand Dutch and Austrian mercenaries to eke out the inadequate number of Regular troops available[1] — it was a singularly inappropriate moment to bring about a further reduction in the Armed Forces.

Yet even when criminals could not be executed at Tyburn unless the gibbet were guarded by troops, and lawlessness was so triumphantly rampant that it was unsafe for magistrates to do their duty unless under the protection of the military, the howl against a Standing Army persisted. The leader of this misguided campaign was 'Downright' William Shippen, who rose in Parliament to move a reduction in the Armed Forces on no less than twenty-one successive occasions. Even Walpole, who had done very well for himself as Paymaster to the Forces, took up the parrot cry during his four years out of office. Thus for nearly two decades the Bloodybacks — of either Service — became little more than something to be deplored and derided. Never was truer word written than when Francis Quarles penned the lines:

> Our God and the soldier we alike adore
> Ev'n at the brink of danger, not before;
> After deliv'rance, both alike requited,
> God is forgotten and the soldier slighted.

Under the inspiration of Walpole and men of like kidney, parliamentary government had degenerated into a deadly rivalry for office and the lavish perquisites that went with it; bribery had become so rationalized as to have been loaned the cloak of respectability; the only asset without a market was probity; the only crime was to be poor. The avid search for easy money might be thrown into a flutter by the bursting of the South Sea Bubble, but it was in no sense abated. What matter if many shipments of rum, sugar and molasses from the West Indies, destined for English warehouses, were swept into the pirates' lair at Tortuga for want of that protection an undermanned and overworked Royal Navy was in no position to afford? India was a burgeoning *el dorado*; the Newfoundland Banks still disgorged their generous yield of fish; while the trade with New England in ship's stores, masting and lumber had never been more flourishing. Indeed, special Crown Surveyors had been appointed and empowered to mark 'all trees of a

---

[1] The entire British Establishment totalled 22,000, of which two-thirds were stationed in Flanders or in Colonial garrisons. (Secretary's Common Letter Book.)

4

diameter of twenty-four inches and upwards at twelve inches from the ground, standing on ground not privately owned, with a broad arrow to signify that they had been reserved for purchase in Great Britain' — although in diminishing number by the Royal Navy.

On the other hand, the Admiralty had taken the far-sighted step of instituting at Portsmouth a Naval Academy where the aspirant for a Commission could be assured of a sound nautical training *before* he went to sea.

So far as the Army was concerned, despite its crippling lack of funds it contrived to turn the four companies of gunners, founded in 1716 by Marlborough on his restoration to the Master-Generalship of the Ordnance, into the Royal Regiment of Artillery; although each infantry formation still retained its quota of battalion guns. The Artillery and their comrades of the still unconsolidated Engineer branch had to wait until 1741, however, to see the establishment at Woolwich of the Royal Military Academy for the instruction of 'raw and inexperienced people belonging to the military branch of the Ordnance in the several parts of mathematics necessary to qualify them for the service of the Artillery and the business of the Engineers'. For the Cavalry and Infantry, of course, there was no such fount of instruction; they learned the art and practice of their calling 'on the job'.

One other event of far from transient importance was the formation, in 1725, of certain independent Highland companies, to preserve order among the clans. These were subsequently expanded to form the 43rd[1] of the Line, better known as *Am Frieceadan Dubh*, or Black Watch; the first of a long line of staunch and sturdy Scottish formations destined to gain many well-earned laurels on the field of battle.

Two years later, on the other side of the Atlantic, the construction was put in hand of a stoutly-timbered fort at Oswego. Situated at the mouth of the Oswego river, hard by the southern shore of Lake Ontario, it guarded the western end of the Mohawk Valley trade route, and constituted an open challenge to the French fur trade, as also to French ambitions south of Lake Erie.

The importance attached to the West Indies by the eighteenth-century politician and man of commerce can only be fully appreciated if it is realized that much which subsequently went to make up the British Empire had yet to come under Parliamentary control. In effect, the

[1] Subsequently renumbered the 42nd (1751), the number originally given to Oglethorpe's battalion in Georgia.

'Sugar Islands'[1] constituted the embryo of that mercantilist expansion on which 'the great cobs of Lombard Street' and their political henchmen had set their hearts. The one thing to be dreaded was servile rebellion on the part of the large number of slaves employed on the plantations. In the February of 1745, for example, the *Gentleman's Magazine* reproduced a letter from Jamaica which reported, 'About 900 negroes had formed a plot to destroy all the white people which was discovered by a negro wench to her mistress, because they refused to spare a child she had nursed'.

In this instance the insurrection was nipped in the bud. But apart from the Islands' vulnerability in time of war, it was the constant fear of negro uprisings which necessitated the stationing of substantial bodies of soldiers throughout the whole of the West Indies.

So far as South America was concerned, it was clear that Spain had bitten off more than she could chew. In the outcome her efforts to enforce a policy of fiscal 'protection' were consistently flouted by clandestine dealers in smuggled commodities — eagerly welcomed by a populace starved of legitimate consumer goods — as by the filibusters of all nations who so ruthlessly preyed on Spanish maritime commerce.

The war between the smugglers, and the Spanish *guarda costa* — who did not hesitate to detain and confiscate foreign vessels, thought to be freighted with contraband, well outside territorial waters — reached a crisis in 1738. For it was in that year that Master-mariner Robert Jenkins presented to the attention of a flabbergasted House of Commons a desiccated ear, carefully wrapped in cotton wool, which he swore had been sliced from his head when a Spanish *guarda costa* had unwarrantably boarded his vessel *Rebecca* in the open Caribbean. So astounded and indignant were Honourable Members that it occurred to no one to lift the outraged seafarer's wig to ascertain whether in fact he was lugless or properly furnished in this particular; while rumour-mongers who suggested that the gallant Captain had been deprived of his ear when condemned, some years earlier, to the pillory, were indignantly hushed into silence.

Public opinion, bored with Walpole's eventless, if superficially prosperous, period of administration, clamoured for retribution to be meted out to 'the Dons'; blissfully unaware of the fact that of a hundred and twenty-nine ships of the line listed by the Admiralty one-third was

---

[1] In addition to sugar and molasses, their prime exports, the Islands also produced a little cotton, coffee, cocoa, dyewoods, and hardwood timber.

beyond repair and another third in such a state of neglect as to be quite unfit for service.

Yielding to the clamour of Parliament and the baying of *mobile vulgus*, on the third Thursday of October tabarded heralds duly proclaimed that His Majesty George II 'relying on the help of Almighty God, who knows the uprightness of our intentions, have thought it fit to declare and do hereby declare war against the King of Spain'.

With Horse Guards to cleave a way for them through the exultant, milling crowds, the heralds rode on to repeat the proclamation at Temple Bar; their voices barely audible through the brazen clangour of the bells and the wild huzzas of the mob.

'They are ringing the bells today', Walpole commented dryly: 'they will soon be wringing their hands.'

With the country committed, the need for positive action was not to be deferred. It was at this juncture that the Board of Admiralty bethought them of a certain Captain Edward Vernon, whose sturdy championship of the lower deck, both in and out of Parliament, had paid little heed to officialdom's susceptibilities. Since he was alleged to have proclaimed his readiness to capture the Spanish American harbour of Porto Bello 'with six ships', he was hastily promoted to the rank of Vice-Admiral, given command of a squadron made up of four 70-gun ships of the line, three of 60 guns, one of 50 and one of 40, and told to proceed forthwith to the Caribbean and there 'sink burn or destroy' enemy shipping, and if possible attack such Spanish men-of-war as might be found either at Porto Bello or Cartagena, with the aim of warding off assaults on the North American Colonies and affording 'full protection to Jamaica'.

An accomplished seagoing officer and staunch patriot, Vernon was as warm-hearted as he was irascible; but he was too familiar with local conditions in Spanish America to entertain projects that were obviously beyond the means at his disposal. His own preference was for an attack on Cuba, which would 'afford Spain the most sensible loss', and which would be the easiest place to retain and colonize. The home Government, however, were urgent that something should be attempted against either Cartagena, on the north-west coast of the Main, or Porto Bello, on the northern coast of the Isthmus of Darien.

Picking up a couple of hundred Bloodybacks at Jamaica, to act as Marines, and with 2,495 seamen manning the six vessels he had been allotted for the venture, on 5th November Vernon weighed anchor and headed for his objective — Porto Bello.

In normal circumstances, unless the assault from the sea is supported by a strong landing party, few enterprises are less likely to end in success than a naval attack on fixed shore defences. Fortunately for Vernon, Porto Bello's means of defence had been grossly neglected for years. In the Castello de Todofierro, on the northern side of the harbour, the gun carriages had rotted so badly that scarcely a cannon could be brought into action. The few that were actually fit to employ were hastily mounted, but several were promptly knocked out when the fleet entered the harbour and opened up its bombardment. As the weight of the cannonade began to take its toll of the defences, a landing party of sailors and Marines was put ashore on the Mole; the former making their way into the castle by climbing on each other's shoulders and clambering through the embrasures under the mouths of the guns.

> The soldiers we took with us from Jamaica [wrote one A.B. subsequently to his wife], were as harty cox as ever took Musket in hand; and Jack Cox my messmate you know he was always a hevy arsed dog and sleepy headed, but had you seen him clime the Wals of the Batry you would never forget him for a cat could not xceed him in nimbleness.[1]

Once within the main works, the Spanish flag was quickly hauled down and the English ensign run up in its place. Deserted by most of their companions, the Spaniards in the upper fort, realizing that further resistance was useless, raised a white flag. Of the original garrison of some three hundred, only five officers and thirty-five men were left to make formal submission, when, on the day following, the Spanish Governor capitulated.

British casualties had been very light, no more than four killed and seven wounded; while the booty acquired included the Spanish Army payroll of ten million dollars. This was immediately distributed *pro rata*, so that the correspondent already mentioned could gleefully inform his wife that, 'Our dear Admiral ordered every man some Spanish Dollers to be immediately given which is like a Man of Honour, for I would rather have 10 dollers in hand than to have 100 for sefen Years together, and perhaps compound it at the last'.

Vernon's concern for his men extended beyond their pockets to their

[1] *Gentleman's Magazine*, 1740.

general health. In the West Indies the sailor had made appreciative acquaintance with rumbullion; and in due course rum had become an official issue, being 'dished out' on the scale of nearly half a pint daily; which, far too often, the hands gulped down neat, to the benefit neither of their health nor sobriety. It was by Vernon's instruction that an Order was promulgated to all his Captains, which ran:

> You are hereby required and directed as you tender both the Spiritual and Temporal Welfare of His Majesty's Service, to take particular care that Rum be no more served in Specie to any of the Ship's Company under your Command, but that the respective daily allowance of half a pint a man for all your Officers and Ship's Company be every day mixed with the proportion of a Quart of Water to every Half Pint of Rum...

Sugar and the juice of fresh limes could be added to taste; and since Vernon was already known as 'Old Grog' owing to his fidelity to an ancient boat-cloak of grograin,[1] the potable jorum he recommended speedily acquired that name of 'grog' by which it has ever since been known.

Although Porto Bello had fallen in the last week of November 1739, it was not until the March of 1740 that the news of Vernon's success reached England; whereat the entire country went delirious with joy. London, Bristol, York, Norwich and many other ports and cities were ablaze with bonfires; both Houses of Parliament joined in an Address to the King congratulating him on 'the glorious success of your Majesty's arms in the West Indies, under the command of Admiral Vernon'; two Bristol privateers were endowed with the victor's name; scores of publicans gave orders for their inn sign to be altered to *The Admiral Vernon*; while the popular hero himself gave directions for a special medal to be struck, for distribution to his followers, bearing his effigy above the legend 'He took Porto Bello with six ships'.[2]

The capture of Porto Bello was a brilliant and heartening exploit, but its importance was magnified beyond all reason; although it was eagerly seized upon as useful window dressing by an unpopular

---

[1] Grograin was a thick, wet-resisting material made of silk and mohair, stiffened with gum.

[2] A less opulent memento was manufactured in cheap zinc and copper alloy as invented by Christopher Pinchbeck. Hence the term for anything spurious, of deceptive appearance but low quality.

Ministry. Unfortunately Vernon's initial success, and his subsequent capture of the lesser haven of Chagre, encouraged the formulation of the far more ambitious design to bring about the submission of Cartagena.

Thus in the autumn of 1740 preparations were going forward on both sides of the Atlantic to concentrate a force powerful enough to undertake the conquest of the richest and most populous city in the whole of New Spain. Orders were given to hasten the recruitment of six regiments of Marines, of 1,100 men apiece; but so persistent was the dearth of volunteers that resort was made to the pernicious device of filling the ranks from existing regiments — which enabled the respective Colonels to get rid of the least desirable of their rank and file. It was an opportunity of which they took remarkably prompt advantage. Indeed Lord Cathcart, assigned to the command of the troops, 'found that part of the force consisted of boys who had not the strength to handle their arms. Such were the first-fruits of the cry of "No Standing Army" '.[1]

On the other side of the Atlantic, however, Deputy-Governor Spotswood of Virginia experienced no difficulty in raising the four battalions — totalling 3,600 officers and men — which the 'Old Dominion', Maryland and Pennsylvania had agreed to contribute to the venture. For 'when the King sent out blank Commissions to his Royal Governors, for Officers who would recruit companies...Americans snapped them up. They relished the idea of authentic military title as well as half-pay for life after the campaign. Other Americans enlisted in the ranks because they knew their Officers and had heard of the streets of gold in Havana.'[2] Amongst the Virginia contingent was the twenty-two-year-old Captain Lawrence Washington, of Hunting Creek on the Virginia shore of the Potomac river.

After considerable delay attributable to bureaucratic confusion and the issue of contradictory orders, and a number of casualties amongst the troops owing to seasonal sickness to which many of the earlier arrivals in Jamaica speedily succumbed, the expeditionary force was finally concentrated by the last days of December 1740. Unfortunately, the casualties had included Lord Cathcart, whose belief that heroic doses of Epsom's salts constituted the best cure for dysentery had proved clinically unsound. At his death command of the troops passed

[1] Fortescue, *op. cit.*
[2] Shy, *op. cit.*

to Brigadier Thomas Wentworth; and with his assumption of responsibility the fate of the expedition to Cartagena was sealed. An experienced, conscientious subordinate, in the exercise of actual command Wentworth emerged as a pedantic formalist, painfully unsure of himself, whose resentment of criticism—unless it could be euphemized as encouragement—produced a sullen irritability which quickly hardened into obstinacy. Two men less likely to pull together than bluff, forthright Edward Vernon and the hypersensitive, over-burdened Thomas Wentworth it would indeed have been hard to find.

Vernon's first task was to immobilize the defences guarding the lagoon and sheltered roadstead leading to the principal objective, and this he accomplished with his customary efficiency and despatch. 'The first attack was by three of my 80-gun ships on the forts of St Jago and St Philip, lying without the Boca Chica Castle', Vernon exultantly wrote his wife; 'and we drove the enemy out of them in less than an hour, and secured a descent to the army, and without their having so much as a single musket-shot fired at them. And my gallant sailors twice stormed and took two batteries on the opposite side of the harbour.'[1]

But from the moment of getting the troops ashore almost everything went wrong that could. Fumbling and hesitant, Wentworth embarked upon all the elaborations of a formal siege—in slow motion—when a speedy and resolute assault held out every promise of carrying the venture to a swift and successful conclusion. Fuming on his quarterdeck, Vernon did nothing to conceal his comprehensible impatience. Thus the rift between the Admiral and the commander of the troops steadily widened. 'Instead of conferring personally, and co-operating with vigour and cordiality, they began to hold separate councils, draw up acrimonious remonstrances, and send irritating messages to each other.'[2]

Fever and other local ailments had taken a heavy toll of the force even before it had left Jamaica; seventeen officers and six hundred men had died before the end of the year, and another fifteen hundred were on the sick list; the losses being made good to a certain extent by incorporating in the expeditionary force the four Independent Companies stationed in the Island.

Once they were cantoned in a badly sited camp on the Tierra Bomba, the afflictions characteristic of the locale—'Yellow Jack', malaria,

[1] E. Hallam Moorhouse, *Letters of the English Seamen.*
[2] Tobias Smollett, *A Compendium of Interesting and Authentic Voyages.* Smollett was serving with the Fleet as a Surgeon's Mate.

smallpox and dysentery — were free to riot through the ranks until the total of sick and wounded had mounted to 3,569. Even so, a brisk assault on the main stronghold of San Lazaro might well have succeeded had Wentworth launched it unhesitantly. But so fatal was his procrastination that when at last the attempt was made it was thrown back by a garrison strongly reinforced in the ample time afforded the Spaniards to work out their measures of defence.

With the respective commanders completely at loggerheads and the rainy season close at hand, almost inevitably the decision was taken to re-embark the troops and artillery and abandon as hopeless an enterprise which had done little more than 'strew the sea with English corpses'.

It is not perhaps without irony that young Lawrence Washington retained sufficient respect and admiration for the British Admiral's handling of his share of the enterprise to change the name of his ancestral home to Mount Vernon.

By 1742 the strife with Spain had merged into the far greater conflict brought about by the dispute over the succession of Maria Theresa to the throne of Austria. Charles VI of Austria's 'pragmatic sanction' ensuring that the Hapsburg domains should descend undivided to his daughter had been endorsed by France, Spain, Prussia and Britain. But with the Emperor's death the first three had recanted on their guarantee, bringing Britain and some of the minor German principalities to Maria Theresa's support.

With France and Britain once again openly in conflict, the unofficial strife on the American borders and in the wilderness flared into a state of open warfare destined to increase in scope and intensity over the ensuing sixteen years. And this despite the reluctance of the more grasping Albany traders to sacrifice their profitable, if clandestine, traffic with New France in the cause of British imperialism, or the complacent pacifism so smugly preached by Quaker Pennsylvania.

Since news of the outbreak of hostilities in Europe was common knowledge in Louisbourg long before it reached Boston, the initiative lay with the French. They took advantage of it to stage a raid in strength on the fishing station of Canceau, at the southern end of the strait separating the Nova Scotia peninsula from Cape Breton Island. A naval and military force, totalling nine hundred of all ranks, escorted by two armed vessels, fell on a garrison of eighty men cantoned in an

4*

extremely flimsy fortification, and speedily compelled their surrender on the condition that they would be given safe conduct to Boston. The rather squalid hamlet, with its inadequate wooden citadel, was then burned to the ground.

Inflated by this easily-won success, Duquesnil, the Military Governor of Louisbourg, went on to plan the capture of Annapolis. Owing to the neglectful indifference of the authorities in Whitehall, the outpost's defences were in the last state of disrepair, 'the sandy ramparts were crumbling into the ditches, and the cows of the garrison walked over them at their pleasure'.[1] For garrison there were about a hundred effective men of the resident Independent Company under a French Protestant expatriate, Major Mascarene, whose family had been driven into exile with the revocation of the Edict of Nantes. A small reinforcement of militia, sent in by Shirley, Governor of Massachusetts, arriving without arms but with extremely healthy appetites, proved less of an asset than a liability.

At the head of his mixed French-Indian force, Captain Duvivier, the proud conqueror of Canceau, appeared before Annapolis in August, and being surprisingly warmly received he retired somewhat precipitously to work out more cautious means of prosecuting the siege. But before attempting any further active operations Duvivier sent to inform the unimpressionable Mascarene that since the beleaguering force was in daily expectation of a substantial accretion of strength, including two French warships, he strongly advised capitulation while favourable terms were still obtainable.

But Mascarene was too old a bird to be caught by chaff; and throughout the three weeks of desultory attacks which ensued, the garrison proved perfectly capable of holding its own. With the end of the third week, instead of the arrival of two French warships and another two hundred and fifty Regulars, a couple of small vessels put in from Boston bringing a reinforcement of fifty Indian Rangers. At this extremely modest addition to his foes, Duvivier threw in his hand, retiring once more to Louisbourg. As a writer in the *Habitant de Louisbourg* somewhat acidly summed it up, 'The expedition was a failure, though one might have bet everything on its success, so small was the force the enemy had to resist us'.

The situation was obviously not one that could be left unresolved; and Boston was soon humming with preparations for nothing less than

[1] Francis Parkman, *Half a Century of Conflict* (vol. II).

an attack on the thirty million livres stronghold of Louisbourg. For this audacious enterprise a force of fifteen hundred militia and volunteers were mobilized by Massachusetts, New Hampshire, Connecticut and Rhode Island; while the Duke of Newcastle wrote instructing Commodore Peter Warren R.N. to support the enterprise with all the vessels under his command.

Warren was a strong-willed, resourceful individual whose native vigour was in sharp contrast to his cadaverous and somewhat sickly appearance. Having married Susanna Delancy of New York, and thereafter developed a keen interest in land speculation in the Mohawk Valley, he was fully in sympathy with colonial aspirations and only too eager to further them. No better man could have been chosen to work harmoniously with the enthusiastic but inexperienced William Pepperrell, a substantial merchant of Kittery, who 'joined to an unusual popularity as little military incompetency as anybody else who could be had'.[1] Truth to tell, actual experience of warfare was lacking amongst the 3,300 men recruited by Massachusetts, the 516 from Connecticut, and the 450 from New Hampshire.[2] A few veterans of the Cartagena campaign, a handful of backwoodsmen, such as Seth Pomeroy, with lively memories of the earlier fighting on the border, were scarcely sufficient to leaven the mass of fishermen, lumberjacks and husbandmen who made up the bulk of the force; although most men in the ranks were accustomed to handling firearms. Prominent amongst them was Parson Sam Moody, a fiery evangelist who had equipped himself with an axe, with which he declared his intention of smashing all the 'popish idols' he could find.

But Louisbourg called for something more potent than an axe, being defended by a garrison of over sixteen hundred trained troops; while the main fortress was encircled by a ditch eighty feet in width and was furnished with a hundred and one cannon, seventy-six swivels and six mortars. In addition, the harbour was defended by an island battery of thirty 22-pounders, and by the Royal battery on the shore, mounting thirty pieces. Fortunately Pepperrell had been given a copy of the plan of Louisbourg's defences, which had been drawn up as early as 1734 by the Engineer Officer John Henry Bastide; so at least the Provincial leader knew something of the nut he proposed to crack.

[1] Francis Parkman, *op. cit.*
[2] Rhode Island recruited a detachment of 300, but they arrived too late to participate in operations. New York contributed some ordnance; Pennsylvania some provisions.

Shirley had wisely insisted that the hundred craft transhipping the force should rendezvous simultaneously at Canceau, about fifty miles from Louisbourg; where Warren added the weight of H.M.S. *Superb*, *Mermaid* and *Launceston*, and a schooner out of Boston, to the eleven privateers rounded up to lend the enterprise support.[1]

Even in the early days of April the waters off Louisbourg were still clogged with ice; but it was essential to push home the enterprise before the two French warships put in their expected appearance. The successful rendezvous in Gaborus Bay was commemorated by an open air sermon from Parson Moody, preaching on the text, 'Thy people shall be willing in the day of Thy power'; concerning which one contemporary diarist commented, 'Several sorts of Busnesses was Going on, Som a-Exercising, Som a-Hearing Preaching'; and the thought is not to be suppressed that one and all would have been better employed under the drill-Serjeant. It was, indeed, characteristic of the haphazard manner in which affairs were conducted that when a landing had been effected at Freshwater Creek, three miles to the westward of the objective, the cattle-pound and abbatoir was casually sited *above* the water-point used by the troops.

But nothing could diminish the enthusiasm of Pepperrell's men; which was maintained at fever heat by the success of the Provincial vessels in beating off the French frigate *Renommée* when it sought to make Louisbourg harbour.

The first overt move in the siege took the form of a close blockade of Louisbourg by all the craft under Warren's command. The enemy stronghold stood on a tongue of land which lay between its harbour and the sea; with a navigable passage no more than half a mile wide commanded *en enfilade* by the Island Battery, and dead ahead by the guns of the Royal Battery.

While Warren engaged the ordnance in the fixed defences, a small party under William Vaughan stole overland to fire the extensive naval stores situated in rear of the Royal Battery; which was then found unaccountably to be deserted. Vaughan and his handful of followers immediately seized the work; a lad of eighteen, William Tufts of Medford, climbing the flagstaff, to fasten his red coat to the pole as a signal that the Provincials were in possession. Four boats, crammed with men, immediately put out from the town quay to reclaim the

---

[1] Warren was subsequently reinforced by the frigate *Eltham*, escort for the annual fleet from New England.

battery; and Vaughan was hard put to it to fend off his assailants until reinforcements could be hurried up under Lieutenant-Colonel Bradstreet.

The twenty-eight 42-pounders and two 18-pounders had been spiked before the Royal Battery had been evacuated, but so indifferently had the work been carried out that Seth Pomeroy and his skilled gunsmith assistants experienced little difficulty in drilling out the touch holes and rendering the weapons fully serviceable. Hitherto, lack of heavy ordnance had constituted not the least of the attacking force's handicaps. But with all the pieces in the Royal Battery in the assailants' hands, 'the enemy', as the *Habitant de Louisbourg* gloomily recorded, 'saluted us with our own cannon, and made a terrific fire, smashing everything within range'.

On the water-front, however, the defences seemed almost impregnable, backed as they were by a loopholed wall of masonry, with a covered way and glacis towering over a ditch twelve feet wide and ten feet deep. Transferring the heavier pieces from the captured Royal Battery, the Provincials toiled to drag them four miles over hills and rocks, through spongy morasses and a tangled web of evergreens; 'block-and-tackle work' in which Peter Warren's seamen were ready to lend a hand. Timber sledges were necessary to tide the heavy pieces over the soggy marsh; with the gun-teams—often of two hundred men—in constant danger of foundering in the mire. And there was little chance of rest and refreshment when the long hours of toil came temporarily to a halt. For there were few tents, and shelter had to be contrived out of old sails or huts built of sods and roofed with spruce-boughs, to keep out the biting cold. Uniforms, underwear, and shoes were all worn out; and the twin scourges of dysentery and scurvy were steadily increasing their grip. Calvinists as the majority of them might be, the one bright spot in their unending round of toil and danger was the daily tot of prime Jamaica rum.

Green Hill, a spur in the line of heights which formed a *demi-lune* about the town was eventually crowned with a battery of six guns; while other ordnance was laboriously dragged into position until there were few areas in the town which could not be brought under fire. Other than by random artillery shot, these preliminary activities— mostly carried out under cover of darkness—went undisturbed. In the previous winter the authority of Duchambon, Louisbourg's Governor, had been badly shaken by a mutiny amongst the troops; and any attempted sortie in strength would only have put a premium on wholesale desertion.

With the besiegers' artillery in position, the dearth of experienced cannoneers amongst Pepperrell's motley throng was readily made good by Commodore Warren, by whose order a number of Naval gun-layers were set ashore, where they found many eager pupils to take advantage of the experts' painstaking instruction.

Pepperrell's men had been far too impatient to 'get at the Mounseers' to make anything but exceedingly sketchy entrenchments, so the only safe course was sedulously to outshoot the enemy. 'Began our fire with as much fury as possible', Captain Sherburn noted in his diary, 'and the French returned it warmly from the Citidale, West Gate and North-East Battery with Cannon, Mortars, and a continual shower of musket balls; but by 11 o'clock we had beat them all from their guns.'[1] Many of the French defences became untenable, while 'the town was ploughed with cannon balls, the streets were raked from end to end, nearly all the houses damaged, and the people driven for refuge into the stifling casemates'.[2] The Royal Navy's gunnery instructors could take a genuine pride in their pupils' prowess.

When not on duty, 'some of our men went fishing', recorded another diarist,[3] 'about 2 miles off, and caught 6 Troutts. One man went to catch Lobsters; caught 30'.

The Island Battery, garrisoned by a hundred and eighty men and equipped with thirty cannon, seven swivels and two mortars, was the core of Louisbourg's defence; and it was clear that until it had been put out of action the stronghold could not be subdued.

A night attack was put in by a party of Provincials, stiffened by a handful of British Marines. But the venture badly lacked co-ordination and was so noisily conducted as to sacrifice all element of surprise. 'They was a-hollerin' and hoorayin' ', wrote one disgruntled Marine survivor, 'as if they was off to Pinner Fair.' It is scarcely surprising that the garrison was able to throw back the assault with a total loss to the assailants of a hundred and eighty-nine dead, wounded and captured. Orders were therefore given to erect a battery on Lighthouse Point to bring the objective under concentrated fire.

It was at this juncture that the Royal Navy scored a striking success

---

[1] Captain Joseph Sherburn, *Diary*.

[2] Parkman, *op. cit.*

[3] Lieutenant Benjamin Cleaves.

that helped tremendously to restore morale, which had wilted badly after the failure of the attack on the Island Battery. An enemy warship —the 64-gun *Vigilant*, manned by 560 hands, and crammed with stores and munitions—had encountered one of the British cruisers well out to sea, and in a running fight had been lured towards Commodore Warren's main fleet. Beset by several vessels of his command, after a gallant resistance and the loss of eighty men, the *Vigilant* had struck her Colours; her captured stores being as thankfully welcomed by the New Englanders as their loss was bemoaned by the undernourished men of Louisbourg's drooping garrison.

With the battery on Lighthouse Point firmly established and a sortie aimed at its destruction resolutely beaten off,[1] a heavy concentration of fire could be brought to bear on the defences, in which the besiegers' cannon on the land side also joined with stunning effect. The town was in ruin; only one house remained untouched by shot or shell. With Commodore Warren's squadron strongly reinforced and moving right into the harbour to bring the town under additional fire, the panic-stricken townsfolk hurried to the Governor with a petition begging him to capitulate.

On the 15th of June Duchambon sent a flag requesting a suspension of arms to enable him to draw up proposals for submission. Articles were eventually agreed whereby the survivors of the garrison were permitted the customary 'honours of war' on condition that they pledged themselves 'not to bear arms against the King of England or any of his allies for the space of a year'. By the 17th Louisbourg was in the besiegers' hands. There was rich prize for the Royal Navy in the many captured French vessels; but Pepperrell's men, to their considerable resentment, were forbidden to loot the town, as they had hoped to at the outset. There was nothing, however, to prevent Parson Sam Moody from hewing at the altars and sacred images in the churches, until they had all fallen victim to his sectarian zeal.

'The victory set the bells ringing in Boston, cannons blasting off joyously in Maine, a bonfire flaring in London.' But Shirley's design to follow up Louisbourg's capture by a full-scale attack on Canada was accorded little support. 'King George's War'[2] had proved anything but an unbroken triumph for British arms. By sheer hard fighting a force

---

[1] An attack on Annapolis Royal by an isolated force under the noted partisan Marin was also repelled with heavy loss to the assailants.

[2] Such was the term by which Americans referred to the War of the Austrian Succession.

of 40,000 Allied troops had managed to extricate themselves from the 'mousetrap of Dettingen', set to snare them by 60,000 Frenchmen. At Fontenoy headlong victory had been snatched from the Duke of Cumberland's hands by the last-minute intervention of Lally's Irish Brigade, serving with the French army. The loss of Ostend had been almost overlooked in the consternation which had shaken the whole country with the Young Pretender's march on Derby; when the military cupboard had proved so scandalously bare that it had been necessary to eke out such few British troops as were available by hiring three thousand 'Bluecoats' from Holland. For the vaunted competence of the militia to defend their native soil had scarcely been reflected in the order to the reserve Brigade of Guards, which ran, 'If the militia are reviewed tomorrow by His Majesty, the soldiers of the three regiments of Guards are to behave civilly, and not to laugh and make game of them'.

Louisbourg was an undoubted victory for the Colonists, but it was far from being the last word in the long struggle between them and their intransigent French neighbours. It was difficult to persuade a moiety of the 'Hostilities Only' New Englanders to stay on to form a garrison for their capture until relieved by three regiments of Bloody-backs — 29th, 30th and 45th Foot — from England; especially as Massachusetts was hard put to it for the necessary funds with which to maintain them until a subsidy from the Home Government resolved the worst of the Colony's and her neighbours' financial difficulties.[1] Ambitious plans to carry operations into the heart of Canada had to be abandoned when the additional naval and military forces promised by Newcastle were foolishly diverted to undertake an amphibious attack on L'Orient; which, in the event, turned out a dismal failure. A French attempt to send a vast armament for the recapture of Louisbourg was frustrated by a terrible storm which littered the coast of Nova Scotia with the expedition's wreckage.

A problem particularly difficult of solution was how best to deal with the native Acadians, whose Francophilia was unlikely to concede anything to British or New England heretics while fanatical priests of the type of the turbulent Le Loutre were at hand to keep racial prejudice and sectarian intolerance vengefully alive.

Hostility found brutally direct expression towards the end of Septem-

---

[1] Massachusetts received £183,649, New Hampshire £16,355, Connecticut £28,863, and Rhode Island £6,332 (Treasury Papers).

ber 1745, when a strong raiding party from Crown Point descended on Saratoga, the northernmost English-speaking settlement in the Hudson valley. A hundred residents were killed or captured and the whole township was left in ruins; with the result that the region north of Albany was speedily denuded of the majority of its inhabitants, who had sought safety further to the east. In the following year the Abenaki and other affiliated tribes hurled themselves against the feeble settlements on the Kennebec; Waldoboro being virtually razed to the ground and the whole frontier reduced to a state of quivering alarm.

In the traditional European cockpit the Duke of Cumberland's inferiority in strength, together with the tepidity and incapacity of his allies had led to the loss of Bergen-op-Zoom — reputedly the strongest fortress on the Continent — and the reverse at Lauffeld, near Maestricht; successes the French were too over-extended to turn to material advantage. In effect, both sides were thoroughly exhausted, a fact reflected in the terms of the Treaty of Aix-la-Chapelle; the French restoring such conquests as they had achieved, while British mercantile interests ensured that Louisbourg should be exchanged for the commercially more promising Madras. *Pecuniae obediunt omnia.*

It was a transaction which in no sense commended itself to the people of New England, since it turned a wilfully blind eye on all they had striven for at such costly sacrifice. Since the usual swingeing reductions had taken place in both the Royal Navy and the Army, Cumberland and Lord Halifax, the President of the Board of Trade, could at least indulge in such atonement as was embodied in the offer of a free land-grant and immunity from taxation for ten years, together with a free passage overseas to all discharged soldiers and sailors who elected to emigrate to Nova Scotia. The bait was taken with some freedom; and the influx of a considerable body of English-speaking settlers, and the foundation of the fortified township of Halifax, did something to offset the presence of the irreconcilable French-Acadians in this highly sensitized 'Tom Tiddler's ground'.[1]

In 1701 the Iroquoian Confederacy and the lesser local tribes they controlled had concluded a treaty with the Governor and Virginian Assembly which had ceded the region north of the Ohio, stretching from the Mississippi and Illinois rivers, to 'the English King'; with additional rights over the territory north of Lake Erie as far east as

[1] In all, four thousand former Bloodybacks took advantage of the offer.

Ottawa. In return, the Five Nations had registered their claim 'to be protected therein by the Crown of England'; and although throughout the intervening years interpretation of the compact had become somewhat misapplied, its fundamental validity had never been openly called into question by either party to it. The contemporary Iroquois, however, were far more susceptible to French influence that had been the case with their immediate forebears. They had therefore been profoundly impressed by the attempt to link Canada and Louisiana by way of Lake Erie and the Allegheny and Ohio rivers, successfully carried through by the Baron de Longeuil in 1739. Then in 1749 their faith in the Colonists' will to resist aggression was badly shaken by the raid into the Upper Ohio Valley staged by Celoron de Blainville. It is not without irony that this same year brought to the newly-formed Ohio Company the regal grant of 600,000 acres beyond the Ohio for the syndicate's exclusive exploitation.

Among its members the Ohio Company numbered Virginia's Lieutenant-Governor, Robert Dinwiddie, Thomas Lee of the Virginia Council, and the frontiersman and land-speculator, Thomas Cresap. Another shareholder was the young Major George Washington, one of the four Adjutants for Virginia and, since the death of his half-brother, Lawrence, owner of the pleasant landed property of Mount Vernon.

In making their 600,000 acre grant the British Government had strongly recommended the construction of a couple of forts near the Ohio river, to afford the territory the necessary protection. While the matter was still in debate by the Virginia Assembly, a party of resentful Shawnee and Delaware Indians, under the leadership of Charles Langlade, had raided the trading post at Pickawillany, on the Miami river; a defiant gesture which the French followed up by the erection of Fort Presqu'ile at the western end of Lake Erie, to stand guardian over the territory between the lake and the Ohio. 'The French', wrote the veteran frontiersman Elisha Williams, 'intend to prevent the English spreading any further on the Continent — to be Masters of the Whole as soon as maybe.'[1]

It was at this juncture that a Franco-Indian raiding party swooped on a trading centre in the domain of the friendly Twightwees. According to an account in the contemporary *London Magazine*, the assailants had boiled and eaten the Twightwee sachem, scalped a white man, taken

[1] Massachusetts Historical Society records.

'out his heart and eaten it, and cut off his fingers and sent them to Canada to justify the reward offered for English victims'.

At the same time a second stronghold, Fort le Boeuf, was constructed, whence canoes could make their way downstream to the Allegheny and Ohio. It was only sickness amongst the French troops and *coureurs-de-bois* which thwarted the authorities' intention to build yet a third fort at the junction of French Creek and the Allegheny; but garrisons were left at Forts le Boeuf and Presqu'île, and the remainder of the force returned to Montreal having firmly secured the line of communications between the St Lawrence and the Ohio.

As soon as these activities were reported to Dinwiddie he wrote to the Commandant at Fort le Boeuf demanding that he withdraw forthwith from territory 'so notoriously known to be the property of the Crown of England'. Delivery of the missive was entrusted to Major George Washington. With the veteran backwoodsman Christopher Gist as his principal henchman, Washington set out from Williamsburg on his five-hundred-mile winter journey by way of Wills Creek and the Great Crossing of the Youghiogheny, and on over successive mountain ridges that carried him to a peak elevation of 3,000 feet. Past Great Meadows and across the snow-swollen junction of the Monongalhela and Allegheny and the windy, desolate peninsula where Pittsburg sprawls today, he plodded on to Great Beaver Creek, the French outpost of Venango, and then, in the twilight of a December day, to his final objective, the grim stronghold of Fort le Boeuf.

Frigidly correct in their reception of Dinwiddie's emissary as they might be, Washington's nervous *sotto voce* humming of the refrain *Lillibulero*, so indelibly associated in the French mind with defeat at the hands of the British, was scarcely calculated to add warmth to his reception. Bluntly the young Virginian was informed that the French Officers' orders were to take possession of the Ohio, and that 'by God they would do it'. With nothing more than an assurance that the Lieutenant-Governor's protest would be forwarded to Montreal, Washington set out on his arduous return journey. It was a trek in the course of which both he and Christopher Gist came close to drowning in the ice-choked waters of the Allegheny. But both survived; and Washington pushed on steadily to Williamsburg, to deliver his message to Dinwiddie. At the same time he strongly recommended him to hasten the construction of a fort at the forks of the Ohio, urging that possession of that lonely peninsula would not only ensure strategic control of the Ohio and Monongahela waterways, but might well determine the future economic fate of all the Middle Colonies.

Dinwiddie immediately besought the Virginia Assembly to vote the money for the fort's construction, backing his appeal by revealing a letter from the Board of Ordnance in England approving the project and offering arms and ammunition; as well as a missive from the King authorizing the work and bidding his representative to meet force with force. But although vaguely alive to the danger menacing the Colony, the Assembly, true to the principle of thwarting their Governor when any opportunity offered, refused to vote a stiver. Dinwiddie, however, was in no mood to permit the situation to deteriorate further; and a second appeal persuaded the Assembly grudgingly to vote a small, totally insufficient sum with which to help subsidize the construction at the Forks of the Ohio.

In mid-April, as the forty men engaged in the erection of the Ohio stronghold were busy about their work, a flotilla of small craft came swarming down the Allegheny bearing a party of five hundred French. The troops landed and summoned the numerically inferior British working party to surrender. Resistance was hopeless; and the French, having demolished the original stockade, proceeded to construct a much larger and stronger fieldwork on the site, and named it Fort Duquesne in honour of Canada's contemporary Governor.

In the circumstances anything less than an appeal to arms would have been futile; although it was scarcely an imposing array — a mere three hundred men — of which Washington was given the command on the death of Colonel Fry, the leader originally nominated, as the outcome of a fall from his horse.

Although the French threat was directed against the Plantations as a whole, Virginia received little practical assistance from the other Colonies; united action in their joint interest was as yet inconceivable — as Benjamin Franklin was to discover at the Albany Congress in the June of 1754.

At the head of his motley following, Washington pushed on until he had reached Great Meadows, some forty miles from his objective of Fort Duquesne. It was at this juncture that he received warning from a friendly sachem, known as the Half-King, that a scouting party of French and Indians were concealed nearby in a certain 'low obscure place'. Determined to try and surprise this enemy band, Washington set out, in pitch darkness and heavy rain, to run them to earth.

In this he was successful, and the small party was silently surrounded. But on the alarm being given the interlopers sprang to their feet, weapons in hand. At this 'Washington promptly gave the order to fire. A volley was given and returned. Coulon de Jumonville, the Ensign who commanded the French, was shot dead, and a few of his men killed and wounded, while the remaining twenty-one were taken prisoners.'[1]

Learning from some unguarded exchanges between his captives that De Contrecoeur, commanding the main force of some five hundred men, was advancing to the support of the Jumonville scouting party, Washington fell back on Great Meadows. Here he found a few reinforcements, including a detachment from the two Independent Companies stationed in New York.[2] With their appearance it speedily became apparent that their ranks were woefully under strength, that they were undisciplined, that they had neither tents, blankets, knapsacks nor ammunition — nothing but their arms, and thirty women and children with whose presence the expedition could very well have dispensed. But the addition of this draggle-tail Bloodyback unit to the force undoubtedly gave rise to a situation of some delicacy. For as an Officer holding a Regular Commission, Captain McKay, the commander of the Independent Company detachment, outranked Washington, although the latter's grade in the militia had now become that of (temporary) Lieutenant-Colonel. This was a state of affairs peculiarly galling to the young militiaman's *amour propre*; for although McKay was lacking in self-assertion and seemed only too ready to leave the conduct of affairs to the local expert, the Virginian's technical subordination to a junior in rank unquestionably rankled. Indeed, it is extremely doubtful if Washington ever managed to pluck this particular burr from his mind.

Ultimately, Washington decided to take up a position the French would be unable to bypass and would therefore be compelled openly to assault. In any case his men and horses were too worn out to march any further. In seeking to train himself in the military art, Washington had been a diligent student of invaluable books such as the Earl of Ossory's *Treatise on the Art of War* and the writings of Richard Elton, Humphrey Bland, Richard Kane, Leonard Fronsperger and

---

[1] A. G. Bradley, *The Fight With France for North America*.
[2] The Independent Company from North Carolina mutinied and virtually disintegrated on the way to the rendezvous.

Fouquières, in which the military wisdom of the European experts was enshrined. But the situation in which he chose to erect a rough entrench-ment surrounded by a log breastwork and a dry ditch was hardly one that would have met with the approval of the theorists on whose works he relied for guidance. For not only was the position in a hollow and remote from any water supply—but it could be brought under fire by marksmen in perfect concealment on the surrounding wooded slopes.

At Fort Duquesne, Jumonville's brother, Coulon de Villiers, thirst-ing to avenge his kinsman's death, set out at the head of a party of French and Indians; and by the night of 2/3 July he had run his quarry to earth. With Washington's men penned within their elementary defences and showered with musketry from the cover of the nearby woods, such return fire as they could bring to bear could scarcely hope to be effective. Their guns were almost useless, since they were so exposed that the loss of life involved in serving them was far greater than any injury they could inflict on the enemy.

In pouring rain, up to their knees in mud and water, with starvecrow rations and failing ammunition, for nine solid hours the beleaguered Provincials and Bloodybacks stubbornly fought back. From time to time the teeming rain forced a lull in the combat, since the opposing forces were completely hidden from one another by sheets of falling water.

The first summons to surrender was ignored; but with the ammuni-tion exhausted and nearly a hundred of the defence force killed or wounded, the second proposal for a capitulation was scarcely to be spurned. Van Braam, one of Washington's own dependents, was the only man with any command of the French tongue, and it was through his intermediation that terms were drawn to which both parties were prepared to agree.

Since the French had no facilities for dealing with more than a few hostages, de Villiers—having first extracted a pledge that the Virginians would not attempt to erect any works beyond the mountains for the space of a year—was quite content that the British force should march out with the customary 'honours of war'; having first surrendered all but one of their swivels and all their baggage other than purely personal effects.

In the articles of capitulation, however, had appeared the phrase 'l'assassinat de Jumonville', which through Van Braam's indifferent translation had been interpreted as nothing more sinister than 'the death of Jumonville'. Appending his signature to the document, Washington quite inadvertently bore witness to the fact that he had brutally slain one who was as much a peaceful emissary as he himself had been on his diplomatic mission to Fort le Boeuf. And by this seeming admission the French had been handed a propaganda weapon of which they made the utmost use.

Amongst the terms of capitulation was a clause regarding the return of the French prisoners who had been taken at the time of Washington's encounter with Jumonville, and sent back to Williamsburg. As hostages for their safe delivery de Villiers retained Van Braam, and a certain expatriate Glaswegian named Robert Stobo, whose subsequent incarceration in Quebec his captors had occasion to rue.

But if the French were temporarily triumphant in the West, the last word on the matter in dispute had yet to be spoken. For as Voltaire tersely summed it up, 'Such was the complication of political interests that a cannon-shot fired in America gave the signal that set all Europe in a blaze' — and, for that matter, launched the Thirteen Colonies on a course which was to determine the ultimate destiny of the whole of America north of the Gulf of Mexico.

5

Challenge in the Wilderness

'It is impossible to satisfy the French.'
Michael ('Lavalette') Bruce

IT IS OFTEN AVERRED that 'trade follows the Flag'. Actually, the exact opposite is far nearer the truth. Enterprise perceives an opportunity to advance its interests and, accepting the risks involved, swings briskly into action to exploit a likely opening. Should opposition be encountered, the 'Flag' is unhesitantly called upon to afford 'trade' the necessary protection and support; the Bloodyback is set to work to 'make safe the field where the building shall be built', and thereafter play watch-dog over it on behalf of its new proprietors.

Just such a situation was the outcome of the rebuff inflicted on the Ohio Company with Washington's surrender at Fort Necessity in the spring of 1754. Not only had enterprise temporarily been thwarted, but local prestige had been so thoroughly besmirched that it was impossible for the mother country to ignore the fact or let it pass without some attempt to help bruised self-esteem recover from the injury it had suffered.

It was not, however, a particularly propitious moment for the Plantations to seek the homeland's active support. Walpole's reasonably capable protegé, Henry Pelham, was dead, 'and the ridiculous Newcastle, as Prime Minister, had succeeded in finding a fool still greater than himself, Sir Thomas Robinson, to be Secretary of State, in charge of the Colonies'.[1] As usual, the Royal Navy was under-nourished and

[1] Fortescue, *op. cit.*

120

over-extended and the military cupboard bare. Nevertheless, in the July of 1754, £10,000 in specie and two thousand stand of arms were sent across the Atlantic to help in the reorganization and re-equipment of the Provincial forces.[1] Then on 30th September orders were given for the 44th and 48th Foot,[2] both of them on the Irish Establishment, to be embarked at Cork. Neither battalion could muster more than three hundred and forty rank and file; and although this total was increased to one of five hundred by drafts of indifferent quality from other formations, the respective Commanding Officer's orders were to make good their numbers with American recruits. Seven hundred stand of arms were to be taken overseas with which to equip the hoped-for additions to the ranks. In November the *Gentleman's Magazine* reported, 'Upwards of £40,000 have been granted by Parliament for defraying the expense of the regiments to be raised in America for the service of the ensuing year; and upwards of £9,000 for defraying the charge of Officers and an Hospital there'.

Command of the small British expeditionary force was awarded to General Edward Braddock. A Coldstream Guardsman of forty-five years' service, a strict disciplinarian, but not devoid of common humanity, his experience of warfare had perforce been confined to the battlefields of Europe; where the technique of combat bore about as much resemblance to the 'bushwhacking' methods employed in America as do the formal measures of a stately quadrille to the rough-and-tumble horseplay of a country dance.

As Braddock's modest force approached Virginia, a body of nearly three thousand French Regulars, under the command of Baron Dieskau, was put under orders for Canada. A British naval attempt to intercept the convoy, when it eventually put to sea, failed to capture more than a couple of transports, carrying at most five hundred men. At precisely the wrong moment Canada had been usefully reinforced.

Before Braddock's departure, Halifax had evolved a plan for the capture of Niagara and Crown Point, with the object of cutting French communications with the Ohio Valley — the strategic *solar plexus* of the whole area in dispute. Unhappily, everyone — and particularly the sponsors of the Ohio Company — was too impatient for speedy results in the immediate vicinity of the Forks of the Ohio for this long-term design

[1] P.R.O., America and West Indies, vol. LXXIV.
[2] Subsequently the 1st Battalion the Essex Regiment and the 1st Battalion the Northamptonshire Regiment.

to find favour. The wish being father to the thought, everyone was serenely confident of swift success; a writer in a contemporary issue of *The Connoisseur* boastfully affirming that 'A Frenchman who piddles on *fricassée* of frogs can no more encounter with an Englishman who feeds on beef, than the frog in the fable can swell her body to the size of an ox'.

So it was at Hampton Roads that Braddock landed from the 50-gun *Norwich* in the mid-February of 1755; proceeding thence to Williamsburg to confer with Dinwiddie—and plunge into the maelstrom of factional politics, conflicting interests, and widely varying response to the needs of the hour. For where the Virginian Assembly had voted £20,000 towards furthering the projected enterprise, and an additional £5,000 was forthcoming from North Carolina, Quaker Pennsylvania had asked to be excused furnishing any troops as they were 'not a fighting people'. (The majority of the Quaker element lived well to the east; those dwelling nearer the borderlands were quite prepared to have their safety ensured at other men's risk.)

With so many waterways seaming the countryside and serving for the passage of goods, overland means of transportation were hard to come by. Thus the demand for waggoners, tumbrils, and horses to draw them could never fully be met; while some of the draught animals actually furnished—at full market price—turned out to be little more than worn-out crocks. Provisions posed another constant problem. For despite a certain number of desertions[1] subsequent to the force's landing, local recruiting—including the illicit enlistment of a number of indentured servants—had brought the 44th and 48th up to something approaching full strength. And as Sir Peter Halkett and Thomas Dunbar, the respective Commanding Officers, were perfectly well aware, men under arms are hungry with great punctuality three times a day.

On 14th April a full Council of Colonial Governors and British Officers produced a master plan for the immediate future. While the principal effort was to be devoted to clearing the French and their Indian supporters from the Forks of the Ohio, subsidiary attempts would be put in motion—to be headed respectively by Shirley and Pepperrell, Brigadier Monckton,[2] and the influential Commissioner for Indian Affairs, William Johnson—against Niagara, the French fort of

---

[1] The sum of 40s was offered for the apprehension of a deserter: Captain Robert Orme, *Orderly Book.*

[2] Second-in-Command to Lawrence, Governor of Nova Scotia.

Beauséjour, on the isthmus joining Nova Scotia to the mainland, and the chain of lakes which led due north from Albany to Canada.

It was an ambitious design, having regard for the fact that Canada's new Governor, de Vaudreuil, could dispose of over three thousand troops of the line — exclusive of the Louisbourg garrison — two thousand Colonial Regulars of the Marine, and a body of militia estimated at fifteen thousand. Moreover, it involved that dispersion rather than concentration which is very rarely known to pay military dividends.

How far the garrison in Fort Duquesne had been reinforced was a matter of guesswork; although Captain Robert Stobo had contrived to smuggle out a detailed plan of the works which in due course reached Braddock's hands. It was a boldly patriotic gesture which, when discovered, inevitably reduced the informant's standing as a hostage to that of prisoner of war. Indeed, but for the fact that France and Great Britain, together with her dependencies, were not officially at war, Stobo might have faced a firing party. As it was, he was promptly removed to Quebec — with consequences which no man at that time could possibly have foreseen.

Having made their approach march in two separate columns, by mid-May the troops of Braddock's command had mustered at the trading station of Wills Creek; where the shaky, green-timbered structure of Fort Cumberland served as official Headquarters.

The warm weather had already produced an epidemic of the itch — attributable to the bite of the chigre, or tick — and the sick list from fever and the 'bloody flux' mounting rapidly, a Field Hospital was established under Master-Surgeon James Napier. In charge of the women selected to tend the patients, at sixpence a day, and their rations, was a certain Mrs Emory Brown, whose post as Matron certainly owed something to the fact that she was a sister of one of the less untrustworthy Commissaries.

Divided into two Brigades, Halkett's force consisted of his own 44th Foot, 230 New York, Virginia and Maryland Rangers, and fifty carpenters. Dunbar's Brigade was made up of the 48th Foot, 650 strong, 230 Rangers from the Carolinas and Virginia, and thirty-five carpenters. The artillery consisted of four 12-pounders, six 6-pounders, four 8-inch howitzers, and fifteen cohorn mortars. Since a certain amount of ferrying and much block-and-tackle work would be involved in getting the ordnance over the streams and rough trail that lay ahead, a landing party of sailors, under Lieutenant Charles Spendlowe, of H.M.S.

Norwich, was detailed to lend the Gunners a hand. Finally, each Brigade was allocated one of the two Independent Companies from New York.

The delay at Wills Creek was far longer than Braddock had contemplated, evoking from Horace Walpole the cynical comment that the General Commanding 'seemed in no hurry to get scalped'. But the problems in logistics seemed almost insoluble, despite the best efforts of Benjamin Franklin, Pennsylvania's able and conscientious Postmaster, to meet Braddock's pressing demand for a hundred and fifty four-team waggons, and the men to work them. But neither threats nor money could produce the total required in 'this drear and desolate country', as Braddock resentfully termed it – not even when a wage was offered of 15s a day for each driver, waggon and four-horse team. Almost in despair, Sir John Sinclair, the Deputy Quartermaster-General, sought to make good the deficiency by rounding up 1,500 pack-horses. But the quality and staying-power of many of the animals brought forward by unscrupulous horse-copers was so indifferent that Braddock's acid comment that Franklin constituted 'almost the only instance of ability and honesty I have known in these provinces' is only too comprehensible.

Fort Cumberland had always been a trading centre; and with the troops *en bivouac* there were plenty of unofficial sutlers to furnish cheap 'moonshine' whiskey – known as 'twenty rod' and 'forty rod'[1] – to eager customers amongst the rank and file and Spendlowe's sailors; and the latter were soon lifting up cheerful voices in the well-known sea chanty,

> Whiskey is the life of man,
> Whiskey! Johnnie!
> I'd drink it out of an old tin can,
> Whiskey for my Johnnie!

Braddock, however, had a remarkably short way with any show of drunkenness. An order was speedily promulgated warning that any soldier caught peddling liquor to his comrades would be 'severely punished'; that any soldier's wife or huckster caught in the act would be 'drummed out of camp'.[2]

In maintaining discipline Braddock's hand could be heavy should the occasion call for it. 'This day', Captain Cholmley's batman noted in his *Diary*, 'there were two men of Sir Peter Halket's Regt that Rec'd a

---

[1] The range at which these appalling distillations were said to be lethal.
[2] Orderly Book of the 44th Regiment.

thousand lashes a piece for Stealing some Money and Deserting. They were drum'd through the lines with halters about their necks.'

On the other hand, given particular circumstances Braddock was capable of real human understanding and compassion, as another diary entry from the same source bears witness. 'This day', runs the note for Monday, 9th June, 'a soldier was tryed for Sleeping when a Sentry, a great Crime here. But he having a good Carractor was forgiven.'

The hundred and six miles from Wills Creek to Fort Duquesne were traversed by no more than an Indian trail. This had to be transformed into a road surfaced and commodious enough to take waggons and the artillery train. For the rank and file, entrusted with the creation of this highway, 'the duty is Excessive hard', Cholmley's batman noted, 'they having only one night in Bed. The day that they are of[f] guard they go to work so that they Either mount guard or go to work Every day, and only salt meat and water to live on, and not having sufficient of that.'

Since the pace of advance was sometimes as slow as three miles a day, and Braddock was resolved to hoard his reserve stock of rations to the last, everyone was on short commons. 'We have been given nothing but carrion for meat', one disgruntled Officer wrote home, 'Indian corn for bread and jades for horses that cannot even carry themselves'; while Cholmley's batman tersely noted down, 'Today we dined on Bear and Rattle Snake'.

After the surrender at Fort Necessity Washington had resigned from the Virginia Provincials; since reorganization of that force fore-shadowed his reversion to the rank of Captain. With rare tact Braddock had invited the Squire of Mount Vernon to make one of his 'family',[1] with his former rank of Lieutenant-Colonel. Although in anything but good health, Washington had gratefully accepted the offer, and had joined the General's entourage at Fort Cumberland.

It was in Braddock's company that the Virginian made reacquaint-ance with Great Meadows, that ill-starred place of bitter memories, when the advance guard of the Bloodybacks and their Provincial com-rades-in-arms reached it at noon on Wednesday the 25th of June.

So far there had been little sign of the French, other than the ribald rhymes and defiant catch-phrases smeared on rock surfaces or pinned to trees; although a number of stragglers had fallen victim to Franco-Indian scouting parties. Three of these strays having been run down and scalped, Braddock's offer of five pounds for any enemy scalp —

---

[1] The contemporary term for the Staff.

French or Indian — went a long way towards restoring somewhat shaken morale.

With the report that five hundred French were on their way to reinforce the Sieur de Contrecoeur at Fort Duquesne, Braddock determined to leave the heavy baggage and most of the womenfolk under a guard commanded by Colonel Dunbar, and push on with twelve hundred of his best troops to capture his objective before its garrison could be strengthened. Thus it was with a relatively small advance guard that Lieutenant-Colonel Thomas Gage made the final crossing of the Monongahela at Turtle Creek, some eight miles from the French stronghold.

No opposition was encountered at the ford, and the men advanced along the trail which led through the woodlands beyond it with all the swing and confidence characteristic of a ceremonial parade. With Colours flying and the still air noisy with the squeal and thump of fifes and drums, the approach march made no attempt at stealth. A little distance from the ford the track passed over a wide and bushy ravine; and it was at this point that a man in Indian garb, but with an Officer's gorget at his throat, sprang into view, turned suddenly and gestured wildly towards the momentarily halted redcoats.[1] A wild war-whoop echoed from the surrounding woodlands, followed immediately by a burst of musketry loosed by assailants scattered amongst the trees. Without hesitation the leading redcoat files swung out of the column into line and replied with a crashing volley.

But this was no open European battlefield, with plainly discernible adversaries. Half the redcoats' missiles buried themselves harmlessly in the timber; few found a human billet. None the less, as volley after volley crashed out, some of the French Canadians in the nearby thickets turned tail and 'fled shamefully, crying "Sauve qui peut" '.[2] But the handful of French Regulars stood firm, and their example had the effect of steadying their Indian allies and sending them back into the fight. 'Yelling like demons but always invisible, they streamed away through the forest along both flanks of the British, and there, from every coign of vantage that skilful bushmen could find, poured a deadly fire upon their hapless opponents.'[3] An attempt to clear the wooded slope on the right flank faltered and was thrown back with heavy loss.

---

[1] Winthrop Sargent, *Journal of the Proceedings of the Detachment of Seamen.*
[2] Captain Dumas in a report to the French Minister of Marine.
[3] Fortescue, *op. cit.*

With the sound of volley fire crashing out up ahead, Braddock, in the words of Cholmley's observant batman, 'galloped towards the noise of battle, with his troops scrambling after him without any form or order but that of a parcell of schoolboys coming our of s[c]hool...But they Continued Surrounding us more and more. Before the whole of the Army got up we had about two thirds of our men Cut of[f] that Ingaged at the First...They continually made us Retreat, they always having a large marke to shoute [shoot] at and we having only to shoute at them behind trees or laid on their Bellies.'

'The greatest part of our Men that were behind trees were either killed or wounded by our own people; even so one or two Officers were killed by their own Platton. Such was the confusion that ye men were sometimes 20 or 30 deep, & he thought himself securest who was in the Centre; during all this time the enemy kept up a continual fire, & every shot took place.'[1]

'In a short time the whole of Braddock's force, excepting the Virginians and Halkett's baggage guard, were broken up in a succession of heaving groups, without order and without cohesion, some facing this way some facing that way, conscious only of the hideous whooping of the Indians, of bullets falling thickly among them from they knew not whence, and that they could neither charge nor return the fire. The Virginians alone, who were accustomed to such work, kept their presence of mind, and taking shelter behind the trees began to answer the Indian fire in the Indian fashion. A few of the British strove to imitate them as well as their inexperience would permit; but Braddock would have none of such things.'[2] Scrambling from saddle to saddle as horse after horse was shot under him, he beat the huddle of bewildered redcoats with the flat of his sword, seeking to hound them back into line, bellowing curses, and entirely oblivious to the fact that he himself constituted one of the most conspicuous targets on the field.

But 'the men could never be persuaded to form regularly, and in great confusion fell back upon the Party which Sir John Sinclair commanded, as did Sir John Sinclair's on Col. Burton's. Every exhortation, entreaty and perswation was used by the General and Officers to make them advance or fall back into the line of March, examples of all kinds were given by the Gen'l and Officers to make them advance, but the Pannock

[1] *Journal of a British Officer*, Anon.
[2] Fortescue, *op. cit.*

was so universal and the firing so executive and uncommon that no order could ever be restor'd.'[1]

'We would have fought if we could have seen anyone to fight with', one survivor ruefully recorded;[2] but both the French and their Indian auxiliaries were employing woodcraft which ensured their own concealment, while condemning their adversaries to bunch helplessly in the open.

Four horses had already been shot under Braddock when he fell from his last mount with a bullet through his arm and lungs. With their leader's collapse, such resistance as the troops had still been prepared to offer dissolved in utterly demoralized rout. In vain Washington and some of the surviving seniors strove to arrest the men's panic retreat; but as Washington himself grimly commented, 'they might as well have tried to stop the wild bears of the mountains'.

Sixty out of eighty Officers had fallen dead or wounded,[3] together with eight hundred and fourteen of the thirteen hundred and seventy-three of the rank and file engaged; while three of the women who had accompanied the advance party had been struck down. 'The Ingagement began at one and ended half an hour after four, when we Retreated. They prosued [pursued] us better than a mile and Cut many of[f] in going through the River.'[4]

Stragglers were set upon and promptly scalped. 'In going Over the River there was an Indian Shot one of our Wimen and began to Scalp her. Her Husband being a little before her [turned and] shot the Indian dead.'[5]

There was no prolonged pursuit, the Indians being far too busily engaged in gathering loot, and in scalping such stragglers and injured as the retreat had left in its wake.

Wounded as he might be, Gage pluckily refused to give up command of the rearguard; with which Braddock also insisted on remaining, being borne along in a litter. 'We marched all night', Captain Cholmley's batman recorded, 'and the Next day without anything to Eat and drink except water.'

In effect, the troops fell back sixty miles to Gist's Plantation before

[1] Captain Orme to Napier.

[2] In a letter of 18th July, 1755.

[3] Sir Peter Halkett and his son were both killed, and among the wounded were Sir John Sinclair and Captain Horatio Gates.

[4] Captain Cholmley's batman.

[5] *ibid.*

Washington—sent to the rear by Braddock for this specific purpose—
was able to meet the weary column with a fresh supply of rations.

Braddock had been in agony from the pain of his wound, but retained
sufficient grip on events, on regaining contact with Dunbar, to order
the destruction of all spare ordnance, ammunition and stores, utilizing
all available waggons for the removal of his wounded. In mid-evening
of Sunday the 13th he breathed his last, almost his final words to the
faithful Orme being a murmur of praise for 'the Blues', or Virginians,
and a whispered hope that he would live to reward them.[1]

'On Monday the dead commander was buried in the road; and men,
horses and waggons passed over his grave, effacing every sign of it, lest
the Indians should find and mutilate the body.'[2]

With Dunbar and the rump of the British and Provincial forces safely
back at Fort Cumberland, it was only too clear that leaders trained in
the formalist Frederickian school of European warfare had much to
learn before they could hope to compete successfully in the 'backwoods
fighting', peculiar to North America. As Washington wrote somewhat
sourly to Robert Jackson, 'When this story comes to be related in future
Annals it will meet with ridicule and indignation, for had I not been
witness to the fact that on that fatal Day, I sh'd scarce give credit to it
now'.[3] Unquestionably, the Braddock disaster had severely damaged the
Bloodyback's reputation as a fighting man in the eyes of a Colonial
population never too inclined to cherish an individual generally regarded as little more than an unwelcome reminder of imperial authority.
Not that universal success was destined to characterize operations
allocated to Shirley and Pepperrell, William Johnson, and Brigadier
Monckton.

New England had responded admirably to the demand for men,
populous Massachusetts raising no less than 4,500 volunteers, and New
York and the remainder of the region nearly three thousand more. For
the attack on the isthmus stronghold of Fort Beauséjour a few Bloodybacks from the Halifax garrison were added to Monckton's Provincials;
and a fortnight's siege delivered the stronghold into the assailants'
hands at relatively small cost; the lesser post of Fort Gaspereau, on the
north shore at Baye Verte, being taken over without opposition. Inevitably, 'this success was followed by the expulsion of the greater part

[1] Francis Parkmen, *Montcalm and Wolfe,* vol I.
[2] *ibid.*
[3] *The Writings of Washington,* edited John C. Fitzpatrick.

of the French population from Acadia, a harsh measure necessitated entirely by the duplicity of the Jesuit priests and of the Canadian Government, who had never ceased to stir up the unhappy peasants to revolt'.[1]

William Johnson's effort against Crown Point, however, was visited with no such favourable fortune. Backed by a motley and untrained body of Provincials,[2] Johnson proceeded up the Hudson, built a stronghold at the Great Carrying Place, subsequently termed Fort Edward, and moved on to Lake Sacrément, which the Indian Agent loyally renamed Lake George in honour of his Sovereign.

But at Fort St Frederick, Crown Point, Count Dieskau, a veteran of the campaigns of Marshal Saxe, had mustered some eight hundred Regulars, twelve hundred militia, and six hundred Indian auxiliaries. Having brushed aside a somewhat naïve attempt to ambush his forces, the Frenchman went on to try and rush Johnson's defensive position on Lake George. The assault was bloodily repulsed, Dieskau himself being wounded and taken captive.

Johnson, however, failed to follow up this golden opportunity, contenting himself by setting his men to work on the construction of a stronghold on the southern end of the lake, which he named Fort William Henry. By the end of November sickness, indifferent rations and worn-out clothing had reduced his men to such a mutinous state of mind that Johnson decided to retrace his steps to the Hudson. After the disgrace of Braddock's sanguinary defeat on the Monongahela, however, the need for a little timely political window-dressing decreed that the Indian Commissioner's rebuff of the French at Lake George should be hailed as an outstanding triumph over the enemy. In the outcome, Johnson's award of a baronetcy and a Parliamentary grant of £5,000 constituted far from ungenerous recognition of services which had contributed little of lasting significance to the general cause.

Nothing further was attempted against Crown Point, and no effort was made to use naval power, based on Oswego, to bar the water passage across Lake Ontario to Fort Niagara and thence by riverway to the Ohio Valley. Moreover, the French were left undisturbed to start work on the erection of an elaborate stronghold at Ticonderoga, to bar

---

[1] Fortescue, *op. cit.*

[2] Although borne on the British Establishment and numbered the 50th/51st Foot, Shirley's and Pepperrell's respective Regiments were made up of raw Provincials, sadly lacking in training and therefore in discipline.

passage from Lake George to Lake Champlain. Named Fort Carillon, it was first built with horizontal log walls, but in the year following reconstructed in stone, on plans worked out by a French-Canadian engineer, Michel Chartier de Lotbinière.

In his turn, Shirley set about his self-appointed task with all the abounding confidence of a lawyer, completely ignorant of the military art, who has bemused himself into the belief that he was a born General.

With Niagara as his objective, Shirley's base for operations was the British outpost of Oswego. With a bland disregard of such humdrum considerations as logistics Shirley, with the shattered remnants of the 44th and 48th Foot, part of his own and Pepperrell's regiments, the four Independent Companies from New York, and a small body of Provincials, arrived at his base well ahead of his supplies, and was compelled to undergo a long wait on half rations. Papers taken at the Monongahela having fully apprised the French of their antagonist's design, they had been at pains to reinforce their garrisons not only at Niagara but at Fort Frontenac at the north-eastern outlet of the lake. This added to Shirley's difficulties, since, unless he first captured Frontenac, the enemy could slip across the lake, once he was fairly on his way to Niagara, capture Oswego and cut him off from his base. As this consideration gradually dawned upon him, Shirley ruefully came to the conclusion that he had taken on a task beyond his powers. Having arrived at this wise if deflating appreciation of the situation, Shirley at least exhibited the moral courage to abandon the enterprise; having first thrown an additional force of seven hundred men into the garrison at Oswego. At the same time outworks were put in hand to bolster up the Oswego post — Fort Ontario on the east side, and an extension of the main stronghold to the west; purely defensive measures but not without their potential value.

With failure attending the British-Colonial effort all along the disputed borderlands, the Francophile Indians needed little urging to swarm out of the Fort Duquesne area into Virginia, Pennsylvania and Maryland, to pillage and massacre virtually without let or hindrance. Washington's fifteen hundred Virginia militia and the Bloodybacks of the available Independent Companies did what they could to protect well over three hundred and fifty miles of frontier. But there was little that could be accomplished with so meagre a force; which the various Assemblies took no steps whatsoever to strengthen; being far too preoccupied in bickering with their respective Governors. There are times when fidelity to a long-cherished tradition can prove a highly expensive form of self-indulgence.

It was in a general atmosphere of frustration and alarm that the unhappy year of 1755 drew to a close. In North America hostilities between the French and British were incessant and undisguised. But as yet there had been no official declaration of war; although everyone, on both sides of the Channel, fully realized that it could only be a matter of time before one party or the other officially threw down the gage. Yet Britain's preparations for the clearly foreseeable clash of arms could scarcely have been more makeshift and perfunctory.

Since the activities of the press had failed to keep the Royal Navy up to strength, it was proposed – by some means undisclosed – to raise five thousand Marines, who would be placed under the direct control of the Lord High Admiral. The strength of the Guards and seven Line regiments was to be raised;[1] while certain treaties with Hesse-Cassel, Bavaria and Saxony would ensure the services of some eight thousand hired mercenaries – at a cost far in excess of that legislated for in previous compacts – should Hanover be invaded. On the other hand, Sir Edward Hawke, in command of the country's only substantial fleet, was sent to sea under instructions of such extraordinary ambiguity as to violate the principles of peace without securing the slightest benefit from the commital of an act of war.

With little more than 34,000 Bloodybacks on the British Establishment, with another 13,000 allocated to the Colonies, Chatham brought forward a Militia Bill which sought to pass the entire eligible manhood of the country through the Reserve Force by ballot, in terms of three years. But although eventually passed, the enactment was never properly enforced; substitution was permitted; and in far too many instances resort was made to the pernicious system of 'raising men for rank'. This signified the grant of a step in promotion to all serving Militia Officers, or the award of a Commission to any civilian – no matter the depth of his ignorance regarding military matters – who could raise a given number of recruits, by the exploitation of personal popularity or by kind favour of the crimps. In effect, the quality of the militia ultimately inveigled or dragooned into serving under the operation of the

---

[1] Ultimately 20 battalions of the Line were raised to the strength of a thousand men; 11 regiments of Cavalry were augmented, and two new companies were added to the Artillery. Miscellaneous Orders, 15th October, 1755, Warrant Books, 21st October, 1755.

Act showed little improvement on the pitiful throng which in earlier days had inspired John Dryden to comment:

> ...raw in the fields the rude militia swarms;
> Mouths without hands: maintained at vast expense,
> In peace a charge, in war a weak defence;
> Stout once a month they march, a blust'ring band,
> And ever, but in times of need, at hand.
> Of seeming arms to make a short essay,
> Then hasten to be drunk, the business of the day.

A far more constructive measure was the introduction of a Bill to enable the King to grant Commissions to foreign Protestants domiciled in America. According to Horace Walpole, the enactment was the outcome of a suggestion emanating from a certain James Prevost, a Protestant refugee, to raise four battalions of Swiss or German Provincials in America, with a British Officer as Colonel-in-Chief, but with a reasonable number of foreigners holding other Commissions. The Bill, authenticating what was nothing more or less than a Foreign Legion in British pay, was duly passed, the formation was designated the Royal American Regiment of Foot, John Campbell, 4th Earl of Loudoun, was appointed Colonel-in-Chief, and Pennsylvania nominated as the regimental recruiting ground. First numbered the 62nd, in the February of 1757 the unit was renumbered the 60th, and so remained.[1]

Yet such was the disgraceful state of neglect into which all departments of the Army had been allowed to fall that John Ligonier, at the Ordnance, could furnish the new formation with nothing better than '3741 long-hand service muskets, serviceable but not fit for regular regiments'.[2]

Throughout the whole of the winter and early spring of 1755–1756 England appeared to lie under threat of imminent invasion. Large bodies of troops were concentrated in the Gallic Channel ports; but although war had at last been officially declared, so inadequate had been Newcastle's preparations to wage it that a considerable body of Hessians and Hanoverians had hastily to be hired to defend an island

---

[1] After many vicissitudes the formation secured a permanent place on the British Establishment as the 60th, King's Royal Rifle Corps, 'the Green-jackets'.

[2] Secretary's Common Letter Book.

which bleakly lacked the trained force with which to defend itself.
But the parade of martial strength along the enemy shore was no more
than a feint, under cover of which the real design was perfected – the
recapture of the invaluable base of Minorca.

To the succour of the elderly but indomitable General Blakeney[1] and
his meagre, under-supplied garrison in Port Mahon – closely beset by
the Duc de Richelieu and 16,000 troops – a weak squadron was sent out
under the command of Admiral John Byng. It was without store-ships,
a siege train or troops to reinforce Blakeney's defence; nor would
General Fowke, Gibraltar's Governor, give heed to the Secretary of
State's directive to make good the last-named deficiency out of the
garrison on the Rock.

Off the mouth of Port Mahon harbour Byng encountered a French
squadron under Galissonière, 'belaboured the French unmercifully, and
the French retaliated by firing at masts and sails, so as to hinder the
English chances of pursuit'.[2] Then giving preference to the safety of
Gibraltar over that of Port Mahon, the Admiral put back to the Rock;
ultimately returning to his home port for major repairs and re-equipment. Abandoned to their fate, Port Mahon's debilitated, scurvy-ridden
garrison was forced to surrender; and with Minorca in French hands
all hope of maintaining the blockade of the fleet in Toulon abruptly
vanished.

Obviously a scapegoat was urgently required to take the blame for
the Government's criminal lack of foresight and scandalous neglect of
its naval resources, and the choice fell on the unfortunate Byng. Tried
under the Twelfth Article of War, he was found technically guilty of
having failed 'to do his utmost to take or destroy' every one of Galissonière's vessels, by a Court Martial confident that the Sovereign would
exercise his royal prerogative and pardon him. But Byng alive and
articulate was a menace to its continued existence which a peccant
Administration was not prepared to tolerate; the ignorant mob was
deliberately encouraged in its demand for retribution, and in the end
'the unfortunate Admiral was shot because Newcastle deserved to be
hanged'.[3]

France, obsessed as ever with the urge to achieve the hegemony of
Europe, could count on the tempered support of Austria, Saxony,

---

[1] He was eighty-four at the time of the siege.
[2] Sir Geoffrey Callender, *The Naval Side of British History*.
[3] Fortescue, *op. cit.*

Sweden and Imperial Russia; Great Britain was sustained only by Hanover and Prussia. Professing a bland neutrality, Holland was, however, quite ready to furnish any of the belligerents, prepared to 'pay through the nose' for them, with a wide variety of warlike stores. Of the gunpowder purchased from the Dutch by Great Britain the contemporary *Gentleman's Magazine* reported, 'We took it away without examination; by which it appeared that they had imposed upon our weakness and credulity, sending us powder that was inefficient as sawdust'. As Canning was one day tersely to point out,

> In matters of commerce the fault of the Dutch
> Is offering too little and asking too much.

Such plans as the flustered Newcastle Administration were capable of evolving were primarily concerned with developments in Europe; although the sum of £115,000 was forwarded to North America in the hope that Shirley would be able to organize the Provinces' defence by the employment of forces raised in New England. The general sense of depression and alarm was further deepened by ill news out of India, where the loss of Calcutta and the horrors of the 'Black Hole' had marked the mid-January of 1756.

One of the fruits of France's newly-gained freedom of the seas was the arrival in Canada of Louis Joseph, Marquis de Montcalm-Gozon de Saint Véran. In his forty-fifth year, the Marquis had seen much service in the campaigns of 1741 and 1744 and in the desperate action under the walls of Piacenza, where he had been severely wounded and taken prisoner; being promoted to General's rank on his subsequent exchange. Shrewd, resourceful and level-headed, he was the most formidable opponent to confront the British in North America since the days of Frontenac.

Accompanying Montcalm as his second and third in command were de Lévis and de Bourlamaque, with Bougainville as senior *aide-de-camp*. With them went twelve hundred Officers and men of the two seasoned Regiments of La Sarre and Royal Rousillon.

In New England Shirley had resigned himself to nothing more adventurous than paper planning until he could transfer responsibility to his successor, for which post it was known that the Earl of Loudoun had received the home Government's nomination.

One matter which should have engaged Shirley's attention, but which he flagitiously neglected, was the reinforcing and reprovisioning of Oswego, on the extremity of the western route into enemy territory. 'On the northern route the French held Crown Point and Ticonderoga, being thus omnipotent on Lake Champlain; while the British, forty miles to the southward, had their outposts at the head of Lake George. It was the obvious task of each to drive the other back—the one on Albany, with a possibility of capturing it; the other on Montreal, with about the same prospect of success.'[1] But if these considerations ever entered Shirley's mind, he gave no sign that he had appreciated their implications; and the fact that Oswego was dangerously 'out on a limb' to all appearances went blandly ignored.

Loudoun did not put in an appearance until the middle of July. He was accompanied by the 35th and 42nd Foot,[2] and by a personal retinue to maintain his nineteen horses, his travelling coach, his chariot, and his street coach; and to wait at table at the elaborate dinners in which he indulged, and at which in one week he and his guests accounted for the consumption of nineteen dozen bottles of claret, thirty-one dozen of Madeira, and a dozen of Burgundy, four bottles of port and eight of Rhennish.

Loudon had been preceded by his second and third in command, Major-General James Abercromby and Colonel Daniel Webb; and the fact is not to be disguised that in the matter of military aptitude a more moderately-endowed triumvirate has rarely ventured on to the Field of Mars.

Loudon's first discovery was that his predecessor had emptied the military chest, with very little to show for the outlay. On inspection, it was clear that Fort Oswego was incapable of defence; while the under-nourished garrison's neglect to observe the most elementary sanitary precautions had sent the sick list soaring. Another report recorded that, 'At Fort William Henry about 2,500 men, 500 of them sick, the greater part of them what they call poorly. They bury from five to eight of them daily... They are extremely indolent and dirty, to a degree. The fort stinks enough to cause an infection, and they have all their sick in it. Their camp nastier than anything I could conceive, their necessary houses, kitchens, graves and places for slaughtering cattle all mix[ed] through their encampment; a great waste of provisions, the men having

---

[1] Bradley, *op. cit.*

[2] Subsequently the 1st Battalion the Royal Sussex Regiment and the 1st Battalion the Royal Highlanders.

just what they please, no great command kept up.'[1] Small wonder
that the men of this garrison were dying at an average rate of thirty a
week.

With the campaigning season swiftly passing, the only event of note
was Johnson's daring penetration of the 'no-man's-land' giving access
to the Six Nations' capital of Onandaga, to strive, with bribes and
exhortations, to win back the Iroquois Federation's allegiance to the
British cause — badly shaken by the Braddock disaster and subsequent
failures to get the better of the French.

In August rumours that the enemy had designs on Fort Oswego sent
Colonel Webb hurrying off to reinforce the garrison with the battered
remnants of the 44th Regiment and a few Provincials. Webb had barely
got as far as the Great Carrying Place, however, before news reached
him that Oswego had already fallen.

Basing himself on Fort Frontenac, and with the regiments of La
Sarre, Guienne and Beárn supplemented by Colonial Regulars and
Indians, Montcalm had invested the disease-ridden Oswego garrison
with a force of over three thousand, supported by a powerful artillery
train, which embodied some of the guns captured from Braddock. To
oppose this formidable array Colonel Mercer could muster barely a
thousand effectives, with eight small pieces of ordnance; although in
addition to its actual defenders the fort housed over six hundred non-
combatants, including a hundred and twenty women and children.

So indifferent was the watch kept on the surrounding countryside
that it was not until the French were within a mile of their objective
that the alarm was sounded which sent the Oswego garrison scurrying
to man their defences.

Mercer's light guns could effect little against the working parties
digging emplacements for the Frenchman's far heavier artillery; nor
was the flimsy palisade of tree trunks, of which the fort's defences were
constructed, capable of standing up to the heavy round-shot that
speedily battered it into ruin.

In Fort Ontario, the outwork on the eastern side of the river, the
defence force of 370 were 'pent up in a Pickitted Fort', as one survivor
recorded, 'with a Ditch begun but not Completed & too weak to admit
of a Sortie. The picketts of this Fort which were fourteen feet high,
were below the level of a little hill to the Eastw'd about eighty Yards,
on which the enemy Battery was raised, so that we could not bring one

---

[1] Quoted in Edward P. Hamilton's *The French and Indian Wars.*

Gun to bear upon the Enemy.'[1] But the men of Pepperrell's Regiment fought gallantly to keep their assailants at bay, until signalled to abandon their position and join the main garrison. Montcalm immediately ordered the erection of a battery on the abandoned height; and it was by a round-shot from this commanding position that Mercer was brought low.

With Mercer's death the garrison had no stomach for further fighting. 'A council of war was called, and it was decided to capitulate. The surrender was practically unconditional. One thousand six hundred and forty prisoners were taken in all, most of whom were forwarded to Canada. Six vessels carrying fifty-two guns fell into Montcalm's hands, with two hundred barges, a hundred and thirteen cannon[2] and mortars, with large supplies of ammunition, pork, flour, spirits, and £18,000 in cash.'[3]

With the captured liquor freely broached, 'the Canadians and Indians broke through all restraint and fell to plundering. There was an opening of rum barrels and a scene of drunkenness, in which some of the prisoners had their share; while others tried to escape in the confusion, and were tomahawked by the excited savages. Many more would have been butchered, but for the efforts of Montcalm, who by unstinted promises succeeded in appeasing his ferocious allies, whom he dared not offend.'[4] None the less, fifteen of the more youthful prisoners were given up to the Indians to be 'adopted' in place of the braves recently slain.

Casualties had barely totalled fifty a side; but with Oswego laid in ashes, and five captured Regimental Colours displayed in Montreal's churches, the French had scored a triumph at remarkably small cost.

With the news from up-country, Webb lost what little nerve he had ever possessed. Giving full credit to the rumour that Montcalm was advancing on Albany at the head of six thousand men, he burned two recently erected forts, filled in the channel of Wood Creek[5] with fallen timber—of which it had only just been cleared, at great labour and expense—and then retired at speed to German Flats, on the Mohawk river.

British military prestige could scarcely have been at a lower ebb.

[1] Quoted in N. J. O'Conor's *A Servant of the Crown.*
[2] Mostly light swivels.
[3] Parkman, *Montcalm and Wolfe*, vol. I.
[4] Bradley, *op. cit.*
[5] Not to be confused with the Wood Creek near Lake George.

'Save in the New England Provinces, there was no spark of military vigour. No answering challenge to the audacity of the French came from the middle and Southern Colonies; the minimum of necessary protection seems to have been the limit of their ardour.'[1] Nor was Loudoun the type of leader to arouse the general mass of the people from their mood of sullen apathy. Conscientious, almost pedantically methodical, he was far too cold and aloof to get on easy terms with the Colonial officials with whom he was called upon to collaborate. Moreover, in many respects he was the victim of the long-established but ill-advised regulation which decreed that all Provincial Officers serving with the British Regulars, whatever their status in their local formations, were to take rank as no more than junior Captains, an ordinance deeply resented by the ten Provincial Colonels, eleven Lieutenant-Colonels and ten Majors shown on the contemporary active list. In addition, Loudoun was called upon to deal with the extremely vexed question of quartering the Bloodybacks and their Officers on the civil population, a necessity arising out of the lack of barrack accommodation in the back areas, which the various Provincial Assemblies gave no thought to remedying. It was a bone of contention destined to play a progressively significant part in the relationship between the civil population and the Bloodybacks in their midst. It was, indeed, a problem for whose solution men far more conciliatory than the stiff-necked Loudoun were unable to find a *modus operandi* satisfactory to all the interests concerned.

There is a degree of fatuity which exceeds what even the complacently indulgent British Parliament is prepared to tolerate; and by the November of 1756 Newcastle had plainly exceeded it. After endless intrigues to retain office, the shifty old jobber reluctantly made way, nominally for the Duke of Devonshire, but in reality for William Pitt. 'England has been long in labour', said Frederick the Great, 'at last she has produced a man.'

Without delay the Electoral troops and the Hessians, brought over for Britain's home defence, were sent back to Germany; for good or ill the guardianship of the island base was to be confided to the militia. On 15th December estimates were submitted to the Commons for a British establishment of 30,000 men, with another 19,000 allocated to the Colonies, besides 2,000 Artillery and Engineers. (The absence of

[1] Bradley, *op. cit.*

Minorca from the list of overseas garrisons furnished a sufficient commentary on the stark ineptitude of the previous Administration.) For fifteen Regiments of the Line orders had already been issued for the recruitment of second battalions. Two years later these battalions were given separate existence as the 61st to the 75th Foot.[1] Pitt then went on, with some daring, to form two regiments of Highlanders, each 1,100 strong, both of which were destined to achieve considerable distinction under the names of their respective Colonels—Fraser and Montgomery.[2] Shirley's and Pepperrell's respective corps were removed from the British Army List, their numbers being taken up by two indigenous formations.[3] Besides drafts for the units already overseas, seven battalions were earmarked for despatch to North America; while the strength of the 49th Foot, stationed in Jamaica, was nearly doubled.

If the regeneration of the Royal Navy took longer to bring about, at least Lord Anson, at the Admiralty, could give validity to his sound belief that 'the best defence for our Colonies, as well as our coasts, is to have a squadron always to the westward as may in all probability either keep the French in port, or give them battle with advantage if they come out'. With Sir Edward Hawke to command the Western Squadron, and the dearth of experienced seamen to some extent made good by adding another thirty companies of Marines to those already established, the progressive strengthening of the Royal Navy could go steadily ahead.

But in warfare, post-outbreak improvisation, however brilliant and energetic, cannot absolve such forces as are actually in the field from the dire consequences of pre-war neglect.

Thus the unfortunate Duke of Cumberland, sent to Germany at the head of an entirely inadequate 'Corps of Observation' to protect Hanover, found himself confronted with a numerically overwhelming enemy force under Marshal D'Estrées. Cumberland's plea for reinforcements was ignored, since the only troops available had been pre-empted for one of those 'operations of detachment' which always seem to exercise so fatal a fascination for the politician. In the event, the abortive amphibious expedition against Rochefort succeeded in 'breaking a few

---

[1] P.R.O. Miscellaneous Orders, 20th December, 1756.

[2] Miscellaneous Orders, 4th January, 1757.

[3] Ultimately to be known as the 1st Battalion the King's Own Yorkshire Light Infantry and the 2nd Battalion Oxfordshire and Buckinghamshire Light Infantry.

French windows with English guineas'; and then trailed home; while for lack of the needful reinforcements Cumberland suffered such complete defeat in the field as left him no option but to sign the humiliating Convention of Kloster Zeven, by which he agreed to disband his troops and leave the French in undisturbed enjoyment of their conquest.

Not that the picture in North America glowed with brighter colours. It was Loudoun's design to organize an expedition against the rebuilt and heavily reinforced stronghold of Louisbourg. But Provincial forces were late in mustering, and reinforcements from England did not put in an appearance until well on into the summer. Another six weeks were wasted before Loudoun decided to move forward to Halifax to rendezvous with Admiral Holbourne and his squadron. It was not until the troops had been landed that steps were taken to ascertain the strength of the opposition likely to be encountered. It was with the discovery that a French squadron, including twenty-two sail of the line, was in Louisbourg harbour and that the strength of the garrison had been increased to seven thousand, that the hopelessness of the enterprise became apparent. Without more ado the expeditionary force turned about and sailed back to New York.

Loudoun's absence from the hub of events, and the partial denudation of the frontier to swell his numbers, had presented Montcalm with an opportunity to strike at weakened defences he was far too good a soldier to overlook. At the end of July he had assembled 8,000 French, Canadians and Redskins at Ticonderoga; and on 30th July some 2,500 of them, under de Lévis, started their march to the western shore of Lake George. Montcalm, with some 5,000 more, embarked in *batteaux* on Lake Champlain. Within twenty-four hours both detachments had united close to Fort William Henry, which was promptly laid under formal siege.

Within the fort—built of crossed logs filled in with earth—Lieutenant-Colonel Monro, of the 35th Foot, had the command of a mixed body of troops, sailors and mechanics, totalling some 2,200; while the quality and care taken of the twenty-four pieces of ordnance with which the Fort was equipped was clearly indicated by the fact that by the third day of the investment six of them had burst.

Montcalm's troops were all in position by five o'clock on the morning of 3rd August; and for the ensuing six days the siege was pressed with the utmost vigour. On 9th August an anonymous diarist entered in his record of events, 'The Ennemy fired very slowly, and run another Boyeau behind the Garden near 300 yards from the Fort. Several Shott came into our Retrenchment Also a mortar, with several Cannon Bursted on the Batterys in the Fort. About 8 a Clock in the Morning a White Flag was hung out from the Fort which proved to be a Signal of Capitulation, which was Confirmed & Ratified by 12: a Clock.'[1]

Although lying no more than fourteen miles away at Fort Edward, Colonel Webb made no attempt to take his four thousand men to his brother Officer's succour; deeming it more advisable to concentrate all available forces on the defence of the approach routes to Albany.

Thus with over three hundred killed and wounded, and smallpox raging among the survivors, Monro accepted the honourable terms offered him by his adversary, which included the proviso that the French should furnish an armed escort for the survivors on their march to Fort Edward. On the road thither, however, the Indian auxiliaries, sweeping Montcalm and his Officers aside, and entirely unhampered by the Canadian militia, threw themselves on the unarmed British, massacring eighty of them and maltreating many more.

The important post on Lake George had been lost, and the British had suffered yet another notable reverse in North America.

Such was the legacy of Newcastle's fumbling incompetence; responsibility for some part of which inevitably fell on the shoulders of the man who was striving so diligently to make good the errors of judgment and the wholesale neglect of the country's Armed Forces of which his predecessor in office had so patently been guilty.

[1] P.R.O., Amherst Papers.

6

The Trampling of the Lilies

'The French have often, and frequently mistakenly, considered that
they had the primacy in the military art.'

Major-General Sir John Davidson

LIKE MOST MEN of outstanding character and ability, William Pitt
suffered at times from the defects of his own qualities. Clear-headed,
clean-cut and decisive in his views, at the outset of his term of office
he was inclined to be both domineering and impatient. It was only
when the faultiness of his judgment was demonstrated by the failure
of his subordinates to carry his policy to success—as in the case of
Loudoun and Abercromby—that he was induced to lend a more atten-
tive ear to the counsel of the veterans at the head of the two Fighting
Services—Anson at the Admiralty, and Ligonier, the newly-appointed
Commander-in-Chief of the Army.[1]

Pitt's overall design, to win America in Germany, demanded a large
increase of troops for operations in Europe, and legislation was enacted
which was calculated to bring the Army's strength up to a total of
100,000. A French breach of the Kloster Zeven convention afforded
Pitt the opportunity to denounce the agreement, keep the Hanoverian
Army in being and place it, together with a strong contingent of
Bloodybacks, under one of Frederick of Prussia's most brilliant subordinates, Prince Ferdinand of Brunswick. With Prussia enheartened

---

[1] Anson had fought with great distinction against both Spain and France, while his
three-year-and-nine-months circumnavigation of the globe had brought him wide *réclame*.
John Ligonier, the expatriated Huguenot, had fought under Marlborough and at Fontenoy,
and at one period had headed the Board of Ordnance.

by the resounding victories of Rosbach and Leuthen, co-ordinated operations by the British, Hanoverians and Prussians could be put in motion against the French on a scale hitherto not even attempted.

At this juncture national morale was given a useful fillip with the news of Robert Clive's victory over the Francophile Surajah Dowlah at Plassey.

So far as North America was concerned, a three-fold advance had been planned against the territories still held by the French. Under Abercromby's personal command a force of 15,000 Bloodybacks and Provincials was to strike northwards from Albany and take Fort Carillon, as the first step in an advance on Montreal. Under Brigadier John Forbes a 'mixed' column of 6,000 was to concentrate on the capture of Fort Duquesne; while a third body of 14,000 Regulars was to undertake the reduction of Louisbourg. Command of the Louisbourg enterprise had been entrusted to Jeffrey Amherst. A Guardsman who had served with distinction at Dettingen, Fontenoy and Roucoux, Ligonier's personal knowledge of his capabilities had gone a long way towards determining his selection for command of the enterprise.

Brigadier James Wolfe was nominated to command the Grenadiers and Light Infantry, and the 42nd Highland Regiment; Brigadier Lawrence had the 13th, 22nd, 35th and 45th Foot, together with the 2nd Battalion of the Royal Americans. The Brigade under Colonel Whitmore consisted of the 1st Royals, the 17th, 47th, 48th and 58th Regiments, and the 3rd Battalion of the Royal Americans.[1]

The request for upwards of 25,000 Provincials to supplement the Bloodybacks had been supported by Pitt's offer to furnish the local forces with all they required in the way of arms, ammunition, consumable stores and tents, leaving to the Provinces the obligation to meet no more than the expenses involved in raising, clothing and paying them. At the same time the invidious regulations regarding the relative seniority of Provincial and Imperial Officers were tactfully reframed far more in favour of the former.

The British troops destined for Louisbourg were to be conveyed by a fleet under 'wry-necked Dick',[2] an armament powerful enough to overpower any hostile naval force it was liable to encounter. A squad-

---

[1] See Appendix C.

[2] Admiral Edward Boscawen—also known as 'Old Dreadnought'. He had been with Vernon at Porto Bello and Cartagena and had served with distinction in Indian waters. Wounded in the shoulder in the Finisterre battle of May 1747, muscular contraction had permanently tilted his head to one side.

ron was also sent under Admiral Osborne to the Mediterranean to intercept any French reinforcements seeking to put out from Toulon; while yet another squadron, under Sir Edward Hawke, cruised with the like object off Rochefort. Both armaments carried out the tasks entrusted to them with complete success; Captain Gardiner's single-ship action against the infinitely more powerful *Foudroyant* ending with H.M.S. *Monmouth*'s colours nailed to her mainmast and the Frenchman's ensign lowered in defeat.

Bad weather seriously retarded Amherst's rendezvous with Boscawen at Halifax, and it was not until the last days of May that the convoy — escorted by twenty-three ships of the line and several smaller Royal Navy craft — set sail for Louisbourg.

With the Chevalier de Drucourt as Governor, Louisbourg's four thousand inhabitants were watched over by a garrison of over three thousand troops;[1] with artillery amounting to two hundred and nineteen cannon and seventeen mortars, plus forty-four pieces of ordnance in reserve. In the harbour rode five ships of the line and seven frigates, equipped in all with five hundred and forty-four guns and manned by approximately three thousand men.

With five hundred Provincial troops to supplement the eleven thousand Bloodybacks, actually under command, Amherst's advantage in numbers was more than counterbalanced by the difficulties of approach to his objective. Of the four possible landing places that in Freshwater Cove offered the best chance of getting ashore in strength; but for five days on end the raging surf forbade any attempt at disembarkation.

It was not until two o'clock on the morning of 5th June that the troops were got into their boats; and as Whitmore and Lawrence organized feints against the other three landing places, Wolfe — at the head of five Companies of Grenadiers, five hundred and fifty marksmen drawn from the different regiments, Fraser's Highlanders, and a body of Provincial Rangers[2] — pulled steadily for the shore of Freshwater Cove,[3] four miles distant from the city. Entrenched beyond the Cove's rock-edged quarter-mile beach a thousand Frenchmen held their fire and that of their eight cannon and swivels, until it could wreak the

[1] The garrison consisted of the battalions of Artois, Bourgogne, Cambis and Volontaires Etrangers, with two Companies of Artillery and twenty-four of Canadian Provincials, some militia and armed Indians.

[2] Eight more Companies of Grenadiers were held in support.

[3] Also known as Coromandière Cove and sometimes as Kennington Cove.

maximum of effect. 'The enemy acted very wisely, did not throw a shot till all the boats were in the Cove and then they threw in a cross-fire of one 24-pounder, four 6-pounders and the fire of the Infantry that had lined the whole Bay.'[1] Fortunately three boats, which had pulled in on the extreme right, were sheltered from the enemy fire by a small projecting spit. Leaping ashore, the Officers and men, with the French caught *en enfilade*, held on gamely until they could be supported by diverting the majority of the troops to the flank which had been so daringly secured. As reinforcements poured in to land—however precariously—in the shelter of the rock spit, Lawrence's brigade also managed to get ashore at the western end of the cove. Assailed on right and left, and fearing to be cut off from the town, the French abandoned their artillery and fled, pursued by their assailants until the fugitives had reached the protection of the fortress guns. At a cost of less than a hundred in killed, wounded and drowned, Amherst's first and most difficult objective had been gained.

Much as in 1745, vile weather and the difficulties presented by the terrain combined to retard the landing of the artillery train and the creation of something of an approach road to the commanding Green Hill position, whence the most effective fire could be brought to bear on Louisbourg's landward defences. 'It was soon evident that there was one operation which alone could reduce the place within the appointed time, and that was that the fleet should enter the harbour. Yet in spite of Pitt's hint, Boscawen seems never to have entertained the idea.'[2] To the impatient Wolfe the canny Boscawen rated as little more than a faint-hearted dodderer. It was not a point of view shared by the foremast hands whom 'Old Dreadnought' had actually led into action, one of whose favourite chanties ended with the lines,

> Sing ho, jolly bucks, we'll set the taps a-flowin'
> And drink health and good luck to Admiral Boscawen.

Not that there was any noticeable alacrity to challenge Boscawen's squadron on the part of the enemy warships in the haven. Indeed, even when Wolfe set about the installation of a powerful battery at Lighthouse Point they made no attempt to intervene, but continued to cower under the protection of the harbour guns.

On 9th July, the French launched a sortie in strength—some eight

[1] Jeffrey Amherst, *Journal*.
[2] Sir Julian Corbett, *England in the Seven Years' War*.

hundred men, 'most of them drunk'[1] — which was driven back into the town with little loss to the Bloodybacks.

Partisan attacks on the British flanks and rear, by Indians and Acadians led by Boishébert — erstwhile commander of the surrendered outpost at Baye Verte — were countered by strengthening the outlying pickets. The difficulties encountered in carrying out their task are sufficiently revealed in an order which ran, 'As the air of Cape Breton is moist and foggy, there must be particular attention paid to firearms on duty, that they may be kept dry and always fit for use, and the Light Infantry should fall upon some method to secure their arms from the dews and the droppings of trees, when they are in search of the enemy.'

Yet hard pressed as the siege operations might be, the courtesies of war were by no means overlooked. The indomitable Madame de Drucour, as well known and as well loved a figure on the ramparts as she was about the shattered streets of the town, was the recipient of two luscious pineapples, just brought in to Amherst from the Azores. Not to be outdone in courtesy, Madame promptly presented the British Commander-in-Chief with several bottles of champagne; which in turn brought her ladyship another offering of pineapples and a firkin of sweet butter. For his part, the Governor offered the services of an exceptionally skilled physician to any of the wounded British Officers who cared to avail themselves of his attentions.

From the outset the French expenditure of ammunition had been recklessly prodigal, so that by 23rd July Amherst was noting in his *Journal*, 'The Enemy fired off all sorts of old Iron Nails &c. on every occasion.' But the besiegers were well dug in; eight hundred seamen having readily come ashore to lend a hand in the incessant work with spade and mattock.

With many of the town's wooden dwellings reduced to smoking ruin and the barracks no more than a fire-blackened shell, with old men, women and children cowering in the shelter of the stifling casements, it was plain that further resistance could only be maintained at the useless sacrifice of life and limb. Negotiations speedily led to agreement on the terms of capitulation. Thus it came about that at twelve noon on 27th July the garrison laid down its arms — '5,000 firelocks', Amherst duly noted, 'and eleven Colours'. Over two hundred cannon and a certain quantity of stores fell into the victors' hands, together with

[1] Amherst, *op. cit.*

5,600 prisoners; the Governor and his undaunted lady being ceremonially received and elaborately dined by Amherst aboard Captain
Rodney's H.M.S. *Terrible*.

After Louisbourg's fall the whole of Cape Breton Island and the
neighbouring Île St Jean[1] passed into British possession; the news of
the successful operation being as rapturously received in the North
American provinces as in Great Britain. While in the homeland bonfires
blazed and church bells pealed from John o' Groat's to Land's End,
New York celebrated with loyal toasts, and Boston indulged in a positive orgy of pulpit eloquence, softened in many instances by certain
concessions to the fleshpots; Amherst, temporarily in the city with five
of his battalions, recording with humorous resignation, 'I could not
prevent the men being quite filled with rum by the inhabitants'.[2]

With the campaigning season no more than half over Amherst was
anxious to push on without delay for Quebec. It was the level-headed
Boscawen who reminded him that the grand design against the capital
of New France was contingent upon the progress of correlated operations
elsewhere; and news from the south-west was anything but reassuring.

If Pitt's judgement had been seriously in error where the Earl of
Loudoun's capabilities as a field commander were concerned, it was
equally at fault in assessing the qualities of that typical military dray-
horse Major-General James Abercromby.

Some of Loudoun's preliminary spadework had shown an admirable assessment of what was demanded by the 'backwoods fighting'
peculiar to North America. Almost from the first he had striven his
best to add a little flexibility to the battle-practice in which the Bloodyback had so sedulously been trained. Furthermore, having recognized
the undependability of the Indians, he had readily agreed to substitute
Ranger Corps in their place – such as that raised by Robert Rogers – as
a fighting force which would combine a trapper's innate woodcraft
with a proper sense of discipline and subordination. Thus it had been
Loudoun who had welcomed Colonel Thomas Gage's offer to raise, at
his own cost, a regiment of Light Infantry, British Regulars trained to
serve as Rangers.[3] In effect, Loudoun could think out the needs of a

---

[1] Subsequently renamed Prince Edward Island.

[2] Amherst to Pitt, 18th September, 1758.

[3] The Regiment was formed early in 1758 and numbered 80th, a number subsequently
assumed by the forebears of the 2nd Battalion the South Staffordshire Regiment.

campaign, but had been entirely unable to energize it and fight it to a successful conclusion.

Of Abercromby it can only be said that he carried orthodoxy well beyond the point of no return. If the situation which confronted him had been legislated for 'in the book', then he was prepared to deal with it according to the line of conduct laid down in standing regulations. But anything heterodox, anything outside the scope of the 'book of the rules' had him completely nonplussed and therefore doomed disastrously to flounder. Yet it was to this well-intentioned but slow-witted man that Pitt confided the task of capturing the outer bastion of Fort Carillon, as the preliminary to a full-scale advance on Montreal by way of Lake George and Lake Champlain.

To carry this mission to success Abercromby had the command of seven thousand Bloodybacks and nine thousand Provincials; although the preliminary work of mustering the latter and getting all the stores and equipment over the three portages between Albany and Fort Edward proved, as always, extremely laborious and vexing.

Fortunately, in a flash of inspiration, Pitt had authorized the appointment, as Abercromby's Chief of Staff, of George Augustus, 3rd Viscount Howe, who had arrived in America in the previous year at the head of his Regiment, the 55th Foot.[1]

The Howe family could claim royal blood in its veins even if *à la main gauche*, the maternal forebear of the line having been Charlotte Sophia Baroness Kielmansegge, *maîtresse en titre* to George I. It followed that the three grandsons of the first Viscount had instinctively gravitated to the Fighting Services, the eldest, George Augustus, having originally been commissioned in the 1st Regiment of Foot Guards.

In the Flanders campaign of 1747 Howe had shown so marked an aptitude for his chosen calling as to linger favourably in the minds of those authorities responsible for the appointment of Officers to posts demanding outstanding adaptability and resourcefulness. It was in the hope that Howe's versatility drive and initiative would do something to counterbalance Abercromby's sluggish rigidity of outlook that the thirty-four-year-old Lieutenant-Colonel had been promoted Brigadier and sent to join the Scottish General as his Chief of Staff.

Nor were the hopes entertained of him in any sense disappointed. He had already spent a year on American soil, and there had been no moment of that time from which he had failed to derive some profit.

[1] Subsequently the 2nd Battalion the Border Regiment.

For much of the year, in the company of such accomplished woodsmen as 'Ranger' Rogers, Israel Putnam and John Stark, he had devoted himself to mastering the art of 'bush-whacking', which he had found to differ in almost every particular from the formalized type of soldiering practised on the traditional battlefields of Europe. In 'backwoods fighting' it was clear that fundamental discipline required to be supplemented by a profound knowledge of woodcraft, infinite resourcefulness and the guile and initiative of the skilled hunter.

In this process of self-education no man could have done more than this scion of the British aristocracy to dispel the belief, so widely held amongst the Colonists, that the Bloodyback Officer was an affected, patronizing 'Macaroni', too dainty for anything more onerous than ceremonial parades. As one simple backwoodsman enthusiastically recorded, 'Lord How was the Idol of the Army, in him they placed the utmost confidence, from the few days I had to observe his manner of conducting, it was not extravagant to Suppose that every Soldier in the Army had a personal attachment to him. He frequently came among the Carpenters, and his manner was So easy and fermiller, that you loost all that constraint or diffidence we feele when adressed by our Superiors, whose manners are forbidding.'[1] Affable and easy without condescension or sacrifice of dignity, Howe was as welcome and at home at a backwoodsman's camp fire as at a fashionable Boston tea table; in his brief hour of universal acceptance no more popular Bloodyback ever set foot on American soil.

Having comprehensively indoctrinated himself in what 'Ranger', Rogers termed 'our methods of marching, ambushing, retreating &c' Howe was all eagerness to impart the lessons he had learned to the force of stolid, formally trained Regulars concentrated at Albany.

To begin with, the Chief of Staff got rid of all hampering 'frills'. Cumbersome 'pigtails' were shorn off[2] as ruthlessly as the hindering long skirts of the scarlet jackets. Leather stocks and pipeclay became taboo; stout leather gaiters replaced the restricting, easily soaked spatterdashes; while musket barrels were browned to eliminate their betraying glitter.

Officers were required to dispense with the services of the camp washerwoman and launder their own shirts and 'smalls'; to cut down

[1] Quoted in John H. Cuneo's *Robert Rogers of the Rangers*.

[2] It is interesting to note that it was the German element in the ranks of the Royal Americans who were most indignant at this departure from orthodoxy.

drastically on the elaborate messing amenities to which they were accustomed; to reduce their personal baggage to the absolute minimum, and to shelter *en bivouac* under a single blanket and a bearskin. But with Howe himself to set the example there were no more than minor grumbles at the spartan simplification of the daily round to which one and all were subjected. 'You would laugh to see the droll figures we make', one of them wrote good-humouredly to a friend; 'Regulars as well as Provincials have cut their coats as scarcely to reach their waists...Only a small portmanteau is allowed each Officer. No woman is allowed in the camp to wash our linen. Lord Howe has already shown an example by going to the brook and washing his own.'

It was, therefore, very largely due to Howe's ruthless scaling down of impedimenta that by the end of June Abercromby's force of 6,377 Bloodybacks and 9,034 Provincials, with all their essential supplies, had been assembled at the head of Lake George. By the morning of 5th July the whole expedition had been embarked in nine hundred *batteaux* and thirty-five whale boats, with a large number of flatboats carrying the artillery.

Under a beaming sky and to the strains of martial music, the formidable armament glided forward, with Rogers's Rangers and Gage's brown-coated Light Infantry sharing the van with Howe's own 55th Regiment of Foot. The sombre blue of the New York, New Jersey, Rhode Island and New England Provincials contrasted soberly with the faded scarlet of the Royal Americans and the four British line regiments of the centre; each corps carefully keeping station on its own flag. Two 'floating castles' bristled with the artillery pieces assigned to cover any forced landing to which the expedition might find itself committed.

Where French preparations were concerned, Fort Carillon had accommodation for a winter garrison of four hundred. Had the assault on it been launched in May, as originally intended, it might well have found the winter garrison unreinforced. As it was, Montcalm commanded a body of 3,500 men; and for his main defensive position had chosen a ridge about half a mile back from the fort. For roughly a quarter of a mile, timber had been cut to make a loopholed zigzag wall —to create salients—six to seven feet high and with the flanks carefully 'refused'. In front of the wall was a deep and thick abatis, with sharpened branches pointing towards the most obvious line of attack. One battalion had been left in the fort itself as a reserve and to help man the guns; while a few scouting parties had been sent out to harass the British in their approach.

Abercromby's main body reached the foot of the lake at ten o'clock on the morning of 6th July. By noon the whole army had been landed on the western shore. Since the French had destroyed the bridge over the channel connecting Lake George and Lake Champlain, the plan was to follow the western bank and fall on Fort Carillon's defences from the rear. Rogers and some of his Rangers were sent forward to reconnoitre the thick virgin forest which lay ahead; the main body thrashing along in their wake. A French scouting party, about three hundred and fifty strong, finding its retreat cut off, had no resource but likewise to take to the woods, where they too lost themselves amongst the maze of trees. Thus both hostile bodies were groping and fumbling their way through the tangled woodlands, lost to all sense of direction, like strangers abandoned in a cunningly constructed labyrinth.

Suddenly the straggling British right-centre column, with Lord Howe and some Rangers at its head, blundered full upon the enemy detachment. A sharp skirmish filled the woods with the angry bark of musketry, with the French caught in the crossfire of the British column and Rogers's advance guard and virtually annihilated. In number, the British losses were trifling, but none the less fatal to the enterprise, for Lord Howe lay dead with a bullet through his heart, and the whole army had lost its inspiration. 'Never Ball had a more Deadly Direction', wrote an eyewitness of the tragedy; 'I was about six yards from him, he fell on his back and never moved, only his Hands quivered an instant and were then still.'[1]

With Howe's untimely death Abercromby was seized with virtual paralysis. It was not until the morning of 8th July that the General, rejecting any suggestion to attack the enemy position from the flanks while employing his artillery to batter the breastwork into splinters, gave the order that the position should be carried head-on with the bayonet.

It was high noon when the shots fired by the retreating French pickets brought Montcalm's garrison of eight Regular battalions and four hundred and fifty Canadians—a little more than a fourth of the British force—to their battle stations behind the breastwork, which

---

[1] Howe's untimely death was as deeply mourned by New England's civilian population as by the Army; the people and Government of Massachusetts combining to erect a monument to his memory in Westminster Abbey.

Abercromby's indecision and delay had given them ample time to complete. Forming in the shelter of the forest, the attacking column moved steadily towards the abatis and the silent, loopholed palisade of logs which lay beyond it. Suddenly the breastwork burst into a sheet of flame, and a whirlwind of musketry and grape-shot swept the ranks from end to end. 'The fire', one survivor[1] subsequently recorded, 'was exceedingly heavy and without intercession insomuch as the oldest soldier never recalled so furious and incessant a fire. The fire at Fontenoy was nothing to it.'

The attack had been led by the Rangers and Light Infantry, but with the 42nd and the 55th coming up in support, the main volume of the enemy musketry was directed against the Black Watch and their red-coat comrades. 'Impatient for the fray', wrote an Officer-Survivor of the former, 'the Highlanders rushed forward to the entrenchments, which many of them actually mounted, their intrepidity was rather animated than dampened by witnessing their comrades fall on every side. They seemed more anxious to avenge the fate of their deceased friends than to avoid a like death.'[2] Some of them drew their claymores and strove to hew a path through the hampering abatis, while others sought individually to return the fire of an enemy they could rarely even glimpse. But for all their toil and sweat they could not force their way through the close-meshed obstruction under the terrible fire that tore into them from front and flank and from the angles of the breastwork; and after an hour's struggle they fell back, cursing and swearing that the position was impregnable. Two miles away from the scene of action, Abercromby's only response to a situation which called for real tactical flair was dourly to direct that the attack should go in again.

And then followed such a scene as had not been witnessed since Malplaquet nor was to be seen again till Badajoz. The men stormed forward anew, furious with rage and heedless of bullets or grape-shot, through the network of trunks and boughs against their invisible enemy. Behind the breastwork the French were cheering loudly, hoisting their hats occasionally above the parapet and laughing when they were blown to pieces, but pouring in always a deadly and unquenchable fire, while the British struggled on,

[1] Lieutenant William Grant of the Black Watch.
[2] Quoted by Frederick B. Richards, *The Black Watch at Ticonderoga.* (New York State Historical Association.)

grimed with sweat and smoke, vowing that they would have the wooden wall at any cost.[1]

But it was not to be. With the greatest difficulty the Highlanders were forced to abandon their fallen comrades, and under cover of the Light Infantrymen's fire the whole battered force withdrew, as de-moralized as they were exhausted, stumbling in wild disorder to the landing place; where Abercromby himself led the retreat to the head of Lake George. Of the Bloodybacks 1,600 had fallen — of which the casualties in the Royal Highlanders accounted for close on five hun-dred — while losses with the Provincial troops totalled 334. With the dispirited Bloodybacks once more in camp, a bad outbreak of dysentery speedily added to the troops' losses. If ever a man had been shown that a combination of delay and tactical inflexibility brings inevitable defeat it was the unhappy James Abercromby.

It is one of warfare's constant ironies that subsidiary enterprises are often visited with far better fortune than a major operation in which the main effort has been concentrated. So it fell out in the fateful year of 1758.

Lieutenant-Colonel John Bradstreet, veteran of the 1745 siege of Louisbourg, was strongly in favour of nipping out Fort Frontenac, that half-way post between Montreal and the remoter western strongholds and the enemy garrisons in the Ohio valley. Thus, after Abercromby's failure at Ticonderoga, Bradstreet was entrusted with the command of 2,500 men — mostly Provincial militiamen — and bidden advance by way of the Mohawk valley, past the site of the former Oswego outpost, to Lake Ontario.

On 25th August the *batteaux* men brought their charges safely to their destination. On the lake the 16-gun *Marquis de Vaudreuil* and two smaller craft of twelve and nine pieces could have blown the *batteaux* out of the water had they but shown a little alertness and resolution. But nothing was done to exploit this naval advantage; and the French garrison — severely reduced to reinforce the troops in Montreal — could make little more than a token resistance. By the 27th the fort was in Bradstreet's possession, together with the entire naval force on the lake — nine vessels, of which two were carried off and the rest burned, since there was now no fort at Oswego to afford them support and

[1] Fortescue, *op. cit.*

protection. Fort Frontenac itself was dismantled; and with this command of Lake Ontario was lost to the French, while their communications north and south were completely severed. Moreover, the wavering sympathies of a number of Indian tribes veered in favour of the British; while the enemy garrison in Fort Duquesne was left isolated.

Command of the expedition for the capture of this long-detested focus of enemy activity had been assigned to Brigadier John Forbes. A former student of medicine turned soldier, no man had a better grasp of the fundamentals of 'backwoods fighting' than this canny, resolute, sexagenarian Scot. Unprejudiced by his lengthy experience of the battle-fields of Europe, he always insisted that 'in this country we must comply and learn the art of warr from the enemy, Indians or anything else who have seen the country and warr carried on in it'; adding to a method of battle practice peculiarly applicable to the local terrain all the advantages accruing to a superior armoury and a properly organized system of supply.

With Forbes's arrival in Philadelphia early in the April of 1758, however, he found that he had virtually nothing in the way of an army to command. The Provincial troops allotted by Pennsylvania, Virginia, Maryland and North Carolina had not even been enlisted, let alone subjected to any sort of training; while of the hard core of Regulars, Montgomery's Highlanders were still in the south and only half of Colonel Bouquet's battalion of the Royal Americans was within reach.[1]

It was not, indeed, until the beginning of July that Forbes had enough Regulars under command to keep his irregulars 'in due decency and order', and could send an advance party forward to Raystown,[2] on the eastern slope of the Alleghenies. This was not the earlier route followed by Braddock, which the merchants with commercial interest in the frontier and the great cobs of the Ohio land company had urged him to take, since it could be anticipated that in due course a highway fully put in repair by the military would be turned over for civilian traffic without charge to the users. It was a development advocated nowhere more fervently than by Colonel George Washington when he arrived in Philadelphia at the head of his Virginia Provincials. But Forbes had little patience with proposals whose narrow self-interest was

---

[1] The Royal Americans had acquired a certain number of rifled carbines, and were therefore prepared to sustain that role of rifleman with which they were subsequently to be identified.

[2] Now the town of Bedford.

so disregardful of all other considerations. He had mapped out his own route, one which would enable him to move forward by short stages, establishing fortified magazines every forty miles, until, within reach of his objective, he would be in a position to march upon it with his entire force and with as few encumbrances as possible.

So far as the local Indians were concerned, the best that could be hoped of them was that the efforts of the Moravian missionary, Christian Frederick Post, would succeed in keeping them neutral.

It was slow going; and Forbes himself was in increasingly poor health. But he pressed on doggedly and by the middle of August 1,600 men had arrived beyond the Allegheny Ridge. Toil had been incessant; rations spartan and monotonous to a degree; one of his Officers writing to Bouquet, 'The salt pork has very nearly dried up [the] spring in this encampment'.[1] As always, the 'bloody flux' had taken its toll, and there had been sporadic outbreaks of smallpox. But it was being committed to march day after day through seemingly interminable woodlands, hemmed in by close-ranked tree trunks under an unbroken canopy of leaves, in a perpetual green twilight, airless and reeking of unwashed bodies – it was this which brought about a depressive sense of claustrophobia almost impossible to shake off. With this morbid sinking of the spirit went the haunting fear of straying from the marching files and failing to regain them. 'Having observed on that march', Bouquet subsequently wrote to Amherst, 'that the Highlanders lost themselves in the Woods as soon as they got out of the Road, and cannot on that Acc't be employed as Flankers, I commissioned a Person to procure me about thirty Woodsmen to march with us' – and play sheep-dog to the strays. A cringing dread of the unfamiliar was a sensation to which every generation of Bloodybacks that fought in North America was to yield in its turn.

Slowly but steadily 'Forbes's Road' moved forward, until by September work had been started on the construction of Fort Ligonier on Pennsylvania's western border. A grim reminder of past events came with the rounding up of half a dozen stray horses, whose Government markings identified them as having once formed part of Braddock's transport train.

It was at this juncture that a party of Highlanders, Royal Americans and Indian auxiliaries, bent on a reconnaissance of Fort Duquesne, suffered a sharp rebuff; a badly handled enterprise which was followed

[1] Bouquet Papers, B.M. Add. MSS., 21640, p. 147.

by an attack by the French on Forbes's main body, encamped at Loyalhanna, which was easily repulsed.

Continuing his forward march, by late November Forbes had arrived within a few miles of his objective. During the night hours of the 24th/25th the British camp was aroused by the sound of a heavy explosion. With daylight it was speedily discovered that the French had blown up Fort Duquesne and abandoned all pretence of exercising suzerainty over the Forks of the Ohio. Bradstreet's destruction of supplies at Fort Frontenac had reaped handsome dividends for John Forbes.

Before the fort's destruction several of the Highlanders, captured during the blundered reconnaissance, had been tomahawked, while five of them had been ceremonially burned at the stake on the parade ground, their blackened skulls stuck on posts sadistically draped with the victims' kilts.[1]

Leaving a small force to garrison the post, Forbes and the main body of his troops set out on their return journey. The enforced desertion of the vital Forks of the Ohio by the French undoubtedly constituted a signal triumph for a desperately sick man. As Bouquet was the first to declare, 'The glory of our success must, after God, be allowed to our General'. It was a *réclame* which Forbes was not destined long to enjoy. So desperately sick was he, indeed, that throughout the last stage of the homeward journey he had to be carried in a litter; and by the time he reached Philadelphia he knew himself to be a dying man. But there was still time to have a medal struck for those who had accompanied him on his successful march; and before his death in the March of 1759 he had the satisfaction of distributing the memento to those who had served him as faithfully as he had served his country's cause.

In no contest in which Great Britain and France were belligerents could the West Indies be safely left out of calculation. Easy to raid and wreak destruction upon – with their highly combustible fields of cane and sugar factories – the islands were difficult to seize and retain unless their captors enjoyed overwhelming naval superiority in local waters.

In the January of 1759 a force of six battalions,[2] shepherded by eight ships of the line, set out from Barbados intent on the capture of

---

[1] This was reported by a lad who had escaped from the fort shortly before its destruction.

[2] Six thousand men of the 3rd, 4th, 61st, 63rd, 64th and 65th Foot. Miscellaneous Orders 27th September–10th October, 1758

Martinique. After an unproductive landing to the north of Port Royal, re-embarkation and a little hovering off the haven of St Pierre, which drew far heavier fire than had been anticipated, it was decided to abandon the attempt on Martinique in favour of a descent on the notorious nest of privateers concentrated in the neighbouring island of Guadeloupe.

Basseterre was known to be defended by a formidable fortress, towering over the town on a lofty eminence. None the less, so brisk and effective was the naval gunfire that the commercial quarter, crammed with sugar, rum and molasses, was soon burning furiously. By nightfall every enemy battery had been silenced and the town was a heap of blackened ruins. 'You never seen such a blaze', wrote a Bloodyback gun-layer to his parents; 'and all that prime licker blazing away to waste.'[1]

With the troops put ashore, the capture of the well protected eastern half of the island proved no easy task; while sickness speedily reduced the landing force by nearly a quarter. It was not until the elderly and somewhat indecisive Major-General Peregrine Hopson[2] had been succeeded by the younger and more resourceful Colonel John Barrington that a vigorous and successful offensive completed the island's conquest—just ahead of the arrival of French reinforcements, which sailed away in great haste upon discovering that they had appeared too late. The capture of Mariegalante effectively rounded off a highly successful little campaign.

The stunning reverse suffered at Fort Carillon in the July of 1758 had made it plain—even to Pitt—that Abercromby would have to be replaced as Commander-in-Chief. For his successor the obvious choice was Jeffrey Amherst; although it was not until the campaigning season for 1758 had drawn to a close that he received official confirmation of his appointment to the chief command.[3]

With the troops he had brought with him from Louisbourg added to those concentrated in and about Albany, Amherst could dispose of twenty-three battalions of Bloodybacks—though none of them was up to strength—while Provincial troops had been promised by the New England States, Rhode Island and New Jersey. Recruiting for these formations, however, was considerably less brisk than in the previous

[1] Letter from A. B. John Wright of H.M.S. *Norfolk.*
[2] A former Governor of Nova Scotia.
[3] His Commission as Commander-in-Chief reached Amherst on November 9th.

year; a return dated 30th May recording '2550 present, 2025 not come up belonging to the Regts of the 2550 which are in the Camp. Col. Worcester's Regt Newhampshires Troop 1000, and 1000 Connecticut not yet come'. The July *Gentleman's Magazine* reported 'An impresse of part of the militia was ordered in New York and by the Massachusetts Government, to prevent which subscriptions were set on foot to engage volunteers by high bounties; some got 91 to 121 sterl: to enlist'.

Obviously it was in every way desirable that the Colonies should actively participate in their own defence. But from a strictly military point of view it is difficult to dispute the view expressed by an American authority, that 'the average Provincial was a poor soldier. He could not well be anything else considering his background and his lack of training, and the fact that those who led him had little or no military qualifications.'[1] His chief defects arose out of his lack of subordination and his resentment of any attempt to subject him to discipline; for an army without discipline is little more than an armed mob. His chief merit lay in his native courage and—in the case of the majority—a reasonable familiarity with the use of firearms.

With a separate force set aside for the enterprise against Quebec, Amherst's only other source of reinforcement lay with the debilitated survivors of the expedition against Martinique and Guadeloupe.

As a preliminary 'clearing' operation, a detached force under Brigadier Prideaux was sent to attempt the restoration of Oswego and the capture of Fort Niagara. The venture was entirely successful, although at the cost of the leader's life. Thus the whole region of the Upper Ohio was left in undisputed British possession, with the French posts to the west hopelessly cut off from Canada.

By late June Amherst had moved as far north as the site of Fort William Henry, where the construction of a new and more formidable stronghold was immediately put in hand. Bad weather and an outbreak of measles slowed down the next stage of the advance; while stray parties, cutting brush and timber, were constantly being ambushed by Indians and Canadian woodsmen, who invariably contrived to elude the Rangers sent after them. It was not, therefore, until late July, that a concerted move was made on Ticonderoga; supported by Captain Joshua Loring's sloop and the *radeaux* bearing the heavy artillery. A note in Amherst's *Journal* for 23rd of the month records, 'The troops having lain on their arms all night, as soon as it cleared in the morning

[1] Edward P. Hamilton, *The French and Indian Wars.*

the Officers commanding the posts opposite Ticonderoga reported to me all their [i.e. the French] tents struck and that the whole was gone off in the Sloops and bateaus'. A rearguard left in the stronghold, however, put up a stubborn defence; and it was not until the night of the 26th/27th that they set fire to the fort and decamped under cover of the darkness. British casualties had come to sixteen killed, fifty-one wounded, and one missing. On the other hand, most of the enemy artillery had been captured.

Early in August Amherst continued his slow progress towards Crown Point. On learning that Fort St Frederick had been blown up and abandoned, with the French retreating northward, Amherst took the precaution of rebuilding Fort Carillon—which he renamed Fort Ticonderoga—his forward move considerably delayed by the necessity to construct a naval force strong enough to compete with that operated by the French on Lake Champlain.

The French had undoubtedly been thrown on the defensive; although they enjoyed the advantage of operating on interior lines. But their capacity to keep the field was bound to suffer from the fact that they were now cut off from all sources of reinforcement and supply.

Pitt and his advisers had always envisaged an offensive against Quebec, by the passage of the St Lawrence, to complement Amherst's advance, by way of the lakes, on Montreal. Originally, a force of twelve thousand had been earmarked for the St Lawrence enterprise, although in the event no more than eight thousand could be mustered to try to carry it through.[1] To the surprise of many and the consternation of not a few, command of the expedition was awarded to Amherst's former subordinate, the somewhat meddlesome and highly opinionated James Wolfe. Only thirty-two years of age, Wolfe had already served in seven campaigns; and to those who had protested that he was 'too impulsive', 'too full of books and theories', and far too prone to 'feel his epaulettes',[2] King George's rejoinder had been, 'Mad, is he? Then I hope he'll bite some other of my Generals!'

Wolfe's three Brigade Commanders were the Hon. Robert Monckton, second son of Viscount Galway, the Hon. George Townshend, and the Hon. George Murray; while his Quartermaster-General was

[1] Supplemented subsequently by two under-strength battalions which had been on duty in the Bay of Fundy.
[2] i.e. to assert his rank.

Guy Carleton, the future Lord Dorchester; all of them men who, in a military sense, had already established themselves as men of energy and talent. Moreover, they were of far greater social standing than the son of an undistinguished officer of the Marine Corps; a consideration by no means to be left out of account in the days when the social milieu from which he derived could materially affect the pace of an Officer's advancement.

Unfortunately, Admiral Durrell, driven into Halifax by floating ice in the Gulf of St Lawrence, had re-emerged too late to intercept a number of storeships with a few men and a considerable quantity of supplies for Quebec, which was thus substantially replenished. However, it was in a mood of high confidence that, on 6th June, the British armament cleared Louisbourg and headed for the river mouth; the toast drunk in all the messes being, 'British Colours on every French fort, port or garrison in North America'.[1]

Since one of the supply ships to reach Quebec earlier in the year had borne Bougainville, carrying an intercepted letter revealing the whole of Pitt's plan for the subjugation of Canada, Montcalm had been in a position to revise his entire scheme of defence. Much faith was reposed in the belief that the British would be unable to overcome the navigational hazards for which the St Lawrence was notorious. But as Killick, the master of the *Goodwill* transport, growled in answer to the protests of a Canadian pilot, 'Damn me, I'll convince you that an Englishman shall go where a Frenchman dare not show his nose'; adding as he triumphantly cleared the tricky shoals of the Traverse, 'damn me if there aren't a thousand places in the Thames fifty times more hazardous than this'.[2] It followed that an outraged de Vaudreuil was presently writing, 'The enemy have passed sixty ships of war where we durst not risk a vessel of a hundred tons by night or day.'[3]

Thus by 26th June Wolfe had been landed on the Île d'Orléans, to contemplate Quebec, four miles away across the intervening basin, and the strongly fortified Beauport lines stretching eastwards for eight miles along the waterway's northern bank, to the river and falls of Montmorenci. Point Lévis, on the southern bank, a little downstream from Quebec, was so obviously a position from which fire could be brought to bear on the citadel that Monckton was sent to seize and

[1] Captain John Knox, *An Historical Journal of the Campaign in North America* (3 vols.).
[2] Knox, *op. cit.*
[3] Vaudreuil's despatch to the Minister of Marine.

6

entrench it before the advisability of fortifying it occurred to the besieged.

Admiral Saunders with his warships and transports was still at his moorings south of the Île d'Orléans, and on the night of 28th June the French attempted the destruction of the anchored vessels by floating seven fireships downstream. The venture was a spectacular fiasco; Delouche, the officer in charge of the operation, having lost his head and given orders to ignite the craft prematurely. A million livres' worth of blazing, shot-spouting shipping 'were certainly the grandest fireworks that can possibly be conceived', wrote the observant Knox, with comprehensible satisfaction; 'many circumstances having contributed to their awful, yet wonderful, appearance'. None the less Saunders found it advisable to shift his anchorage until he was sheltered under the lee of Point Lévis. Two miles westward of this miniature promontory another position was established at the Point des Pères, where only the width of the river separated Quebec from the artillery which promptly brought it under fire. At the same time Wolfe passed a body of troops to the east of the Montmorenci; a dispersion of the British forces which failed to entice Montcalm into a false move which might afford his adversary an advantageous opportunity to attack him.

On 27th July the French made another attempt to set the British fleet ablaze. But the fireships were gallantly grappled by Saunders's bluejackets and toused ashore before they could work any mischief. 'Damme, Jack', one cheerful Bloodyback was heard to call to a comrade, 'didst thee ever take hell in tow before?'[1]

Since it had been left to Wolfe to initiate some stroke calculated to further his general design, he elected to embark on a full scale attempt to force the Beauport lines; a combined operation demanding not only the most carefully planned co-operation between the two Services, but the most meticulous preliminary reconnaissance. That the latter had been anything but carefully carried out was only too painfully demonstrated in the subsequent operation.

It had been discovered that the existence of the 'Beauport Bank' — a wide expanse of shallows in front of the enemy position — rendered it impossible for the fleet to close to within effective bombarding range. What perfunctory soundings had failed to reveal was the existence of a ledge lying short of the flats. The outcome was that when the assault

[1] Knox, *op. cit.*

against the Beauport position went in on the morning of 31st July the landings were made piecemeal instead of simultaneously. Thirteen companies of grenadiers were the first ashore followed at intervals by elements of the Royal Americans; and 'as soon as we landed', recorded one grenadier survivor,[1] 'we fix'd our Bayonets and beat our Grenadier's March, and so advanced on. During all this Time their Cannon play'd very briskly on us; but their Small Arms, in their Trenches, lay cool 'till they were sure of their Mark; then they pour'd their Small-Shot like showers of Hail, which caus'd our brave Grenadiers to fall very fast.' In effect, the impetuosity with which the grenadiers had hurled themselves into the fray, without pausing even to form, and the delay in landing troops for their support, meant that the assault entirely lacked control, co-ordination and disciplined impetus. Isolated in a redoubt they had rushed at the foot of a hill crowned by the main line of enemy defence, the grenadiers sought desperately to climb the slope, while 'the troops and Canadians at the top poured upon them a hailstorm of musket-balls and buck-shot, and dead and wounded in numbers rolled together down the slope'.[2] At this critical juncture a hovering summer storm abruptly burst in a deluge of rain. On both sides ammunition was drenched and rendered useless, while the grassy slopes became so treacherous as to inhibit all movement upon them. Realizing that the whole attempt had gone awry, Wolfe gave the order to withdraw; and the troops fell back and scrambled into their boats; the grenadiers and Royal Marines having lost between them five hundred officers and men, or well-nigh half their numbers, in killed, wounded and missing.

Partly owing to faulty reconnaissance and partly to the uncontrolled impetuosity of the grenadier landing party, Wolfe's opening offensive had been a disastrous failure; and for the moment he could think of nothing more constructive than to lay waste all the settlements in the neighbourhood of Quebec in the hope of provoking desertion amongst the Canadian militia and exhausting the colony generally. Since Montcalm had a number of Indians and the 'white Indians' of the militia at his disposal, hideous reprisals were exacted for every act of desolation perpetrated by the British; while in a constructive military sense affairs remained at a standstill.

[1] Anon, *A Sergeant-Major of Hopson's Grenadiers*. Appendix of Part II of A. Doughty's *The Siege of Quebec*.

[2] Parkman, *op. cit.*

Earlier in the month, however, Admiral Saunders had succeeded in passing several of his vessels upstream without the slightest injury to them; and when troops were also landed upriver, direct communication between Montreal and Quebec was severed. But what to do next was a problem which clearly had Wolfe nonplussed. To try and force a crossing of the Montmorenci some distance upstream would obviously run into prepared defences of such strength as to be almost unassailable. Even if overcome, the Charles river, on Quebec's outskirts, still remained a formidable obstacle barring direct approach to the city. In effect, where the capture of Quebec was concerned Wolfe was like a dog confronted with a plate of food too hot for him, at which he sniffs hungrily at one edge and then at another, hoping to find a place where he can get an effective bite without painfully burning himself in the process.

Then, towards the end of August, word flew around the British lines that the General lay sick abed. Like many of his contemporaries, Wolfe had long been a victim of rheumatism and the gravel, afflictions which the deepening depression begotten of an abiding sense of frustration did little to alleviate.

With day-to-day operations and planning for the future temporarily handed over to a consortium of Saunders and the three Brigadiers, the idea of a landing on the north bank on the upstream side of Quebec took on firmer definition the more its possibilities were explored. Visual reconnaissance from the southern bank to pick out a potential landing place at the foot of the almost vertical cliffs on the northern side of the stream had not overlooked the possibilities of the little cove known as the Anse du Foulon. It was a choice of locale fully endorsed by Captain Robert Stobo, whose third attempt to escape from imprisonment in Quebec had been successful, and whose knowledge of the city and its environs, gained during the course of his long captivity, could scarcely have been bettered.[1] Difficult and arduous as it was bound to be, a landing immediately west of the objective was the only plan which held out any hope of success. When put before him by the members of the consortium, Wolfe accepted without demur a course which had been marked out by the fleet from the moment the leading warship had passed above Quebec.

At least the troops were ready and eager to put fortune to the test,

[1] At one period Stobo had been a prisoner on parole and free to wander about Quebec and its neighbourhood as he listed.

as Serjeant Ned Botwood's confident doggerel had made abundantly
clear:[1]

> Come, each death-dealing dog who dares venture his neck,
> Come, follow the hero that goes to Quebec:
> And ye that love fighting shall soon have enough;
> Wolfe commands us my boys; we shall give them hot stuff.

On 12th September intelligence reached British Headquarters that
on the next ebb tide a convoy of provisions would seek to steal down-
river to Quebec. This was precisely the 'cover' required to validate the
British plan.

Thus it came about that at 1 a.m. on 13th September two lanterns,
swung to the maintop of H.M.S. *Sutherland*, gave the signal for thirty
boats, bearing Wolfe and 1,700 men, to set forth on their desperate
enterprise. In command of the 'forlorn hope', made up very largely of
his own light infantry, was 'Good-natured Billy' Howe, with Captain
William Delaune, of Wolfe's own 47th Foot, crouching at his side;
while Captain Chads, the appointed beach-master, groped his way hopefully for the shore. 'Our army in high spirits', Knox noted; 'weather
favourable, a starlight night.' At the same time a feint by the vessels
still opposite Beauport helped to distract attention from activities
further west; Montcalm, completely deceived, massing the bulk of his
troops in the lines, where he kept them under arms to repel the expected
attack. As Wolfe and the ships' boats approached the Anse du Foulon,
the sloops and frigates stole silently in his wake. But 'when ye first corps
for disembarkation was passing down ye N. Side of ye River', Townshend subsequently noted, 'and ye French Centries on ye banks chal-
leng'd our boats, Captain Frazer, who had been in ye Dutch service &
spoke french—answered—la france et vive le Roy, on which ye French
Centinels ran along ye Shore in ye dark crying laissez les passer ils
sont nos Gens avec provisions'.[2] As hoped, the assault force had
been mistaken for the convoy transporting provisions for the Quebec
garrison.

Once ashore, Howe and his light infantrymen had little difficulty in
overpowering the picket posted to keep watch and ward over the Anse

---

[1] The rhyme was written prior to the attempt on the Beauport Lines, during which
Botwood met his death.

[2] Northcliffe Collection: Townshend Papers.

du Foulon.[1] With the crest safely in British possession, the main body of the troops could be set ashore; with the bluejackets lustily engaged in helping the landing of cannon and ammunition until 'before the sun was well up the whole force of forty-five hundred men had accomplished the ascent, and was filing across the plain at the summit of the heights'.[2]

Deliberately, the British force had accepted a very considerable risk. Ahead of them Montcalm commanded a numerically superior army; a mere eight miles in their rear Bougainville controlled a sufficiently numerous body of men to break through the meagre scattered detachments under Howe, which Wolfe had deployed to fend off any attempt to assail his forces in reverse. But as Wolfe himself had once observed, 'War is an option of risks', and if nothing is ventured nothing can be gained.

By nine o'clock in the morning the rival lines of battle were both formed; with the Regiments of Béarn and La Sarre on the right, with the men of Guienne and Languedoc in the centre, and those of the Royal Roussillon on the left. Canadians and Indians in their scores skirmished forward to harass the British flanks.[3]

It was with the fire of these sharpshooters that the action opened, but the fusillade soon became general; the British steady platoon fire culminating in a crashing volley from the whole front which tore the advancing French line into shreds.

Wolfe had been wounded in the wrist quite early in the engagement, but it was at the height of the shooting that he took the hurt that was to prove mortal. Struck in the groin, 'he desired those who were about him to lay him down; being asked if he would have a surgeon, he replied, "It is needless; it is all over with me". One of them then cried out, "They run, see how they run!" "Who runs?" demanded our hero, with great earnestness, like a person roused from sleep. The Officer answered, "The enemy, sir. Egad, they give way everywhere". Whereupon the General rejoined, "Go one of you, my lads, to Colonel Burton—: tell him to march Webb's Regiment with all speed down to

---

[1] The picket commander, Louis Vergor, was in bed and asleep; and a large proportion of his militiamen had been given leave to return home to attend to the demands of their farms.

[2] Fortescue, *op. cit.*

[3] From right to left the British line was made up of the 35th Louisbourg Grenadiers, 28th, 43rd, 47th, 78th, 58th and 15th Foot; with the 48th and the Royal Americans temporarily held in reserve, and with Howe's Light Infantry guarding the flanks and rear.

Charles's River, to cut off the retreat of the fugitives from the bridge". Then, turning on his side, he added, "Now, God be praised, I will die in peace", and thus expired.'[1]

The French advance, shattered to a halt, had turned into a scrambling confused retreat; with the men of the 35th Foot playing such havoc with the fugitives of the Royal Roussillon that for forty years thereafter they were authorized to sport the white Roussillon plume in their headgear.[2]

Montcalm too had been mortally stricken, and with his death Vaudreuil gave the order to retreat, 'and the entire French (field) force streamed away in disorderly and disgraceful retreat to the post of Jacques Cartier, thirty miles up the St Lawrence. The only instructions left with the garrison of Quebec were to surrender as soon as provisions should fail.' By 18th September the British were in possession of the city; with Brigadier James Murray commanding a garrison of 7,500 men, his battalions strengthened by drafts from the 62nd and 69th Foot, which had been serving temporarily aboard the fleet.

Quebec, Duquesne, Crevelt, Minden—where French defeat would have ended in absolute rout had Lord George Sackville exhibited the courage to obey orders and lead the cavalry in pursuit of the fleeing French[3]—the capture of Guadeloupe, Boscawen's success against the French off Lagos and Hawke's triumph amidst the treacherous reefs of Quiberon Bay: in such a 'year of miracles' it is small wonder that Walpole wrote in mock complaint that 'one can never afford to miss a single copy of a newspaper for fear of missing a British victory somewhere'.

But the main issue had yet to be determined. In India Clive was making slow but steady progress. In Europe Ferdinand of Brunswick and Frederick the Great confronted French forces so numerically superior that even such brilliant victories of Emsdorff and Warburg— where the British cavalry fully redeemed their good name under the

---

[1] Knox, *op. cit.*

[2] Subsequently the plume was embodied in the Royal Sussex Regiment's cap badge. The captured Roussillon Colours, of course, bore the Bourbon lilies, earning for the 35th, with their tawny facings, the nickname of 'the Orange Lilies'.

[3] Sackville was courtmartialled for his disgraceful dereliction of duty and adjudged 'unfit to serve His Majesty in any Military Capacity whatsoever'. The pity was that the Court did not add the words 'or Civil'.

personal leadership of the Marquis of Granby—had little effect upon
their ability to carry on the struggle.[1]

And Canada had yet to be won; the news of Quebec's surrender
reaching Amherst while he was no further advanced than Crown Point
—and while more cynical tongues in Boston and New York were
bandying about the little doggerel rhyme:

> Oh, Lord Jeffrey Amherst was a soldier of the King,
> And he came from across the sea;
> To the Frenchmen and the Indians he didn't do a thing,
> In the wilds of this wild countree,
> In the wilds of this wild coun—tree!

But the distinctly gastropodic pace of Amherst's advance was not
altogether wanting in excuse. An outbreak of smallpox, the rising tide
of desertions, especially amongst the Provincials, who, as he noted in
his *Journal*, 'have now got home in their heads & will now do little
good', trouble with the Indian auxiliaries ('as idle, good-for-nothing
crew as ever was') above all, his determination thoroughly to consolidate his lines of communication—all these factors must be taken into
consideration before dismissing the British advance as unduly cautious.
Unfortunately, the principal victims of Amherst's particular *modus
operandi* were the garrison in Quebec. Throughout the winter of 1759–
1760 all ranks had suffered severely from disease and the biting cold;
by April not more than three thousand men were fit for duty, even
those still capable of turning out being afflicted with scurvy in greater
or lesser degree.

It was at this juncture that De Lévis, at the head of an army of seven
thousand and a fleet of *batteaux* escorted by two frigates, was reported
in the neighbourhood of St Foy. Quebec's fortifications were in no
condition to withstand heavy, concentrated bombardment, so Murray
sallied forth to confront his antagonist on the deeply snow-covered
Plains of Abraham, where he took up much the same position as that
which had been occupied by Montcalm's troops in the previous
September. Action was promptly joined; Murray paying dearly in
casualties for his temerity, but dealing his enemies so hard a knock that
his own troops were able to withdraw into Quebec without molestation.

Immediately all ranks set to work further to strengthen the defences;
'Officers yoked themselves to cannon and plied pick and spade; and the

[1] Emsdorff was the first 'Battle Honour' officially awarded to British troops.

men, with such an example before them, strained themselves to the utmost. In a short time one hundred and fifty guns were mounted and at work on the walls of Quebec, while the French, however they might toil at their trenches in the stubborn soil of the plateau, had hardly brought up a single cannon to answer them.'[1]

On 9th May all eyes turned anxiously to the St Lawrence, where a single frigate was seen ploughing her way upstream. A roar of cheering greeted her identification as H.M.S. *Lowestoft*, bearing news that a British squadron was hard on her heels.

With British men-o'-war destroying all the enemy ships containing the French reserve of supplies and ammunition, De Lévis hastily raised the siege, retreating with such precipitancy as to abandon all his guns and stores, and every one of his sick and wounded. Quebec was saved; and the coming of Spring, with plentiful supplies of fresh wholesome food, soon turned Murray's sickly battalions into an army fit for service in the field.

News of the successful issue of the struggle for Quebec had reached Amherst at Albany, whence he had returned after a winter visit to New York. Administratively the trip was doubtless of value. But it had done little to hasten his own preparations and the subsequent resumption of his march on Montreal; before which all that was left of the French forces in Canada was now concentrated. Moreover Amherst had been forced to denude his none too adequate force of the three thousand men needed to quell an uprising of the Cherokee Indians. But at length when high summer was almost past, the net he had so carefully woven began to close around the French.

The first move came from Murray, whose *batteaux* moved up the St Lawrence, skirmishing all the way, until by 24th August he was within nine leagues of Montreal, ready to move up to the Île Sainte Thérèse, just below the city. Meanwhile a force of 3,400 Regulars, Provincials and Indians, under Brigadier William Haviland, had landed at Île aux Noix to bring Bougainville's defences under brisk fire, severing his communications with St John's, the next post down the river. Driven from Île aux Noix, Bougainville proceeded to join Bourlamaque on the banks of the St Lawrence; their joint force rapidly melting away through desertion. By this time Murray and Haviland were in communication, and eagerly awaiting the arrival of the main force under Amherst.

With eight weak battalions totalling less than six thousand men, plus

[1] Fortescue, *op. cit.*

6*

five hundred Provincials, on 10th August Amherst crossed Lake Ontario at the head of nearly eight hundred whale-boats and *batteaux*, escorted by Joshua Loring's gunboats. Delayed by the necessity to subdue Commandant Puchot's defence of Fort Lévis, on an islet at the head of the rapids, it was not until the 30th that the flotilla could attempt the descent of the rapids themselves. The water being exceptionally high, it proved a hazardous and costly passage, Amherst recording in his *Journal*, 'We lost 24 men, 20 batteaus of Regt's, 17 of Artillery, 17 whaleboats, one Row Galley, a quantity of Artillery stores & some guns that I hope may be recovered'.

By 6th September, however, the last boat glided safely down to La Chine, nine miles from Montreal on the left bank of the St Lawrence. Junction was made with Murray and Haviland, and Montreal's close investment was immediately put in hand.

The Canadian militia had melted away almost to a man, accompanied by many deserters from the Regulars. With Amherst's heavy ordnance moving into position, de Vaudreuil called a council of war which speedily resolved that resistance was hopeless. The Governor's original suggestion that terms of submission should include the garrison's right to march out 'with the honours of war' being unfavourably received by Amherst, who was unable to overlook the constant efforts of the French to stir up the Indians to every kind of treachery and barbarity, de Vaudreuil had no option but to capitulate unconditionally. Including the soldiery's womenfolk, a total of 3,894 surrendered, to await repatriation with the end of the conflict in Europe.

On 10th September Amherst noted in his *Journal*, 'I dined with the Marquis de Vaudreuil; was very civilly received, and he appeared to be very communicative, talked of his situation, of what he had asked from France, of the impossibility of defending himself against three such Armies.'

The French have ever been fecund in excuses for their military failures; but the fact was not to be gainsaid that while conflict might still rage in Europe, in India, and in the Caribbean, so far as New France was concerned the Bourbon lilies had been trampled firmly in the dust.

At this stage in events it demanded an exceptionally penetrative eye to perceive that in freeing the Thirteen Colonies from the menace of the French the British had removed the most practical restraint on the growth of separatism, and in so doing had ensured their own eventual expulsion from the Thirteen Colonies.

7

The Years of Unease

> 'As there are certain hollow blasts of wind and secret swellings of the sea before a tempest, so there are in States.'
>
> *Francis Bacon*

WITH THE DEATH OF George II in the October of 1760 the succession had passed to his grandson, eldest offspring of 'Poor Fred'[1] and Augusta of Saxe-Coburg. In his twenty-second year, George III was conscientious and fundamentally well-intentioned; but for the best part of a decade the young King was too callow and inexperienced to do much more than echo the sentiments of his strong-willed mother, the Dowager Princess of Wales. Furthermore, he had the misfortune to be subjected to the counsel of a concatenation of ministerial advisers far too immersed in the intrigue and jobbery of party politics to devote their attention to the development of a far-sighted policy for the organization and administration of the empire their Armed Forces were in process of consolidating. When, for example, the successful trader and Indian agent, George Crogan, paid a visit to London as late as the March of 1764, he could write back to Sir William Johnson, 'Nothing has been Don Respecting North America...There has been Nothing Don Sence I came to London by the Grate ones butt Squebeling & fighting [to] See who will keep in power'.[2]

There was, of course, much still demanding close attention. In India the battle of Wandewash had gone in Great Britain's favour, while Dutch support for Clive's enemies had been sharply rebuffed at Badara.

---

[1] Frederick Prince of Wales, whose death had occurred in 1751.
[2] Johnson Papers, vol. IV

In Europe the numerical superiority of the French had proved of little avail against Ferdinand of Brunswick's resourceful generalship; while Spain's misguided entry into a 'Family Compact' with France had brought about the seizure of the French islands of Martinique, St Lucia, St Vincent and Grenada, the capture of Manila, and the submission of the Spanish *entrepôt* of Havana after a two months' siege. A British expeditionary force, sent to the support of Portugal under the command of 'Gentleman Johnny' Burgoyne, had saved Lisbon from Spanish clutches, and gone on to inflict sanguinary defeat at Valentia d'Alcantara and Villa Velha; in reporting which Burgoyne was at pains to emphasize that 'I am conscious that the chief merit of the success was due to the admirable though not uncommon valour and activity of the troops I had the honour to command' — the first tribute ever to be paid to the rank and file Bloodyback in a public despatch.

To the capture of Senegal and Goree had been added the seizure of Belle Île, off the coast of France, as 'a place of refreshment' for the fleet engaged in the wearying task of blockade; a success which largely offset the failure of the attempt on Buenos Ayres.

Notwithstanding the fact that troops had been sent out from England for operations in the Caribbean, Amherst's battalions had also been laid heavily under contribution; and although the casualty rate from enemy action had not been excessive, losses from disease, as always in this latitude, had grievously thinned the ranks. In the major enterprise against Havana, for example, losses in killed and wounded had totalled less than a thousand; yet within three months five thousand men of the army of occupation had perished of fever and kindred ailments. Nor did the return of the troops from Cuba to North America serve to abate the mortal sickness decimating their ranks, for the brigade drawn from the Canadian garrison lost three hundred and sixty men within a month of its return to its northern cantonments.[1]

This terrible rate of wastage ruled out any hope of organizing an expedition against the French in Louisiana; although when a French squadron and fifteen hundred enemy troops fell upon and overwhelmed the hundred-strong garrison in Newfoundland, Amherst promptly despatched his brother William to restore the situation; a task he carried out with exemplary skill and despatch.

Furthermore, there remained a number of remote French outposts

[1] Lord Albemarle (General Officer Commanding) to the Earl of Egremont (Secretary of State, Southern Department), 21st August, 1762.

over which the Bourbon lilies still floated defiantly — Detroit, Michili-mackinac on the shores of Lake Huron, La Baye, St Joseph, and lonely Fort de Châtres in Illinois. Indeed, at Detroit the French commandant had 'Set up a high flagg Staff with a wooden Effigy of a Man's Head on the Top, & upon that a Crow, that the Crow was to represent himself, the Man's Head mine [i.e. that of the writer, 'Ranger' Rogers], and the Meaning of the Whole that he would scratch out my brains'.[1]

One by one these pockets of resistance had to be brought to submission; although it was not until 1765 that Captain Thomas Stirling and a detachment of Highlanders marched a thousand miles from their base at Fort Pitt to bring about the surrender of isolated Fort de Châtres.

In the homeland Pitt, like Achilles, was temporarily 'sulking in his tent'. The brief period of his ascendancy in the King's councils enjoyed by the Earl of Bute — 'the best-hated man south of the Border' — had brought about the conclusion of a peace treaty with the Bourbon dynasties of which Pitt was not the only indignant critic. While undoubtedly leaving much to be desired, it formally ceded Canada to Great Britain while permitting the French to retain the adjacent islands of St Pierre and Miquelon as a harbourage for their fisherfolk trawling the Newfoundland Banks. In America the Mississippi was to be the dividing line between British and French territory; but Florida, having earlier been secretly made over by the French to the Spaniards, was exchanged with the latter for Havana. In the Caribbean, Guadeloupe, Mariegalante, Désirade and Martinique were returned to France, while certain so-called 'neutral' islands were divided between the British and the French, the former securing St Vincent, Dominica and Tobago, the latter obtaining St Lucia. Returning the island of Goree to French possession, the British retained Senegal, while gladly exchanging Belle Île, for the Mediterranean base of Minorca.

In effect, the compact which terminated seven years' bitter and costly struggle exhibited all that vacillation and lack of political firmness of purpose characteristic of a land which had become the prey of a weak Government and a powerful Opposition. All that the party in office desired was to terminate 'a bloody and expensive war'; while the man in the street was far more immediately concerned with the enormity of the proposal to tax perry and cider at 4s a hogshead.

With the signatures on the Paris peace treaty scarcely dry, the disbandment of all cavalry regiments junior to the 18th Light Dragoons,

[1] Robert Rogers, *Journals*.

and all infantry of the line junior to the 70th Foot, left the Army with a nominal Establishment of 17,500 — including nearly 3,000 of the Corps of Invalids.[1] The total fixed for the Colonies — exclusive of the 4,000 allocated to Gibraltar and Minorca — was 10,000.

Even on paper this was scarcely an adequate force with which to garrison an enormous area of still unconsolidated territory twelve times the size of England, and stretching from Quebec in the north to Mobile and Pensacola in the deep south. Moreover of the 8,000 men shown as actually being under Amherst's command a considerable number were ailing, debilitated survivors of the campaign in Cuba. His sick list, indeed, was only a thousand less than his fully effective strength. Yet of the 85,000 French-Canadians still in the country at least 20,000 were capable of bearing arms. Moreover, in the north-west alone there were Indian tribes totalling over 200,000, whose attitude towards the victors in the recent struggle was dangerously ambivalent. While some of the sachems were prepared to declare their readiness to 'take fast hold of the chain of friendship',[2] others greeted the arrival of the British victors in their midst with anything but enthusiasm.

For Dryden's 'noble savage' was no longer the self-reliant, self-sufficient child of nature he once had been. Contact with the white man had destroyed the primitive tribal economy to such an extent that the Indian had come to rely on trade with the 'Palefaces' to furnish him, in return for his valuable peltry, with everything from rum to blankets. His demand was constant for clothing, axes, hoes, knives, kettles, innumerable trinkets, and even food, in lean times; while the gifts he looked upon as being his of right included a plentiful supply of powder and ammunition, and the free service of a gunsmith to keep his weapons in repair. Presents had been lavished on him by the French, who fully recouped themselves for the outlay by the usurious trading terms they imposed on all with whom they chaffered. Thus a precedent had been created to which all who had dealings with the tribes were expected to conform.

With the British, however, the tribes soon found that affairs were on a very different footing. Echoing the policy of Shelburne, the responsible Minister, Amherst informed Sir William Johnson and George

---

[1] i.e. men not passed fit for general service but retained on the strength as an emergency force. The Irish Establishment accounted for another 12,000 men, while the Artillery and Engineers totalled 1,800.

[2] The term employed by the Ottawa chieftain Oulamy.

Crogan that largesse of all kinds should be strictly curtailed, since 'they will be able to supply themselves with these [requirements] from the traders for their furs. I do not see', he went on, 'why the Crown should be put to that expense. I am not either for giving them any provisions; when they find they can get it on asking, they will grow remiss in their hunting, which must industriously be avoided, for so long as their minds are intent on business they will have no leisure to hatch mischief.'

Like his Minister, Amherst failed to appreciate that the donation of presents was less a corrupting form of bribery than a traditional technique for maintaining friendly relations; that withholding them would add to suspicions already dangerously inflamed. For in addition to their resentment at the unexpected parsimony displayed by the British, the tribes were concerned at the wholesale encroachment on their territories which was an immediate consequence of the French defeat—particularly in the valley of Monongahela, beyond the intervening mountains, and in the Susquehanna valley. For the tribal sachems did not appreciate that the French, by a process of gradual infiltration, had been in a fair way of achieving that penetration of the Indian reserves which the British were seeking to consummate by the establishment of large-scale settlements.

The febrile spirit of unrest common to all the tribes had been greatly stimulated by Spain's entry into the war in the January of 1762. For rumours were quickly in circulation that the Spanish and French would soon be sending a mighty force up the Mississippi to retake Quebec and drive the perfidious British into the sea. With frustrated and bewildered savages, uncertain whether the British victors regarded them as allies or as a vanquished people, such *canards* found only too ready an acceptance; and as early as 3rd July of that year Captain Donald Campbell, writing to Colonel Bouquet from Detroit, ended his letter with the warning that the local Indians were seething with unrest and that 'I assure you that they only want a good opportunity to fall upon us, if they had encouragement from an enemy'.[1] It was a sentiment echoed by George Crogan when he wrote, 'Ever since ye Reduction of Canada the Indians in these parts have appeared very jealous of our Growing Power.'[2]

Later in the year a secret council met at which many of the tribal leaders were present, as were two Frenchmen, disguised as Indians;

[1] Bouquet Papers, series 21648.
[2] Louise Phelps Kellog, *The British Regime in Wisconsin and the North-West.*

while wampum war-belts were hopefully circulated by the ever turbulent and unpredictable Seneca. In the May of 1763 Amherst recorded,
'I received a letter from M'r Gladwin [commanding at Fort Detroit]
with accounts of the Indians having some bad designs'; and early in
the next month the Commander-in-Chief recorded, 'I had a letter from
Col. Bouquet enclosing one from Capt. Écuyer, Commanding Officer
at Fort Pitt, with an account that the Indians had some evil intentions,
that they had murdered two soldiers at the Saw Mill on 29th May, and
Mr Clapham and his family before that.'

These were storm signals which could not be ignored; but any insurrectionary movement demands a leader if it is to gain the cohesion
and impetus demanded of open defiance. And in the early spring of
1763 the Indian conspiracy found its predestined paladin in the person
of Pontiac, former partisan of the French on the Monongahela, in 1755,
and venerated sachem of the Ottawa.

It was Pontiac's design that the tribes should rise simultaneously,
destroying the minuscule British garrisons in their immediate neighbourhood and then, in a concerted movement, overwhelm the intrusive
settlements along the frontier. The initial coup was to be the capture,
under his personal direction, of Fort Detroit,[1] hard by his habitat on
the river of that name.

But news of the pending attack leaked out and reached the ears of
the garrison commander, Major Henry Gladwin, a survivor of the
Braddock disaster, and a man far too steeped in the Indians' peculiar
psychology to be easily deceived. Thus on 7th May, when Pontiac and
a select cohort of braves approached the Fort under pretext of seeking
a conference, but with sawn-off, loaded muskets concealed under their
blankets, they found the gates of the stronghold open, but guarded by
double sentries — with fixed bayonets — while the men of the garrison
were drawn up at full muster on the parade ground, under arms.[2]
Perceiving that his treacherous design had been penetrated, Pontiac led
his sullen followers away; avenging himself by killing and scalping the
British-born inhabitants of a nearby farm. The braves then closed in on
the Fort and brought it under heavy but largely ineffective fire.

With a garrison of some 120 officers and men and a score or so of

---

[1] The former French stronghold of Fort Pontchartrain.

[2] Two companies of Royal Americans and one Company of Queen's Rangers — formed
in 1762 — all under strength, plus the crews of the sloop *Michigan* and the schooner *Huron*,
both attached to the Fort.

traders to lend a hand in the stronghold's defence, Gladwin's chief problem was one of supplies, since his stock of provisions was due for replenishment, with rations for a fortnight all there was in hand. Pontiac's six to seven hundred braves were much more happily circumstanced; they simply requisitioned anything they were short of from Antoine Cuillerie and other of the French residents who had furtively urged them on, under threat of slaughtering off their cattle should they demur at giving practical expression to sympathies so often vocally protested. For the investment of Fort Detroit threatened to be a protracted operation; the effective conduct of a siege being something the Indian had yet to master.

Elsewhere, however, the flame of insurrection flared with astonishing vigour and startling success. A twelve-man military detachment on the St Claire river was set upon and all but one of them slaughtered. Fort Sandusky — only completed in the previous November, and garrisoned by Ensign Christopher Pauli and fifteen men[1] — was overrun in a surprise attack; Pauli being the only survivor. Forced to run the gauntlet by his captors, he emerged from this ordeal cruelly battered but resolved to make his escape at the very first opportunity. This he contrived to effect after a few weeks in enemy hands, reaching Fort Detroit early in July.

The forts at Le Boeuf and Venango were both destroyed, the former being set ablaze by fire-arrows and burning to the ground. On 7th July Amherst recorded in his *Journal*:

> This day I had an express from Colonel Bouquet with intelligence that a soldier of Captain Cockrane's company was come into Fort Pitt and declared he left Presq' Île on 22nd June, and that on the 19th, being Monday, that post was attacked by Indians. The Garrison defended themselves that day, and the next day Ensign Christie capitulated; they [the Indians] were to escort the garrison on to Pittsburg with six days' provisions, but after pillaging the Blockhouse they massacred the Garrison, this man and two others excepted, who flew to the woods. The Indians were of four different nations — Ottawas, Chippewas, Wiandots and Seneca.

At Michilimackinac the ostensibly friendly Indians had gained access

---

[1] Undermanning was not peculiar to America. Pendennis Castle, guarding the entrance to Falmouth harbour, and furnished with 46 cannon, was garrisoned by a master-gunner, ninety years of age, aided by a single assistant.

to the Fort by 'accidentally' tossing a ball inside the works during a carefully staged game of lacrosse. Swarming in to recover it, they snatched their weapons from the squaws who had concealed them in their blankets and fell on the scattered Bloodybacks, who were taken completely by surprise and overcome by sheer weight of numbers. One of the few survivors subsequently related, 'I beheld...the ferocious triumph of the barbarian conquerors. The dead were scalped and mangled, the dying were writhing and shrieking under the unsatiated knife and tomahawk, and from the bodies of some, ripped open, their butchers were drinking the blood, scooped up in the hollow of joined hands and quaffed amid shouts of rage and victory.'[1]

On 25th May Fort St Joseph had fallen; and three days later a relieving force of a hundred men, with stores and ammunition from Niagara, was cut to pieces within a day's march of Detroit. By the middle of June there was not a British soldier to be found in the region of the Great Lakes save those serving under the indomitable Major Gladwin; who had received a welcome reinforcement and was full of fight, despite the fact that his enemies had by now increased fivefold.

On the route from Pennsylvania to the Ohio, Forts Pitt, Ligonier and Bedford still held out gamely; although the intervening country had been thoroughly pillaged and laid waste, with whole communities streaming eastward in demoralized flight. Fort Ligonier was held by a mere twelve men, 'yet not one of the flying settlers would remain to stand by them';[2] everywhere alarm mounted into blind panic as word passed that nine forts had already fallen and one been voluntarily abandoned.

At Fort Pitt the murder of William Clapham,[3] two women and a child, in the nearby settlement of West Newton, had embodied a warning whose significance had been anything but lost on the garrison commander, Captain Simeon Écuyer of the Royal Americans. Without hesitation he ordered all the settlers in the neighbourhood to move into the Fort, the better to come under his protection.

It was a timely move, since Fort Pitt offered a refuge the Indians would find it a hard task to overwhelm. With stout walls, encompassed by a deep ditch, the garrison totalled two hundred and sixty men — Regulars and militia — while sixteen pieces of ordnance were mounted

---

[1] Alexander Henry, *Travels and Adventures in Canada.*
[2] Fortescue, *op. cit.*
[3] See above, page . 176

on the walls. As events were to demonstrate, Fort Pitt was in excellent condition to give a good account of itself.

Although incredulous at first of the extent and venomous spirit animating the Redskins' insurrection, Amherst was not slow to initiate such counter-measures as were within his scope. His principal handicap was sheer dearth of troops. The tremendously heavy casualties suffered at Martinique and in Cuba had never been made good; hundreds of the survivors transferred to North America had been rendered unserviceable by sickness. Application to the Pennsylvania Assembly to strengthen his ranks with local levies had failed to produce a single man.

Amherst had wisely decided that such punitive field force as he could get together should move along the line of posts — Bedford, Ligonier and Pitt. By the end of June Colonel Bouquet had managed to muster five hundred Bloodybacks, consisting of detachments of the 42nd, 60th, and Montgomery's Highlanders, brought relatively up to strength by drafts from other corps. 'Even so, many of Montgomery's were so much enfeebled by the West Indian campaign as to be quite unfit for duty, and no fewer than sixty, being unable to march, were carried in waggons to reinforce the posts on the way.'[1]

Amherst, indeed, was so desperately short of vigorous and active troops that he did not flinch from resorting to the desperate expedient of biological warfare. 'Could it not be contrived', he wrote to Bouquet, 'to send the Small Pox among these disaffected tribes of Indians? We must, on this occasion, use every Stratagem in our power to Reduce them.' Bouquet readily agreed, and the records contain a charge of £2 13s 6d for two blankets and two handkerchiefs 'got from People in the Hospital to convey the Small Pox to the Indians'.[2] Bouquet also proposed to employ 'the Spanish Method to hurt them with English Dogs, supported by Rangers and some Light Horse, who would... effectually extirpate and remove that Vermin'.

But it was the Bloodyback, of course, aided by such Provincials as eventually came to his support, who ultimately quelled the uprising, although not without much hard fighting and considerable sacrifice. Setting out at the end of June 1764, Bouquet's relieving column was delayed at Carlisle, awaiting a convoy of provisions, and it was eighteen days before he could resume his march, by way of the old rough-hewn

[1] Fortescue, *op. cit.*
[2] Bouquet Papers, 21652. Smallpox had broken out amongst the garrison in Fort Pitt.

Forbes road, to reach Fort Ligonier on 2nd August. At this point he discarded his heavy waggons in favour of three hundred and fifty pack-horses and a few driven cattle; designing to push on to a stream called Bushy Run, rest there till night, and pass through the dangerous defile of Turtle Creek under cover of darkness.

Early on the morning of the 5th the march was resumed and the troops were soon in dense forest land. It was after a tramp of seventeen miles that a sharp fire in the van gave warning that the advance guard had run into trouble. Two companies, hurrying forward, cleared their immediate surroundings with the bayonet; but renewed firing made it plain that the Indians, faithful to their usual tactics, had developed a simultaneous assault on both flanks and in rear. Bouquet promptly re-called all his troops to form them in a ring about the pack-horses, where they were assailed again and again by whooping savages until, after seven hours of deadly combat, nightfall brought the action to a tem-porary halt.

Waterless and therefore too thirsty to relish food, the troops lay on their arms all night, knowing that dawn would bring a renewal of the struggle. It came with first light, the assailants rushing furiously at point after point; but although British losses were severe the ring of bayonets remained unbroken.

At this juncture Bouquet deliberately withdrew two companies, ex-tending the files on each flank to fill in the gap, as though to cover a retreat. Tremendously encouraged by this move, the Indians rushed forward furiously and seemed on the point of carrying all before them when they were staggered by a tremendous volley which crashed full into their flank. Taking advantage of a fold in the ground, Bouquet had sent the two withdrawn companies to fetch a compass through the forest, to reappear on the periphery of the circle, to pour in their fire in enfilade. Dismayed and demoralized, the faltering savages were blasted by the fire of another two companies, which had worked round to their rear. In wild flight the Indians dispersed into the depths of the forest.

Although Bouquet had lost the services of eight Officers and ninety-six men, killed or wounded, the column proceeded to Fort Pitt without further molestation, arriving on 10th August. A detachment was imme-diately despatched to Fort Ligonier to bring up the bulk provisions, and then returned with all the refugee women and children. It was a comprehensible precaution; but in actual fact the crisis in western

Pennsylvania was virtually over; Fort Pitt was no longer the target for barbarian assault.

At Detroit conditions had virtually reached stalemate. Pontiac was reluctant to incur the heavy casualties that an all-out attack on the stronghold would be bound to involve, the more so as dissension and a weakening of resolution among the tribes had seriously impaired the leader's authority. The stronghold seemed impervious to anything but direct assault.

Faltering enthusiasm for the cause among the Potawatomie, Shawnee and Chippewa was further undermined by the Ottawas' failure to capture the *Michigan*, returning from Niagara with fresh supplies and a reinforcement of fifty-five Bloodybacks. Subsequent attempts to destroy the schooner by floating a fire-raft downstream were frustrated by the skilful manœuvres whereby Captain Newman evaded the blazing menace.

Then in the early hours of 28th July the leading craft of a line of twenty-two *batteaux* stole out of the morning mist and pulled into the water gate of the Fort. Crammed with two hundred and sixty Bloodybacks and a handful of Provincials, including 'Ranger' Rogers, the force was commanded by Captain Dalyell, who had long served as Amherst's senior *aide-de-camp* and was all too eager to display his talents in the field. Somewhat against his will, therefore, Gladwin assented in his junior Officer's urgent demand to launch an immediate attack on Pontiac and the tribesmen still supporting him. 'The General wanted the Indians broken up and wiped out',[1] Dalyell insisted; and since he appeared to be speaking with Amherst's direct authority, he was scarcely to be gainsaid.

At two o'clock in the morning of 31st July, therefore, a force of 247 of all ranks, led by two guides, set out from the Fort to march on Pontiac's encampment by way of the bridge over Parent's Creek, two miles from the objective. But there was to be no surprising Pontiac and his wily followers, whose French friends had apprised them of the impending enterprise long before the tramping, clanking column had started on its way.

At Parent's Creek Pontiac was in wait at the head of four hundred savages; and the leading files were no more than half-way across the bridge when they were met by a wall of fire which strewed the planks with dead and wounded; Dalyell himself being grazed by a bullet in the

[1] Howard H. Peckham, *Pontiac and the Indian Uprising*.

hip. Further down the column heavy firing made it plain that the rear-guard had been caught in flank. With darkness hampering all attempts to rout the enemy out of concealment, there seemed every chance that the entire force would be cut off and annihilated. Leading a charge to try and scatter the attacker, Dalyell fell mortally wounded; and but for the fact that 'Ranger' Rogers contrived to organize a covering party to hold the assailants in check, there would have been very few survivors to regain the Fort. As it was, with the loss of sixty-one Officers and men, killed and wounded, the balance of the force contrived to stumble back to the protection of the stronghold's walls. As James Sterling, one of the survivors, wrote in a letter to his father, 'You never Saw the like, such a damn'd Drubbing the Savage Bougres gave us the 31st'.[1]

But the ambush at Parent's Creek was a success which brought Pontiac no lasting benefit. On condition that punitive war should be prosecuted primarily against the Western Indians, Massachusetts and Connecticut had agreed to support the Bloodybacks with a strong body of Provincials; New York and New Jersey had given a pledge to furnish a thousand men between them; and Virginia had already sent a force to protect her outer settlements. Pennsylvania, however, had persisted in her refusal to vote a single man; and when fifty-seven Pennsylvanians, known as the 'Paxton Boys', had indulged in personal reprisals against a band of perfectly peaceful, friendly Indians—killing and scalping twenty of them in their Conestoga encampment—Philadelphia expressed its horror and indignation, but took no steps whatsoever to bring the desperadoes to justice. So far as another small band of Christianized Indians were concerned, it was left to the Bloodybacks to furnish the guard required for their protection.

Actually, it was the success of Colonel Bouquet's expedition against the Delawares and Shawanoes of the Ohio Valley which broke the insurrectionary movement's back; efficiently paralleled as it was by another column which set out from Albany for the relief of Fort Detroit, under the command of Colonel John Bradstreet. The reoccupation of the posts in distant Illinois was not accomplished without a certain amount of sporadic fighting; but for all practical purposes the Indian uprising had been brought to an end. But although Pontiac was discredited, and a Royal Proclamation forbidding emigration beyond the Allegheny watershed gave some assurance to the Indians of immunity from unwanted intrusion on their territories, the fundamental

[1] Quoted in Cuneo, *op. cit.*

issue had by no means been settled. For the succeeding hundred years the irresistible surge westward was to wear down all their attempts to arrest it, and eventually present the world with the most comprehensive example of successful colonization it has ever witnessed.[1]

'Gratitude', said Tallyrand, 'is a test which friendship rarely survives.' And the gratitude of a people towards the belauded fighting man who has presented them with victory is as evanescent 'as snow upon the desert's dusty face'. In this respect the North American Colonies only too faithfully reflected the mother country's rapid change of attitude towards the Bloodyback from grateful appreciation to the traditional aversion and peevish complaint.

For victory had been followed by the usual casting up of accounts. Doubtless Great Britain had won an empire—although France and Spain, humiliated by defeat and loss of territory, only awaited the moment to seek their revenge—but the cost of gaining it had left the country financially exhausted. In seven years the National Debt had risen from £72,000,000 to £132,000,000; and with the cessation of ephemeral wartime demands, the normal ebb and flow of trade showed little sign of speedy revival. Money was 'tight', and there was a sharp rise in everyday prices which sent the cost of the 4-lb loaf, normally retailed at 1d, soaring to 2d and even 2½d, while beef and mutton, previously to be bought at 3½d and 4d the pound, commanded up to 11½d.

Post-war reductions in the Armed Forces had promptly been demanded by Parliament, and they had been carried out despite the fact that the Pontiac uprising had clearly demonstrated the need for a stronger garrison in North America. For there was no guarantee that the settlement arrived at by Sir William Johnson and the tribal chiefs would prove enduring. Benjamin Franklin, indeed, did not hesitate to pronounce that the quartering of Regular troops in North America was entirely to be recommended, and openly welcomed the prospect for its promise of security 'not only as a guard against foreign invasion but against intestine disorder'.[2] Furthermore, it had to be recognized that

[1] With the possible exception of the Russian empire, which, in the space of 400 years, expanded from a satrapy of under half a million square miles to an enormous Tsardom of over nine million square miles; to which the Communists have added a further five million square miles.

[2] Benjamin Franklin, *Works*, vol. IV, 89–90. Franklin even went so far as to recommend the appointment of a Viceroy to supervise the governance of the Thirteen Colonies.

possessing no Fighting Marine of their own, the Colonies had perforce to look to the Royal Navy for maritime protection; and the Royal Navy needed overseas bases, which had to be garrisoned.

When it came to the question of adjusting post-war credits and liabilities, it was not to be gainsaid that, apart from Americans enlisting in British formations, the various Colonies had, together, put more men into the field than had been sent across the Atlantic by the motherland. But it had also to be borne in mind that to 'win Canada on the banks of the Elbe' Pitt had subsidized a force of 60,000 on the Continent of Europe, and maintained fleets in the Mediterranean and the Channel, whose activities had contributed quite as much to the conquest of Canada as the armies commanded by Amherst and Wolfe, and the squadrons sailing under Holmes and Saunders.

That this state of affairs had been given full consideration by the Colonial authorities was made sufficiently clear by the Massachusetts' representatives who, speaking for the Colonists in general, while firmly denying the British Parliament's right to impose any form of tax on the Colonies without their prior consent, gave assurance that if a letter came from the Secretary of State asking them, in the King's name, to contribute something from their general resources to the needs of empire, 'it will be their indispensable duty most cheerfully and liberally to grant his Majesty their proportion of men and money'.[1]

Could matters have been maintained on this elevated, non-controversial plane, the whole issue could have been settled satisfactorily and amicably. But the idea that Parliament could thus be short-circuited was altogether too much for its dignity; to question its right to impose taxation as it listed was to strike at the very core of its self-importance.

It followed that on succeeding the Earl of Bute as First Lord of the Treasury[2] George Grenville promptly turned his eye on the working of the Acts of Trade and Navigation, whose proceeds constituted the only source of revenue for defraying the cost of protection for the Colonies. Enquiry revealed that the Acts had been violated on so wholesale a scale that the revenue actually accruing was insufficient to pay even a third of the cost of its collection. For generations the Colonies had practised free trade in the form of smuggling with such impunity that the running of contraband had come to be regarded as a perfectly normal procedure, devoid of all stigma or reproach—even when

[1] Calendar of State Papers (Colonial).
[2] Bute resigned office in April 1763.

trafficking with the French West Indian Colonies during the war. As Governor Nicholson put it, 'they were good honest men, except in the matter of illegal trade'. It was, in effect, the accepted thing to set at defiance regulations which the local authorities had made small effort to enforce. It was a traffic in which many of the less scrupulous hucksters of Mincing Lane also slyly participated. Indeed, a correspondent in the *New York Journal* went so far as to affirm that 'nine-tenths of this commerce is more profitable to the mother-country than to the Colonies'.[1]

To the upright but somewhat pedantically-minded Grenville such an insouciant disregard of an enactment duly endorsed by Parliament was no longer to be condoned. Accordingly, not only were stringent measures devised for enforcing the Acts, but new duties were proposed in addition to those already existent; tempered by the grant of additional bounties and by the removal of certain of the earlier restrictions. It was made perfectly clear, of course, that the terms of the Act strictly reserved the revenue raised under its provisions for defraying the costs involved in affording the Colonies full naval and military protection. In the same session Grenville carried a resolution in favour of the imposition, by Act of the British Parliament, of certain stamp duties,[2] applicable in the Colonies, as a further contribution to regional defence. There was nothing abnormal or unprecedented in all this. Governor Shirley had suggested the adoption of a similar fiscal device as early as 1756. Moreover, as far back as the days of Charles II the local Assemblies in Barbados and the Leeward Islands had granted a duty on exports, on condition that the proceeds should be devoted to local defence; while Jamaica had not only raised a regiment of Light Dragoons at its own expense, but had undertaken to meet the pay demands — plus a special Colonial allowance — of both Officers and men.[3]

The whole question was clearly one of imperial defence, and could it have been spared hectoring Parliamentary interference it is very possible that good sense and goodwill would have prevailed, and a solution agreed upon satisfactory to all the parties concerned. But it was not to be. Dragged down into the murky shallows of party politics, it was made to serve as a stalking-horse for a whole host of contentious points of disagreement which were the outcome of Treasury Bench arrogance on the one hand, and on the other the heady sense of freedom begotten

[1] Issue of October 24th, 1768.
[2] 5 Geo. III, Stat. I, cap. 13.
[3] The Regiment was none the less shown as being borne on the Home Establishment.

of the Colonists' release from the age-old fear of what might be brewing on the other side of the border.

Thus despite the covert Indian menace still lurking on the north-western frontier, and regardless of the continued presence of the French in Illinois, and the dubious activities of the Spaniards along the Gulf Coast and in New Orleans, many Americans began to voice the strongest objections to the maintenance of anything in the way of a standing army on their soil. The cherished image of the 'embattled farmer' once more emerged, despite the fact that all recent experience conspired to demonstrate that 'although volunteer units could perform well under certain circumstances, they generally suffered from low morale and slack discipline'.[1]

Following the expulsion of the French from Canada, the Colonies' militia had been divided into two categories — 'minute men', approximately twenty-five per cent of each unit, pledged to turn out like volunteer fire companies on alarm, and the 'regular' militia, existing mostly on paper. In most of the Colonies these men turned out only once a year for muster, the occasion being 'more a combination of barbecue-roast and whiskey-guzzling than anything else'.[2] To entrust the safety of the country to so precarious a body would have been little less than a betrayal of its manifest destiny.

But essential as the retention of the Bloodybacks on American soil might be, it was not long before their presence gave rise to indignant clamour and complaint — sometimes petty and frivolous, sometimes of a legitimacy which it was difficult to confute.

To begin with, the Commissions of the local military commanders and the Provincial Governors were plainly incompatible, since *both* were endowed with supreme authority in the areas for which they were responsible. So once again the echoes reverberated of John Winthrop's century-old plaint, 'To erect a standing authority of military men might well overthrow the civil power.' Since this dichotomy was never authoritatively rationalized, it led to endless friction[3] where the individuals concerned failed to devise a rough-and-ready delineation of function, and abide by what had been agreed between them.

Of more general concern was to determine what constituted the most

---

[1] John W. Shy, *A New Look at Colonial Militia*. (William and Mary Quarterly, 3rd Series, vol. XX, no. 2.)

[2] Colonel R. Ernest Dupuy, *A Compact History of the United States Army*.

[3] See below, p. 197.

prudent and advantageous disposition of the available troops. Before handing over to General Thomas Gage, Amherst had divided Canada into three military districts. In America, whatever the mental reservations with regard to its ultimate efficacy, there was substantial official endorsement for Sir William Johnson's demarcation line along the watershed of the Alleghenies, as for his design to concentrate the traffic in furs to eleven specific frontier posts. Hitherto many traders had penetrated deep into the Indian territories to make their purchases of peltry. With the traffic confined to definite trading posts, it was hoped that it could be brought under control; with some sort of check on the too-liberal dispensation of rum to sweeten a bargain in which sharp practice had certainly not been absent; some sort of say in the amount of powder and ball that could be handed over as a bonus on some particularly profitable transaction.

With the selected posts garrisoned by Bloodybacks, it was thought that the sly trickery indulged in by the more unscrupulous type of trader, no less than the drunkenness and savage outbreaks of violence so common amongst the Redskins, would be sharply curtailed. But it would have demanded the wisdom of a Solon to determine whether the Bloodyback's prime responsibility was to guard the noble savage from the rapacity of the nefarious trader, or protect the innocent trader from the murderous onslaught of some drink-crazed savage. In any case, with no martial law in operation, to employ the Bloodyback for the enforcement of the civil code was flying in the face of all constitutional precedent and therefore open to every sort of objection.

Apart from such considerable strongholds as Michilimackinac, Detroit and Fort Pitt, there were, of course, many other small military posts strewn along the frontier, garrisoned for the most part by the Royal Americans, 'separated into many small Bodies, seen by nobody and seeing none but Indians for Years together'.[1] Situated perhaps a hundred miles and more from the nearest settlement, the cost of provisioning these lonely outposts and conveying the supplies to them was an obligation at which the Assemblies jibbed consistently, fruitfully as some of their members might profiteer out of the contracts involved. Where the more inaccessible posts were concerned, the cheeseparing by which supplies were characterized, and the tardiness of their delivery, is fully reflected in a letter written by a member of the isolated garrison at Presqu'Île. 'We have no Kind of Flesh nor Venison nor Fish, and

[1] Bouquet Papers; Bouquet to Viscount Barrington, Secretary at War.

that We would suffer with Patience; but the Porck is so Bad that neither Officers nor men can Eat it...and Self lief [I myself have lived] more than Seventeen Weeks upon Flour and Peace-soup, and have Eat no Kint of Meat but a little Bear at Christmas.'

Posts were not only under-nourished but under-manned, the paucity of troops along the vulnerable Pennsylvania–Virginia border being starkly revealed in another illuminating screed: 'My garrison', wrote the Officer in command at Fort Ligonier, 'consists of Rodgers, unfit for any kind of fatigue, Davis, improper to be entrusted on any duty, Shillem, quite a little boy, my servant, an inactive simple creature, and one more. Two stout fellows would beat the whole five of them.'[1]

With a permanent force in America averaging seven thousand Officers and men, the question of how best to provide them with adequate shelter also posed problems of no little complexity. In mid-century, barracks had been built at Albany and Schenectady at Crown expense. There were permanent quarters on Castle Island in Boston Sound;[2] New York town council had provided barracks for the four Independent Companies; there was limited and somewhat decrepit quarters in South Carolina and Pennsylvania; while New Jersey had put up five barrack blocks on the line of march between Elizabeth town and Burlington — on the route between Philadelphia and New York.

Elsewhere — apart from the frontier forts — for troops wintering or in movement the dearth of taverns and ale-houses with more than a single room necessitated resort to billeting on the local inhabitants. The alternative was to spend the biting winter months *en bivouac*.

Strictly speaking, under the terms of the Bill of Rights of 1689, and of the Annual Mutiny Act, quartering soldiers on private householders without their consent was contrary to the law. But under Loudoun the exigencies of war had compelled the Americans to follow the practice, not of England, but of Ireland and Scotland, where the military could lawfully be billeted in private dwellings should the necessity arise; and similar procedure under peace conditions was authorized under the terms of the Quartering Act[3] passed by the British Parliament in 1765.

In a sparsely settled country instances of hardship were bound to occur; while the inconveniences attached to having an uninvited stranger thrust upon an already overcrowded household scarcely call

---

[1] Bouquet Papers; Ensign Schlosser to Colonel Bouquet.
[2] Originally constructed for Shirley's 50th and Pepperrell's 51st Regiments.
[3] 5 Geo. III, Stat. I, cap 33.

for elaboration. An unwilling host makes for a surly and resentful guest, while mutual suspicion soon hardens into mutual antipathy. It is true that the Commandant of Fort Bedford reported to Colonel Bouquet that, 'the Inhabitants have used me and the Troops under my Command extremely well, and upon every Occasion show their readiness in Serving us'.[1] But these particular Bloodybacks were not billeted but housed in quarters, and dependent on the local inhabitants for no more than trivial amenities and the provision of a few trifles to vary their dietary. For the most part the average American regarded the Bloodyback, if not with actual distrust, with that wariness so often to be observed in the attitude of the bucolic hind towards the more worldly and sophisticated 'townee'. As early as 1701 Governor Nicholson of Virginia had noted, 'the people are beginning to have a sort of aversion to newcomers, calling them strangers'; and the years had done nothing to modify this acute sense of parochial separatism.

It is not, of course, to be denied that the arrival and distribution of a body of troops, even in a sizeable settlement, inevitably occasioned considerable domestic upheaval and hardship. A memorial from the householders of Princeton, on the line of march between Philadelphia and New York, delineates a state of affairs in no way peculiar to New Jersey. 'Although many of your Petitioners are poor, have small houses and numerous families, with not more than one room, they have yet been obliged to entertain sometimes ten, twelve, or fifteen Soldiers for a night...During the two winters last past they have been obliged to quarter in their houses, some two, some three, others four of his majesty's troops.'[2]

Above all, the Bloodyback was dealing with the descendants of a stock which had founded the Plantations as a means of escape from unacceptable religious, political, economic and social conditions, rather than as part of a process of national expansion. The settlements founded by the Pilgrim Fathers had been a rejection of the contemporary English way of life, not a transposition of it to another clime. And what could more glaringly epitomize the spurned English way of life, and the detested authoritarianism it embodied, than the Bloodyback garbed in his royal livery of scarlet?

For all that, quite a considerable number of redcoats found sufficient welcome to encourage them to stay on in America after their discharge

[1] Bouquet Papers, Lieutenant Nathaniel McCulloch to Colonel Bouquet.
[2] Quoted by John W. Shy, *op. cit.*

from the ranks, 'time expired'. Many of them married local wenches and started farming on their own; others found work as hired help, and were gradually assimilated into the local community. Much the same applied to a certain number of their Officers, some of whom purchased property in one or other of the Provinces, on which to settle down on retirement. It was the man in uniform and still under military discipline and subject to military orders who was looked upon with aversion and mistrust.

At best it was an uneasy atmosphere, which appreciably worsened when, failing any voluntary contribution from the Colonies towards the cost of their defence, the Stamp Act[1] was passed by both Houses of the British Parliament. It provided for the raising of £100,000 annually, or rather less than a shilling a head of the white inhabitants of the North American Colonies.[2] Yet opposition to the enactment, as oppressive and entirely unacceptable, was immediate and widespread. Furthermore, as the provisions of the Acts of Trade — particularly the Molasses and Sugar duties — underwent more vigorous enforcement, the profits of smuggling dwindled appreciatively. Vessels were seized, condemned and forfeited. Employed in support of the Revenue Service, the King's ships — once regarded as the symbols of British protection — came to be loathed as the instruments of imperial tyranny. It wanted little to ignite the spirit of disaffection, and the Stamp Act set the match to the smouldering train. The Boston mob, with no such thing as a properly organized police force to restrain it, broke loose to wreck the house of the Commissioner of Customs, sack and burn that of the Chief Justice, who had had the temerity to proclaim his resolution to uphold the law, and release from jail such few of their number as had suffered arrest. To stay the tumult was impossible, since the only force at the disposal of the executive was the militia — most of whose members were already heavily engaged in rioting.

The news of the general outcry in Boston was received in England with astonishment and a dismay which was little short of consternation; and there was much legalistic straw-splitting as to the distinction between external taxation for the regulation of commerce and internal taxation for the purpose of raising revenue; with Pitt declaiming in the Commons, 'I rejoice that America has resisted' — more with a view to

---

[1] 5 Geo. III, Stat. I, cap. 12.
[2] The annual cost of the upkeep of the British forces in North America averaged £500,000, much of which expenditure found its way, of course, into American pockets.

scoring off his political opponents than with any idea of comforting the Bostonians. The Stamp Act was thereupon repealed.[1] But Pitt, when called upon to form a Government on the fall of the feeble Rockingham Administration, found that the problem of Imperial defence was still as far from solution as ever it had been. Moreover, it had been so enmeshed in extraneous issues that its overriding importance had become blurred and minimized.

An immediate consequence of the open expression of opposition to the regulation of American affairs by the British Parliament was the widespread evasion or disregard of the provisions of the 1765 Quartering Act. 'Magistrates made captious difficulties over granting sites for military store-houses, and were even suspected, in one case, of inciting a mob to destroy a store-house and pillage its contents.'[2] Officers were even imprisoned for daring to occupy the billets allotted to them, and should an Officer arrest a deserter, the man was promptly claimed from him as an 'indentured servant',[3] while he himself was prosecuted and fined. In Massachusetts, New York and Georgia obstruction to the working of the Quartering Act rose to such a height that, in 1767, Parliament passed a Restraining Act prohibiting all legislation of any kind by the New York Assembly until provision should have been made for the King's troops.

Ironically enough, the contention that there was need for an army in America and that it was therefore entitled to a revenue from America had been fully substantiated as recently as 1766. Riots in Albany and elsewhere in New York, over a dispute as to the ownership of certain lands, had proved quite beyond the power of the local militia to deal with them — especially as many of them were personally embroiled in the wrangle. The Bloodybacks had therefore been called in to deal with the situation, and having stood the copious but ragged fire of the rioters had dispersed them with a single volley. Fleeing to the Massachusetts border, the refugees had been welcomed by an armed mob, fully prepared to offer militant resistance should either their neighbours or the Bloodybacks attempt to cross the border line. To so ludicrous but dangerously anarchic a state of confusion had domestic politics degenerated.

By 1767 Pitt — now Earl of Chatham — had become so tormented by

---

[1] 6 Geo. III, Stat. I, cap 11.   [2] Fortescue, *op. cit.*
[3] The man would be furnished with false indentures ante-dating the time of his desertion.

suppressed gout as to be quite incapable of transacting any public business. The effective control of affairs therefore passed into the hands of the Chancellor of the Exchequer, Charles Townshend, a man who was clearly of the conviction that opportunism is as essential to the practice of politics as is the glib enunciation of principles to public oratory.

Pledged to the reduction of the highly unpopular land tax, 'Weathercock' Townshend – temporary head of a weathercock Administration – sought to make good the deficiency in revenue by imposing import duties on a host of commodities in everyday demand in America – including tea. But the sum derived from these new duties – estimated at £40,000 *per annum* – was to be devoted, not to the upkeep of the Army in America, but to the formation of a Civil List for the support of the Governors in each Province, of the judges, and of such placemen as could contrive to sidle their way on to the payroll. Thus the perfectly valid proposals with regard to Imperial defence, upon which Great Britain had hitherto based her pretension to tax the Colonists, were jettisoned in favour of a measure which was little more than a pettish assertion of Parliament's right to legislate for the Dependencies at will. Constitutionally Parliament was doubtless acting within its rights. But there are some rights which are all the more respected for being implied rather than insisted upon too explicitly.

Opposition to the Townshend enactment was instantaneous and almost universal throughout the Colonies. Although the interests of the various Provinces were far better looked after by their respective Agents than ever they could be by Parliamentary delegates, the general cry went up of 'No taxation without representation'.[1] Unfortunately, the validity of the retort 'No protection without contribution', had very largely been undermined by the waspish irresponsibility of the Townshend Act.

Events were swift to demonstrate that Massachusetts was the focus of the most active spirit of resistance. The Customs authorities' seizure of the sloop *Liberty* – property of the prosperous Bostonian tycoon John Hancock – for an open violation of the revenue code, was promptly followed by widespread rioting and the destruction of the Collector's boat. If mob rule were not to prevail, immediate steps would

---

[1] The quibble that the Plantations, being technically within the Manor of Greenwich, were represented in the British Parliament by the Hon. Member for Kent made little appeal to Boston constitutionalists.

have to be taken forcibly to hold it in check. In the June of 1768, there-fore, General Gage was ordered to send a military force to Boston sufficient in number to support magistrates and revenue officers in enforcing the law in general, and in particular the Acts of Trade. If nothing else, the Bloodyback would serve as a useful cockshy on which the populace could vent its spleen.

Thus on 30th September Colonel Dalrymple, with the 14th and 29th Foot,[1] together with a Company of Artillery, arrived from Halifax, Nova Scotia; all three units being well under nominal strength.

Since the neglected barracks on Castle Island were too remote should speedy intervention by the troops be called for, there was no alternative but to billet them in the town, a procedure which at once gave rise to trouble. For it was the civic authorities' contention that the barracks on the island must first be filled to capacity before any question of providing other quarters at the Province's expense could arise. Gage countered this move by affirming his readiness to quarter the troops 'at the King's cost'. Eventually, for want of other accommodation the bulk of the nine hundred men of the rank and file were distributed between the Assembly's Chamber, the Court House, and Faneuil Hall; while certain Bostonian citizens found themselves prepared to lease their private premises to the troops in consideration of a far from negligible rental. Since the 29th possessed tentage, they were put under canvas on the Common.

In the circumstances scarcely anything could have been more unwise than this scattering of the troops throughout the town. Men concen-trated under the immediate eye of authority can be kept under proper control, their discipline maintained, and their off-time diversions sub-jected to reasonable supervision. But dispersed in billets, once their formal duties have been carried out they are divorced from all con-straint, free to comport themselves responsibly or irresponsibly as circumstances and the prevailing mood may dictate. Since they met with no more welcome from the 'mohairs'[2] than a sullen antipathy liable at any moment to expand into active hostility, their own mood responded in like fashion; many altercations between townsfolk and Bloodybacks ending in an exchange of blows. At the outset the hand of authority did its utmost to impose restraint on the men of the rank

[1] Subsequently the Prince of Wales's Own (West Yorkshire Regiment) and the Worcester-shire Regiment.
[2] The soldier's name for the American civilian.

7

and file, and deal out punishment to those who became embroiled in acrimonious disputes and their bellicose outcome. 'This morning', a local newsheet recorded early in October, 'nine or ten soldiers of Colonel Carr's Regiment, for sundry misdemeanours, were severely whipt on the Common. — To behold Britons scourg'd by Negro drummers was a new and very disagreeable spectacle.'[1] It was one to which Bostonians grew considerably more accustomed, and to some onlookers the sight of the detested redcoat in process of acquiring his bloody back was not without its morbid satisfaction.

With the troops scattered in all quarters of the town desertion presented scarcely any problem, especially as many of the local inhabitants, as well as those further afield, proved only too ready to 'give aid and comfort' to any man seeking to slink away from his sworn allegiance. Indeed, in some instances soldiers were deliberately encouraged to desert so that they might 'instruct the inhabitants in the modern way of handling the firelock and exercising the men'. Even when one recaptured fly-by-night, Richard Arnes, a Private of the 14th Foot, was executed by a firing party on Boston Common, the desertion rate showed little sign of diminution.

For no retribution awaited those who aided the deserter. 'A countryman named Geary, who was taken up and bound over by the Chief Justice to answer the Superior Court, to the complaint of his having endeavoured to entice some soldiers to desert from one of the regiments quartered in this town, had his trial last Thursday, and was acquitted by the jury'[2] — who would have called down the unbridled wrath of their fellow-citizens on their heads had they brought in any other verdict.

In the same way, there were virtually no applicants for the reward of ten guineas 'for information relating to any person seeking to persuade a soldier to desert'. On the contrary, it was reported that 'A Serjeant and some soldiers, having apprehended two deserters, were surrounded on the road ... by 100 or 150 armed men, who obliged them to release their prisoners'.[3]

It was useless for the military to appeal to the magistracy for support, for they had become entirely subservient to the dictates of the people.

---

[1] *Boston Evening Post*, October 6th, 1768; a day which saw Faneuil Hall given up to the troops.

[2] *New York Journal*, 28th November, 1768.

[3] *New York Journal*, 2nd February, 1769.

'On one occasion a constable came round to the [improvised] barracks and arrested a soldier who was not named in his warrant; but when his Officers appeared on his behalf in court, they were indicted for riot and rescue, and fined ... Again, one justice openly threatened an Officer from the bench with the vengeance of the populace; while another encouraged the rabble in court to hail an Officer as a "bloody-back rascal".'[1]

On occasion this despicable abuse of authority went even further. For Major-General Mackay reported to Gage that 'a soldier was lately confined to gaol for some petty offence, tried by the justices, condemned to pay damages to the amount of £70, and, for not paying, has been indented as a slave and sold for a term of years'.

The Bloodyback, of course, was not without his share of responsibility for the unhappy state of affairs that everywhere prevailed. Regiments were not, unfortunately, made up exclusively of 'respectable, docile country lads, brought up by careful, thrifty parents in a decent cottage home'. They also included far more than a sprinkling of undesirables, brought in by the crimps; many of whom had known the stocks and the pillory, or the inside of a prison—men whom only constant supervision and a real fear of the lash could keep in something approaching order. In Boston they were so scattered in makeshift quarters as virtually to be loose upon the town. It was with this minority of ne'er-do-wells that much of the worst trouble originated.

Moreover, the generally abrasive relationship between the townsfolk and the Bloodybacks in their midst was in no sense bettered by the proliferation of dram-shops, which sprang up all over the town, retailing rum and raw whiskey at prices which even the ill-paid redcoat or mariner could afford.[2] As a race the British were prone to indulge themselves too freely in liquor; from the wine-bibbing frequenters of Crockford's and Almack's to the gin-soaked lower orders; whose boozing-kens in London's 'Alsatia' confidently gave assurance that their patrons could rely on getting 'Drunk for 1d: Dead drunk for 2d'. In this propensity the Serviceman differed in no way from his contemporaries. So in Boston drunkenness soon became all too common, leading to many unseemly brawls between the troops and the trouble-seeking Sons of Liberty; who daily accosted the man in uniform with

---

[1] Fortescue, *op. cit.*

[2] With pay at 8d a day, less stoppages and 'off-reckonings', the British Infantry soldier was fortunate if he were left with 3s to 3s 6d 'spending money' a week.

such endearing epithets as 'lobster scoundrel', 'red herring', or the ever-recurrent 'bloodyback'.

To the 'unco'guid', the troops' habit of marching off, after Sunday service, to the music of their band, was nothing less than a profanation of the Sabbath, especially as one of the favourite items was the provocative little melody *Yankee Doodle*.

The voluntary embargo on the import of British goods — only to be evaded at the risk of a public tarring and feathering — and the consequent decline in the profitable disposal of exports, had sharply curtailed the town's prosperity. Such, indeed, was the shortage of silver and bullion that pressing debts were often discharged by the sacrifice of a piece of family plate in lieu of cash. With Boston's lower orders and the destitute expatriates from a Halifax almost stripped of its former garrison,[1] grinding poverty lead in many instances to prostitution; of which the less scrupulous Bloodyback was not slow to take advantage; which lead to yet more trouble.

Furthermore, there was a perpetual feud between the Town Watch and the soldiery, both Officers and men; while reputable citizens were hustled on their own doorsteps; respectable womenfolk roughly accosted in the street. Even worse, small bands of roystering Officers roamed the highways and byways 'trailing the tails of their coats' in a manner which did as little credit to their sense of responsibility as to their standing as men of ostensible birth and breeding. The arrest of eight of the worst offenders during the winter of 1774–1775 did little to abate the truculence of the more aggressive among the corps of Officers, who would have swaggered and bullied wherever they might have been stationed. These graceless rowdies were not, however, typical of the Officer corps as a whole. For as one chronicler has frankly recorded, the British troops 'were under good Officers and good discipline, and there was no more reason why they should have occasioned trouble there [in Boston] than in any provincial garrison in England'.[2] Yet the fact remains that in local eyes they were anathema. They were even charged with the responsibility for a number of petty thefts, although there is every reason to believe that the bulk of these minor larcenies were perpetrated by the lesser fry amongst the town's own malefactors, disguised in uniforms sold to them by deserters.

---

[1] To furnish an adequate number of troops for Boston the garrison in Halifax had been reduced to one Officer and twenty-five men.

[2] James Truslow Adams, *The Epic of America*.

Furthermore, in some quarters it was even alleged that the Bloody-backs were guilty of inciting Boston's many negro slaves to rebel against their masters.

Matters were not bettered by the arrival of yet more potential trouble-makers in the shape of the 64th and 65th Regiments, which were landed at Boston in the January of 1769. Actually, they were just in time to lend an additional hand in dealing with a dangerous outbreak of fire which, had not the Bloodybacks turned out *en masse* to cope with it, might well have consumed the very centre of the town.

But the goodwill momentarily generated by the Bloodybacks' ready aid was not destined to endure. Long-cherished enmity had begotten counter-animosity to so parlous a degree that Boston continued to live in what amounted to a state of internecine running warfare – oblivious to all outside events such as the conflict in Florida between the Gover-nor and General Haldimand over the distribution and employment of the troops; the mounting dispute with Spain over the Falkland Islands, and the riots in London occasioned by the supporters of the ranting demagogue John Wilkes. With John Hancock, Samuel Adams and James Otis,[1] Boston was in no danger of running short of her own particular breed of ochlocrat; subtly encouraged as they were by the network of Gallic agents organized by the Baron de Kalb – with a hopeful eye on the future – almost before the last shot in the Seven Years' War had been fired.[2]

The appetite grows by what it feeds on as much with the hunger of the mob for violence as with the gourmet at a Lucullan feast. Such was the case in Boston. A grenadier of the 14th Regiment, John Riley, intervening when a small boy was being unmercifully beaten, knocked down the lad's assailant in the public market. He was brought imme-diately before Justice Edmund Quincey, who found him guilty of assault and fined him 13s 4d; remanding him in custody until such time as the forfeit should have been paid.[3] The day following twenty of Riley's comrades swarmed down to the lock-up to rescue him. In the

[1] Lieutenant-Governor Hutchinson has a note in his *Diary and Letters*, 'Mr Otis stopped at my home and after salutations desired to see me in private, tho' in the morning about 8 or 9 he smelt strong of rum'; a characteristic also shared by the notorious Tom Paine, whose consumption of the spirit averaged three quarts a week.

[2] De Kalb was a native of Alsace who had received his military training in the French Army. 'Towards the close of the Seven Years' War he was despatched to the British Colonies in America as a secret agent of the French Government.' B. J. Lossing, *Field Book of the Revolution.*

[3] C.O. 5/88.

mêlée many bystanders went to the constable's assistance, swords were
drawn and some slight injuries inflicted before Riley could be spirited
away and smuggled out of Boston.

Ensign John Ness, Officer of the guard at the post on Boston Neck,
became involved in a quarrel with a certain Pierpont over the quality
of the fuel delivered to the guard house. There was an angry scene as
Pierpont rallied his supporters, with Ness forced to turn out the guard
to protect his post. The next morning, during the march back to
Boston, the little column was set upon by a yelping mob; a blacksmith
named Whiston forcing his way amongst the troops to strike Private
William Fowler so violent a blow that he had to be supported by his
comrades for the rest of the homeward route; an N.C.O. using the butt
of his halberd to keep the raging, half-crazed blacksmith at bay. Fortunately Ensign Ness had his men under control, or the incident might
well have ended on an even grimmer note. Private Fowler, however,
was debarred from prosecuting his assailant for want of *civilian* witnesses.

Such a condition of seething unrest was bound to reach flash point,
and it came with the events of 5th March. Two days earlier the ropemakers of Atkinson Street had jeeringly enquired of a Bloodyback of
the 29th whether he wanted spare-time work,[1] and when he said he did,
derisively informed him that he could clean out their privy. There was
an altercation, from which the soldier staggered away with blood
streaming from his head. Thomas Walker — a drummer of the 29th —
and some of his comrades determined, in Walker's own words, to 'in-
quire down at the ropewalk'. The outcome was another sanguinary
brawl; and 'next morning as Walker was being carried to the hospital,
he remembered hearing some ropemakers ask the litter bearers where
the 29th planned to bury its dead'.[2] On the following day any Bloodybacks seen on the streets — particularly in the vicinity of the ropewalks
— were likely to be snowballed and attacked with lead-weighted clubs;
while a Serjeant was reported to Colonel Dalrymple as missing believed
to be dead. Since it was known throughout Boston that the sentries had
been given orders that in no circumstances were they to fire their
muskets, isolated men *en poste* or soldiers passing through the streets
alone were easily abused and victimized; and the troops were wisely
ordered back to quarters. With this the mob turned on the solitary

[1] Many of the troops supplemented their pay with spare-time work as cobblers, tailors
and the like.
[2] John W. Shy, *op. cit.*

Bloodyback on guard before the Customs House; and a scatter-brained boy in the forefront of the press shrilly cried out at the immobile sentry, 'That's the scoundrel who knocked me down!'

Instantly a score of voices shouted, 'Let us knock him down!— Down with the bloodyback!—Kill him!' The sentry loaded his musket, the mob in the meanwhile pelting him with pieces of ice and other missiles, and finally attempting to seize him. He ran up the Customs House steps, but, unable to procure admission, called to the main guard for assistance. Captain Preston, the Officer of the day, detailed a picket-guard of eight men with unloaded muskets, and sent them to the relief of the sentinel. As they approached the mob pelted them more furiously than they had the sentinel; and a stout mulatto named Crispus Attucks, who was at the head of a party of sailors, shouted, 'Let us fall on the nest! The main guard! The main guard!' The soldiers now loaded their guns. Attucks dared them to fire; and the mob pressed so closely upon them that the foremost were against the points of their bayonets. The soldiers perfectly understanding the requirements of discipline, would not fire without orders. Emboldened by what seemed cowardice, or, perhaps, by a knowledge of the law which restrained soldiers from firing on their fellow-citizens without orders from the civil magistrates, Attucks and the sailors gave three loud cheers, beat the muskets of the soldiers with their clubs, and shouting to the populace behind them, 'Come on, don't be afraid of 'em—they daren't fire! Knock 'em over! Kill 'em!' At that moment Captain Preston came up, and endeavoured to appease the excited multitude. Attucks aimed a blow with a club at Preston's head, which was parried with his arm, and, descending, knocked the musket of one of the soldiers to the ground. The bayonet was seized by the mulatto, and the owner of the musket was thrown down in the struggle. Just then mocking voices in the crowd behind Preston cried, 'Why don't you fire? Why don't you fire?' The word 'Fire' fell on the ears of Montgomery, the soldier struggling with Attucks, and as he rose to his feet he fired and shot the mulatto dead. Immediately five other soldiers fired at short intervals: three of the populace were instantly killed, five dangerously wounded, and a few slightly hurt.[1]

[1] B. J. Lossing, *op. cit.*

With that, the mob broke up and dispersed in considerable panic. In the sequel, however, it was Preston and his men who were stigmatized as the aggressors and clapped into gaol; and Samuel Adams, by threat of a general insurrection, actually cowed Lieutenant-Governor Hutchinson into withdrawing the two battalions left in the town—now numbering at most five hundred effectives[1]—to Castle William, on an island in the harbour; while the Assembly reiterated its demand that the inhabitants 'provide themselves with arms for their defence'.[2]

Under the envenomed prompting of 'Sam the Maltster' the whole unhappy episode was immediately dressed up in the exaggerated terms of partisan propaganda. Dubbed the 'Boston Massacre', a fracas brought about by the unbridled lawlessness of the local mob was distorted by inflammatory woodcuts and incendiary broadsheets into a sweeping indictment of the whole system of gubernatorial control by the British Parliament. Nor were there wanting 'friends of the Colonies' in the Homeland to contend that everything Great Britain had done in America throughout the past decade had been inspired by an ignoble arrogance, selfishness and greed.

The tattered fabric of kinship had been rent beyond all hope of immediate repair.

---

[1] By Government orders the 64th and 65th Regiments, with the Artillery Company had already proceeded to Halifax, the 14th Regiment going to New York.

[2] A demand first put forward by a vote of the Assembly of March 1769.

Part Two
Kindred in Conflict

'Two stars keep not their motion in one sphere.'
William Shakespeare

'No quarrel is so bitter as a family quarrel.'
George Gissing

8

At Open Odds

> 'Rebellion, if unsuccessful, is the most extravagantly heinous of crimes; if successful, the most glorious of virtues.'
>
> *Hegel*

A MOMENT OF acute crisis is often followed by a period of inaction, attributable rather to bruised apathy than to a sober attempt to rationalize a situation which has got dangerously out of hand. Such was the prevailing state of mind in Boston as the weeks went by and the events of 5th March fell a little more into perspective.

Preston and his men, clapped into gaol on a charge of murder, were exceedingly fortunate to secure John Adams as their defending counsel. A cousin of the ineffable 'Sam the Maltster', he was a man whose impersonal sense of justice was as strong as his personal integrity was unimpugnable. His rebuttal of the capital charge was supported by two independent witnesses who, despite their secessionist beliefs, were prepared to testify under oath that the soldiery had used their weapons only under extreme provocation. In effect, the defence was put so clearly and so forcibly that Preston and six of his men were set free. The other two — a man named Killroy, and Montgomery, whose musket had fired the initial shot — were found guilty of manslaughter, branded on the hand in open court, and then discharged.

Boston's more chastened mood owed not a little to the influence of world events on the general climate of opinion. A slave-owning population living in perpetual dread of a servile insurrection in their midst,[1]

---

[1] There had been servile uprisings in New York in 1712 and again in 1741. In 1774 the slave population in the North American Colonies was estimated to total between five and six hundred thousand.

the outcome of the war against the revolted Caribs in the Island of St
Vincent was something in which all classes of the community were
deeply concerned. Bostonians could not fail to be impressed by the
fact that the suppression of this dangerous uprising—covertly supported as it had been by the French in Martinique—had called for the
services of no less than 2,500 Bloodybacks; of whom one hundred and
fifty had been killed or wounded, while another hundred had perished
of endemic diseases. It was always possible that what they had accomplished in St Vincent might be demanded of them in New York or
Massachusetts. Furthermore, a Spanish attack on the British Colonists in the Falkland Islands had threatened to bring on a general
war which would not only have imperilled the settlements in
Florida, but seriously impeded New England's trade with the West
Indies.

With the Carib uprising finally squashed and the difference with
Spain composed without a resort to arms, something of the old spirit
of loyalty to the mother country enjoyed a brief St Martin's summer.
British recruiting parties sent out by General Gage garnered quite a
number of American volunteers; while disputes with the Assemblies
over the quartering of troops were almost unknown. Indeed, on the
removal of a battalion from New Jersey, in the ordinary routine of
service, many voices were raised in a plea that their capital should not
be denied a regiment in permanent garrison.

Here was a most opportune moment in which to remove the irritating tea duty, the only one of the Townshend imposts to be retained by
Lord North on his succession to Grafton as Prime Minister. Since the
suspension of all but one of the obnoxious taxes was accompanied by
North's pledge that the Government would seek no further revenue
from America, the reservation of the duty on tea, although constituting
no legitimate grievance, amounted to folly at its most extravagant. For,
while bringing practically no money into the Treasury, it furnished the
incorrigible Sam Adams and others of his kidney with sufficient pretext
to continue their fuming and fulmination against the British Government and all it represented. But the East India Company, responsible
for the tea's import, was paying the price of jobbery and mismanage-
ment, and was desperate for revenue; and the East India Company
controlled something like two hundred votes in the House of Commons[1]—a fact which no one appreciated more acutely than Lord North.

[1] Sir Charles Petrie, *The Four Georges*.

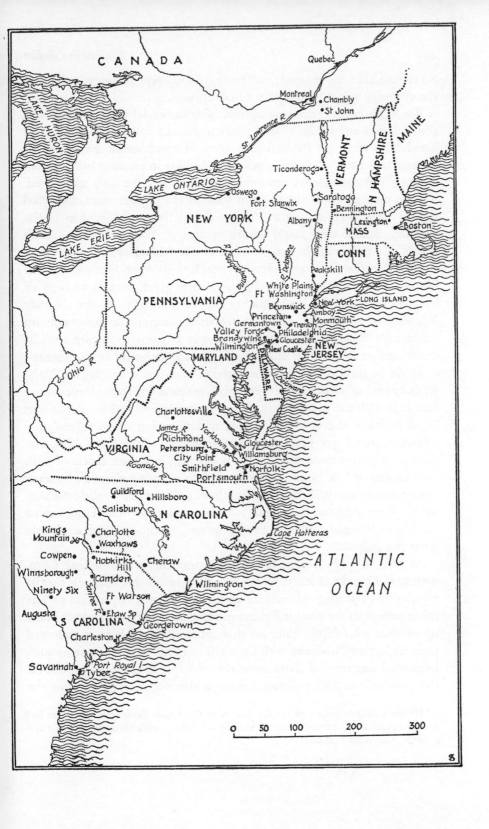

CANADA

LAKE HURON

Quebec

Montreal

Chambly
St John

LAKE ONTARIO

VERMONT

N HAMPSHIRE

MAINE

Ticonderoga

Oswego

Fort Stanwix

St Lawrence R

NEW YORK

LAKE ERIE

Saratoga
Bennington

Albany

Lexington
MASS
Boston

R Hudson

CONN

Peakskill

R Susquehanna

PENNSYLVANIA

R Delaware

White Plains
Ft Washington
Brunswick
Princeton
Germantown
Valley Forge
Brandywine
Wilmington

New York
Amboy
Trenton
Philadelphia
Gloucester
New Castle

LONG ISLAND

Monmouth

NEW JERSEY

Ohio R

MARYLAND

DELAWARE

Delaware Bay

Charlottesville

James R

Richmond
Petersburg
City Point
Smithfield
Portsmouth

VIRGINIA

Roanoke

Yorktown

Gloucester
Williamsburg

Norfolk

Guildford
Hillsboro
Salisbury

N CAROLINA

Cape Fear R

King's
Mountain
Cowpen
Winnsborough
Ninety Six

Charlotte
Waxhaws
Hobkirks
Hill
Camden
Ft Watson

Cheraw

Wilmington

Cape Hatteras

ATLANTIC

OCEAN

Augusta

Santee R

S CAROLINA

Etaw Sp

Georgetown

Charleston

Savannah

Port Royal I
Tybee

0   50   100   200   300

8

So the tea tax was retained; and the agitators were presented with just the ammunition of which they stood in need.

Briefly, however, the resumption of commercial relations between the Colonies and the mother country fostered a spirit of harmony and goodwill which the Bloodybacks were at considerable pains not to jeopardize—even when the workmen engaged in erecting barracks for expected reinforcements went on strike and left the task unfinished. Troops moving about the town in their off-duty hours were instructed not to wear their side-arms. There should be no bloodshed if the absence of cold steel could insure against it. Furthermore, on such potentially inflammable occasions as St Patrick's Day, all units were confined to their quarters. Similar precautions were taken every 5th March, when Boston's meeting-houses were given over to an orgy of longwinded homilies, culminating in an 'Oration on the Bloody Massacre of 5th March, 1770'—a distorted harangue on the events on Atkinson's Wharf which Sam Adams was at pains to inspire with as much venom against the Bloodyback and the authority he represented as could be compressed into the diatribe's context. For Sam the Maltster's hatred of Great Britain and all she stood for burned ever more furiously with the years, accompanied as it was by a lurking dread that his default, to the tune of £8,000, when serving as an official tax-collector, might yet give grounds for official action.[1] For him, any change of government must be for the better. It was an article of faith fully shared by 'the black regiment' of the dissenting clergy, who were in no mind to see their power and authority challenged by the establishment of an Anglican episcopacy. As Massachusetts' Governor wrote bleakly to the authorities in the homeland, 'Sedition flows copiously from the pulpits'.

As early as 1772 Adams had been prominent in establishing Committees of Correspondence, which served as invaluable channels for the circulation of propaganda and the encouragement of opposition to 'any infringement of their natural constitutional and chartered rights'. Made up of men who firmly believed that their original Charters endowed their respective Provinces with the right to home rule, it was from such influential sources that there arose the widespread embargo on tea. As the only commodity yielding even the shadow of a revenue to the

---

[1] Hancock had secured a reprieve for Adams on the default charge, but the matter had yet to be determined. Adams's effort to succeed as a brewer, after his suspension as a tax-gatherer, had ended in failure.

Crown, many town meetings — inspired by the local Committee members — adopted the resolution that anyone who purchased or consumed the leaf 'should be looked upon as an enemy to this town and to the country, and shall by this town be treated with neglect and contempt'.[1]

It was while this hardening mood was steadily in the making that the British Administration was guilty of the incredible folly — from the point of view of timing — of seeking to reimpose the Acts of Trade. Opposition to their reinforcement was immediate and unrestrained. Rhode Island had long rivalled Boston in its indulgence in 'free trade'; everyone from the Governor downwards having an interest in the illicit traffic. Indeed, as far back as 1763 one of the island batteries had fired upon a Royal Navy vessel which had been in pursuit of a smuggling craft.[2]

In attempting to suppress the running of contraband after the reimposition of the Trades Acts no vessel had been more active than H.M.S. *Gaspée*, commanded by Lieutenant Duddington. In chase of the local packet *Hannah*, Duddington struck on a submerged sandbank at Namquit Point, which was only just covered by the ebbing tide. With the waters falling fast, the *Gaspée* was hopelessly grounded, a fact which Captain Lindsey, of the *Hannah*, lost no time in reporting to a certain John Brown, one of the leading merchants of the busy township of Providence.

Knowing that the schooner could not be got off till flood tide, after midnight, Brown thought this a good opportunity to put an end to the vexations caused by her presence. He ordered the preparation of eight of the largest long-boats in the harbour, to be placed under the general command of Captain Whipple, one of his most trusted ship-masters...At dusk, a man named Daniel Pearce passed along the Main Street beating a drum, and informing the inhabitants that the *Gaspée* lay aground at Namquit Point, and inviting those who were willing to engage in her destruction to meet at the house of James Sabine. The boats left Providence between ten and eleven o'clock, filled with sixty-four well-armed men. Between one and two in the morning they reached the *Gaspée*, when a sentinel on board hailed them. No answer being returned, Duddington appeared in his shirt at the starboard gunwale, and waving the boats

[1] Report by the Committee of Correspondence adopted by the town of Lexington.
[2] Admiral Montagu to the Admiralty, 18th April, 1772.

off, fired a pistol at them. The discharge was returned from one of the boats. Duddington was wounded in the groin, and carried below. The boats now came alongside the schooner, and the men boarded her without much opposition, the crew retreating below when their wounded commander was carried down. A medical student among the Americans dressed Duddington's wound, and he was carried ashore at Pawtuxet. The schooner's company were ordered to collect their clothing and leave the vessel, which they did; and all the effects of Lieutenant Duddington being carefully placed in one of the American boats to be delivered to the owner, the *Gaspée* was set on fire and at dawn blew up.[1]

The British response to this act of defiance was less exemplary than tepidly legalistic. Large monetary rewards — up to five thousand dollars — were offered for information leading to the conviction of the incendiaries. But although the identity of the perpetrators of the outrage was widely known, no one could be persuaded — or had the temerity — to come forward. A Commission to investigate all the circumstances of the affront was baulked and baffled by the same carefully feigned ignorance of events, and no conclusion being possible, the enquiry was adjourned *sine die* without attempting to come to one. Admiral Montagu shrugged aside the suggestion that he should take a squadron to Rhode Island 'to support the investigation'. 'I am clear that nothing will come of that Commission', he wrote to Lord Sandwich, First Lord of the Admiralty; later giving it as his firm opinion that the Bostonians were 'almost ripe for independence, and nothing but the ships prevents them going greater lengths'.[2] From other correspondence it is clear that General Gage also regarded Massachusetts in general, and Boston in particular, as the storm centre of opposition to British rule; and his precautionary aim was to concentrate as many troops as possible in New York and New England.

Yet the Bloodybacks had hardly marched out from Fort Pitt before Governor Penn was beseeching their return. For the surge into Indian territory had brought about an association of Virginian settlers whose members openly avowed their intention to resist Pennsylvanian authority; while a state of open war was rapidly developing between the Virginia land-grabbers and the Shawnees. In the outcome the struggle

[1] Lossing, *op. cit.*
[2] Montagu to Sandwich, 18th March and 1st June, 1773.

for the reassertion of authority was one which had to be fought out by the local militia without any Bloodyback support.

Boston, meanwhile, had been only too dangerously preoccupied in defeating all attempts to raise revenue by the importation of tea.[1] The matter came to a head in the December of 1773 with the arrival in Boston harbour of the *Dartmouth* and two other vessels, all freighted with consignments of the leaf; for by this time the North administration had become little more than a plausible façade to mercantilism.

Unable to discharge their cargoes, yet forbidden by Hutchinson, the Lieutenant-Governor, to put about and return whence they had come, the *Dartmouth* and her consorts remained secured at Griffin's Wharf; the consignees — with the windows of their residences smashed by the mob — having taken refuge in Castle William.

Immediately the *Boston Evening Post* came out with a warning, signed by the Committee of Tarring and Feathering, against any traffic in the leaf; and from threat to action was no more than a step. On the 16th an overflowing mass of Bostonians gathered at the Old South Meeting-house, to be addressed by Josiah Quincey in a fiery harangue which owed not a little of its inspiration to the embittered promptings of Sam the Maltster. When, finally, the question was formally put, 'Will you abide by your former resolutions with respect to not suffering the tea to be landed?', the vast assembly, as with one voice, gave an affirmative reply; while a hothead in the gallery shouted, 'Boston harbour a tea-pot tonight! Hurrah for Griffin's Wharf!'

It was already dusk when the meeting broke up; and with nightfall a party about one hundred and forty strong, led by about twenty men very thinly disguised as Narragansett Indians, made its way from the 'Green Dragon' to Griffin's Wharf, where

> ...on the gently swelling flood,
> Without jack or pendant flying,
> Three ill-fated tea-ships rode.

No hand was raised to stay them. For what amounted to little more than a Corporal's guard of Bloodybacks had been segregated over three miles from the scene of action; and with the militia dedicated to the

---

[1] Ninepence had been remitted on the 1s tax on tea, so that Americans could purchase the leaf at considerably less cost than consumers in Great Britain. This, of course, tended seriously to diminish the profits of the 'free-traders' in the leaf.

congenial task of heading off the Customs officials from the performance of their duty, authority had abdicated.

Under the pale cold moonlight of the wharfside, the 'Narragansett
Indians' swung their axes briskly to open up the holds and broach
cargos. Within a couple of hours three hundred and forty tea chests
had been splintered and cast into the water. 'Who knows', one of the
'Boston Boys' had speculated, 'how the tea will mingle with salt water?'
And in the strangest and most costly[1] brew of the leaf the world has
ever seen, he found the answer.

Clattering along the turnpikes to New York and Philadelphia,
couriers hastened to spread the intelligence which made it starkly clear
that what hitherto might optimistically have been construed as Boston's
little private war with the East India Company bade fair to develop into
a nation-wide challenge to the whole concept of Parliamentary authority.
And that is exactly how it was interpreted, despite one would-be con-
ciliator's attempt to dismiss the whole affair as no more than 'a pic-
turesque refusal on the part of the people of Boston to pay a tax'.[2]

Tea drinking, of course, was now entirely taboo. 'Committees have
been appointed to inspect into the Characters and Conduct of every
tradesman', recorded a youthful English traveller, 'to prevent them
selling Tea or buying British Manufactures. Some of Them have been
tarred and feathered, others had their property Burnt or Destroyed by
the Populace. All trade', he added, 'is almost at a stand.'[3] Addicts,
deprived of their favourite beverage, rather forlornly sought to appease
their craving with an infusion of ginseng tips.[4]

With Boston's posture of defiance supported by the equally challenging attitude of New York and Carolina's Charlestown, and despite the
expressed wish of certain of Boston's more sober-minded merchants to
indemnify 'John Company' for its loss, Parliament was prompt to give
the North administration assurance of support for all reasonable efforts
'to preserve order in the Colonies'. It was a gesture as much designed to
restore members' own somewhat battered good conceit of themselves
as to endow the Government with the power to initiate measures of
reprisal.

But it is very questionable if, without hearing a word from the

[1] According to the *Monthly Review and Literary Journal* the gross value of the tea freighted
by the three vessels came to £300,000.

[2] Quoted by Senator Lodge in *Boston* (*Historic Cities*).

[3] Nicholas Cresswell, *Journal* 1774–1777.

[4] The plant Aralia ginseng.

Colonists in their own defence, the closure of the port of Boston to all sea-borne traffic until outstanding differences had been rationalized and the East India Company indemnified for their loss, could be regarded as a legislative master-stroke. For the Boston Port Bill had been accompanied by additional enactments which very significantly modified the Massachusetts Bay Charter. For the future the Council would be nominated rather than elected;[1] while provision was made for the removal to England for trial of any official indicated by the civil courts for murder in the suppression of a civil disturbance. Finally, the right was reserved to quarter troops in Boston at local expense. This legislation was shortly followed by the passage of the Quebec Act, which extended the frontiers of Canada in such a manner as very largely to inhibit large-scale American emigration north of the Ohio river. This, of course, cut right across the interests of such land-exploiting corporations as the Virginia group sponsored by Washington and the Lees, and the Pennsylvania group—which had been soliciting the grant of a modest 12,000,000 acres—headed by the Philadelphia firm of Baynton, Wharton and Morgan.

In some quarters even greater offence was taken over Parliament's endowment of the French-Canadian Catholics with the right to practice their own faith—a right still obdurately withheld from their co-religionists in Great Britain and Ireland; entailing the loss of the services of hundreds of admirable Irish soldiers, barred from the British Army by sectarian prejudice.[2]

On both sides of the Atlantic bigotry raised an immediate outcry against this last provision; New England Calvinism notching up yet another deep-seated grievance against a Parliament which could countenance such ungodly licence. Pastors grew hoarse with their perfervid denunciations of the contaminating proximity of the 'Scarlet Whore of Babylon, the Mother of Harlots and the Abomination of the Earth'. Tolerance, never a noticeable feature of New England, had gone into exile.

A violent attack on the Quebec Act was the immediate outcome of the assembly, at Philadelphia, on 5th September, 1774, of the extra-legal Forst Provincial Congress. This was followed by the issue of addresses

[1] The rights of the Lower House of Assembly, however, suffered no abridgement, save in the matter of electing a Council, which hereafter was to be appointed by the Governor.

[2] So late as 1800 the Army Half-pay Lists contained the annotation against a number of Officers' names, 'Suspected Papist'.

to the people of Great Britain, the Colonies and Canada, distinguished by a girding rodomontade as biased as it was inflammatory; and the tinder of unreflecting public opinion was speedily ignited. It did not take long, indeed, to render it absolutely clear that it was not the King's writ which ran throughout the North American Colonies, but the mandate of the First Provincial Congress.

'Nothing talked of but war with England', the observant Nicholas Cresswell noted on 16th October; recording a little later, 'Independent Companies are raising in every County'; and a few days after, 'The people are arming and training in every place. They are Liberty mad.'

In Massachusetts the coercive Acts had already become a dead letter, from the sheer absence of sufficient means to enforce them. 'The whole working of the new Government was defeated by intimidation of every official appointed by the Crown, and by the setting up of a rival government, which was omnipotent everywhere except under the shadow of British bayonets.'[1] For General Gage—on his return from a visit to England, to replace Hutchinson as Lieutenant-Governor—found himself in command of a mere four battalions; a force which possibly might have dealt with the situation in 1769, but was now far too small to be effective. For of the nominal ten thousand troops allocated to North America, by far the greater number were in Canada; Boston's garrison barely totalling sixteen hundred Officers and men.

Unable to assert the authority with which he had been invested, Gage[2] was fully determined to avoid anything which would provoke an armed clash between the Bloodybacks and the local populace. He did take the precaution, however, of fortifying Boston Neck, although the completion of the task was seriously retarded for want of carpenters; no local craftsmen daring to undertake the work for fear of the retribution which would be visited upon them by Sam the Maltster's more ruffianly followers. Ultimately the Royal Navy came to the rescue, 'Chips' and his assistants expeditiously carrying the job to conclusion.

By this minor concession to prudence Gage, of course, laid himself open to the charge that he designed to reduce Boston to subordination by famine. But in every other respect the restraint he exercised over the troops, as well as himself, could scarcely have been more circumspect. There were no more race meetings on the Common to disturb the gloom of Boston's Sabbath. No longer were the meeting-houses' interminable

---

[1] Fortescue, *op. cit.*

[2] 'My mild General', in the words of George III.

sermons profaned by the thump of drums and 'the vile squeaking of the wry-neck'd fife'. So far as the Sunday was concerned, the military bandsmen rejoiced in a life of fatted idleness. The troops were further warned not to attend the cock-fights and card-playing sessions with which some of the less reputable Bostonians were wont surreptitiously to relieve the Sunday tedium.

At the first hint of trouble on the part of the Bloodybacks — Officers or men — Gage did not hesitate to crack the whip, as an entry in the diary of one of the Boston garrison bears sufficient witness. 'As there was some disturbance last night', runs the note for 21st January 1775, 'and a quarrel between some Officers and the Town Watch, the General has ordered a Court of Enquiry, composed of five Field Officers, to examine into the Cause and Circumstances of it, and to report thereon to him.'[1] Subsequently, a sharply-worded memorandum on the subject was circulated to all four Regiments.

When a man was caught trying to bribe a soldier of the 47th Foot[2] into selling his arms and ammunition and the Bloodyback's comrades grabbed the rascal, stripped him, tarred and feathered him, and then paraded him through the streets, Gage expressed his strongest disapproval. Yet the offence was all too common to be condoned by anyone save a man determined to do his utmost to keep the peace. Even when it was reported to him that waggons were being driven out of Boston with a load of munitions concealed beneath a top dressing of hay and manure, he was reluctant to institute a check at the Guardhouse on Boston Neck. When a stricter system of surveillance was finally instituted, 'a countryman was stopped at the Lines, going out of Town with 19,000 ball cartridges, which were taken from him. When liberated, he had the insolence to go to Head-quarters to demand the redelivery of them.'[3] Since the authorities had not dared to prosecute him, his impudent demand only too faithfully reflected the immunity from all processes of the law which he and his kind had come to enjoy.

There was no attempt on the part of the extremists to obscure their aims. Samuel Adams had openly demanded a patriot army of 18,000; while the Congress had as openly appealed for £21,000 for the purchase of munitions. With a steady, if clandestine, traffic in arms and ammunition to supplement the firearm, pound of powder and bag of bullets

---

[1] Captain Frederick Mackenzie, *Diary*, 1775–1781.
[2] Subsequently the Loyal North Lancashire Regiment.
[3] Mackenzie, *op. cit.*

which, by Massachusetts law, every citizen was entitled to possess, the Province was fairly bristling with weapons and warlike supplies. Nor was Massachusetts the only Colony where preparations for conflict were busily going forward. 'Mustering in every village', noted Creswell; 'they will all be soldiers by and by.' And a little later, he was present when the hundred and fifty members of the Gentlemen and Mechanics' Independent Company were reviewed by no less a person than Colonel George Washington.

It was the responsibility of the Committee of Safety, appointed by the Provincial Congress to ensure that the individual store of arms and ammunition was supplemented by every means that could be devised and successfully carried into execution. Thus, with the Earl of Dartmouth momentarily counselling the velvet glove rather than the iron hand, the Bloodybacks were allowed to take no retributive action when forty pieces of ordnance were brazenly 'filibustered' from Newport harbour and a quantity of warlike stores filched from Port Piscataqua. The best Gage could do was to bring in a trifling quantity of arms and powder which had been stored in nearby Cambridge, and impound another small cache unearthed in Salem; thereafter somewhat ineptly spiking, instead of gathering in, all the cannon on Fort Hill.

The descent on Cambridge undoubtedly stirred up considerable ferment; with 'all those who had taken an active part in favour of Great Britain obliged to screen themselves in Boston. Even in Boston itself the company of cadets, consisting wholly of gentlemen who used to attend the Governor, disbanded themselves, and returned the Standard he had (as was the custom) presented them with on his accession to the Government. This was occasioned by his having deprived the celebrated John Hancock of his Commission as Colonel of the cadets.'[1]

But the raid on Cambridge was no more than a gesture. With the Proclamation warning the Colonists of the consequences of rebellion completely ignored, his half-hearted attempts to stem the illicit accumulation of warlike stores coolly resisted, and his Loyalist supporters in Boston subjected to the indignity of tarring and feathering and aggravated assault, Gage found himself in the unenviable position of being 'denounced by the King for his mildness, and by the Colonists for his tyranny'. Only the Loyalists of the neighbouring townships of Marblehead and Marshfield had a good word to say for him; their request for a sufficient number of troops to afford them protection having been

[1] Serjeant R. Lamb, *Journal of Occurrences during the Late American War.*

complied with so promptly and effectively that there had been 'no brush with the townspeople, no clash with the local militia, not even bitter resolutions';[1] a state of affairs which had aroused Sam the Maltster to foaming indignation.

Adams might be angrily disappointed with the relatively supine attitude adopted by the people of Marshfield and Marblehead, but where Boston and its outlying districts were concerned he can have had little cause for complaint. Substantial stocks of arms, powder and ball were steadily building up, while the militia was already organized in rural detachments; some of their number even keeping the extra-mural activities of the Boston garrison under regular surveillance. 'The Advanced Guards at the Lines', Mackenzie noted on 10th March, 'have of late been ordered to send out patrols towards Roxbury. A patrol going out last night fell in with a party of Roxbury people, with Arms, patrolling towards our Lines, but as soon as the latter saw our people they took to their heels towards Roxbury.'

These night patrols betokened a new alertness on the part of the garrison, stimulated to far greater activity by a distinct hardening in Dartmouth's attitude as reflected in his instructions to the Commander-in-Chief.

It was at this juncture that Gage received intelligence that a considerable quantity of warlike stores had been assembled at Concord, a small township some twenty miles to Boston's north-west. For he was not without his private sources of information. Dr Benjamin Church, high in the councils of the Provincial Congress as he might be, had shown himself quite prepared to keep the Governor primed as to all that was going forward, in return, of course, for the usual 'consideration'.

And it was at this juncture that Gage, with a slightly larger body of troops under command,[2] had come to the belated conclusion that further temporizing with a rapidly deteriorating situation was as impossible as it was unwise; that the time had come when the Crown's authority must sternly be asserted.

For some time past the troops had been regularly exercised by means of route marches—the men equipped with arms, knapsacks and full kit—which had taken them deep into the surrounding countryside. On

[1] Arthur Bernon Tourtellot, *William Diamond's Drum*.

[2] At this period the garrison consisted of the 4th, 5th, 10th, 18th, 23rd, 29th, 38th, 40th, 43rd, 47th, 52nd, 59th, 64th and 65th Foot; but no battalion could muster more than 477 effectives. The same was true of the 1st and 2nd battalions of the Marines.

occasion they had even lain out all night *en bivouac*, returning to base on the following day. It was under the guise of an ostensible route march that the Commander-in-Chief designed to stage the raid on Concord. The better to preserve 'security' and ensure secrecy, a night approach march had been determined upon; but Gage had reckoned without the superlatively efficient intelligence service organized by Dr Joseph Warren and that craftsman in copperware and conspiracy, Paul Revere. With a round-the-clock watch on the garrison's activities in smooth working order, the conspirators were so fully apprised of the Commander-in-Chief's design that on the evening of 18th April Brigadier Earl Percy was coolly informed by a substantial Bostonian that the troops would be certain to 'miss their aim'.

'What aim?' his lordship had demanded.

'The cannon and stores at Concord', had come the immediate answer.[1] Whereupon Percy, on reporting the incident to Gage, had been informed by that flabbergasted Officer that 'his confidence had been betrayed, for that he had communicated his design to one person only besides his lordship'. But where that 'one person only' was concerned, it has to be borne in mind that Gage was an uxorious husband, and that the sympathies of the enchanting Peggy Gage — *née* Kemble[2] — were of such partial complexion that by the following August it had been thought wiser to despatch her to England in a homeward-bound transport pleasantly named *The Charming Nancy*.

In any case, ships' boats were required to transport the troops from the waterside at the foot of Boston Common across the harbour and the mouth of the Charles river to their starting-point at Phipps's Farm, near Cambridge. A number of these craft had had to be put under repair; an activity whose significance had by no means been lost on Sam Adams's watchful spies. Neither had reconnaissance of the route by which the troops would proceed gone unremarked. Furthermore, on Saturday 15th April the light infantry and grenadiers of the respective regiments in garrison had been relieved of their routine duties and brigaded together as a special task force; another move whose implications were easily interpreted by any man of military experience.

From Saturday the fifteenth onwards it was clear that some overt coup on the part of the Bloodybacks was in active preparation. Only its

[1] Hugh Earl Percy, *Letters*.
[2] Or Kembal. She was a native of New Jersey and was related to the influential Van Courtlands of New York.

exact purpose and destination left room for speculation; and Dr
Warren and Paul Revere, together with their immediate henchmen,
William Dawes and Richard Devens, were on the *qui vive* for any hint
which would reveal the actual nature of the troops' assignment. By
Tuesday the 18th little doubt remained as to the nature of the mission
or the date set down for its accomplishment.

At ten o'clock on the night of Tuesday 18th April the seven hundred
light infantry and grenadiers of eight battalions, brigaded under the
command of the portly Colonel Francis Smith—with Major John Pitcairn as his Second-in-Command—mustered on the waterside at the
foot of Boston Common. There was considerable and entirely unneces-
sary delay in getting the men embarked, so that it was between midnight and one o'clock before the entire complement had been landed at
Phipps's Farm, in East Cambridge, and were ready to take the road.

'After getting over the marsh', an Officer of the 4th Foot subsequently recorded, 'where we were wet up to the knees, we were halted
in a dirty road and stood there until two o'clock in the morning, waiting
for provisions to be brought from the boats and to be divided, and
which most of the men threw away, having carried some of 'em.'[1]
Celerity, the key to the vast majority of successful military enterprises,
was obviously not within Colonel Smith's circumscribed professional
philosophy. His over-confidence that the mission would be accomplished without running into opposition was reflected in his unforgiv-
able omission to ensure that his detachment was accompanied by a
surgeon.

In Boston there had been ample time for Paul Revere to set the signal
lanterns agleam in North Church, as a warning to watchers in Charlestown that troops were actually on the move; while Billy Dawes, who
had contrived to slip past the guard on Boston Neck, was spurring
furiously towards the Rev. Jonas Clarke's house at Lexington, where
both John Hancock and Samuel Adams were privily known to be
temporarily in residence. All along the way the warning had been
passed, and with the ringing of church bells and the firing of guns the
whole countryside was quivering on the alert. Three members of the
Committee of Safety, Elbridge Gerry, Jeremiah Lee,[2] and Azor Orne,

[1] Lieutenant John Barker, *A British Officer in Boston*.
[2] Not to be confused with the former British Officer, Charles Lee, who sided with the
Americans.

temporarily lodged at Menotomy (Arlington), had already made good
their escape; while the Minutemen in both Concord and Lexington
had lost no time in mustering under arms, to debate the order issued by
the Provincial Congress during their recent meeting at Concord. For it
affirmed in unequivocal terms that, 'whenever the army under command of General Gage, or any part thereof to the number of five
hundred, shall march out of the town of Boston, with artillery and
baggage, it ought to be deemed a design to carry into execution by force
the late Acts of Parliament, the attempting which, by the resolve of the
late honourable Continental Congress, ought to be opposed; and therefore the military force of the Province ought to be assembled, and an
army of observation immediately formed, to act solely on the defensive
so long as it can be justified on the principles of reason and self-preservation'.[1] The point to determine was – when did self-preservation
demand that defence should go over to the attack? Doubtless it was
this consideration which persuaded the Congress subsequently to stiffen
their instruction and call upon their armed supporters to 'oppose their
march to the last extremity'.

Steadily tramping along throughout the hours of darkness, at 'about
five o'clock the next morning the British troops had reached Lexington,
fifteen miles from Boston: here the militia and Minutemen had assembled on the green in order to oppose the British troops. Major Pitcairn,
who commanded the advance guard, rode forward, and called out to
them to disperse, but they still continued in a body.'[2]

Before their circumspect departure from the scene of potential
danger, both Hancock and Adams had consulted with Captain John
Parker, in command of the local militia, counselling him to 'make a
show of strength upon the Common, but not to fire';[3] fully aware, no
doubt, that a show of strength which is not carried to its logical conclusion amounts to no more than a confession of weakness. And as they
had every reason to know, weakness was not a characteristic of the men
they were callously prepared to make use of in the furtherance of their
overall design.

On and around the little Common stood perhaps a quarter of the
town's population. Serjeant Munroe had got some forty of his
Minutemen in line, perhaps thirty more were milling around,

[1] General William Heath, *Memoirs*.
[2] Journal of the Second Provincial Congress.
[3] Serjeant Lamb, *op. cit.*

going to the meeting-house for ammunition, coming in across the meadows and pastures from their houses, crossing the road from Buckman's Tavern. Other townspeople, unarmed but curious, stood around the Common, in the yards of the three houses, or behind the stone walls of the pastures and meadows...Seventy militia, more or less; a hundred spectators, most of whom would be getting up at this hour anyway—this was the formidable force that confronted Major Pitcairn and his five companies of light infantry as they came in sight of the Common.[1]

Pitcairn was no irresponsible fire-eater, bent on provoking trouble, but a level-headed Officer concerned only to carry out the task entrusted to him without bloodshed and, if possible, without the necessity of taking prisoners. On the other hand he was aware that an Officer of a mounted patrol, earlier sent forward, had been fired on, and that the small body of men confronting him were armed. He had no mind to let them scatter, weapon in hand, very possibly to open fire on the troops at some later and more propitious moment. So he took the only course left open to him: 'I instantly called to the soldiers *not to fire* but to surround and disarm them.'[2]

As the troops moved forward to carry the order into effect 'the Van Comp'y of the Light Troops was staggered by seeing a Flash of a Pan from a man with Arms, and soon after a Report and whistling of two Balls fired on it, on which the Light Company hearing a shout from the leading Company, immediately formed, and a Fire was given on their running off which killed most of them. For my part', the narrator sums up, 'I was amazed when I heard the Shout, and being the third Company that led in the front, took it for granted we were surprised, not imagining in the least that we should be attacked or even molested on the march, for we had but that instant Loaded and had marched all night without being loaded.'[3]

Who first gave fire can never be absolutely determined, but the probability is that the 'shot which echoed round the world' was loosed by some impulsive hothead, aiming from the cover of an adjacent stone wall. But the Rubicon had been crossed, to the infinite satisfaction of the hard core of the separatists. From the safe retreat at Woburn to

[1] Tourtellot, *op. cit.*

[2] Pitcairn's report to Gage, *Gage Correspondence*.

[3] Major W. Soutar, *Correspondence*. Serjeant Lamb's version of events runs, 'At this moment some shots were fired at the British troops from a house in the neighbourhood.'

which he and Hancock had hastily departed, Samuel Adams listened exultantly to the distant crackle of musketry which told him that out-right revolution was now within his grasp. Then turning to the absentee Lieutenant-Colonel of Militia, he ecstatically cried out, 'Oh, what a glorious morning is this!' Hell knows no fury like that of a non-combatant.

Although Pitcairn was not slow to take the situation in hand, it was Colonel Francis Smith who claimed the credit for bringing the over-excited troops back to some semblance of order. 'I endeavoured my utmost to stop all further firing', he subsequently recorded, 'which in a short time I effected.'

One Bloodyback had been nicked in the leg; Pitcairn's horse struck in two places. But eighteen of the militia had been killed or wounded.

In chastened mood, the closed-up British column pushed on as speedily as fatigue permitted, intent on reaching Concord and accom-plishing its mission with the least possible delay.

As they approached the pleasant sylvan little retreat, another con-tingent of militia, which had been drawn up in their front, tailed off to join in the fight again when their numbers had been strengthened by the two companies of Minutemen in Concord, commanded by Colonel James Barrett.

At Concord the light infantry hastened to take post at the North and South bridges over the river. For it was from the hinterland beyond the waterway that reinforcements of militia might be expected to make their appearance. Once the light troops were in position, the grenadiers set busily to work to destroy such *matériel* as had not been effectively concealed or earlier spirited away. Since the troops had been sternly warned to treat the local inhabitants with 'consideration and forbear-ance', they missed as much in the way of illicit stores as ever they found. The chest of the Treasurer of the Provincial Congress, for example, was in a room which a spirited young woman claimed to be her own sleeping-chamber. Since she barred the entrance to the room and could not be bundled out of the way by brute force, the chest remained undiscovered.

Even so, there was plenty of work to do. For in addition to the cannon concealed in the town gaol, there were stores of beef, pork, rice, linen and hides; while the Account Book of the militiamen's Waggon-master, John Goddard, itemized such miscellaneous military equip-ment as, 'Spades, billhooks, iron pots, wooden mess bowls, cartridge paper, powder and fuzes, grape and roundshot, bombs, mortars, musket balls and flints, molasses, salt fish, oatmeal and flour'—much of which there had been no time to remove or conceal. Very soon a bonfire of captured provisions and equipment was blazing, whose flames and smoke were speedily misinterpreted by the militiamen on the far side of the river as arising from their burning homesteads.

While the work of destruction was going forward, Major Pitcairn, being the practical man he was, repaired to the inn for breakfast—which he was careful to pay for in 'hard' money. At other homesteads about the scattered township payment was also punctiliously forthcoming for the food and drink the famished troops demanded; while at the house of Amos Wood two guineas were rendered as *solatium* for having subjected the place to the indignity of search. One chamber, indeed, had been chivalrously exempted from investigation, since it was alleged to be occupied by a sick woman. Needless to say it was the room which contained the military stores the Wood household had been entrusted to secrete. In the dogma peculiar to New England theology, mendacity in the patriot cause rated as no more than a venial slip of the tongue.

On the far side of the North Bridge, overlooked by a wooden slope swarming with constantly reinforced militia, the seven companies under Captain Parsons—numbering no more than one hundred and ninety-six men—had been under the necessity of detaching a sufficient force for the search of the Barrett homestead, alleged to be the repository of a large quantity of illicit military stores. Inevitably, Parsons was committed to the military enormity of splitting up his forces, leaving a mere eighty-four men, widely scattered, in the vicinity of the bridge, and marching off the remainder to carry out their search.

Not unnaturally, this division of forces was an open invitation for the Minutemen and general body of the militia to show a bolder front. 'During this time', wrote Lieutenant Barker subsequently, 'the people were gathering together in great numbers and, taking advantage of our scattered disposition, seemed as if they were going to cut off the communications with the bridge.'[1]

The smoke from the bonfire of burning stores had fully persuaded the militiamen out by the North Bridge that Concord had been put to the torch; and in far angrier mood they began to close in on the handful of Bloodybacks actually stationed by the bridge itself. By this time the

[1] Barker, *op. cit.*

original militia force had been heavily strengthened by contingents from Bedford, Lincoln, Acton, Carlisle, Westford, Chelmsford and Littleton.

Ensign Lister, posted with an outlying picket a quarter of a mile west of the bridge, subsequently noted, 'We had not long been in this situation when we saw a large body of men drawn up with the greatest regularity, and approached us seemingly with an intent to attack.' Hastily weighing up the situation relative to the troops' general distribution, Lister added that, 'they still approached and in that force [strength] that it was thought proper by the Officers, except myself, to join the Forty-third's company at Concord Bridge'.

With no more than three companies concentrated at the bridge, Captain Laurie, in command at this point, sent a hurried message requesting reinforcements, and then turned to confront the oncoming Provincials, now totalling between three and four hundred. After a sharp exchange of fire the bridge was carried by sheer weight of numbers, the Bloodybacks being driven in on Concord; the detached party at the Barrett homestead being enabled to rejoin the main body owing to the lack of any authoritative voice amongst their adversaries to give the orders which would have sent a contingent to cut them off.

On their hurried march back, it was the men of this party who glimpsed the body of one of their comrades who, lying wounded on the river bank had had his head wantonly bashed in by a passing boy, who had armed himself with an axe. It was this incident which gave rise to the entirely unwarranted *canard* that the Provincials were scalping the helplessly injured.

With the grenadiers' abortive labours hurried to a close, Colonel Smith dared not rest his tired, hungry men as he would have wished— indeed it is fair criticism to suggest that he had delayed overlong as it was. With the Minutemen and their supporters everywhere gaining in strength, it was high time to pull out and fall back on those reinforcements for which the Colonel had already made urgent application.

For 'the Country by this time had took Ye alarm, and were immediately in Arms, and had taken their different stations behind Walls &c. on our Flanks and thus We were harassed on our Front, Flanks and Rear,...by a Continual Fire for eighteen miles, it not being possible for us to meet a Man otherwise than behind a Bush, Stone, Hedge or Tree, who immediately give his fire and off he went. Our Companies were not able to march half of its [their] Front on the open Road, or more properly speaking in two Platoons, the second in Rear of the first.

'On our leaving Concord we were immediately surrounded on every Quarter, and expected to be cut off every moment. Sometimes we took possession of one Hill, sometimes of another; at last it was determined to push forward to Lexington, which we did through a plaguey Fire, when we were joined by Lord Percy with the first Brigade, with four[1] Pieces of Cannon, otherwise I do believe that not one of us had got into Boston again...'[2] This was no longer something which could be re-garded and dealt with as no more than a sporadic uprising by a few hot-headed malcontents: this was war—naked and undisguised.

By the time Colonel Smith's urgent call for reinforcements reached British Headquarters in Boston, General Gage had already decided it was advisable to send out supports for the original raiding column. Orders had therefore been issued that the 1st Brigade, consisting of three infantry regiments, a battalion of Marines,[3] with some artillery, should parade in time to march off at 4 a.m., under the command of Brigadier Earl Percy. But such was the almost incredible incompetence of the Headquarters Staff that the written instructions reached no one in time for them to be punctually obeyed. The Adjutant of the 23rd Foot, for example, did not receive his orders until 7 a.m. and had personally to hustle Officers from their billets to get the Fusiliers on parade without further waste of time. The Marines denied the receipt of any directive whatsoever, a perfectly legitimate plea, since the written orders had been addressed to Major Pitcairn—absent with the con-tingent at Concord!

It was not, therefore, until nine o'clock that the troops got on the road; marching by way of Cambridge. Here they found that the militia had removed the planks from the bridge over the River Charles. How-ever, as the springers had been left in position and the planks thought-lessly stacked close handy, Percy soon had the structure sufficiently under repair to enable the troops to pass over it; although the hold-up of necessity added to the day's delays.

Marching towards Menotomy, the Brigade Commander noted the singular emptiness of the countryside. 'All the houses were shut up', he subsequently recorded; 'there was not the appearance of a single

---

[1] Two is the number given in Duncan's *History of the Royal Regiment of Artillery*.
[2] Soutar, *op. cit.*
[3] Eight companies each of the 4th, 23rd and 47th Foot, and the Marines.

inhabitant. I could get no intelligence of them [the Provincials] until after I had passed Menotomy.' Neither was he to know that the provision waggons, following an hour's march behind him, had been allowed to pass over the Charlestown bridge before being ambushed by a picked band of militia.

The first intelligence of events further up country came when the column was met by two wounded Officers, being driven towards Boston in a commandeered chaise. From them the Brigadier gained some idea of the progress of events and of the gravity of the situation which had developed.[1]

'I therefore pressed to the relief of the advance party as fast as good order & not blowing the men would allow', Percy subsequently noted down. 'By now the Rebels were in great no'r, the whole country having collected for 20 m. around.'[2]

Grimly the column quickened its pace; and when an Officer naïvely remarked to Percy that in his opinion little opposition need be anticipated, since all the windows of the houses were shut and they appeared to be deserted, the hard-headed Brigadier curtly retorted, 'So much the worse, for we shall be fired at from those very houses'.

As the march continued Provincials made their appearance in ever-increasing number, lurking behind the stone walls and amidst the trees; and every man had a weapon in his hand.

It was 2.30 p.m. by the time Earl Percy made contact with Colonel Smith, the former approaching Lexington Common from the southeast as the latter stumbled in from the west. Halting his men on the Common's edge, by Munro's Tavern, Percy posted field pieces on the two hills to the right and left of the road and formed a large hollow square into which Smith's hounded men thankfully threw themselves, sinking to the ground through sheer exhaustion.

'The village of Lexington lay between both parties', Mackenzie duly noted; 'we could observe a considerable number of the Rebels, but they were much scattered, and not above fifty of them to be seen in a body in any place. Many lay concealed behind the stone walls and fences. They appeared most numerous in the road near the Church, and in a wood in the front and on the left flank of the line where our Regiment was posted. A few Cannon Shot were fired at those on and

[1] Both Officers were subsequently waylaid and captured by a party of militia, who sent their prisoners off to Medford.
[2] Hugh, Earl Percy, *Letters*, (Edited by C. K. Bolton).

near the Road, which dispersed them...During this time the Rebels endeavoured to gain our flanks, and crept into the covered ground on either side, and as close as they could in front, firing now and then in perfect security. We also advanced a few of our best Marksmen, who fired at those who shewed themselves.'

It was the field pieces which kept the militiamen at a respectful distance. But once the light infantry and grenadiers had been sufficiently rested to take the road again, the cannon had to be withdrawn; and the Provincial marksmen were free to resume their galling fire from every coign of vantage that offered on either side of the homeward road.

Percy's dispositions were as sound as any could be in the prevailing circumstances. With the weary and demoralized light infantry at the head of the column and therefore furthest from the fire on flanks and rear, the rearguard was taken over in turn by the battalions of the 1st Brigade. They also furnished the strong flank guards which did so much to keep down the volume of the snipers' fire. Houses bordering the road were thoroughly searched for concealed marksmen; in three instances the sharpshooters being smoked out by setting the dwellings afire. For the most part, however, there was no time to linger and start a blaze.

But although William Heath[1] – appointed to General's rank by the Second Provincial Congress – and the indefatigable Dr Joseph Warren sought to organize a full-scale, concerted flank attack, the militiamen preferred to go their individual way and carry on the fight as best suited their personal inclinations.

'Before the column had advanced a Mile on the Road', Mackenzie later noted, 'we were fired at from all quarters, but particularly from the houses on the Roadside and the adjacent Stone Walls, and the Soldiers were so Enraged at suffering from an unseen Enemy that they forced open many of the Houses and put to death all those found in them...As the Troops drew nearer to Cambridge, the number and Fire of the Rebels increased, and although they did not shew Themselves openly in a Body in any Part, except on the Road to our rear, our Men threw away their Fire very inconsiderately and without being certain of its Effect: this emboldened Them [the Provincials] and induced Them to draw nearer, but whenever a Cannon Shot was fired at any considerable number, they instantly Dispersed.'

[1] Heath had been a Captain in the Ancient and Honourable Artillery Company of Boston, and Colonel of the 1st Suffolk County Militia.

8

It was the Monongahela all over again, with the Provincials employing similar 'bush-whacking' tactics to those which had wrought such
sanguinary mischief on that June day of 1755.

Earl Percy possessed quite sufficient military acumen to realize that
by this time the bridge over the River Charles would be held in
strength; and indeed Heath did contrive to get sufficient regard paid
to his orders to ensure that any attempted passage across the river
would be hotly disputed.

But the Provincials were in no need of Dr Joseph Warren's exhortations to persuade them to maintain their harassment of the Bloodyback
column to the bitter end. As militia from the peripheral townships
around Boston joined in the fray, the scale of the fighting steadily increased, reaching its fiercest in the relatively open terrain about Menotomy. Here the field pieces were again brought into action with excellent effect. Sharpshooters who risked seeking concealment within the
four walls of a house or in some snug wall-angle, were given little time
in which to realize that in mobility lay their only hope of safety. A party
of seven Danvers Minutemen, for example, thought themselves perfectly secure behind their improvised barricade of piled-up shingles.
But they had scarcely opened fire before Bloodyback flankers, stealing
up on their quarry's left-rear, despatched all seven of them with the
bayonet. Three Cambridge men were killed in one spot by flankers who
caught them by surprise; and even Dr Joseph Warren lost the pin from
a wing of his hair to an errant musket ball.

On the whole, however, the wearying Bloodybacks had little opportunity to bring effective fire to bear, 'as the rebels hardly ever fired but
under cover of a stone wall, from behind a tree, or out of a house; and
the moment they had fired they lay down out of sight until they had
loaded again, or the column had passed. In the road, indeed, in our
rear, they were most numerous, and came on pretty close, frequently
calling out, "*King Hancock for ever!*" '[1] 'In this manner', Percy noted,
'we retired for fifteen miles under an incessant fire, wh. like a moving
circle surrounded and follow'd us wherever we went, 'till we arrived
at Charlestown at 8 in the ev'g & having expended almost every
cartridge.'[2]

Wearily, the battered column stumbled across the narrow isthmus
leading to Charlestown Heights; encompassed by waters in which the

[1] Mackenzie, *op. cit.*
[2] Percy, *op. cit.*

64-gun *Somerset* offered a measure of protection the Provincials were not disposed to challenge.

Darkness had fallen before the last Bloodyback had marched, drag-footed, across the Neck; which the Brigadier at once set about fortifying, Captain Montressor, of the Engineers, constructing a small redan on the slope of Bunker Hill. 'Thus ended this Expedition', wrote the disgruntled Lieutenant John Barker, 'which from beginning to end was as ill planned and ill executed as it was possible to be'; an expedition in which the Bloodybacks had suffered 273 casualties and inflicted 93[1]— and in the process started a conflict whose outcome no man could possibly foretell. What was even more deplorable was the fact that the troops had been given the wrong objective. For the capture of Hancock, Warren and the fanatical Samuel Adams would have been of far greater consequence than the confiscation of all the hidden military stores in Massachusetts.

The plain tale of events on that fateful 19th of April would in any event have embodied implications of the very grimmest. Seized upon by 'Rumour, with her thousand lying tongues', the outcome was calamitous. For to skilled propagandists of the calibre of Samuel Adams and Dr Joseph Warren, the day of Lexington and Concord was a gift from the gods. There was no need for fabrication at the fountain head; the known facts, suitably coloured, were sufficient for rumour to build up an edifice of half-truth and fantastic exaggeration which was staggering in its effect upon the popular mind. By the time the chronicle of events had reached the news-sheets of Pennsylvania, Carolina and Georgia, the substructure of hard fact had become so overlaid by the most viciously irresponsible fantasy as to have become almost totally obscured. According to some of the more hysterical fabulists, the British soldier was nothing less than a sadistic, blood-boltered monster. According to the *Massachusetts Spy* the redcoat, 'unmolested and unprovoked, wantonly and in a most inhuman manner fired upon and killed a number of our countrymen, then robbed them of their provisions, ransacked, plundered and burned their houses! Nor could the tears of defenceless women, some of whom were in the pains of childbirth, and the cries of the helpless babies, nor the prayers of old age, confined to beds of sickness, appease their thirst for blood!—or divert

[1] British, 73 killed, 174 wounded, and 26 missing. Provincials, 49 killed 39 wounded, and 5 missing.

them from their design of MURDER and ROBBERY!'[1] Mendacity even went to the length of affirming that 'women in childbed were driven by the soldiery naked in the street';[2] while the number of ancient men alleged to have been slaughtered out of hand went far to suggest to the statistically-minded that Massachusetts was almost exclusively populated by octogenarians, still capable, however, of consigning a vast number of women to child-bed.

Not a word, of course, of Captain Parker's Minutemen drawn up belligerently on Lexington Common; for in its own particular way *suppressio veri* constitutes a very telling form of propaganda. With the exception of rape—which the rumour-mongers neglectfully omitted to include in their indictment—the wretched Bloodyback was charged with every enormity in the calendar; and since where propaganda is concerned 'truth' is anything you can persuade the gullible to believe, the day of Lexington and Concord proved, if nothing else, a triumph for the unscrupulous propagandist.

Nor was the propagandists' receptive audience to be found on one side of the Atlantic only. The American Colonists were far from without friends and sympathizers in Great Britain; and since nearly all of them were at odds with the party in office, it imposed no great strain upon their credulity to accept without question the version of events which portrayed the responsible authorities in the darkest possible hue.

When propaganda comes in at the door conciliation flies out of the window. With good will on both sides, the actual events of 19th April could have given rise to those second thoughts which prefer the give-and-take of mutual accommodation to a hot-headed resort to war. But with the legend which so speedily crystallized about the events of that fateful day, the only outcome was a direct descent to that last measure of desperation—an appeal to arms.

[1] Issue of 3rd May, 1775.

[2] One of Dr Warren's higher flights; though why women in childbirth should all have lain naked in their beds was given no explanation.

9

The Iron Hand of War

'You can control the mobilisation, but after the first shot has been fired you sail out into a completely unknown sea.'

Helmuth von Moltke

ONE IMMEDIATE CONSEQUENCE of the day of Lexington and Concord was the endowment of Samuel Adams and Joseph Warren with the army for which they had so long been agitating—or at least with the raw material from which an army could be fashioned.

News reached Jonathan Hastings's homestead in Cambridge, where both Artemas Ward and the Committee of Safety had set up headquarters, that forces were hastily being recruited in Connecticut, Rhode Island and New York; although for the moment there was no word from Philadelphia or the southern Provinces. Men swarmed in from near and far; students from Yale, farmers from New Hampshire, a company from New Haven under the command of the energetic Benedict Arnold. The veteran Indian fighter, Israel Putnam, rode a hundred miles in eighteen hours, from his home in Connecticut to the scene of action; while Brigadier-General Nathanael Greene headed a contingent recruited 'in His Majesty's service and in the pay of the Colony of Rhode Island, for the Preservation of the Liberties of America'—the clearest possible indication that the Colonists' quarrel was not with the Sovereign, but with the overweening British Parliament. 'The ardour of our people is such', Hancock openly rejoiced, 'that they can't be kept back.' Numbers swelled so rapidly that within a matter of days Cambridge and its immediate neighbourhood was crammed with some 20,000 militia and volunteers.

At the outset, subsisting the inchoate legion of Provincials presented no particular difficulties; the richly productive Massachusetts countryside could furnish ample provender for the time being. It was the want of a sufficient number of arms and an adequate supply of ammunition which posed by far the gravest problem. For not every man had brought his own firearm; many weapons having been left at home for the protection of the family. A good musket was worth all of two pounds 'hard' money, and speedily increased in purchasing price. For the rest it was with a wide variety of hardware that the militia and volunteers had come into the field. 'Here an old soldier carried a heavy "Queen's arm", with which he had done service in the conquest of Canada, while by his side walked a stripling boy with a Spanish fusee, not half its weight or calibre, which his grandfather might have taken at Havana; while not a few had old French pieces that dated back to the reduction of Louisbourg.'[1]

The want of ammunition was an enduring cause of anxiety. For although every contemporary calendar included instructions on how to make gunpowder, the requisite ingredients were in short supply. An adequate amount of ball was equally hard to come by; and the urgent call went out for clock and window sash-weights to melt down as bullets. It is questionable if at this stage the men under arms had more than nine rounds apiece.

As with all hastily improvised forces, sanitation and camp hygiene were rudimentary; it was a fortnight after the camp began to form before anyone thought of digging a latrine. The outcome was the inevitable outbreak of those diseases which invariably accompany the herding together of large numbers of men in a condition of mounting filth and personal uncleanliness. 'The Men are growing Sickly and Daily Dying out of the Barracks', young Joseph Trumbull wrote to his father.

In the whole of the camp there were but two medicine chests; and since women were not allowed anywhere near the lines, there was no one to do any laundering or mending, and everyone grew progressively more ragged and unkempt.

It was anything but a stable host; men marched into the camp and drifted away from it as their inclination might dictate. At Roxbury numbers fell away so swiftly from six thousand to a mere two thousand that General John Thomas, in local command, took to marching the

[1] Tourtellot, *op. cit.*

same men round and round Roxbury hill — stage-army fashion — to give the necessary impression of numerical strength.

Nevertheless, there were ample militia and volunteers left in Cambridge and its immediate neighbourhood to prompt Captain Frederick Mackenzie to record in his diary for 21st April, 'The Town is now Surrounded by Armed Rebels, who have interrupted All Communication with the Country.'

With an amorphous mass of men more or less under arms, but under no pledge with regard to continuity of service, the Congress resolved to seek the establishment of a force of 30,000, enlisted for a definite period, of whom 13,600 were to be furnished by Massachusetts. This hard core was to be supplemented by militia companies, of variable strength and reliability, under their own officers. Working on the British model, it was the Committee of Safety's design to organize the men enlisted for a definite term in regiments of ten companies; to which Congress proposed to appoint the appropriate Officers. But the rank and file insisted on following the custom rigidly observed with the militia, who chose their own Officers, and could dismiss any one of them at will, in favour of some other individual who had momentarily taken their fancy. The obstinate spirit of localism enshrined in this cherished right was to prove the cause of more trouble throughout the ensuing years than any other single factor.

In daily contact with the surge of threatening unrest which had characterized the whole period of his governorship, Gage had always maintained that so far as the North American Colonies were concerned the British Government should 'lop them off as a rotten limb from the empire and leave them to themselves, or take *effectual* means to reduce them to authority'. If the latter course were decided upon, he insisted that a minimum of 20,000 Bloodybacks would be required 'to get the business over'. As he quite rightly emphasized, 'If force is to be used at length, it must be a considerable one; for to begin with small numbers will encourage resistance and will not terrify, and in the end cost more blood and treasure; a middling force will gain no friends.'[1]

But as has so often been the case, the considered opinion of the man on the spot was entirely ignored by the muddle-headed office-holders in London. Thus the belated orders Gage had received early in the April of 1775 had been entirely irrelevant, since they had not been

[1] *Gage Correspondence*, Gage to Barrington, October and November, 1774.

substantiated by any addition to the force under the General's command. Equally, Dartmouth's plan[1] for military action which would cut off New England from the rest of the Colonies omitted all mention of the increase in numbers necessary to carry it into execution. There can be little wonder, therefore, that the condition of stalemate Gage had earlier envisaged had duly come about.

It is to be recognized, of course, that the Administration found itself confronted with considerable contrariety of viewpoint in seeking to arrive at a definite policy for the North American Colonies, not only from leading parliamentarians such as Edmund Burke and Charles Fox, the Marquis of Rockingham, the Marquis of Granby, the Earls of Shelburne and Abingdon, Viscount Midleton and Sir George Savile, Franklin's regular correspondent, but also from men like Joseph Priestley, Thomas Bentley, Josiah Wedgwood, Richard Price and John Horne Tooke. Even the fluttering James Boswell confided to the private pages of his *Journal*, 'I am rather inclined to the American side of the present grand dispute, notwithstanding Dr Johnson's eloquence'. Furthermore, even in official circles there were grave doubts of the wisdom of trying to reassert authority by a recourse to arms. Harvey, the Adjutant-General, had roundly affirmed that 'taking America as it at present stands, it is impossible to conquer it with our British Army. To attempt to conquer it by our land forces is as wild an idea as ever controverted common sense'.[2] He wrote later to Howe, 'Unless a settled plan of operations is agreed upon for next Spring, our army will be destroyed by damned driblets'. Lord Barrington, with his lengthy experience in the War Office, was equally outspoken, if a little more imaginative. 'The Americans', he declared, 'may be reduced by the fleet, but never can be by the army.'

Then on 10th June, with 'hawks' and 'doves' still spinning dialectical subtleties across the dining-table, London was stunned by the news of Lexington and Concord. The capital had barely recovered from its initial astonishment and dismay when *The Gentleman's Magazine* for 24th June announced, 'By the shipp *Watt* arrived from Virginia, in 32 days, there is advice that Lord Dunmore [the Governor] had suppressed an insurrection at Williamsburgh that was of a dangerous tendency, 150 men from the back settlements having attempted, with Mr Patrick Henry, one of the delegates, at their head, to oblige the Governor to

---

[1] Drawn up four days before the march to Lexington and Concord. P.R.O. Co/5, V, 92.
[2] *Commander-in-Chief's Letter Books*, Harvey to General Irwin.

bring on shore a quantity of gunpowder belonging to the King, which he, for security, had put on board one of the men-of-war'.

Dr Warren might still be writing to his London correspondent, Arthur Lee, in terms which more than hinted that reconciliation should still be possible—needless to say on conditions laid down by Congress. But the general mood throughout England had appreciably hardened; 'Gentleman Johnny' Burgoyne was howled down in the House of Commons[1] when he expressed the hope that, 'where the error of her ways was concerned, America could be convinced by persuasion, and not by the sword'. In any case the King had already written to Lord North, 'The New England Governments are in a state of rebellion; blows must decide whether they are to be subject to this country or independent'.

Indeed, even before the news of Lexington and Concord had reached England, steps had been taken to muster the reinforcements Gage had for so long been soliciting—if not in anything like the number he regarded as requisite.

Seven battalions of Infantry and one of Light Dragoons[2] had been ordered to ready themselves for embarkation; although all the formations were so woefully under establishment that their numbers could only be raised to passable strength by heavy drafts from other corps; a process scarcely conducive to the upkeep of the unit's general quality. The Light Dragoons, trying to uphold their generally high standard, failed to increase their strength beyond a total of three hundred Officers and men.

With warfare on a considerable scale now a moral certainty, a number of senior naval and military Officers found themselves in a painful dilemma. For the sympathy they felt for the attitude taken up by the Americans was at hopeless variance with their instinctive sense of loyalty to the Crown. Since the death of Granby, Ligonier's successor, in 1770, the office of Commander-in-Chief had been in abeyance, the routine duties of the Army's titular chief being carried out by the Adjutant-General. The move to re-institute the post now was temporarily baulked by Jeffrey Amherst's initial refusal to accept it, on the score of his advancing years; an admirable plea with which to cloak his reluctance to 'take sides'. Admiral the Honourable Augustus Keppel refused to accept any command that would commit him to action

---

[1] He had been returned as Member for Preston in 1768.
[2] The 4th, 22nd, 35th, 42nd, 63rd and 65th Foot and the 17th Light Dragoons.
8*

against the Colonists. 'Although professional employment is the dearest object of my life', he wrote, 'I cannot draw the sword in such a cause.' General Harvey, the Adjutant-General, was firmly opposed to any resort to force, less, perhaps, out of partiality for the Americans than from his knowledge of the contemporary British Army's inadequate resources; although the exact reverse can be said to have motivated the politically wavering General Henry Seymour Conway. The Earl of Effingham resigned his Commission, as did Chatham's son, Viscount Pitt, Captain Peregrine Bertie, M.P. for Oxford, and many others amongst the more radical element in the Services. Major-General Lord Cornwallis, on the other hand, while warmly espousing the Colonial cause in Parliament, lost no time in soliciting a command in the impending theatre of war.

A similar dichotomy confronted the three general officers—Henry Clinton, William Howe and John Burgoyne—nominated to proceed forthwith in command of the additional troops earmarked for employment in North America. Clinton, the son of Admiral of the Fleet the Hon. George Clinton, a former Governor of New York, had actually been born on American soil. Securing a Commission in the Foot Guards, he had fought with distinction throughout the Seven Years' War and achieved Major-General's rank at the early age of thirty-four. Burgoyne had already established a sound reputation by his leadership in the Portuguese campaign of 1762, while Howe's services at Louisbourg and Quebec had won him considerable standing in the eyes of his contemporaries.

All three were Members of Parliament; and while Burgoyne in the House had pleaded the cause of moderation where the North American Colonies were concerned, Howe (a friendly acquaintance of Benjamin Franklin and his Craven Street circle of ultra-radicals) had openly informed his Nottingham constituents that he would not accept a command which committed him to fighting against the Colonists. When instructions reached him to proceed across the Atlantic, he immediately asked if they were to be regarded as a request or an order. Informed that they must be accepted as an unequivocal command, he bowed to the inevitable with the comment that 'he could not refuse without incurring the odious name of backwardness to serve my country in distress'. As a cousin of the King, albeit *à la main gauche*, his sense of loyalty could scarcely have demanded less of him. The same was equally true of Burgoyne and Henry Clinton. They were under oath to their Sovereign and there was an end to the matter; although in later years Clinton was at some pains to point out, 'I was not a volunteer in that war. I was ordered by my Sovereign and I obeyed.'

Thus it came about that on 5th March Captain James Chads, commander of H.M.S. *Cerberus*, received instructions from Lord Sandwich, as head of the Admiralty, to the effect that 'The King having thought fit that Major-Generals Howe, Burgoyne and Clinton should be employed upon His Majesty's Service in North America, and that they should repair as soon as possible to Boston, it is His Majesty's command that you receive them in your Vessel, together with their Attendants, Servants & Baggage, and proceed with them without loss of time to Boston'. A few days later 'Good-natured Billy' Howe was introducing his companions to the bluff naval officer whose vessel he had last boarded in the waters off the Anse de Foulon.

It is to be hoped that the warmth of the reception accorded the three voyagers atoned in some degree for the fact that they had left a metropolis convulsed with mirth at the topical witticism, 'Our Generals may terrify the enemy; they certainly terrify me!'

It can be advanced with some show of reason that had Gage launched a vigorous full-scale offensive immediately after the return of the troops from Lexington and Concord, the Provincials' lack of organization and want of central control would have led to their certain defeat. But Gage had been deeply impressed by Earl Percy's judicious comment on his opponents that 'whoever looks upon them as an irregular mob, will find himself much mistaken; they have men among them who know very well what they are about, having been employed as Rangers against the Indians and Canadians; and this country being much covered with wood, and hilly, it is very advantageous for their method of fighting...You may depend upon it that as the Rebels have now had time to prepare, they are determined to go through with it, nor will the insurrection here turn out so despicable as it is perhaps imagined at home.'[1]

Moreover, it was impossible to estimate how many of Boston's civil population would be prepared—given the opportunity—to strike a blow in the cause of independence. Certainly it would not be through lack of subtly conveyed encouragement on the part of the emissaries the French Court had been prompt to send across the Atlantic to foster

[1] *Letters of Hugh Earl Percy*, Percy to General Harvey.

any design that would work to the detriment of *perfide Albion* and the men entrusted with her destiny. In the circumstances Gage was strongly of opinion that it would be folly to sally forth into the countryside with the whole force available and leave Boston soldierless and at the mercy of a citizenry who might well rise and seize it in his absence. Until the arrival of substantial reinforcements Gage resolved to 'play safe', even to the extent of abandoning the Charlestown Heights and the embryonic fortification Captain Montressor had erected on the crown of Bunker Hill.

So far as Boston's own defences were concerned, immediate steps were taken to strengthen and expand them. A battery was installed at the Blockhouse commanding the narrow isthmus carrying the road to Roxbury; while Lieutenant Barker noted in his diary, 'There is an Abbatis in front of the left Bastion, and across the road a triple row of *chevaux de frise*...Another Battery is erecting for four Guns close under the Blockhouse, to command the Marsh to the left of the Dyke.' Altogether, the strongpoint found accommodation for ten 24-pounders.

Fort Hill dominated the lower rim of the crescent-shaped bay to the eastward; while to the north-west Barber's Point — opposite Lechmere's Point on the mainland — had also been fortified.

Lying at their moorings in Nantucket roads or at the mouth of the Charles river were H.M.S. *Mercury, Nautilus, Falcon, Preston, Boyne, Glasgow* and *Merlin*, with Samuel Graves, Vice-Admiral of the Blue, wearing his flag in H.M.S. *Somerset*.

In earlier days Graves and Gage's father had been seriously at loggerheads, and the elder man quickly showed a determination to nag and obstruct the son of his old enemy whenever the opportunity should offer. It was Graves who complained that the whole of Boston's western flank, below the Common and at the foot of Beacon Hill, was bleakly open to assault. For the tidal waters hereabouts were far too shallow to afford safe anchorage even for one of the smaller warships. And the hill itself was crowned with no more than a flimsy earthwork, flanked by a few small batteries. Dissatisfied with what he deemed entirely inadequate defences, and with no more than perfunctory consultation with the Governor and Military Commander, Graves set his bluejackets to work erecting an extremely solid battery on Copp's Hill, facing Bunker Hill, less than three-quarters of a mile away on the far side of the intervening waterway. Armed with 24-pounders, the work inevitably acquired the name of the Admiral's Battery.

Reasonably well furnished with defences, Boston was an exceedingly difficult objective to assail—except from the sea, or by long-range bombardment. Equally, it was a profoundly awkward stronghold from which to debouch; a factor Gage doubtless took into consideration in rejecting Graves's proposal to put Charlestown to the torch as a preliminary to the seizure of Charlestown and Roxbury Heights, the only points from which Boston could be commanded. For morale with the troops generally was low; and the four companies of the 65th Regiment from Halifax and the six hundred Marines who came to reinforce the garrison early in May scarcely amounted to a significant accretion of strength. As Lieutenant Baker confided to his diary in mid-month, 'We are anxiously awaiting the arrival of the Gen'l Officers and Troops that are expected; we want to get out of this Coop'd-up Situation. We cou'd now do that, I suppose, but the G—[Gage] does not seem to want it; there is no guessing what he is at. Time will show.'

For the moment Gage's whole attention was concentrated on bolstering up his defences and dealing with the many problems arising from the fact that he had a civilian population to control as well as a military garrison to keep under discipline.

In a grossly overcrowded township, completely cut off from the countryside, the want of fresh provisions quickly made itself felt. For although access to Boston by sea was not as yet seriously impeded, supplies had to be very sparingly eked out until sufficient time had elapsed to permit provision ships to arrive from Halifax or the other side of the Atlantic. In the meantime an undermanned foray to Grape Island[1] to secure hay had ended in the foragers scuttling for their boats with a cutting-out party of Provincials hard on their heels. A subsequent attempt by H.M.S. *Diana* to prevent the enemy from removing all the cattle from Hog Island had wound up with the vessel running aground and being set ablaze.[2] Thereafter Noddles's Island had been cleared by local militia of all stock, green food and dairy produce, with the result, as Lieutenant Barker sourly recorded, that 'The worst of it is we are ill off for fresh Provisions; none to be bought save now and then a little Pork'.

Moreover, although the Provincial forces had been quiescent enough so far, there were no means of ascertaining what dark designs they might have in mind. Gage's intelligence service was as meagre and

[1] Off Weymouth, S.E. of Boston.
[2] P.R.O. Admiralty Papers, 1/485, North America, 1774–1777.

unreliable as that of his opponents was widespread and dependable; lack of a good reserve of money in his military chest depriving the Commander-in-Chief even of the services of the hired spy. Writing to his brother in England, Peter Oliver, son of a former Chief Justice, dourly recorded, 'We are Besieged this moment with 10 to 15,000 men, from Roxbury to Cambridge; their Rebell Sentries within call of the Troops' Sentry on the Neck. We are every Hour expecting an Attack by land and water. All Marketing from the Country stop't and since the Battle [Lexington and Concord] Fire and Slaughter hourly Threatened.'

As a local poetaster summed it up:

> The Saints, alas, have waxen strong;
> In vain your fasts and godly song
> To quell the rebel rout!
> Within his lines sulks valiant Gage,
> Like Yorick's starling in the cage,
> He cries, 'I can't get out!'

For that matter, the Provincials had let slip as big an opportunity as had their opponents. Given the necessary control, initiative and sense of urgency, a striking victory might have been snatched from the aftermath of Lexington and Concord, 'when they were flushed with the triumph of a superior Victory, and when part of the British Troops were greatly harassed & fatigued with their long march,…& the Rest with Double Duty in their Absence'.[1] But much of warfare is no more than a catalogue of attempts to retrieve lost opportunities – and all wars can be wonderfully well fought in retrospect.

But if deadlock persisted in front of Boston, further afield two violently antipathetic individualists had momentarily combined to engineer a coup whose consequences neither of them could possibly have foretold.

Amongst the men who had instantly sprung to arms with the news of Lexington and Concord was a certain Ethan Allen, who had already achieved more than local notoriety by virtue of the defiant part he had played in a land dispute between his native New Hampshire and the State of New York. Realizing that the whole of Canada was defended by no more than two weak battalions,[2] unable to spare more than token garrisons to guard the traditional line of approach to the Colony by

---

[1] Richard Reeves, *Correspondence*.
[2] The 7th and 26th Foot.

way of Lake George and Lake Champlain, it was Allen's plan to rush these outposts and push on at speed to the assault of Montreal and Quebec. A precisely similar design had been evolved by Benedict Arnold, as the preliminary to a descent on Canada before General Guy Carleton could be reinforced by fresh troops from England.

Allen was the first off the mark, at the head of some two hundred and seventy guerrillas picturesquely styled 'Green Mountain Boys'. Despite the impressive parchment authorizing his activities which Arnold flourished in his rival's face, Allen refused to acknowledge his authority; and it was as no more than a 'volunteer' that the New Haven Colonel attached himself to the enterprise.

The garrison of Ticonderoga, Allen's first objective, consisted of forty-eight men of the 26th Foot, under the easy-going Captain Delaplace; an uxorious husband whose attractive wife commanded far more of his attention than the maintenance of discipline and alertness among his troops. Acquainted with Allen as he was, and entirely ignorant of the warlike state of affairs prevailing elsewhere, Delaplace found nothing strange in his visitor's guileful plea for the loan of twenty men to aid in some heavy work going forward on the nearby lake. The request having been duly granted, and this substantial part of the garrison having been reduced to a condition of helpless intoxication by a lavish distribution of New England rum, Allen and his 'Green Mountain Boys' experienced little difficulty in overpowering the solitary sentinel and cowing the sober but somnolent remainder of the garrison into submission; thereafter demanding the formal surrender of the stronghold from a custodian scarcely looking his military best in the exiguous shirt and drawers which served him as night attire.

'By what authority do *you* demand it?' stammered a comprehensibly bewildered Delaplace.

'In the name of the great Jehovah and the Continental Congress', thundered Allen; which for a metempsychosist and professed freethinker was as nice a concession to the dramatics demanded of the moment as could reasonably be expected.

Far more valuable than his haul of prisoners was Allen's capture of a park of a hundred and twenty thoroughly good cannon, and large quantities of powder and ball — all of which were in desperately short supply with the forces beleaguering Boston.

Allen's next move was on Crown Point, which, being ungarrisoned, despite its small store of artillery pieces and munitions, called for no expenditure of effort—or even of New England rum—for its seizure. Thereafter, Arnold, possessing himself of the only British vessel on Lake Champlain, surprised and subdued St John's. Carleton's subsequent efforts to recover the lakes with elements of his garrison of less than eight hundred effectives proved unsuccessful; although he did contrive to reconquer St John's.

Ironically enough, the Congress announced that 'the cannon taken at Ticonderoga were to be returned to Great Britain when the former harmony between Great Britain and the Colonies should be restored'.[1] Actually, that admirable Bostonian bookseller and gifted amateur of artillery, Henry Knox, was in the throes of conducting the best of the pieces on their difficult journey from the lakes to the lines before Boston.

Such ambiguities arose inevitably from the fact that neither England nor America could speak with one voice; both were as a house divided against itself. And in the babel of contentious tongues and the confusion of contradictory assumptions, it was the single-minded fanatic who prevailed. For at least he knew what he wanted, and reinforced that knowledge with a ruthless determination to achieve his ends.

It was 25th May before the *Cerberus*, after a passage of thirty-four days, sighted Cape Anne and Boston lying in its bay a little to the south-west. If the three Generals' departure from England had been accompanied by a scalding jape, a local versifier's welcome for them was scarcely less blistering:

> Behold the Cerberus the Atlantic plough,
> Her precious cargo, Burgoyne, Clinton, Howe;
> Bow, wow, wow!

As the three newcomers made their way to the Province House to report their arrival to Gage, the gossips were already circulating Burgoyne's somewhat cocksure mid-ocean prophecy, 'Well, let us get in, and we'll soon find elbow-room'. (It was a comment which, as the weeks of inactivity lengthened, was to earn him the derisive title of 'General Elbow-room'.) For Gage, it seemed, was anything but minded to put to the test of action his earlier boast that 'the Rebels would be Lyons whilst we are Lambs; but, if we take the Resolute part, they will undoubtedly prove very weak'. A state of *impasse* still prevailed; while

[1] John Marshall, *The Life of George Washington*.

conditions in Boston steadily grew more difficult and distressful. With a garrison of approximately 3,500 effectives and a floating population which averaged 6,700, the town was uncomfortably crowded, since the hospital had been unable to accommodate all the wounded from Lexington and Concord and private property had perforce been requisitioned in which to house them.

With incoming victualling ships often the prey of New England privateers, and Admiral Graves's coastal raids for cattle and fresh provisions singularly unproductive, the dearth of supplies posed a problem of increasing gravity. 'We have been obliged to live entirely on salt provisions and what stores we have in this house', wrote Henry Pelham to his half-brother, the artist, John Singleton Copley; 'tis inconceivable the Distress and Ruin this unnatural Dispute has caused this Town and its Inhabitants. Almost every Shop and store is Shut. No business of any sort going on…The Cloaths on my back and a few Dollars in my Pocket are now the only Property I have the least Command of.'

On the other hand, the letter from an Officer in beleaguered Boston records an instance of military chivalry in the very best tradition: 'Why should I complain of hard fate? General Gage and his family[1] have for this month past lived upon salt provisions. Last Saturday General Putnam, in the true style of military complacence, which abolishes all personal resentment and smoothes the horrors of war, when discipline will permit, sent a present to the General's lady of a fine quarter of veal, which was very acceptable, and received in return a very polite card of thanks.'[2]

Shortage of necessities had, as always, brought an immediate rise in their cost. When procurable, beef and mutton, which had sold at 3½d a pound, with veal at 3d a pound and chicken at 9d the pair, soon commanded double, treble, and quadruple their old prices; while fish, at one time so plentiful as to be retailed at 1½d the pound, virtually disappeared from the market. The fishermen of Boston, Salem, Gloucester and Marblehead were looking forward to the day when, as privateers, the sea would yield them an infinitely richer harvest.

Even the reserves of flour were far from adequate for the demands of anything like a lengthy investment, while the price for deliveries to the military soon reached 15s the hundredweight. But for the moment

[1] i.e. his Staff.
[2] Quoted by the *Constitutional Gazette* as originally appearing in an unspecified London newspaper.

there was no shortage of rot-gut rum of such rasping potency that in the opinion of one Bloodyback who survived sampling it, it 'would scour the rust off a dirty bayonet'.

On the 12th June Gage had put his signature to a Proclamation, drawn up for him by Burgoyne in terms so pompous and verbose as to arouse more ribald laughter than respectful attention. It ended by instituting martial law, and by promising clemency to all who were prepared to reaffirm their allegiance to the Crown — with the exception of Hancock and Samuel Adams. (No mention was made of Dr Joseph Warren, by far the most intelligent, as he was certainly the most resolute, of all those who had set the supremacy of the British Parliament at defiance.)

The only response on the part of the Provincials to this fulmination was the redoubling of their efforts to perfect the fortifications, thrown up at Roxbury and in front of Cambridge.

Almost from the moment of their arrival Clinton, Howe and Burgoyne had been appalled by Gage's apathy and irresolution. But even with his resources substantially increased by the reinforcements sailing in from England, it was not until several days after the issue of his Proclamation that the Commander-in-Chief called a council of war, attended by Admiral Graves as well as by Clinton, Howe and Burgoyne. As the best tactician present Howe proposed that a detachment should be sent to erect two strong redoubts on Charlestown Neck, and that an attack should then be launched on the insurgents' post at Roxbury. Once Boston were free from the threat of attack from this direction, a powerful force should sally out by way of Charlestown to assail the Provincials in Cambridge from the flank. The plan was agreed, and the attempt to put it into execution was scheduled for 18th June.

Such was the efficiency of Warren's espionage network that the Command at Cambridge was fully apprised of the projected enterprise within a matter of hours. The outcome was that on the morning of the 17th the lookout aboard H.M.S. *Lively* peered through the rising mist to discern that Bunker Hill, the main feature of Charlestown Heights, had been fortified overnight by a strong party of Provincials who, at sun-up, were still labouring to strengthen the works. Aroused by this startling news, Captain Thomas Brown R.N. promptly put a spring on his cable to swing the *Lively* so that her guns could be brought to bear on the newly dug redoubt. To the thunder of cannon, sleepers in Boston, as in the lines at Cambridge, tumbled from their beds in bewilderment and alarm.

The redoubt had not yet been properly 'refused' on either flank, and it was clear that for the moment it was manned by not more than 850 men, wearied by their strenuous labours throughout the night hours. So there was much to commend Clinton's urgent plea to hurl in an attack without a moment's delay, before the strongpoint's defenders could be reinforced.

But Gage was not to be hurried. While agreeing that an early attack was highly advisable, he insisted that everything should be done in due form, and with a proper plan drawn up to ensure collaboration with the Royal Navy, whose vessels could offer no substantial support until high tide had set in. It was not until 1.30 p.m., therefore, that the first of the twenty-eight barges loaded with twenty companies of light infantry and grenadiers, under General Howe, and the two line battalions,[1] under Brigadier-General Robert Pigot, set out of Morton's Point on the extreme easterly tip of the Charlestown peninsula. Every man was loaded down with his full kit, which, with knapsack, blanket and ammunition, totalled at least a dead weight of one hundred and twenty-five pounds. The sun blazed out of a cloudless sky, and ahead lay the slopes of Breed's Hill[2] —with a steep bank on its western, or Charlestown, flank —and beyond it the steeper incline of Bunker Hill. A stone-based rail fence ran from the Bunker Hill redoubt in a north-easterly direction towards the Mystic river, a roughly constructed *sangar* carrying the defence to the water's edge. In many places the rank grass was knee-high, while the uneven ground was intersected by a number of rail fences obstructing the direct line of advance. It was going to be uphill work in all senses of the term; and Howe was sufficiently impressed by the number of opponents now discernible in and about the redoubt to send for the two battalions held in immediate reserve. Pending their arrival the troops were ordered to fall out and eat their dinners; three days' rations having formed part of each man's load. No one realized better than 'Good-natured Billy' Howe that few victories are won on an empty stomach.

With the arrival of the two battalions Howe had sent for, the whole detachment was drawn up in three lines; the grenadiers, 5th and 52nd Foot in column of battalions forming the left wing under Howe, with Pigot commanding the light infantry, 38th and 43rd Foot on the right.

To the roar of the eight field pieces and howitzers directing their

---

[1] The 43rd and 52nd Foot.
[2] Sometimes known as Breed's Pasture.

somewhat ineffectual fire against the redoubt, the Bloodybacks began their advance across the six hundred yards which separated them from their objective; deploying so that the light infantry confronted the rail-fence and *sangar* on the Provincials' left, while the grenadiers and main body of the infantry launched themselves straight for the redoubt. In their front marched Howe, who had already assured his men that he would not ask a single one of them 'to go a step further than where I go myself—at your head'.

Unfortunately the Bloodybacks—committing a fault that could rarely be laid to their charge—opened with their musketry prematurely; while the Navy's floating batteries, arrested by a vagary of the tide, could not proceed far enough up the flanks of the peninsula to bring really effective enfilade fire to bear. The Provincials, on the other hand, were careful to reserve their fire until it could be relied upon to wreak the maximum damage, exhorted as they were by 'Old Put's' wily counsel, 'Wait till you can see the whites of their eyes![1] And when you fire, aim at the gorgets and the fancy vests!'[2] Restraining themselves until the Bloodybacks were within fifty yards of their sheltering earthwork, the Americans loosed such a blast of fire into the scarlet ranks that they staggered to a halt, stumbling over the bodies of the many Officers and men brought low by a sleet of missiles aimed with deadly accuracy by picked marksmen, supplied with a succession of loaded weapons so that they could wreak the greatest possibly injury. It was 'a discharge of cannon and musketry that poured down a full half hour upon them like a torrent. The execution it did was terrible, insomuch as some of the oldest Officers and soldiers declared it was the hottest service they had ever seen'.[3] 'The fire was so terrible that the British, after a gallant attempt to reload and return it, gave way, broken to pieces by their losses, and fell back out of range, when they quickly rallied and re-formed for a second attack.'[4]

Throughout the course of this first assault the Bloodybacks' left wing had been viciously galled by the stream of musketry poured out by scores of sharpshooters ensconced in the houses in Charlestown. In response to an urgent signal, therefore, the battery at Copp's Hill was

[1] A piece of advice first given by Gustavus Adolphus of Sweden to his Reiters, and echoed by Lord Stair at the battle of Dettingen.
[2] i.e. at the silver or brass 'duty' gorgets worn at the throat, and the gold-laced waistcoats, by which the Officers were distinguished.
[3] Serjeant R. Lamb, *Journal of Occurrences During the Late American War.*
[4] Fortescue, *op. cit.*

brought swiftly into play, its red-hot shot and 'carcasses' speedily setting Charlestown fiercely ablaze.

The right wing, under Pigot, had suffered no less severely than the men detached for the assault on the redoubt. But there was no thought of abandoning the fight; although the British guns had fallen silent, since, through sheer muddle-headed carelessness, the reserve of ammunition had been made up with the wrong calibre of shot—12 lb balls for 6-pounder guns. As one infuriated Gunner Officer subsequently recorded, 'The wretched blunder of the over-size balls sprung from the dotage of an Officer of Rank[1] in the Corps, who spent his time dallying with the schoolmaster's daughters'. Furthermore, a patch of swampy ground to their immediate front prevented the weapons being moved forward to an appropriate range for the discharge of grapeshot, of which there was a reasonable supply available.

But nothing daunted by lack of artillery support, Howe coolly set to work to organize a second attempt on the reinforced objective; directing the right wing to abandon their effort to overcome the beach defences and bend their energies to mastering the rail-fence position, so that they could swing round and assail the redoubt in flank.

'And now ensued one of the greatest scenes of war that can be conceived', the onlooking Burgoyne subsequently wrote;[2] 'Howe's corps ascending the hill in the face of the entrenchments, and in a very disadvantageous ground, was much engaged; and to the left the enemy pouring in fresh troops by thousands over the land; and in the arm of the sea our ships and floating batteries cannonading them; straight before us as a large and noble town in one blaze; the church steeples, being made of timber, were great pyramids of fire above the rest. The enemy all anxious suspense; the roar of cannon, mortars, musquetry; the crash of churches, ships upon the stocks, and whole streets falling together.'

As Howe's scarlet-coated men moved steadily forward they met with an even more searing blast of fire, but with sheer dogged determination continued to force their way against it. 'Our light infantry were served up in companies against the grass fence', recorded one survivor, 'without being able to penetrate it—indeed, how could we penetrate? Most of our grenadiers and light infantry, the moment of presenting themselves lost three-fourths, and many nine-tenths, of their men. Some had only eight or nine men a company left, some only three, four, or five.

[1] Colonel Samuel Cleaveland.   [2] In a letter to his nephew, Lord Stanley.

On the left Pigot was staggered and actually retreated. But our men were not driven back; they actually retreated by orders.'

The assault, under the hail of lead which raked it, had faltered to a standstill, with the men's heads bowed as though stricken by the blast of a tornado. Then, with Officers and men still dropping fast, the ragged line split up into little milling groups which drifted blindly down the slope, whose trampled grass was now sown thick with the bodies of the injured and the slain.

On the tower of Boston's Christ Church Gage lowered his perspective glass in what was little less than a gesture of despair. Nearer the scene of action, Clinton, observing two battalions which had fallen back on the beach in great disorder through want of Officers to rally them, hurried across the intervening waterway to their swift reanimation. With Midshipman Cuthbert Collingwood in charge of the boats, a reinforcement of the 47th Foot and a battalion of Marines followed hard on Clinton's heels; their timely appearance helping materially to put fresh heart in Howe's appallingly diminished ranks.

Not that Howe and his troops were in any mood to accept defeat. However profoundly 'Good-natured Billy' might 'hate business', in the ordinary routine of soldiering, on the field of action he could still command the ready obedience of the men at whose head he was always to be found, sword in hand. So far, he had come scatheless through the fray, although every one of his Staff Officers had fallen at his side, while Thomas Evans, his soldier-servant (who had followed his master everywhere with a liberal supply of liquid refreshment) had had a wine bottle shot out of his hands and sustained a badly bruised arm in consequence. But Howe, with his white breeches and silk stockings splashed with the blood of the fallen, had firmly rejected the protest of some of his subordinates that to take the men in again could only lead to useless slaughter, and had resolutely replied, 'To be forced to give up Boston would, gentlemen, be very disagreeable to us all'. Then, with his sword tucked under his arm, this queer contradiction of a man, whose unflinching courage on this momentous day won the awed respect of every Bloodyback who followed him, turned coolly away and continued his dressing of the ranks.

Deliberately flouting regulations, the men were ordered to cast aside their cumbersome packs and blankets, loosen their belts, and instructed that in the coming assault they should go in at top speed, not pausing to fire, but to put their trust in the cold steel.

Abandoning the folly hitherto practised of trying to attack with equal strength all along the line, Howe merely feinted at the American left, concentrating his main drive on the central redoubt. Advancing at mended pace, the sweating, short-breathed scarlet files once more breasted the slope; the Provincials waiting, as before, until their assailants were close upon them before giving fire. 'When we came close under the work', a survivor of the day wrote home,[1] 'we were checked by the severe fire from the enemy, but we did not retreat an inch. We were now in some confusion after being broke [i.e. broken up] several times in getting over the rails, etc. I did all I could to form the two companies on our right, which at last I effected, losing many of them while it was performing. Major Pitcairn was killed close by me, with a Captain and Subaltern, also a Serjeant, and many of the Privates; and had we stopp'd there much longer, the enemy would have picked us all off. I saw this, and begged Colonel Nesbitt of the 47th to form on our left, in order that we might advance with our bayonets to the parapet. I ran from right to left, and stopp'd our men from firing; while this was doing, and when we got into tolerable order, we rushed on, leap'd the ditch, and climbed the parapet, under a most sore and heavy fire.'

For a moment the action again hung in the balance. 'Then suddenly our men grew impatient', Lord Rawdon subsequently recalled, 'and all saying "Push on! Push on!" advanced with infinite spirit to attack with their small arms. As soon as the Rebels perceived this, they rose up and poured in so heavy a fire upon us that the oldest Officers say they never saw a sharper action. They kept up this fire till we were within ten yards of them; nay, they even knocked down my Captain[2] close beside me, after we had got in the ditch of the entrenchment...I can assure you I saw several pop their heads up even when some of us were upon the berm.'

Suddenly the American fire spluttered and 'went out like an old candle'. It was sheer want of powder which had grounded many a weapon hitherto busily employed. And with the waning musketry came the first sign of flinching in the redoubt's defenders. Not a few of them stood bravely to the end, but under the glittering menace of the thrusting steel the main mass wilted and began to give way. 'Nothing could

---

[1] Lieutenant J. Waller, Marine Corps, in a letter headed '22nd June, 1775, Camp of Charlestown Heights'.

[2] George Harris. Rawdon was a Lieutenant in the 5th Foot.

have been more shocking than the carnage which followed the storming of the work. We tumbled over the dead to get at the living as they
crowded out of the gorge of the redoubt in order to form under the
defences[1] which they had prepared to cover their retreat.'[2]

But it was when the ruck of the withdrawal, seeking to crowd across
Charlestown Neck, came under the fire of the Royal Navy's floating
batteries and the heavy ordnance of H.M.S. *Somerset* — despite the gunners' difficulty in giving their cannon sufficient elevation — that the
fugitives suffered the most serious losses incurred throughout the day;
many men falling beneath a constant rain of roundshot and shells. It was
a barrage which had equally prevented insurgent reinforcements in
making their way down the peninsula in anything like real strength.

There was no pursuit of the fleeing militiamen on the part of the
British. Badly shattered and shaken, completely exhausted by their
efforts under the broiling sun, only an entirely fresh body of troops
could have undertaken such a task. In any case it would have been work
best suited to the cavalry; and the 17th Light Dragoons, having been
unable to make good the heavy loss in horseflesh incurred in their
passage across the Atlantic, were for all practical purposes immobilized.
Once beyond the range of gunfire, the survivors amongst the men who
had so valiantly held on to the redoubt on Bunker Hill made the best
of their way to the shelter of the lines at Cambridge, or to those scattered homesteads from whose walls so many of them had snatched
down musket or deadly fowling-piece only a matter of days before. As
Burgoyne ungrudgingly recorded, the rival host which earlier he had
too hastily dismissed as a mere 'rabble in arms', had organized a defence
which was 'well-conceived and obstinately maintained; the retreat was
no flight, and it was even covered with bravery and military skill, and
proceeded no further than the west hill, where a new post was taken
up and new entrenchments instantly begun'.[3]

Denied an immediate follow-up pursuit, Clinton grimly noted in his
Journal, 'A dear-bought victory; another such would have ruined us'.
For the toll which had been exacted was out of all proportion to the
number of Bloodybacks engaged — from first to last a total of 2,300
Officers and men. Of these 1,054 had fallen, the number of killed coming
to 226. Losses had been particularly heavy, among the Officers, of

---

[1] Defences rather sketchily put together on the reverse slope of Bunker Hill.
[2] Waller, *op. cit.*
[3] Plowed Hill.

whom nineteen had been killed and seventy wounded.[1] As the chival-rous author of *The Fall of British Tyranny* put it, 'Many powdered *beaux*, *petits maîtres*, fops, fribbles, skip-jackets, macaronis, jack-puddings, noblemen's bastards and whores' sons fell that day'; but as was to be said of the fallen in another equally sanguinary encounter, 'every wound was in front'.

The Americans had fought honourably and well; while 'the return of the British infantry to the third attack after two such bloody repulses, is one of the very greatest feats recorded of them, and points to fine quality among the men, grand pride in the regiments, and supreme excellence of discipline'.[2]

Compared with the British, American losses, out of the 3,500 men engaged, had been comparatively light, although they included the fire-brand Dr Joseph Warren amongst the 138 killed. The wounded totalled 276, and there were 36 reported missing; while all the field pieces save one remained in British hands.[3]

As the sun went down and darkness fell over a stunned and mourn-ing Boston, 'carts and waggons of every description pulled up at Long Wharf, coaches, chariots, chaises, even hand-barrows, sent by loyalists to haul the desperately wounded men — and lurched off on the agoniz-ing journey to hospital or home, wherever a hurt soldier might be tended'.[4]

Reviewing his resources in the days subsequent to the costly tussle of 17th June, Gage was brought to the reluctant realization that, until he had been powerfully reinforced, the passive defence of Boston was the most he could hope to achieve. The hard-won Charlestown Heights were of course retained and their fortifications strengthened; command of this sub-area being entrusted to General Howe. But although a plan was evolved for the seizure of Dorchester Heights, the attempt was never put in hand.

Shortage of fresh food, the humid, oppressive heat, and the over-crowded accommodation bred a wave of sickness in Boston which accounted for as many as thirty funerals a day.[5] In the improvised

---

[1] Eight subsequently died of their wounds.
[2] Fortescue, *op. cit.*
[3] These are the figures given by Washington in a private letter. Artemas Ward's Orderly Books record 115 killed, 305 wounded, and 30 missing.
[4] Richard M. Ketchum, *The Battle of Bunker Hill.*
[5] At this period the civilian population of Boston was estimated at 7,000.

military hospitals dysentery, fever, smallpox, gangrenous and suppurating wounds claimed more and more victims until out of a nominal strength of 13,000 Bloodybacks it is questionable if the Commander-in-Chief could actually call upon the services of more than 6,500 effectives; too many to subsist in unproductive idleness, too few for positive action. In any case, where the troops in Boston were concerned morale was particularly low; one Officer writing home, 'All you have sent by way of Troops to this Continent are but a Mouthful. If you send more to add to Us, you may make them a Dinner, and you may continue to supply them with a Supper, and then it will be "Good-Night".' Another correspondent, in acid reference to Burgoyne's jaunty prophecy, sourly commented, 'We have now got a little *elbow room*, but I think we have paid too dearly for it'.

In England the King's reaction to the news of Bunker Hill was to authorize the promulgation of a Proclamation 'for Suppressing Rebellion and Sedition', which in effect ignored the quasi-olive-branch held out by the Congress in its 'Petition of Right'. The point of no return had been reached and passed. But, in the ultimate, authority can never be stronger than the armed strength it can call to its support; and Army recruiting was going anything but well. 'Unless it rains men in red coats', John Pownall wrote to Clinton, 'I know not where we are to get all we shall want.' Indeed, it might well become necessary to hire mercenary troops; in the meantime five of the King's Hanoverian regiments were posted to help garrison Gibraltar and Minorca, and thus set free the Bloodybacks stationed on the Rock and at Port Mahon for active duty elsewhere.

Not that the self-constituted American authorities were without their troubles. On 16th June the second Continental Congress had designated George Washington Commander-in-Chief, and on 3rd July he had ridden into Cambridge to take up his appointment — and to try and create a properly integrated army out of the heterogeneous elements assembled in the lines before Boston. With no Staff, nothing in the way of a command structure, a chronic shortage of every variety of warlike material, and with an amorphous mass of human beings to whom the very thought of disciplined subordination was an affront to their sense of manly independence, it was a task to daunt the stoutest heart. Nor was it in any way lightened by jealous, fussy Congressional attempts to interfere in its halting progress. That the patient, upright, unpretentious but intrepid squire of the Potomac was the one man to carry the undertaking to success, the history of the ensuing years bears sufficiently clear witness.

Only a few days after the news of the Bunker Hill battle reached London, it had been decided to recall Gage 'to report on the situation'. By 26th September intimation of this decision reached Boston, and a fortnight later Gage set sail for England, having handed over the command to William Howe; who thankfully exchanged the sparse amenities of Charlestown Heights for the snug shelter and reasonably well-stocked cellar of the Province House. Nor was the ample leisure in which he indulged himself devoid of stimulating female companionship. For 'in Boston', as one observant onlooker put it, 'he found his Cleopatra in an illustrious courtesan'. This was putting it a little brutally, since Elizabeth Lloyd came of quite a reputable family. She was married to Joshua Loring (son of that Commodore Loring who had commanded the naval element in Amherst's campaign of 1759–1760) and her accommodating husband was easily placated for the wandering nature of her affections by appointment to the rewarding office of 'sole vendue master and auctioneer in and for the town of Boston'. In addition, he was nominated Sheriff, which invested him with considerable control over such Provincial prisoners as fell into British hands. A born *mari complaisant*, the unendearing Joshua was quite prepared to surrender himself—for a consideration—to the protection of good St Cornelius.[1] And 'Good-natured Billy' was the last man to be niggard in the matter of the necessary 'consideration'. It was not long, therefore, before Boston was delightedly repeating the rhyme from Francis Hopkinson's *Battle of the Kegs*:

> Sir William, he, snug as a flea,
> Lay all his time a-snoring,
> Nor dreamed of harm as he lay warm
> In bed with Mrs Loring.

But self-indulgent as Howe might be where he himself was concerned, the discipline of the garrison and control of the civil population were maintained at a remarkably high level. Insubordination, neglect of duty, interference with or theft from private property, were dealt with promptly and exemplarily. Thomas McMahon, of the 43rd, made grim acquaintance with the lash 'for receiving sundry stol'n Goods knowing them to be such'. When the shortage of fresh meat tempted

---

[1] The patron saint of cuckolds.

one camp follower to line her pockets by a departure into private enterprise, the outcome, as recorded in the Orderly Book, revealed that 'Winifred McCowan, retainer to the Camp [was] tryed by General Court Martial for having stolen the Town Bull and Causing him to be killed, and is found Guilty of the Same & Sentenced to be Tyed to a Cart's Tail, and thereto to receive 100 Lashes on her bare Back in different portions of the most Public parts of the Town and Camp, and to be imprison'd three months'. Sentries were sternly warned 'not to give any Molestation to the peaceful Inhabitants of the Town'; while Privates John Wrenshaw and Edward Slator, of the 36th Foot, were tried and sentenced by Court Martial for robbing a Mr William Taylor of a quantity of flour.

Tap-to[1] was at 8 p.m., whereafter order was maintained throughout the town by patrols furnished by the Light Dragoons. To relieve the strain on the troops, some of the work of manning the defences was undertaken by the Royal American Fencibles, a corps of local loyalists, who subsequently shared the duty with two other loyalist contingents, known respectively, as the Royal North British Volunteers and the Loyal American Association.

Within his limited means Howe did his utmost for his sick and wounded, brewing spruce beer as an antidote to scurvy, trying to secure *sauerkraut* for those already suffering from the scourge, setting aside 'wyne and oatmeal' for those for whom these rarities had been ordered by the surgeons; while full rations and pay at 6d a day, in sterling,[2] rewarded those women who volunteered to help in the work of nursing.

With colder weather clamping down on wind-blown Charlestown Heights, a special issue of watch coats and extra blankets was made to troops in the outposts, together with a daily tot of rum. Smuggling liquor into the camp or barracks—whether by male or female delin-quent—was, however, visited with the severest penalty.

With 'Gentleman Johnny' to give them inspiration, amateur theatri-cals helped to furnish a little welcome distraction for soldiers and civilians alike; Lord Rawdon reciting an original—and highly topical— Prologue to a translation of Voltaire's *Zara*, in which Burgoyne's con-temptuous dislike of the disapproving local Puritans found expression in the reproachful line:

[1] From the Dutch *de taptoe slaen*—'the taps turned off'.
[2] The dollar stood at a nominal 4s 8d.

>   Then fell the stage, quell'd by the bigots' roar,
>   Truth fell with sense, and Shakespeare charm'd no more.

On another occasion, when Burgoyne's own farce *The Blockade of Boston* was being given, the performance suffered a rude interruption. The Americans, who knew at exactly what hour the entertainment would be given, took the opportunity to attack the mill at Charlestown — in reprisal, maybe for a British raid on Phipps's Farm. The alarm was given, and a Serjeant rushed on to the stage shouting, 'Turn out! Turn out! They're hard at it, hammer and tongs!' Being mistaken for one of the characters in the play, he was vigorously applauded; and it took quite a little time to sort out the situation properly.

Then in November the cause of American independence received an inadvertent but enormous bonus with the appointment of Lord George Germain to the post of Secretary of State for the Colonies, in place of the Earl of Dartmouth. The fact that as Lord George Sackville his alleged cowardice at the battle of Minden had resulted in trial by Court Martial and dismissal from the Army with ignominy had proved no bar to his re-entry into public life. Changing his name to Germain on inheriting the fortune left him by an old friend of his family,[1] he had exploited his social position to acquire an office in which his combination of arrogance and incapacity could work the maximum of harm. The man who had ruined a golden opportunity on the field of Minden was to be entrusted with the day-to-day conduct of a campaign three thousand miles distant from his desk in Whitehall; whence flowed a stream of instructions which, even if they had not been inept in themselves, were completely outdated and inapplicable by the time they reached the actual scene of operations.

One of the first fruits of Germain's assumption of responsibility for policy-making was the organization of a task force, out of Howe's meagre resources, and under Clinton's command, to 'make a demonstration in the South which would rally loyalist support';[2] the expedition to rendezvous at Cape Fear with a strong naval and military force coming from England. The design entirely ruled out any prospect of seizing the line of the Hudson promptly, and by so doing cut off New England from the Provinces further south. In any case the belief was speedily taking root that far greater reliance should be placed on

---

[1] Lady Betty Germain.
[2] William B. Willcox, *The American Rebellion*, Introduction.

the active help forthcoming from the loyalists scattered throughout the length and breadth of the Thirteen Colonies, and particularly in the South. That their support would tip the balance in favour of the insurrection's suppression was a fond delusion which was to persist throughout the whole duration of the struggle.

What was almost entirely lost sight of was that the loyalism of the strong Scots and Irish element in the South was to the House of Stuart[1] rather than to the Hanoverian succession; that if they took the field at all it would be rather in opposition to American republicanism than in support of the still semi-Teutonic occupant of England's throne.

In the outcome, Clinton's wandering commission achieved nothing, while being attended by considerable military misadventure. To begin with, the convoy from England, with Commodore Sir Peter Parker in command of the Royal Navy vessels and transports and Lord Cornwallis of the troops, was extremely late in putting in an appearance, having taken three months to cross the Atlantic. In the meantime the loyalists who had agreed to support British operations, being unable to postpone their appearance in arms, had risen prematurely and, being entirely unsupported, had easily been dispersed. As nothing could be done in the Cape Fear area, Clinton was persuaded by his naval coadjutor to join in a combined attack on Fort Moultrie on Sullivan Island, the capture of which would endow the British with command of Charleston Harbour.[2]

Once again indecision and delay so fatally held up the execution of the design that ample time was given General Charles Lee to put Charleston in general and Sullivan Island in particular in so admirable a condition of defence that when the assault on it was finally launched the outcome was little short of disastrous. Failure properly to reconnoitre an intervening water obstacle and an impassable swamp prevented Clinton's troops even from approaching close enough to their objective to assail it. Out in the bay Sir Peter Parker in H.M.S. *Bristol*, and the other ten vessels of the squadron, expended an enormous quantity of powder and shot to very little purpose. With one frigate set ablaze and over two hundred casualties among the other craft, the unfortunate Commodore was in process of assimilating the painful truth of the dictum which lays down that 'ships are intended to fight

---

[1] 'The Quakers in Pennsylvania were Jacobite to a man.' Petrie, *The Four Georges*. One of the rebels' favourite marching songs was the Jacobite melody 'The White Cockade'.

[2] As the South Carolina port had now become termed.

ships, not forts, against which they are always at a disadvantage'. Himself injured in the thigh and knee, the Commodore sustained the further indignity of losing his breeches through the 'wind' of a passing shot; a calamity promptly memorialized in the ribald rhyme:

> If 'honour in the breech is lodged',
> As Hudibras has shown,
> It may from this be fairly judged
> Sir Peter's honour's gone.

With battered hulls and shredded sails, the armament put about and headed north for Halifax. For Boston no longer offered even a quasi-harbour of refuge.

As the wet, dreary winter had hardened, a fugitive from Boston reported to the *Pennsylvania Journal* that

> the distress of the troops increases fast, their beef is spent, their malt and cider all gone; all the fresh provisions they can procure, they are obliged to give to the sick and wounded;...that no man dared to be seen talking to his friend in the street; that they are obliged to be within every evening at ten o'clock according to martial law, nor can any inhabitant walk the streets after that time without a pass from the General;...that last week a poor milch-cow was killed and sold at a shilling sterling a pound;...that the soldiers' duty is hard, always holding themselves in readiness for an attack, which they are continually in fear of.

For at long last Henry Knox had completed the difficult transportation of the cannon captured at Ticonderoga and Crown Point, so that in the newly improved field works on Dorchester Heights powerful batteries could be installed which already dominated the town beneath. The attempt to stage a full-scale assault on this new menace was frustrated by a sudden storm, which pinned the troop-laden whale-boats to the wharfside. The next morning Washington's batteries beat at the town and its defences with a sustained and heavy bombardment, under cover of which new works were pushed forward to Nook's Hill, a promontory which flanked the British lines on Boston Neck.

Obviously the Americans were now in a position to render Boston untenable, and Howe was sufficient of a realist to resign himself to the fact that the time had come to organize the town's evacuation.

By 7th March preparations were well in hand for the removal not only of the Bloodybacks, but of those loyalists whose openly professed sentiments rendered their continued presence on American soil an open invitation to reprisals. With the sick, the convalescents and the women-folk given priority in boarding the waiting transports, by 13th March Long Wharf, together with Hancock's, Wheelwright's and Wills's quays, were all a-swarm as more and more Bloodybacks and grim-faced civilians were herded on to one or other of the seventy-eight over-crowded vessels available;[1] loyalist men and women being forced to confront a dubious future with little more in the way of worldly possessions than the clothes they stood up in, and such few treasured personalia as they could bundle together and carry in their hands.[2] Such military stores as could not be transported, including a hundred pieces of ordnance, were thrown into the sea. Throughout the whole bustle of departure the guns on Dorchester Heights held their fire on the tacit understanding that if there were no bombardment, Boston would be spared being put to the torch.

At the very last moment Lieutenant Adair of the Marines set out to sprinkle the no-man's-land beyond the Town Gate with a liberal sowing of caltrops—four-pointed irons which lay on the ground with one spike jutting upward. 'Being an Irishman', one of his fellow-Officers recorded, 'he began scattering the crowsfeet about the gate towards the enemy, and of course had to walk over them on his return, which detained him so long that he was nearly taken prisoner.' On this somewhat wry note of comedy the British occupation of Boston was brought to an end. With twenty miserably under-strength battalions of Infantry and Marines, plus a handful of Artillery and Light Dragoons, removed from Boston and heading for Halifax, Nova Scotia, not a single Bloodyback re-mained in arms on American soil. Indeed, the only thing of British origin still in unchecked circulation was the English guinea. For such was the distrust already generated for Congressional paper money that the golden effigy of 'Farmer George' had never enjoyed a warmer or more universal popularity.

Pecunia non olet.

---

[1] They averaged a mere 250 tons burden.
[2] In all, 1,100 loyalists were given passage to Halifax.

Sword — and Olive Branch

'We are never ready for war, yet we never have a Cabinet which
dare tell the people this truth.'

Field Marshal Viscount Wolseley

IT IS THE inveterate habit of British Administrations first to commit
themselves to a conflict, and then to start extemporizing the means
wherewith to fight it; ever forgetful of the fact that improvisation
doubles the cost of war while gravely imperilling the chance of victory.
Moreover, time and time again, from the Landen action of 1693 to the
German *Blitzkrieg* of 1940, the initial lack of resources has committed
such few troops as could be put in the field to costly but unrewarding
'holding' actions, to stave off defeat while the country sought frantically
to organize itself for the contest that lay ahead.

The early months of the struggle between Bloodyback and American
militiamen had conformed only too faithfully to traditional pattern.
The march to Lexington and Concord had conferred little military
réclame upon anyone but Brigadier-General Earl Percy, who had extri-
cated Colonel Francis Smith from his predicament with reasonable
finesse. For the Bloodybacks, the Bunker Hill encounter had been no
more than a Pyrrhic victory; thereafter the battered, increasingly sickly
survivors had been immured for over eight months behind their makeshift defences, in a state of military inactivity which had afforded
Washington every opportunity to turn an unwieldy mob of 'embattled
farmers' into something approximating to an organized fighting
force.

The American invasion of Canada by the former British Officer,

Richard Montgomery, and Benedict Arnold, had culminated in their joint appearance before Quebec, garrisoned, in Montgomery's contemptuous term, by 'sailors unacquainted with the use of arms, citizens incapable of a soldier's duty, and a few miserable emigrants'.

Fortunately, at this critical juncture, General Carleton's pitiful garrison of sixty Bloodybacks had been reinforced by four hundred men of the Royal Highland Emigrant Regiment,[1] hastily recruited by Colonel Allan Maclean.

With Montgomery killed and Arnold wounded, the assault on the city had been rebuffed; although the Americans had doggedly maintained its blockade. For the moment Canada had been spared having 'liberty' forced upon her by conquest. But with the St Lawrence frozen over, Quebec had been even further removed from succour from the homeland than beleaguered Boston. For that matter, no such thing as adequate help was immediately available.

King George, with sounder soldierly instincts than the majority of his ministers, had long inveighed against the dangerous weakness of the country in the event of war; and early in the summer of 1775 had pressed that recruiting should begin at once for an Army Establishment which Parliament had grudgingly consented to increase from 33,000 to 55,000. It was an Establishment administered by three Departments, with whom the need for integration and co-operation went almost entirely unrecognized. Although nominally subordinate to the Commander-in-Chief (when there was one), the Master-General of the Ordnance and his Board dealt directly with the personnel of the Artillery and Engineers, as with the supply of guns and certain military stores; and pursued their autonomous way virtually without check. The Treasury Board was responsible for pay and provisions. The Navy Board controlled the overseas transportation of the troops, their horses, clothing, tents and camp equipage.

The Royal Navy itself was a tangle of overlapping rather than interlocking Departments, presided over by the fourth Earl of Sandwich, more generally known by the sobriquet of 'Jemmy Twitcher', after the extremely dubious character in the current theatrical hit, John Gay's *Beggar's Opera*. Unstable, corrupt, an inveterate jobber,

---

[1] The Regiment took rank as the 84th Foot; a second battalion being raised in Nova Scotia, which subsequently served under Cornwallis in Virginia and the Carolinas. Both battalions were disbanded in 1784; the number 84 being bestowed on the 2nd Battalion the York and Lancaster Regiment.

> Too infamous to have a friend,
> Too bad for bad men to commend,

Sandwich's reign at the Admiralty was characterized by falsified Estimates, the commissioning of ships to oblige supporters, but without any intention of fitting them for active service, the appropriation of large sums of money for the repair of vessels which were actually left rotting in harbour, widespread malfeasance in the dockyards, and a score of similar abuses. Sandwich, indeed, had even assented in the reduction in the number of seamen in the Royal Navy's employ from 20,000 to a mere 16,000. Little wonder, therefore, that the November of 1775 should have witnessed the American capture of the unescorted ordnance brig *Nancy*, with her holds crammed with 2,000 muskets, 100,000 flints, 30,000 round shot, 30 tons of musket balls, and an enormous 13-inch, 2,700-lb mortar. Small wonder that the Island of New Providence had fallen without resistance to Ezek Hopkins and his freebooter squadron; that a Philadelphia privateer could raid Bermuda for powder without the slightest effort on the part of the Royal Navy to intervene; that the hands manning a transport full of reinforcements for Howe had left it to the redcoats to fight off an American privateer unaided. Bounties and other minor inducements had failed to bring in the right type of seaman, as a letter to his Admiral from the Captain of H.M.S. *Viper* clearly demonstrates. 'I am very much disturbed', he wrote, 'for Petty Officers as well as Warrant [Officers]. My Carpenter infirm & past duty; my Gunner made from a livery servant—neither seaman nor gunner; my Master hardly a man in years, never an Officer before, made from a boy on one of the guardships, he then keeping a public house at Gosport. Petty Officers I have but one, who owns himself mad at times. A Master's Mate I have not, nor anything I can make a Boatswain's Mate. I have not one person I could trust with the charge of a vessel I might take, to bring her in.'[1]

With the inefficient Graves making the least rather than the best of his limited resources in the New England coastal waters, it had been small consolation to learn of Lieutenant Dawson's successful action off Plymouth, Massachusetts, in which the brig *Hope* had forced ashore and sunk an enemy privateer in the North river; or to know that Captain Tyringham Howe, in the 20-gun *Glasgow*, had more than held his own against Hopkins's armada of two frigates, two brigs and a sloop.

[1] Robert Beatson, *Naval and Military Memoirs* (6 vols.).

In effect, the cheeseparing which had characterized the period immediately following the termination of the Seven Years' War had never been made good in either the Royal Navy or the Army, whose numbers were quite inadequate to meet the demands made upon it.

Two battalions had been despatched to Boston in the August of 1775, and by the end of November the 16th Light Dragoons and five more infantry formations—the 15th, 37th, 53rd, 54th and 57th Foot—had received orders to take ship. Eight more had been directed to embark from Ireland, but out of deference to the Irish Executive the number had been reduced to six—the 9th, 20th, 24th, 34th, 53rd and 62nd Foot. All the formations were under strength; while only one new regiment had been raised, to whit, Frazer's Highlanders, of which there were two battalions.[1]

With Gibraltar and Minorca to garrison, and commitments to be met in India, it was clear that the demands of the theatre of war in North America could only be met by the employment of mercenaries.

The decision was, of course, immediately received with indignant cries of protest, not only in the Provincial Congress, but from many members of the Parliamentary Opposition. Yet it was a procedure 'fully sanctioned by time and custom', from the days of John Hawkwood and his White Company in medieval Italy to the recruitment of the Scottish *Regiment de Douglas* into the French service, and the flight of thousands upon thousands of 'Wild Geese' to fight under the Bourbon lilies, the Austrian eagle, or the red lion and golden castle of Castile. For that matter, the Officer corps and the ranks of the 60th (Royal Americans) had always shown a preponderance of Swiss and German soldiers of fortune; but no American Province had ever protested against the formation's employment in the French and Indian wars, while its services had frequently been called upon in the border disputes between neighbouring States.

The principle of employing mercenaries having been accepted, and the Empress of Russia having proved uncooperative, application was made to certain independent German Princelings. Eventually, an agreement was concluded[2] with the Duke of Brunswick to furnish and equip 3,964 Infantry and 336 unmounted Dragoons, and to supply drafts to

---

[1] The Regiment no longer exists, but it rendered yeoman service in its day.

[2] Dated 9th January, 1776. In due course a considerable number of foreign *chevaliers d'epée* took service with the American forces—von Steuben, Kosciuszko, de Kalb, Pulaski, du Portail, to name no more, and clearly as mercenaries.

make good such losses as might be incurred. Since the levy money was fixed at £7 10s per head, the Landgrave of Hesse-Cassel was equally eager to enter into a contract for twelve thousand men. Subsequently, agreements were ratified with the rulers of Hesse-Hanau, Waldeck, Anspach-Baireuth and Anhalt-Zerbst, which, over the years, sent some thirty thousand German hirelings across the Atlantic. Since the respective Princelings were allowed a fixed sum for every man killed or for every three men wounded,[1] casualty replacements were always promptly forthcoming; although there was no monetary recompense for deserters —who in the aggregate came very appreciably to outnumber the killed and wounded.

Offers of contingents from Bavaria and Wurtemberg were rejected owing to the poor quality of the troops and their equipment.

General Howe and the nine thousand Bloodybacks he had brought away from Boston reached Halifax on 2nd April; but it was not until the end of the month that the reinforcements for Canada were embarked; not until the beginning of May that the first division of Hessians and a composite battalion of Guards set sail for Nova Scotia. Meanwhile Howe lay helpless in Halifax,

> a wretched city. The streets are sandy roads with a row of barracks each side in which cobblers, brewers (who brew with bark a beer that is very good) and the like live. The churches are a couple of houses twenty-odd paces long; the arsenal and Government House fair. Poverty, crude art, want of culture show everywhere. Houses merely boarded in standing on a meadow with no other foundation …All the forts and batteries are just thrown up with fresh sod.[2]

Accommodation was so limited, indeed, that as Howe's forces were gradually increased by new arrivals, many of the troops had to be kept aboard their transports—to the detriment both of their health and their comfort.

A plan of campaign had been formed, with the capture of New York as its ultimate objective. But 'we at present have little more than a month's provisions', Major Charlie Stuart wrote to his father, the Earl of Bute, 'having most of the fugitives from Boston to sustain, and are

---

[1] The Company Commander also received a small sum for each man wounded.

[2] Letter from an anonymous German officer, *Letters of German Troops*, edited Ray W. Pettengill, PhD.

without camp equipment at a very advanced season, and I am very much afraid that if these wants are not speedily supplied, all schemes for this campaign will be rendered abortive...'[1]

Troops and supplies took so long to straggle in that it was not until 10th June that Howe was in a position to set out from Halifax; arriving at Sandy Hook, after what Stuart described as 'a tedious passage', on the 29th of the month.

Meanwhile, Canada had seen the reanimation of activities which had perforce been suspended throughout the worst of the winter; during which, however, Arnold had stolidly maintained the blockade of Quebec. None the less his troops had been so seriously reduced by smallpox and desertion that he was on the point of retiring when three small British vessels forced their way up the ice-cluttered St Lawrence, severing all communication between the two divisions of his force, which lay on opposite banks of the river. The opportunity was too good to miss, and Carleton, with the first of his reinforcements,[2] sallied forth to drive Arnold's men into retreat, capturing the whole of their artillery and stores. With further reinforcements, which appreciably raised the total of troops under command, Carleton pushed up river to engage American forces which had been strengthened by a considerable body of men under General Thomas. A head-on encounter between Thomas and Frazer, at Trois Rivières, ended in Thomas's capture, together with two hundred of his men, and the hasty withdrawal of the remainder to Sorel, the junction of the routes to Lakes Ontario and Champlain. Here Carleton was seized with a most untimely hesitancy, only belatedly despatching columns along both routes; the western force was entrusted to General Burgoyne,[3] who was, however, given strict orders not to fight unless supported by the eastern detachment. But for this ill-judged precaution it is very probable that Burgoyne would have reached Crown Point ahead of the retreating Americans – who had already lost five thousand effectives – and compelled the whole of them to surrender. As it was, operations came temporarily to a halt for want of boats, for which no provision had been made. Once again

[1] *A Prime Minister and his Son*, edited by the Hon. Mrs E. Stuart Wortley, C.B.E.

[2] Carleton was ultimately reinforced by the arrival of the 9th, 20th, 21st, 24th, 29th, 31st, 34th, 47th, 53rd and 62nd British Foot, and a contingent of Brunswicker troops under Baron Riedesel.

[3] Burgoyne had received permission to return from Boston to England in the November of 1775. He proceeded to Canada early in 1776 to act as Second-in-Command to General Carleton.

improvisation was called upon to make good the defects begotten of lack of preparation.

As the fleet, shepherded by Graves's successor, Rear-Admiral Molyneux Shuldham, came to their moorings off Staten Island, the New York 'Jenkeys' (as the German auxiliaries elected to term their opponents) braced themselves for the bloody work which obviously lay ahead.

Royalist Governor Tryon had long since found safety in a warship, while the handful of British troops, which for many months had been in a virtual state of siege in their barracks at Fort George, also sought refuge aboard H.M.S. *Asia*. Known loyalists had been forced to surrender any arms in their private possession, and were entirely at the mercy of the mob, who tarred and feathered them, rode them out of the city on rails, taunted them unmercifully, and had many of them clapped into gaol on trumped up charges their victims were given no real opportunity to refute. By mid-June, it was said, 'hardly a Tory face was to be seen'; but even so a committee was appointed to 'detect conspiracies'. On the Bowling Green a lumpy statue of George III in gilded lead had been torn down, less on aesthetic grounds than because the effigy could be turned into 42,000 bullets so that, as a certain Ebenezer Hazard put it, 'the bloody-backs could have melted Majesty fired into them'.

In the February of 1776 General Charles Lee had arrived in New York to put the city, as far as possible, in a proper state of defence. A former British Officer, who had served under Burgoyne in Portugal, and thereafter hawked his sword in Poland and then in Russia, he had finally removed himself—and his standing grievance against the British Government's failure to recognize his claim to military genius—to America.[1] Cantankerous, self-opinionated and devious, events were to demonstrate that the high opinion originally entertained of him by the quidnuncs of Congress was scarcely justified by events. But he was practical soldier enough to put New York in a reasonable state of defence, paying particular attention to the field works at Brooklyn Heights, guarding the Brooklyn-Manhattan ferry.

Washington himself had arrived in the city, on a tour of inspection, on 25th June; four days before Shuldham and the troop transports had appeared off Sandy Hook.

---

[1] Lee was a born cavalryman. When in the Russian service he wrote to a friend, 'I am to have a command of Cossacks and Wollacks, a kind of people I have a good opinion of. I am determined not to serve in the line infantry; one might as well be a churchwarden.'

Coincidentally with the fleet's arrival in the roads, a British deserter, Thomas Hickey, was hanged before a concourse of twenty thousand for his complicity in a desperate loyalist plot to assassinate the American Commander-in-Chief at his Headquarters in the Kennedy House, Broadway.

Shepherded by a squadron detached by Shuldham, 'On the 3rd of July the transport fleet moved up to the Narrows; the grenadiers and light infantry, under cover of the frigates and sloops of war, being dis-embarked in the greatest order on Staten Island, and effected their landing without opposition. Such of the rebel troops as had been posted on the island fled with the greatest precipitation on the approach of the King's ships. The remainder of the Army was landed in the course of the day, and the whole distributed in cantonments. The Headquarters were at Richmond.'[1]

On the 12th July Admiral Lord Howe—elder brother of 'Good-natured Billy'—arrived in the 64-gun *Eagle* to take over the Naval command. Together with his junior, he had been appointed a 'Commissioner for Restoring Peace', with authority to extend 'full and free pardon from their Sovereign Lord the King' to 'all persons who should desist from rebellion and assist in restoring tranquillity'. The primary difficulty was in lighting upon some means by which His Majesty's 'gracious declaration' could be made generally known. Since, in official British eyes, the acephalous Continental Congress had no substantive existence, no official communication could be addressed to it. So, in his capacity as one of the country's leading citizens, a letter conveying the substance of the manifesto was addressed to 'George Washington Esquire', and sent into New York under a flag of truce. Receipt of the letter, however, was refused, 'Colonel Reed[2] informing Lord Howe's messenger that there was no person in the army with that address'. Seeking a compromise, the courtesy superscription of '&cet,&cet,-&cet' was added to the original form of address. But this produced no greater readiness to accept the missive. ' "You are aware, sir, of the rank of General Washington in our army?" demanded the American repre-sentative. "Yes, sir, we are", answered the British Officer; "I am sure my Lord Howe will lament exceedingly this affair, as the letter is of a civil and not of a military nature".'[3]

Unquestionably, the arrival of a communication couched in this

---

[1] Beatson, *op. cit.*   [2] Washington's Military Secretary.
[3] John Fiske, *The American Revolution* (2 vols.).

particular form placed the American Commander-in-Chief in a peculiarly awkward dilemma. As a knowledgeable, cultivated *homme du
monde* he was perfectly well aware that the contemporary style of
address more often than not omitted the military title, even with a
serving Regular Officer. In Wolfe's correspondence, for example, there
are many references to 'Mr Amherst' and 'Mr Boscawen'. Charles Lee,
a stickler for military punctilio, invariably referred to 'Mr Howe' and
'Mr Burgoyne'; while Washington himself had served on the Staff of
'Mr Braddock', and in so doing must have become familiarized with
this quite usual mode of address. So much so, indeed, that he had himself inscribed a letter from his Cambridge Headquarters to 'The Hon.
William Howe, Esquire'.[1]

But Washington, in rejecting Admiral Howe's letter as being im-
properly addressed in its omission of his military title, was thinking less
of his own dignity than that of a fledgling Congress; it would be a slur
upon his nominators not to insist upon recognition of the rank they had
assigned him. Moreover, in his personal capacity he had no mandate to
negotiate in any other than specifically military matters, and the very
last thing he desired was to flout Congress in the eyes of the British
authorities by arrogating to himself powers with which he had not been
invested.

In any delicate negotiation timing is of the essence, and whatever
hopes might have been entertained from the success of Howe's mission
at the hour of its inception had been rendered nugatory by the time
H.M.S. *Eagle* dropped anchor off the tip of Manhattan Island. For on
4th July, Congress—insidiously egged on by the French mission in
Philadelphia—had promulgated its formal Declaration of Independence.
Although there was anything but unanimity of sentiment and opinion
among the inhabitants of the Thirteen Colonies,[2] the Congressional
pronunciamento had committed them to continued resistance. In turn,
the British were automatically committed to more positive action; and
General Howe set about marshalling his resources.

Reinforcements had reached him, even if not in the number he had
hoped for. For owing to over-extended and faulty communications
several transports had inadvertently headed for deserted Boston; where
a desperate fight had ensued against a flotilla of privateers, which had

[1] Washington's own directives were issued under the heading, 'Orders by his Excellency
George Washington, Esquire, Commander-in-Chief of the forces of the United States'.
[2] As a State, Georgia still hung back.

9*

ended in the death of a number of Officers and men and the surrender of the remainder, including Lieutenant-Colonel Archibald Campbell and two companies of the newly raised Frazer's Highlanders. On the other hand Clinton and Cornwallis had rejoined Howe with the survivors of the abortive attempt on Sullivan Island. With this accretion of strength Howe could dispose of some 25,000 effectives.

It was at this juncture that the question of enlisting loyalists and organizing them regimentally demanded serious attention. At the outbreak of the quarrel between Parliament and the North American Colonies it had been estimated that approximately one third of the population was actively opposed to British pretensions, one third so generally disinterested as to be regarded as neutral, and one third sufficiently loyal to the Throne and existent Constitution to furnish an element upon whom the British authorities could rely for active support.

What was consistently overlooked was the fact that the loyalists were scattered widely throughout the Thirteen Provinces, rarely forming a majority in any one district; while the fealty of a very considerable number of them was rather to the concept of constitutional monarchy — preferably with a Stuart Sovereign — than to the contemporary occupant of England's throne. It is scarcely surprising, therefore, that in due course Captain Mackenzie somewhat dourly noted, 'When the Army was on Staten Island we were made to expect that as soon as we should land on this [Long] Island, many thousands of the Inhabitants would show their loyalty and join the Army. But we have seen very little to induce us to believe that the Inhabitants are more loyal than others.'

Certain New York companies of Loyalists formed part of Howe's forces however, and were destined, in the forthcoming action, to give a reasonably good account of themselves.

With the troops only awaiting the assembly of the special landing craft devised to facilitate the descent on Long Island, the initiative had passed into British hands.

To oppose Howe and his legions Washington could muster some 18,500 effectives out of a nominal total of 28,000; Brooklyn Heights being garrisoned by 7,000 men under General Putnam; while guardianship of the rest of the island had been entrusted to General Sullivan and General Stirling,[1] in command of another 5,000 Provincials. The balance of Washington's force was retained as a garrison for New York.

---

[1] William Alexander, who had seen service in the French and Indian wars, and who claimed the Scottish Earldom of Stirling, by courtesy was known by that name.

A daring thirty-five day reconnaissance up the Hudson—or North River—under Captain Hyde Parker,[1] in the 44-gun *Phoenix*, supported by *Rose* and *Tryal*, had penetrated as far as Tappan Zee, forty miles above New York. A number of small craft were sent to attack the *Phoenix* and the *Rose*; but 'one of they galleys Split her Best Guns, and another received a Shot between Wind & Wharter so that they thought it Best to Retreat'.[2]

Yet the Howes made no use of this opportunity to land troops above New York, which might conceivably have cut off the forces on Long Island *in toto*. It was the British field commander's firm belief that the best way to ensure New York's capture was to inflict defeat on the American host based on Brooklyn Heights. But it was not until 22nd August—too late in the year to inaugurate a campaign—that the leading division of the allied troops was landed at Gravesend Bay, on Long Island, close to the Narrows; their disembarkation covered by three frigates and two bomb-ketches. The force had been organized in seven Brigades and a Reserve embodying the German contingent; with the grenadier and light infantry companies massed in separate battalions.

There was little resistance at the point of landing, the American advance parties retiring to a ring of wooded heights which barred the approach to their lines before Brooklyn; burning all the houses, granaries, and barns as they fell back. The grenadiers and light infantry therefore pushed on to the village of Flatbush, which was occupied in strength as an advanced post. The main body of the troops was then free to land and encamp between the villages of Flatbush and Utrecht, two miles in rear.

Since it was clear that the Americans intended to dispute the wooded heights beyond Flatbush, four days were spent in reconnoitring, and by the 26th Howe had worked out his plan of action.

Three highways led towards Brooklyn, of which the westernmost, or Gowan's Road, skirted the base of the hills close to the coast. This was defended by the force under Stirling. Nearly three miles to the north-east the Flatbush-Flushing Road lead over the very crest of the hills, astride which was the American main body under Sullivan; whose left wing, however, did not extend as far as the Jamaica Road to the east, which traversed the hills a mile from their eastern extremity, passing through them to descend on the village of Bedford.

[1] Subsequently Nelson's Commander-in-Chief at Copenhagen in 1801.
[2] Letter from A. B. Joseph Hodgkin to his wife Sarah, dated Long Island, August 1776.

The interval between Sullivan's left and the neighbouring body of American troops was intermittently patrolled by a handful of rather casual militiamen. These were easily snared on the eve of the general attack, leaving Putnam in complete ignorance that his line of defence embodied an extremely vulnerable gap.

Howe's plan was based upon the exploitation of this flaw in his opponents' line, his aim being to turn the American left. At nine o'clock on the evening of the 26th, therefore, Clinton moved off with the 17th Light Dragoons, the grenadiers and light infantry, together with the 4th, 15th, 27th and 45th Foot of First Brigade, Frazer's Highlanders and fourteen field pieces. Halting two hours before daybreak, he sent a battalion to seize and hold the still undefended gap.

'The way being thus open', Serjeant Lamb subsequently recorded, 'the whole army descended into the level country which led to the American lines at Brooklyn. At half past eight o'clock on the morning of the 27th, the attack was commenced by the light infantry and light dragoons, upon large bodies of the Americans, who retreated towards their camp. Here they were met by the Hessians and exposed to the fire of two parties; Generals Heister and Grant in their front, and General Clinton in their rear; they were immediately thrown in the utmost confusion; and in their efforts to retreat back to their lines at Brooklyn, great numbers were killed or taken prisoner.' As Charles Stuart put it, 'The Rebels were surrounded before they were aware; they made some resistance, and the skirmish continued all day, till, finding they could not retire, 1,400 gave themselves up, and were taken prisoners. Amongst them were Gen. Sullivan, Lord Stirling, and another General, besides many of their best Officers. By all account near 1,500 of them were killed.'[1] Six field guns and twenty-six heavy pieces were also taken. British casualties came to less than four hundred killed and wounded.

Victory had gone to the British in the sort of 'set-piece' Frederickian action for which all their training had been designed to prepare them, although it is scarcely in question that they were materially advantaged by the Americans' failure to make the best use of the terrain they had occupied, very possibly owing to the absence of General Nathanael Greene—on the sick list with a bad attack of malaria—the only one of their leaders with an intimate knowledge of the local countryside. But Howe did not follow up his initial success with any attempt to overrun the American lines preparatory to storming the entrenched position on

[1] A nearer estimate would be 2,000.

Brooklyn Heights. Content with having administered 'a good sharp lesson', which might conceivably promote a greater readiness to reopen negotiations for some form of accommodation, the British Commander had rejected the opportunity to wipe out virtually all the organized opposition that Washington could get into action; and by his very restraint put a premium on the tenacious continuance of the struggle. In warfare 'kid-glove' methods invariably defeat the very purpose they seek to promote.

One thing emergent from the Long Island encounter was the fact that 'Old Put's' generalship had been nowhere equal to the demands made upon it; which may be said to account for the following advertisement appearing in the columns of the contemporary *Middlesex Journal*:

> LOST, an old black dog of the American breed; answers to the name of PUTNAM: had on a yellow collar with the following description, '*Ubi libertas ibi patria*', Long Island, 1776. Is an old domestic animal, barks very much at the name of North, and has a remarkable howl at that of Howe. Was last seen in Long Island some time ago, but is supposed to have been alarmed at some British troops who were exercising there, and ran off towards Hell Gate. As he was a great favourite of the Washington family, they are fearful that some accident has happened to him.

With Howe breaking ground before the Brooklyn defences as though intent on opening formal siege, Washington resolved to evacuate Long Island and concentrate all his troops for the defence of New York. The great question was—could withdrawal be accomplished without sacrifice of a disproportionate number of the American garrison? For with the tide and breeze in their favour the Royal Navy could easily command the Narrows between Brooklyn and New York. As it transpired, however, both elements strove on behalf of the Americans. A strong tide and a powerful north-easterly wind saw to it that Howe's warships kept well clear of the scene of action; as the 'Pea-jackets' of Colonel Glover's Marblehead Regiment—very largely made up of deep-sea mariners and fishermen—toiled to ferry the cream of the patriot forces across the mile of waterway which separated Brooklyn from the mainland.[1]

[1] They were materially assisted in their task by Salem and Danvers seafarers of Hutchinson's 27th Regiment.

Although a localized blanket of mist served to obscure what was going forward, it was an all-night task to transfer the bulk of the American troops and their impedimenta to the Manhattan shore. Even when dawn found a few of the rearguard on the wrong side of the ferry, 'under the friendly cover of a thick fog', one of the last evacuees subsequently recorded, 'we reached the place of embarkation without annoyance from the enemy, who, had the morning been clear, would have seen what was going on, and been enabled to cut off a great part of the rear'.[1]

'It is difficult to understand why the British commanders neglected to provide for this contingency. The large fleet...could have provided a very strong flotilla of armed boats to control the waterway,'[2] and might well have frustrated the whole operation. Possible failure to make such an attempt constituted yet another manifestation of the Howe's deliberate policy of restraint. Thus Washington was allowed to evacuate the best part of nine thousand men, with their supplies and weapons, virtually unimpeded; British gains consisting of no more than a few heavy guns and a handful of stragglers.

Naturally enough, the outcome of the Long Island encounter had seriously lowered both public morale and that of the defeated troops; and Washington, far from contemplating further peace negotiations, was only concerned to devise some stroke by which general confidence in the cause of independence could be substantially restored.

An amphibious raid on the British forces on Staten Island might easily misfire and in any case would be bound to entail heavy casualties. So finally it was decided to attempt the destruction of the British flagship by means of an explosive charge transported and placed in position by the one-man crew of the hitherto untried 'submersible' constructed by the Connecticut inventor-mechanic, David Bushnell.

With Serjeant Ezra Lee at the controls, the *Turtle*, as this strange new craft was named, contrived to approach H.M.S. *Eagle* unseen and unheard. But Lee's laborious attempt to attach the explosive charge to a strake running just below the waterline was completely frustrated by the thick coating of coal-tar and fibre-strands by which the hull was protected against the ravages of the toredo worm,[3] and the attempt had

---

[1] Alexander Graydon, *Memoirs of His Own Times*.

[2] Admiral Sir William James, *The British Navy in Adversity*.

[3] Copper sheathing had first been tried out in 1761, but had not become universal so early as 1776.

eventually to be abandoned. Two other craft were tackled, but with no greater success; and with the dawn light strengthening, Lee had no option but to put back; pursuit of his slow, unwieldy craft, when it was spotted by watchers on Governor's Island, being distinctly discouraged by the explosion of the 150-lb *fougasse*, which Lee had slipped into his wake after setting in motion the time clock which would ensure its detonation.

As the story of Ezra Lee's gallant failure swiftly circulated, its stimulative effect was almost as great as if the whole venture had proved an overwhelming success.[1]

If Howe had entertained the hope that the restraint exercised after his Long Island victory would encourage Congress to reopen negotiations for a settlement, he was to be speedily undeceived. Nothing but the capture of Washington's entire army would have persuaded the politicians in Philadelphia to parley; and the bulk of Washington's force had been safely transferred to New York. It is true, as Captain Mackenzie noted in his diary, that 'the Rebel Army' was 'much dispirited by their late defeat and the abandonment of their lines at Brooklyn, which had cost them so much time and pains'; and that the number of deserters exhibited a noticeable increase.

But the *pourparlers* on Staten Island, of 11th September, between the Howes and Benjamin Franklin, John Adams and Edward Rutledge led nowhere; the issue had become one which only the sword could decide.

Haarlem Creek, separating Manhattan Island from the mainland, was spanned by two bridges only; and General Howe quickly realized that were it possible to seize the northerly one at Kingsbridge by a *coup de main*, any garrison left in New York would lie at his mercy.

It was the Council of War of Congress which had rejected Washington's and Nathanael Greene's proposal to put New York to the torch and regroup the troops garrisoning it in a defensive position to the north. So five thousand men were retained in the city, with ten thousand concentrated at Kingsbridge, and the remainder scattered piecemeal about Manhattan Island. The Hudson River was navigable to ocean-going vessels for the best part of a hundred miles, so two redoubts, Fort Lee and Fort Washington, were erected eight miles above New York to close the waterway; while at the latter an armed

[1] For a detailed account of this curious episode see 'Submarine Offensive A.D. 1776', by Reginald Hargreaves. (*U.S. Navy Magazine*, vol. VI, no. 3. March 1963.)

camp was speedily added. In effect, the amateur strategists of the Council of War had committed the primary fault of seeking to be strong everywhere at one and the same time, which meant in practice that they were equally weak at all points.

On 15th September Admiral Howe sent some of his men-of-war up the Hudson to Bloomingdale, four miles above New York; while other vessels penetrated the Narrows to reach Turtle Bay, where the Americans were driven from their trenches by concentrated naval gunfire. Troops were then hurried across to Kips Bay, some three miles above New York, and set about throwing a cordon across the island to Bloomingdale.

As the Bloodybacks pushed on across country to 'close the neck of the bag', a *sauve qui peut* ensued among the refugees from Kips Bay and Putnam's demoralized forces in New York, in a frenzied dash to the safety of Haarlem Heights. Even the prompt appearance of the Commander-in-Chief at the landing point was not enough to stop the rot. In his rage and despair he drew his pistols on the fugitives, flailing at them with his cane and beating at Officers as well as privates, in an agonized attempt to halt the rush. But for the stout rearguard action put up by Glover's 'Pea-jackets', Putnam's unruly mob would have been cut off to a man. As it was, a narrow corridor of escape was held open long enough to permit all but three hundred of the fugitives to scramble through to safety; although a considerable quantity of small arms and military stores—including Knox's cherished heavy cannon—fell into British hands.

It was Howe's aim to secure control of the Hudson and by moving up country to the east of the waterway, to secure a junction with Carleton's forces moving down Lake Champlain and Lake George on Albany. This would cut-off New England, the heart of the rebellion, from all support from the more southerly Provinces.

Howe therefore progressively extended his right; a movement with which Washington perforce had to conform, with the effect that the Colonial Army, in a vain attempt to cover the solar plexus of New England as well as the Hudson Valley and New Jersey, found itself extended on an eighteen-mile line, far too wide a front for the numbers available to man it.

At this juncture Howe's general plan suffered delay owing to a *contretemps* he can scarcely be blamed for not anticipating. 'A little after 12 o'clock last night', Captain Mackenzie recorded on 20th September, 'a most dreadful fire broke out in New York, in three different places in the South, and windward part of the Town. The alarm was soon given, but unfortunately there was a brisk wind at South, which spread the flames with such incredible rapidity, that notwithstanding every assistance was given which present circumstances admitted, it was impossible to check the Progress 'till about 11 this day.'

The fire—which was almost certainly the work of supporters of the cause of independence—broke out in several places simultaneously near the Exchange,[1] consuming all the houses on the west side of Broad Street almost as far as the City Hall. Thence it roared onwards to engulf the dwellings in Beaver Street and almost every building on the western side of the town between Broadway and the Hudson, as far as the College, whose open grounds helped materially to check the conflagration's headlong progress.

Both soldiers and Royal Navy men were quickly marshalled to tackle the outbreak; and the Army sent in a hundred waggons to help remove such of the inhabitants' household goods as could be saved; a task in which the Bloodybacks' unstinted labours proved invaluable.

Dearth of fire engines, however, and lack of water supply severely hampered the fire-fighters' efforts to bring the blaze under control. Some of the incendiaries 'were caught by the Soldiers in the very Act of setting fire to the inside of empty Houses at some distance from the Fire...One or two who were found in houses with Fire-brands in their hands were put to death by the infuriated Soldiery and thrown into the Flames.'[2] In all, some six hundred houses were destroyed, constituting, with various other buildings, close on one fourth of the city.

In addition to this hindering disaster, 'Good-natured Billy' was confronted with the repugnant obligation to confirm the death sentence passed on Nathan Hale, the very gallant espionage agent Washington had sent to Long Island to report on the activities in the British camp established at Brooklyn. A self-confessed spy, there could be no alternative to his condemnation to the gallows.

There was also the question of raising three battalions of Loyalists and selecting from among them those best fitted to undertake the responsibility of Commissioned rank. As Brigade Commander the choice fell on Oliver De Lancy, a wealthy landowner of Bloomingdale and and brother of Chief Justice De Lancy.

It was not, indeed, until the October arrival of a fresh contingent of

[1] And on a wharf near Whitehall Slip.   [2] Mackenzie, *op. cit.*

Hessians, a number of Officer replacements, and the 16th Light Dragoons, that Howe once more prepared to take the field. Advancing from the Bronx at the head of a force of thirteen thousand men, at considerable cost[1] he succeeded in driving Washington from his strongly-prepared position at White Plains, at the foot of the Western Highlands. A renewed attack ordered for the 31st had to be postponed owing to an exceptionally heavy and persistent rain storm; and on 1st November Washington crossed the Croton River and established himself in a position from which it was deemed impractical to dislodge him. But with the German General Knyphausen in firm possession of Kingsbridge and Howe himself at Dobb's Ferry, on the eastern bank of the Hudson, ready either to attack Fort Washington or cross the waterway into New Jersey, the American Commander-in-Chief was in an extremely embarrassing position. His aim was to make safe three principal objects—to secure his line of retreat northwards into the Highlands on the *east* bank of the Hudson, to safeguard his supply line from the *north-east*, while at the same time maintaining his communications with the terrain *west* of the Hudson. Howe, in effect, had taken up a position from which a telling blow could be struck in any one of several directions. Willy-nilly, Washington was committed to a dispersion of force, which left Lee with seven thousand men on the Croton, detached three thousand to Peekskill to guard the Highlands, and sent Putnam with another contingent across the Hudson to take post at Hackensaw, about seven miles south-west of Fort Lee, in New Jersey. Given freedom of action and the Commander-in-Chief would have evacuated both Fort Lee and Fort Washington, particularly the latter. But Greene and some of the other Generals were strongly of opinion that it should be held. Even more important, so was the opiniated Council of War of Congress. Washington, who joined Greene near Fort Lee on 14th November, had no option but reluctantly to acquiesce.

Fort Washington, built up on two parallel ridges, with its rugged approaches covered in many places by dense forest, constituted a formidable obstacle; with the five-bastioned central work, lying on the river, covered by three lines of abattized entrenchments.

For his part Howe had constructed field works and batteries on the eastern bank of Haarlem Creek, to cover an attack from that direction; and on 15th November he summoned Fort Washington, threatening to

---

[1] British loss, 214 killed and wounded, Hessians 99 killed and wounded. The Americans admitted to 140 killed.

put the whole garrison to the sword unless it were surrendered. A defiant answer being returned, at daybreak on the 19th the guns of H.M.S. *Pearl*, on the Hudson, supported by those on Haarlem Creek, opened up a heavy fire.

With the infantry closing in on every side—five thousand Hessians against the north front of the Fort; the Guards and 33rd Foot, with the grenadiers and light troops, pressing on the east; the 42nd Highlanders a little to the south, and a brigade of Hessians and nine British battalions[1] under Earl Percy thrusting up from due south—the Americans were greatly advantaged by the difficult nature of the ground to be traversed and the skill of their marksmen in thinning the ranks of their opponents with scarcely a single shot wasted.

The Hessians in particular suffered severely. Led by General Knyphausen, 'they had to pass an almost impervious wood, which was rendered more dangerous by abbatis of brush-wood and felled timber, covering both sides of the declivity. Nevertheless, after great labour, they penetrated through the wood, and fixed themselves on the top of the ascent. The second division was equally successful; the light infantry made good their landing, and forced the enemy from their rocks and trees up a steep and rugged mountain.'[2] Percy had cleared all the entrenchments on his sector of the front; and 'their outworks being carried, the Americans retreated from their lines and crowded into the Fort; Colonel Rahl, who led the right column of General Knyphausen's attack, pushed forward and lodged his column within one hundred yards of the Fort, where he was soon after joined by the left column'.[3] On the eastern flank, 'the Guards and light infantry drove all before them';[4] and nothing was left to the hemmed-in garrison but virtually unconditional surrender.

American losses amounted to about 3,300 killed, wounded and captured, of whom two hundred prisoners—including ninety Officers— had been taken during the course of the assault; which had cost Howe's forces 458 killed and wounded, two-thirds of the loss falling on the Hessians.

Howe lost no time in following up this successful stroke. For while operations were going forward on the east bank of the Hudson, 'Lord Cornwallis, with a considerable force, passed over the North River in

---

[1] The 4th, 10th, 15th, 23rd, 27th, 28th, 38th, 52nd, and Frazer's Highlanders.

[2] C. Stedman, *The History of the Origin, Progress, and Termination of the American War* (2 vols.).   [3] Lamb, *op. cit.*   [4] Mackenzie, *op. cit.*

order to attack Fort Lee, and make a further impression on the Jerseys. The garrison, consisting of two thousand men, were saved by an immediate evacuation, at the expense of their artillery[1] and stores.'[2]

With a remnant of resentful and dispirited troops, Washington drew warily back towards the Delaware River, pursued—if so extravagant a term can be legitimately employed—by a plodding Cornwallis; with one eye anxiously fixed on the Croton, where Charles Lee, at the head of a respectable body of troops, dallied in puzzling inaction. It is true that, based on North Castle, he was so poised that he could, if he chose, move against Cornwallis's flank and rear. Moreover, he had every confidence that once he took the field—even with no more than seven thousand men under his command—victory would easily be his. Cornwallis he regarded as a mere bummeler. As for 'Good-natured Billy', he once wrote, 'Howe shut his eyes, fought his battles, drank his bottle, had his little whore, advis'd with his Counsellors, receiv'd his orders from North and Germain, one more absurd than the other, shut his eyes and fought again'.[3]

For the moment, Lee was far too busy intriguing with certain of the military and members of the Congress to supplant, as Commander-in-Chief, the leader who with infinite skill had contrived to pilot his stricken army safely to the far side of the Delaware. Moreover, he had taken every craft on the river with him, leaving his pursuers to gape across the empty waterway at the camp rapidly forming in the neighbourhood of Thomas Barclay's 'Summer Seat', in the region subsequently to be known as Morrisville.

It was at this juncture that, 'acting on information received', a strong patrol of the 16th Light Dragoons set out from the British lines under the command of Colonel Harcourt, the advance guard headed by the swashbuckling Banastre Tarleton. Their objective was White's Tavern at Baskenridge,[4] where report had it that General Lee was lodged in some isolation from his troops.

Entirely unimpeded, Harcourt's troopers clattered up to the inn, where the men of Lee's escort, lazing in the pallid rays of the December sun, mistook them for a contingent of the Connecticut Dragoons, whose uniforms—save for the curve of the sabre—closely resembled

[1] One hundred and forty cannon.
[2] Lamb, *op. cit.*
[3] The Lee Papers. (New York Historical Society.)
[4] Sometimes known as Basking Ridge.

those worn by the British. Alarmed by the scuffle consequent on the rounding up of his guards, Lee—who, in a *négligé* of slippers, breeches and flannel *robe de chambre*, had been engaged in the congenial task of penning a conspiratorial letter to Horatio Gates—swiftly sought a hiding-place in the chimney. It was from this inadequate refuge that he was plucked by the men of his own erstwhile Regiment. 'Without his hat or outside coat', he was bundled on to a spare horse and hurried away to the British camp; a remarkably crestfallen figure, haunted by a guilty fear that the fate awaiting him might well be that of a deserter from His Majesty's Army.[1]

In the event, Lee was to be exchanged in 1778 for the bullying block-headed Major-General Prescott, kidnapped from his quarters on Rhode Island in the July of 1777. It is virtually impossible to determine which side had the worse of the bargain.

Benedict Arnold may well have rued the five thousand casualties his headlong and unsuccessful plunge into Canada had cost him. But he was not the man to throw in his hand; and by the end of September he had been able to botch together no less than sixteen small vessels,[2] mounting seventy guns between them, with which to dispute the mastery of the Lakes.

But Carleton was in possession of far superior resources, both in material and the craftsmen to handle it. Gunboats sent out from England had been dismantled, dragged up to Lake Champlain in sections, and there reassembled. By the beginning of October, therefore, he was ready to meet Arnold with a superior Naval armament and a force of twelve thousand men.

Gates's orders were that Arnold was to stay at the lower end of the Lake, retiring on Ticonderoga if in any doubt of getting the better of his opponents. But although the New Haven 'General-at-Sea' complained that 'We have a wretched motley crew in the fleet, the Marines the refuse of every regiment, and the seamen very few of them ever wet with salt water', he was not one to try and evade an encounter even

---

[1] The *Freeman's Journal* solemnly recorded that the British were so jubilant at Lee's capture that they celebrated the event by 'making his horse as drunk as they were themselves'. When it became necessary to fit out the captive with a few necessary garments the regimental tailors of the 16th refused to 'work for such a rascal'.

[2] Two of the vessels had been captured from the British in the year previous. The armament was made up of three schooners, a sloop, three galleys, a cutter and eight gondolas.

with more powerful adversaries. Thus in early October the American armada had set out up the Lake, the hastily rigged galley *Trumbull* in the lead, and Arnold wearing his flag in the schooner *Royal Savage*.

With news that the British force was cruising in the vicinity, Arnold had taken up a strong defensive position west of Valcour Island, whence he had been able to observe the enemy force—led by the ship-rigged *Inflexible*, armed with a battery of 12-pounders—sailing southwards towards Crown Point.

As Arnold's *Royal Savage* had emerged from the bluffs which had sheltered her the British flotilla had come about into the wind, opening up with their heavier pieces. Hard hit by the *Inflexible*'s 12-pounders, Arnold's flagship had been driven on to the tip of Valcour Island, where she grounded and had to be abandoned, Arnold himself transferring to the galley *Congress*.

As the British had clawed their way into the narrow channel, the action had become general; the *Congress* alone being hulled a dozen times and taking seven shots between wind and water. The fight, across a mere hundred yards of water, had been kept up doggedly, hour after hour, with heavy damage wrought by both sides; one British gunboat, armed with brass field pieces and a howitzer, being sunk. In another vessel all the Officers had been hit with the exception of Midshipman Edward Pellew, who had taken over command and continued to fight his ship with outstanding bravery and skill.[1] It had been when the *Inflexible*, catching a favourable gust, had closed to within short range that the struggle had been brought to a summary end. After five of her broadsides, the American line had fallen silent. With sixty of his men killed or wounded, the *Royal Savage* set ablaze and the gondola *Philadelphia* sent to the bottom, Arnold had been only too thankful to take advantage of nightfall and a heavy mist to steal past the English vessels and push on down the Lake. With dawn revealing that their quarry had stolen a march on them, Captain Thomas Pringle's flotilla had immediately given chase, forcing Arnold to abandon what was left of his armament and take to the woods.[2]

But the delay the American leader had imposed on the British advance had frustrated the design for a junction between Howe's and Carleton's

[1] In 1793 Pellew's good service in the Mediterranean was rewarded with a knighthood, and in 1814 he was gazetted full Admiral and created Viscount Exmouth.

[2] Of the 16 American vessels all but three were taken or destroyed.

forces on the upper Hudson. The season was too far advanced to permit of any further campaigning, and both British commanders retired into their respective winter quarters.

With New York in British possession, William Tryon had been reappointed Governor; although for all practical purposes the city was under military direction and control. By virtue of an amendment to the Prohibitory Act,[1] permission had been given for local merchants to reopen trade with foreign ports; although a really healthy revival of commerce was stultified to a very considerable degree by the enterprising activity of the ever-increasing swarm of American privateers. In consequence, the price of all commodities rose steeply; a state of affairs in no sense alleviated by the steady inflow of refugee loyalists, swarming in from Westchester and the Jerseys. Their influx also added appreciably to the problem of accommodation, already rendered sufficiently acute by the great fire of 20th September. For from a population which had declined to approximately five thousand, the number of civilians seeking sanctuary in New York speedily rose to twelve thousand; and the best part of a quarter of the town lay in incinerated ruin. Unhappily, the 'Tories' were just as open to pillage by roaming Bloodybacks as were those of less loyalist cast. For certain veterans of the 64th Foot were only too ready to avenge themselves on the civil population for the indignities to which they had been subjected by the Boston mob in 1769. Until Howe clamped down on such delinquencies, loyalists were abused and plundered just as freely as those suspected of supporting the cause of independence.

A second fire, which had been started accidentally, early in August, had added to the devastation in the region of Cruger's Wharf, Little Dock and Dock Street; and the whole wasted area had degenerated into a sordid 'Alsatia', where drunkards and deserters mingled with the Bloodybacks, who took their pleasure with the many refugees who had been driven to prostitution as the only means of keeping body and soul together.

The City Vestry did what it could for the many indigent, helped privately by the more responsible among the soldiery; the aged poor being supported by the fines exacted for the infringement of military regulations—which extended to the control of retail prices and the penalization of those who sought to exceed them.

The great fear was of further incendiarism. So the two hundred and

[1] 16 Geo. III, Stat. I, cap. 5.

sixty men of the Fire Companies were not only exempted from military service, save in an emergency, but supplemented by eighty Fire Wardens, who regularly patrolled the town's seven Wards.

Honoured with the red ribbon of the Bath for his capture of New York,[1] 'Good-natured Billy' relaxed in company with his 'Cleopatra', in full enjoyment of his long sessions over the post-prandial port, and at the card table. The news that Washington had been empowered to 'raise and collect sixteen battalions of Infantry;...appoint all Officers below the rank of Brigadier; and take, wherever he may be, whatever he may want for the use of the Army', left the Britisher Commander-in-Chief quite unperturbed. If the constant stream of deserters stealing into New York were anything to go by, 'the Gentleman from Virginia' would experience more difficulty in retaining the men in his ranks than he had undergone in persuading recruits to join them in the first place. Moreover, the proclamation offering pardon and protection to all citizens who, within sixty days, declared their readiness to swear an oath of allegiance to the British Crown, had already been responded to by over three thousand sail-trimming waverers.

With an eye to future developments, on 1st December Howe despatched Clinton, at the head of six thousand men, to take possession of Rhode Island. Occupied without opposition, the welcome accorded the Bloodybacks by a predominantly Quaker population was almost as chilly as the New England winter to which they found themselves committed.

In New York, on the other hand, as preparations for the Christmas festivities went busily forward, the military outlook had never seemed more promising.

Christmas was barely over, however, before there came the stunning news that on the night of 25th December Washington had headed a dash across the Delaware to raid and rout the Hessian outpost at Trenton, capturing commander, men and stores — not to mention a full-size brass band — in a dynamic lightning stroke which had paralysed all opposition.

From rosy dreams of present well-being and future success, no man can have experienced more rude an awakening than 'Good-natured Billy' Howe.

---

[1] This was taken almost as a personal affront by Edmund Burke, as by Charles James Fox, who had stigmatized intelligence of the Brooklyn victory as 'terrible news'.

11

Mid-Channel

'The statesman has nothing in his gift but disaster so soon as he leaves his own business of creating or obviating wars, and endeavours to conduct them.'

General Sir Ian Hamilton, G.C.B.

WASHINGTON'S slashing counterstroke at Trenton was precisely the tonic needed to restore the separatists' confidence — and persuade a good number of timorous sail-trimmers hastily to conceal, or destroy, the certificates of loyalty recently issued to them from Howe's Headquarters.

Something had obviously to be done, and done quickly, to restore British prestige. But if Howe had been at fault in manning his advanced posts with Germans more interested in 'maroding' than in keeping a wary eye on their opponents, he displayed equally poor judgment in sending the pedestrian Cornwallis to 'restore the situation'.

With Trenton's fall, Colonel von Donop, in command at neighbouring Bordentown, had hastily fallen back on Princeton, abandoning his sick and wounded. By the time Cornwallis had brought his troops from Princeton to Trenton — seriously harassed *en route* by a force under Nathanael Greene — Washington had taken up position behind the Assunpink waterway, with sufficient show of strength to deter any attack by the British until the morrow could bring them reinforcements.

But Washington was intent in outmanœuvring an opponent he was not yet prepared openly to encounter. Leaving his watch-fires briskly burning, he set out on a forced march, under cover of darkness, which would take him around Cornwallis's left flank and bring him to Princeton, where his desperate want of stores could be made good.

281

At sunrise Colonel Charles Marwood's 17th Foot—part of the column marching to Cornwallis's support—perceiving in their rear what they took to be a stray party of Americans, faced about to attempt their round-up. Actually, the hostile contingent consisted of the left flank-guard of Washington's advance guard, stalwart Virginia troops under that doughty veteran of the Monongahela campaign, General Hugh Mercer.

As the two forces sighted each other through the thinning mist, they promptly swung into action, Mercer's men taking up a defensive position in an orchard facing the Trenton road and opening a brisk fire. But there was no quailing on the part of the Bloodybacks. Closing to point-blank range, they paused only to loose one crashing volley and then went in headlong with the bayonet. Such was the impetus of their onslaught that Mercer's Virginians faltered and began to give way; and over-excited by the success so far achieved, the two hundred and twenty-four men of the 17th burst through the orchard to behold the whole of Washington's main body strung out along the valley road a few hundred yards away. Outnumbered by nearly twenty to one, the idea of turning tail never even occurred to the Leicestershire men, who opened up such a hail of musketry on the leading enemy brigade that for the moment it wavered and hung back.

It was a critical situation for the American Commander-in-Chief; for if the 'green' militia faltered before inferior numbers, the cause of the Colonists in arms would be in serious jeopardy. Without a moment's hesitation Washington rode straight into the press of disordered men, and by rousing exhortation and unflinching personal example, steadied the tumbled ranks and swung them into action.

Overlapped on both flanks, the men of the 17th grimly closed their files and turned to fight their way out of the trap their own uncalculating valour had sprung for them. Throwing off their encumbering knapsacks, they gave three rousing cheers and charged; a tossing spume of scarlet about which the sombre mass of the militia closed in purposefully. It was thrust and stab and cleave a path clear with cold steel and musket butt; and if many fell by the way, the majority won through, bearing their Colours with them. At their best pace, the battle-weary survivors made their way to Trenton, stoically reporting to Cornwallis for immediate duty.[1]

With Washington concentrated to the north, at Morristown, and

[1] One Officer and 35 men fell captive to the Americans and there were 66 casualties.

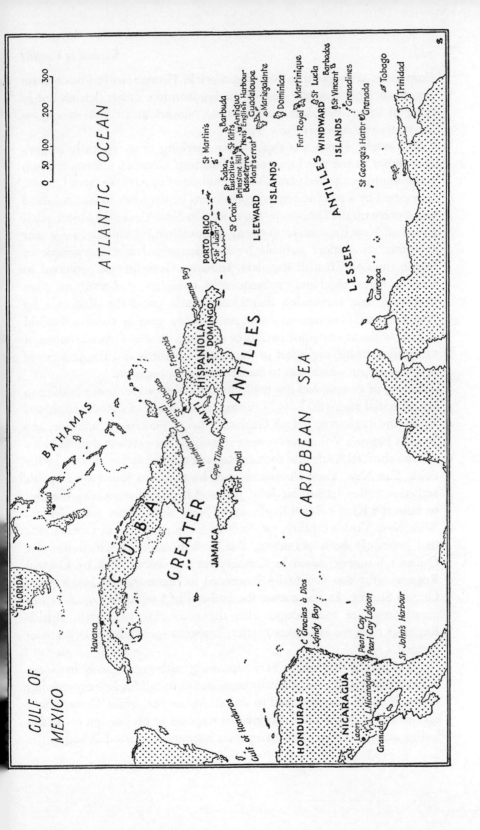

Cornwallis withdrawn to New Brunswick, Howe resolved to contract his advance posts on the west of the Hudson to a rather narrow line in front of Staten Island, from Amboy to Newark and Paulus Hook, on the waterway opposite New York.

In a sense, Howe was deliberately marking time. As early as 30th November in the previous year he had sent Germain a memorandum outlining his projected plans. These envisaged an advance from Canada, supported by a complementary movement by the force in Rhode Island and a drive up the Hudson by the troops in New York; the object being to cut off New England from the more Southern Provincials. To render this combined effort possible he had demanded a reinforcement of fifteen thousand British Regulars. Initially, Germain had promised to furnish eight thousand, subsequently reducing this total to three thousand, and suggesting that Howe made good the difference by raising Loyalist formations – and, presumably, putting them in the field *ec dum*, without any prior period of training. It was a manifestation of Germain's stultifying belief in the loyalist element as a decisive factor in the struggle which was to harden into an obsession.

Howe, of course, had not neglected this obvious means of adding to his potential strength. Loyalist units – Alan Maclean's Royal Highland Emigrant Regiment, Joseph Gorham's Royal Fencible Americans, and Francis Legge's Volunteers – were already doing garrison duty in Nova Scotia, thus releasing the former Regular garrisons for service in the field. The New York Volunteers had hastened to join Howe on his arrival at Staten Island; Sir John Johnson had been awarded a Warrant to raise the King's Royal Regiment of New York in the June of 1776. With New York's capture, recruitment for further Loyalist formations had promptly been organized, the most notable of which was the Queen's Rangers, raised in Connecticut and New York by Colonel Rogers, who was eventually succeeded in command by Major John Graves Simcoe. In due course the embryo of a separate Loyalist command structure took shape with the seconding of certain British Regulars to serve as Muster-master, Inspector-general and Paymaster-general.

On paper, all this looked very promising; although in most instances the raw material was so militarily unskilled as to call for lengthy training before it could be committed to action. Moreover, while 'Government assumed that they would continue to respond in proportion to British inducements to serve, more often their response was conditioned by the counter-exertions of the revolutionaries, the location of operations, and the type of support required'.[1]

The loyalist whose property had been pillaged by marauding Bloody-backs or prehensile Hessians, as well as by his own compatriots, would comprehensibly be unenthusiastic about committing himself to either side. Moreover, not a few alleged loyalists were guilty of seeking to foist troop-raising schemes on the British authorities, whose real purpose was to furnish the promoters with lucrative military employment involving the minimum of personal risk.

Another extremely vexatious problem with which the British Com-mander-in-Chief and his senior subordinates had to contend was the steadily deteriorating relationship between the Bloodybacks and the German auxiliaries. Unwilling conscripts, with no real interest in the struggle between Britain and the Thirteen Colonies, the 'Husshins' – as the Americans in general termed them – made easy prey for the artfully-turned propaganda to which Congress insidiously subjected them. To peasants, torn from their native holdings to don a detested uniform, the promise of a substantial land-holding in return for their withdrawal from active participation in the contest put a premium on desertion, which steadily increased as the months went by. This did nothing to dissolve the attitude of dislike and distrust with which so many of the Bloodybacks regarded the comrades-in-arms they were prone to con-sider quite as unreliable in action as they were incompatible in camp and billet.

On the auxiliaries' side there was bitter resentment for what one of their chaplains described as 'the proud, insulting look the English are wont to cast on the Germans. This not infrequently caused a bloody scene. A Subaltern of the Jäger, to whom an Englishman in his cups said, "God-damn you, Frenchy, you take our pay!", replied coldly and boldly, "I am a German, and you are a sot". Both drew on the spot and the Englishman received such slashes that he died of his wounds.' The diarist adds, 'Not only was the brave German pardoned by the English General, but strict orders were published that the English should treat the Germans as brothers'[2] – a vain hope with those Bloodybacks with Jacobite sympathies, to whom the Teuton, on the throne or in camp or billet, was something alien and unacceptable.

Denied the Bloodyback reinforcements he considered needful, Howe

---

[1] Paul H. Smith, *Loyalists and Redcoats*.
[2] Pettengill, *op. cit.*

contented himself with the organization of raids on the enemy stores at Peekskill—fifty miles above New York—and Danbury, in Connecticut, which was put to the torch. In return, the Americans successfully swooped on the stores and shipping at Sag Harbour, on Long Island.

It was presumably the lack of any major operation which prompted the contemporary poetaster to pen the lines:

> Awake, awake, Sir Billy,
> There's forage in the plain.
> Ah! leave your little filly,
> And open the campaign.
> Heed not a woman's prattle,
> Which tickles in the ear,
> But give the word for battle,
> And grasp the warlike spear.

In the November of 1776 Burgoyne had received permission to return to England before the ice in the river St Lawrence rendered passage of the waterway an impossibility. He took with him a memorandum entitled 'Thoughts for Conducting the War from the Side of Canada', an able 'appreciation of the situation' in the north-east, and a plan for its conquest which immediately won the Sovereign's interest and support. Even Germain condescended to approve, although not without insisting on certain radical alterations in the plan which seriously constricted its flexibility, and by so doing jeopardized its chances of success.

The overall design, however, was adopted; and Germain wrote to Carleton—whom he personally detested[1]—informing him of the number of troops to be allocated to Burgoyne and of those to be retained in Canada; adding that it had become 'highly necessary that the most speedy Junction of the two Armies [i.e. Howe's and Burgoyne's] should be effected'. At the end of the letter he added, 'I shall write to Sir William Howe by the next packet'. As it transpired, that is precisely what he failed to do.

In his acknowledgment of this communication, Carleton pointed out with unimpugnable good sense that 'any Officer entrusted with supreme

---

[1] Carleton was in bad odour with the Cabinet owing to his failure to press on and capture Ticonderoga in 1776. He was personally detested by Germain, one of whose protégés had failed to win Carleton's favour, even though especially recommended to his notice by the Minister.

command ought upon the spot to see what was most expedient to be done better even than a great General at three thousand miles distance'. And there would be few — other than Germain himself — to put the 'Great Incompetent of Minden' in the category of 'great Generals'.

Burgoyne arrived back in Quebec on 6th May; and whatever his private feeling of disappointment and chagrin, Carleton supported his junior's preparations for his forthcoming campaign with a soldierly loyalty which grudged nothing to the cause which both men had at heart. With some seven thousand troops to organize for the difficult venture which lay ahead, 'Gentleman Johnny' and his 'family' were kept at remarkably full stretch.

The gravamen of Burgoyne's design was the junction of his own with Howe's army moving up the Hudson to make contact with the Canada-based force somewhere in the neighbourhood of Albany. Carleton and Burgoyne were, of course, in possession of orders to this effect; but, incredible as it may seem, no such directive ever reached Howe. As William Knox, the Under Secretary for the Colonial Department, subsequently revealed, 'There certainly was a weak place in Lord Sackville's [Germain's] defence, which was want of an official communication to Howe of the plan and Burgoyne's instructions, with orders for his co-operation'. After Burgoyne had been appointed to his command, and the necessary documents were being drawn up, Knox discloses that, 'when all was prepared and I had them to compare and make up, Lord Sackville [Germain] came down to the office on his way to Stoneland, when I observed to him that there was no letter to Howe to acquaint him with the plan or what was expected of him in consequence of it. His Lordship stared and D'Oyly[1] started but said he would in a moment write a few lines. "So", says Lord Sackville, "my poor horses must stand in the street all the time, and I shan't be to my time anywhere." D'Oyly then said he had better go, and he would write from himself to Howe and inclose copies of Burgoyne's Instructions which would tell him all that he would want to know, and with that his Lordship was satisfied, as it enabled him to keep his time, for he would never bear delay or disappointment.'[2]

Whether D'Oyly ever wrote the missive, or, if he did, how it got lost between being 'fair copied' and sealed for despatch, does not emerge;

---

[1] Deputy Secretary.
[2] Knox MS., B.M. See also Lord Edmond Fitzmaurice's *Life of William, Earl of Shelburne*.

only the fact that it was never delivered into William Howe's hands. Considering that a contemporary note from the Secretary-at-War to the Secretary for America, 'inclosing the Last Return of the Forces under Sir William Howe', had a postscript which ran 'Inclosure mislaid',[1] it would seem that the care of State documents was sometimes slipshod, to say the least.

In Canada the difficulty in securing the services of sufficient *batteaux* men, adequate wheeled transport or enough spare gun-teams, combined with a spell of particularly rainy weather to retard the Northern Army's departure from its base until late June. This delay afforded Burgoyne ample time in which to produce a proclamation addressed to 'the hardened enemies of Great Britain', who were sternly warned to make submission lest they fall victims to the 'Messengers of Justice and Wrath which await them in the Field'. Greeted with more hilarity than awe, when copies of this grandiloquent effusion reached certain members of the Opposition it promptly earned for its author the title of 'the Hurlo-Thrumbo of North America'[2] – 'the Chrononhotonthologos of War'.[3]

Far more serious was the fact that Burgoyne's whole plan of campaign was the common gossip of both Montreal and Quebec, 'almost as accurately', he indignantly protested, 'as if it had been copied from the Secretary of State's letter'. The leak, of course, had originated in London; for as a contemporary diarist perceptively recorded, 'We have more dangerous enemies at home than any we have to encounter abroad'.[4] American 'Intelligence' was, of course, fully acquainted with all that had been planned; and the only man who remained in total ignorance of the grand design, its limitations and possibilities, was General Howe.

Burgoyne's field force consisted of the 9th, 20th, 21st, 24th, 47th, 53rd and 62nd Foot; whose flank Companies – plus those of the garrison units – had been detached to form a corps of grenadiers and light infantry under Major Acland and the Earl of Balcarres. The artillery complement was made up of fifty-four field pieces – apart from some heavier

[1] Dated 14th May, 1777. P.R.O. CO/5, V, 169. No. 48.
[2] From the Haymarket Theatre burlesque of that name, by Mr (not Doctor) Samuel Johnson.
[3] From Henry Carey's *The King of Queerummania*.
[4] Thomas Anburey, *Travels Through the Interior Parts of America*.

metal for service on the Lakes[1] — tended by 511 rank and file, including a hundred Germans. The British forces were organized in three Brigades, under Major-General Phillips — 'Phillips of Minden'[2] — and Brigadier-Generals Frazer and Hamilton. The Hessian Rifles, a mixed force of Brunswickers, and a corps of dismounted Dragoons, were under the command of Major-General the Baron Riedesel; with Colonel Breymann as his chief subordinate. Canadian Militia, to the number of 148, rather than the total of 1,500 Germain had sanguinely expected, brought the total under Burgoyne's command to 7,399. A detachment of sailors was allocated for duty on the Lakes; some of them continuing to serve with the troops throughout the balance of the campaign. It had also been proposed to recruit some five hundred Indians, and although this total was never fully achieved, a certain number of Redskins were brought in by the sinister, dubiously reliable la Corne Saint-Luc — who had fought under Montcalm — and the ageing French-Canadian Charles de Langlade; neither of whom was conspicuous for his enthusiasm in the British cause. From the outset Burgoyne had been doubtful of the advisability, let alone the morality, of employing 'savages'. His doubts were reflected in his orders, in which he sternly pronounced, 'I positively forbid bloodshed when you are not opposed in arms'; adding, 'Aged men, women, children, and prisoners must be held secure from the knife or hatchet, even in the time of actual conflict'. In effect, as Lieutenant Digby duly recorded, 'they [the Indians] received the most positive orders not to scalp, except the dead'.[3]

To garrison Canada, Carleton retained the 29th, 31st and 34th Regiments, less 'a hundred men from the latter going with Brigadier Gen'l St Leger. He [Carleton] also had 2 German Reg'ts and 50 men from six of the Regiments going with Gen'l Burgoyne; in all 3,500 Men, including the Sick in Hospital, which are by no means numerous.'[4]

With some Canadian Militia and Indians to supplement his Bloody-backs, St Leger was to conduct a diversionary movement towards Fort Stanwix and the Mohawk River, thereafter joining up with the main army between Saratoga and Albany.

[1] Field pieces with the columns, 38; six 24-pounders, six 12-pounders, and four howitzers.
[2] At Minden, Phillips had handled his guns with such dexterity and dash as to win promotion to the rank of Colonel in the Army. With his appointment as Major-General for service in America the rule forbidding a Gunner Officer to command an infantry force was waived in his favour.
[3] Lieutenant William Digby, *Journal* (edited by James P. Baxter).
[4] Lieutenant James Hadden, *Journal and Orderly Book.*

10

With a trusted and truly beloved commander at their head, it was in remarkably good heart that the Bloodybacks set out to march to their point of embarkation at St John's; with the drums thudding and the fifes squealing out the steady cadence of 'The English March' and the gaily impudent rhythm of 'Lydia Fisher's Jig', which the Americans had come to know and to loathe under its later name of 'Yankee Doodle'.[1] After a spell of singularly unhelpful weather, the sky had cleared, and a beaming sun struck sparks of fire from the men's winking belt buckles and the brass plates on the grenadiers' towering fur caps. With their varicoloured facings, the Bloodybacks' red tunics contrasted sharply with the more sombre garb of the Hessians; while the light infantry, in close-fitting skull-caps, jauntily feathered, grinned feelingly at the clumsy swords and clumping thigh-boots of Baum's Brunswicker Dragoons.

On the eve of setting out, Burgoyne's Order of the Day had explicitly affirmed, 'The services required of this particular expedition are critical and conspicuous. During our progress occasions may occur in which nor difficulty, nor labour, nor life are to be regarded. *This Army must not retreat.*'[2]

Once embarked on Lake Champlain, 'in front the Indians went with their birch canoes, containing twenty or thirty in each; then the advance corps in a regular line, with the gunboats; then followed the *Royal George* and the *Inflexible*,...with the other brigs and sloops following; after them the first brigade in a regular line; then the Generals Burgoyne and Phillips and Riedesel in their pinnaces; next to them were the second brigade, followed by the German brigades; and the rear was brought up with the sutlers and followers of the army'[3]—almost an army in themselves.

For several of the Officers had somewhat rashly arranged for their wives to accompany them on the expedition; their ranks being headed by 'Frau Generalin' Frederica Baroness Riedesel, complete with three female offspring of from four years and nine months to a bare ten weeks. Looking as though she were made of nothing more substantial than Dresden china, in actual fact the enchanting little Baroness was as tough in fibre as the brawniest *hausfrau* in the whole length and breadth

---

[1] The melody had been brought from Holland to England by British soldiers of fortune returning from service with Dutch to fight in the Parliamentary 'New Model' Army.

[2] General John Burgoyne, *Orderly Book.*

[3] Anburey, *op. cit.*

of her native Germany. Quite prepared to make do with a bowl of rattlesnake soup and a hunk of half-cooked bear's paw by way of dinner, even her one fear — that the aroma of burning cedar branches was liable to bring on a miscarriage — was not allowed to diminish the infectious ardour of her spirits or disturb the cheerful alacrity with which she confronted and confidently mastered each novel or vexatious problem as it arose. A close friend of the adorable 'Fritzchen' was handsome, high-hearted Lady Harriet Acland; and of much the same mettle were the wives of Major Harnage and Lieutenant Reynels. It was a little female coterie which pointedly ignored the presence in their midst of Mrs Commissary Lewis — the *chère amie* who constituted the principal item in 'Gentleman Johnny's' military baggage. With the normal quota of wives 'married on the strength' and the usual clutter of draggletails, picked up in the *bas-quartiers* of Montreal and Quebec, who had elected to brave all and follow the men of their choice, the horde of camp followers came to well over a thousand. And although not a few dropped out during the early stages of the march, there were not wanting those to see the venture through to the bitter end.

The British progress down Lake Champlain went entirely undisputed, and by 1st July Burgoyne's advance corps had debouched in front of the Ticonderoga defences, guarding the Lake's long, narrow southern outlet.

Under the command of General St Clair, some three thousand American troops were distributed between the main stronghold, on the western bank of the narrow waterway, and the outwork of Fort Independence on the further side of the stream. A substantial bridge, with a stout boom, joined the two posts. But the one position St Clair had failed to put in a state of defence was the nearby eminence known as Sugar-loaf Hill; and Sugar-loaf Hill 'was a post of great consequence, since it commanded a great part of the works of Ticonderoga, all their vessels, and likewise afforded the means of cutting off their [the Americans'] communication with Fort Independence, a place also of great strength, and the works very extensive'.[1] The ascent of the hill's sharply raking slopes would certainly be no easy matter. But 'where a goat can go', Phillips stoutly insisted, 'a man can go; and where a man can go he can haul up a gun'. And with the words the fate of Ticonderoga was sealed.

With bluejackets aiding the gunners in the heavy block-and-tackle

[1] Digby, op. cit.

work, two 12-pounders were dragged into position on the hill-crest and Ticonderoga had ceased to be a stronghold and became a trap. Having been guilty of a similar laxity to that displayed by Howe in 1775, when he had failed to seize and fortify the Dorchester Heights, St Clair had no alternative but to evacuate his somewhat sickly garrison while escape was still feasible. With the minimum of stores, he slipped down the Lake by way of Skenesborough, to take temporary refuge in Fort Edward, on the upper waters of the Hudson. A rear-guard was left to fend off the British to the last possible moment; but 'allured by the sweets of plunder and liquor, instead of obeying their orders, they were found dead drunk by a case of Madeira'.[1]

Ticonderoga, with its 128 pieces of cannon, was once more in British hands. But it was not until 7th July that a way was forced through the boom, and Burgoyne was free to push on towards Skenesborough. Meanwhile Brigadier-General Frazer had followed up hot-foot on one contingent of the American troops falling back towards Hubbarton. Coming up with an enemy rearguard of twice his strength, Frazer impetuously went into the assault, only to find that the counter-attack launched against him seriously threatened to overwhelm him. 'The situation was critical, until General Riedesel came up with his advanced guard and made with it a fresh attack on the opponents' right flank, which changed the complexion of affairs so much that the enemy was beaten with considerable loss; and Brigadier Frazer, as well as all the Officers of his corps, expressed to the General their most lively gratitude.'[2]

Right from the outset the rank and file of the 62nd, temporarily functioning in what for them was the novel role of light infantry, were so alert, and did so well, as to earn for themselves the nickname of 'The Springers'.

> The Americans left Colonel Francis and over two hundred dead upon the field, and about the same number prisoners in Frazer's hands. The British loss did not exceed one hundred and forty killed and wounded, nor would the figures have been so high but for an unfortunate occurrence. In the course of the action about sixty Americans approached two companies of grenadiers with rifles clubbed in token of surrender, and were allowed to come within ten yards unharmed; when they suddenly stopped, fired a

---

[1] Anburey, *op. cit.*

[2] General Baron von Riedesel, *Military Memoirs*. Riedesel and Frazer were old comrades-in-arms, having fought together throughout the Seven Years' War.

volley, disabling many of the grenadiers, and ran away to the shelter of the forest.[1]

Though rare, such unscrupulous methods of warfare added painfully to the feeling of personal venom with which the Bloodybacks went into action against their opponents.

Continuing the pursuit, the 9th Foot drove their quarry as far as Fort Anne, fourteen miles beyond Skenesborough. The American rearguard fought on gamely until the 9th were reinforced, whereupon the defenders set fire to the stronghold and made good their escape in the general direction of Fort Edward.

As far as Skenesborough the expedition had made reasonably good time; and at this juncture speed of movement was more than ever vital. But as Digby uneasily recorded, 'We have been obliged to remain a long time at Skenesborough on account of getting horses and wagons from Canada; the Contractor of which must have realized a great sum, each horse standing Government in about £15[2] if lost or killed in the service, exclusive of paying the driver, et...'

Yet there were four hundred American waggons, with four horses to each, less than thirty miles away at Fort George, guarded by no more than seven hundred men. Had Burgoyne made for this objective with all the speed attainable in this difficult terrain, 'this', Digby soundly comments, 'would have enabled us to push forward without waiting for horses from Canada to bring on our heavy artillery, which was much greater than we had the smallest use for'.

In response to Burgoyne's appeal — prompted by the egregious Philip Skene, founder of the settlement to which he had given his name — several hundred professing loyalists had come in with offers of service; many of them armed. But further south the revolutionary committees were 'using their utmost endeavours to counteract it, by watching and imprisoning all persons they suspected, compelling the people to take arms, to drive their cattle and burn their corn, under the penalty of immediate death'.[3] Matters had reached the stage when the Americans, at any rate, were prepared to act on the hard-and-fast assumption that 'he who is not with me is against me'.

In a despatch dated 3rd March, 1777, Germain had contradictorily

[1] Fortescue, *op. cit.*

[2] In spending value the equivalent of about £100 in present-day English money.

[3] Anburey, *op. cit.*

signified his approval of a plan submitted by Howe for an offensive designed to bring about the capture of Philadelphia, and in so doing rally what was wishfully believed to be the very considerable loyalist element in the South. 'Gen'l Howe has hopes, or assurances', wrote Colonel Charles Stuart to his father, 'that Maryland will return to obedience.'[1] Nor was he the only one to write in similar strain. In the absence of any explicit order to concentrate his immediate energies on effecting a junction with Burgoyne at Albany, therefore, it was for his project against Philadelphia that Howe proceeded to elaborate his plans.

Washington had cannily refused to commit himself to a general action until his small cadre of Continental Line and remnant of militia had been powerfully reinforced. But his rapidly growing army was so placed as to bar both overland route to the capital and dispute any northward move by the British towards Albany. For as early as the 2nd of July the American Commander-in-Chief had written, 'It seems beyond question that the enemy will attempt to unite their two armies, that under General Burgoyne and the one arrived here'[2] — that is, at New York.

For once Washington had misread his opponent's intention. For in the early days of July Howe, having insufficient men and transport to go by land, embarked some 15,500 Bloodybacks and German auxiliaries at Amboy, intent on approaching his objective of Philadelphia by water. Delayed by contrary winds, it was not until the 23rd that the convoy actually got to sea.

It had been Howe's intention to approach Philadelphia by sailing up the Delaware River, but this the Naval authorities pronounced to be impossible, owing to the obstructions with which the waterway had carefully been furnished. There was nothing for it but to sail up the Chesapeake to land at the 'head of Elk', fifty miles from Philadelphia. This, however, had involved a 350-mile detour, which contrary winds had turned into a twenty-four day passage. So it was not until 25th August — with the campaigning season half gone — that the Bloodybacks were disembarked at the mouth of the Elk, with 'Black Dick', dressed as an Ordinary Seaman, line and plummet in hand, guiding the fleet to its anchorage.

This was the signal for a somewhat bewildered Washington to march

[1] Stuart-Wortley, *op. cit.* As a captive Charles Lee — ever anxious to 'hedge his bet' in case the British should come out victorious — had never ceased to hymn the loyalty of the Philadelphians and Marylanders.
[2] *The Writings of George Washington*, edited by Worthington C. Ford.

his troops to Wilmington, to place himself between Howe and the capital on which he obviously had designs.

Twenty-five miles south-west of Philadelphia, the Delaware is joined by the swirling waters of Brandywine Creek. Overlooked by formidable cliffs where it was crossed by the road from the hamlet of Kennett Square to Philadelphia, at Chad's and Brenton's fords, the situation was of a natural strength of which Washington was prompt to take full advantage. His Continental Line divisions, under Nat Greene and Sullivan, were deployed to right and left of the fords, with his militia further down the creek. By 9th September the American forces — which by now slightly outnumbered Howe's battalions — were well entrenched along their formidable position; with the British concentrated a few miles away at Kennett Square.

To hearten the unfledged American rank and file, propaganda had obviously been resorted to on unstinted scale, since one British memorialist noted down, 'Mr Washington, in an involved rhapsody, has persuaded them they were to exterminate us, and had generously given up to his troops his own share of our baggage, and had committed the fate of America, on which the world was intent, to battle'.[1]

For the impending action Howe had divided his force into two columns, one under the command of Cornwallis, the other under the German veteran, Knyphausen; and as part of the screen skirmishing ahead of the latter's troops prowled Captain Patrick Ferguson.

Ex-dragoon and experienced light infantryman, Ferguson was the inventor of a breech-loading, rapid-fire rifle capable of loosing off six aimed shots a minute. Having reported for service in America, the young Scot had been given command of a small corps of picked marksmen, all armed with the new rifle. Scouting ahead in the thick timberlands, Ferguson and one of his men were making a cautious reconnaissance of an open glade when the sound of horses' hoof-beats drove them to seek cover. 'We had not lain long', Ferguson subsequently recorded, 'when a Rebel Officer, remarkable by a Hussar dress, passed towards our Army, within a hundred yards of my right flank, not perceiving us. He was followed by another dressed in dark green or blue, with a remarkable large hat. I ordered three good shots to steal near to them and fire at them; But the idea disgusted me and I recalled the order. The Hussar, in returning, made a circuit, but the other passed within a hundred yards of me, upon which I advanced from the

[1] Major John André, *Journal*.

wood towards him. On my calling, he stopped; but, after looking at me, proceeded. I again drew his attention, and made signs to him to stop, but he slowly continued his way. As I was within that distance at which, in the quickest firing, I could have launched half a dozen balls in or about him before he was out of my reach, I had only to determine: but it is not pleasant to fire at the back of an unoffending individual, who was acquitting himself very coolly of his duty; so I let him alone. The day after I had been telling this story to some wounded Officers who lay in the same room with me,[1] when one of the Surgeons, who had been dressing the wounded Rebel Officers, came in and told us they had been informing him that General Washington was all this morning with the light troops, and only attended by a French Officer in Hussar dress, he himself dressed and mounted in every point as above described. I am not sorry that I did not know at the time who it was.'[2]

In effect, had he been aware of the identity of his potential target, Ferguson's natural repugnance at the idea of 'potting a sitting bird', might well have been overcome by his soldierly instinct to bring down the one man upon whom the cause of America in the field so vitally depended.

Howe's plan of attack at Brandywine was simple enough in design, but its execution demanded exceptional exertions on the part of the column led by Cornwallis. For the intention was for Knyphausen, deployed along the banks of the creek opposite the two fords, to hold the Americans by a cautious but sustained frontal attack, while his British colleague made an exceptionally wide circuit by way of the upper forks of the Brandywine, twelve miles away, to swing round and come in on Washington's right flank and rear, by way of Dilworth, three miles east of the creek.[3]

For once, British Intelligence — aided, maybe, by information volunteered by local loyalists — proved superior to that of the Americans. Two of Washington's scouts, sent out early to make a reconnaissance on the right flank, brought in word that there was no enemy movement in the area where Cornwallis was actually on the line of march. By this time Washington's rather undernourished attempt to overwhelm Knyphausen had been beaten back; and Cornwallis, with Howe in

---

[1] Ferguson's right elbow was shattered shortly after the encounter.

[2] Patrick Ferguson, *Narrative*. See also John Andrews's *History of the Late War* (1786), vol. IV.

[3] For the constitution of the two columns, see end of chapter.

general command, had brought his men to the end of their lengthy detour, and their increasing pressure on the American right was beginning to make itself felt.

Well in the van marched the Light Company of the 46th Foot, the feathers in their head-dress deliberately dyed red, the better to ensure that the vengeance sworn against them by the survivors of an earlier encounter should not be misdirected. For some of Anthony Wayne's troops had taken oath to extend no quarter to the 'Light Bobs' of the 46th, who had handled them so roughly.[1]

With his realization where the more potent source of danger lay, Washington was prompt to send Sullivan's division hurrying to the right flank, where it deployed on a miniature range of heights above Birmingham Meeting House. With his artillery well posted and both wings protected by dense forest land, Sullivan was admirably placed to hold the British thrust, now developing in strength.

With the swelling roar of the fighting away to the east for cue, Knyphausen seized the moment to attack across Chad's Ford in real earnest; and by so doing he pinned down the American troops in this sector in such a manner as to prohibit the transfer of any of their number to the threatened flank.

With the Bloodyback line thickening against them, Sullivan's men began to waver. 'The militia gave way like sheep on the right flank, and the rout began.'[2] At one moment the supply of ball for the men of the 15th Foot threatened to give out. Entangled in thick woodlands, they had pressed forward with such eagerness that their antagonists momentarily outnumbered them by three to one. But their resourceful Commanding Officer was quite equal to the occasion. 'No ball?', he cried; 'then snap at 'em and be damned!' And 'snap' they did, all the available ball being distributed to the best shots, while the rest of the battalion kept 'snapping off' small but spectacular charges of blank powder, to try and hold their opponents at bay until ammunition and supports could be hurried to the scene. With Sullivan's already demoralized militia element the ruse proved entirely successful;[3] and 'jaded with a long march, loaded with knapsacks, and unrefreshed by any halt', the

[1] The red hackle distinction was preserved in modern times by the brass feather and red cloth helmet and cap badge of the 2nd Battalion Duke of Cornwall's Light Infantry.

[2] Major William A. Ganoe, *History of the United States Army*.

[3] 'The Snappers' remained the nickname of the East Yorkshire Regiment right into modern times.

10*

Bloodybacks 'drove the rebels from wood to wood on every side';[1] and thus the British advance continued its relentless pressure even when Nat Greene was sent hurrying to Sullivan's support. But the flight of Sullivan's demoralized legions was not to be arrested, despite the solid sheet-anchor of Stirling's brigade in the centre.

Then suddenly debouching from a tangle of woodlands where they had been floundering and out of the fight for the best part of an hour, a battalion of the Guards, followed by a contingent of Hessian *chasseurs*, threw themselves violently on the right flank of the Americans contending with Knyphausen's solid wall of advance. With their appearance, Washington's only hope was that retreat would not degenerate into a chaotic flight. With the hard core of Greene's and Stirling's Continental Line as its indomitable rearguard, and aided by oncoming nightfall, what was left of the mangled American force struggled clear and made its way along the road to Chester.

Howe's handful of cavalry were mounted on horses of such miserable quality as to render a brisk pursuit of their broken enemies a physical impossibility.[2] Rain, descending darkness, damp powder, and sheer physical exhaustion equally ruled out any energetic follow-up by Howe's famished and utterly exhausted infantry.

Though far from decisive, Brandywine was a skilful action, very creditable to Howe considering he had little or no superiority of numbers. There has always been a conspiracy to belittle Howe, but, whatever his failings, he could fight a battle and handle his troops on occasion with uncommon ability.[3]

There was excuse enough, therefore, for the camp ditty, extemporized to commemorate the occasion:

> At Brandywine,
> At Brandywine,
> We whipped the Continental Line;
> An' Generals Wayne and Sullivan
> Have lost a thousand soldier men.

---

[1] André, *op. cit.*

[2] Of a shipload of 950 horses sent to America in the April of 1776, for example, only 400 reached their destination, in very poor condition.

[3] Fortescue, *op. cit.* British losses at Brandywine came to 577, of whom 18 Officers and 81 other ranks were killed. American losses totalled over 1,000, including 400 men and 4 guns captured. For the composition of the British forces see end of chapter.

> There lie the Yankee rebel dead,
> The river fords are running red,
> At Brandywine,
> At Brandywine,
> The glorious field of Brandywine.

Twenty-odd miles ahead of the Brandywine runs the Schuylkill River, nearby which, on the banks of the Delaware, lay Philadelphia. Heavy rains had rendered the stream impassable at its mouth, so Washington withdrew across the Schuylkill by several fords, leaving a detachment under 'Mad Anthony' Wayne to menace Howe's left flank.

To deal with this threat Howe despatched General Grey, with three battalions, to tackle it forthwith. Deciding on a night attack, to ensure that no alarm should inadvertently be given, Grey ordered the flints to be removed from his men's muskets. Stealing stealthily towards Wayne's sleeping camp, the Bloodybacks brought off a complete surprise, going in with the cold steel, which they wielded with a fury altogether out of normal character.[1] Quite ruthlessly they 'put to the bayonet all they came up with and, overtaking the main herd of the fugitives, stabbed great numbers and pressed on their rear until it was thought prudent to order them to desist'.[2] Having inflicted three hundred casualties and taken a hundred prisoners for a total loss of eight killed and wounded, 'No-flint' Grey could report the road to Philadelphia free from menace; and on 25th September the capital was occupied by a British advance party under Lord Cornwallis.

The distance from Skenesborough to Fort George, at the southernmost tip of the Lake of that name, is no more than twenty miles. But more appalling territory for an army to traverse it would be impossible to conceive. Heavily wooded areas, with tangled thickets, were interspersed by creek-laced broken ground which in many places the heavy rains had turned into a veritable morass. To add to the natural difficulties of the terrain, Schuyler had set a thousand men to work felling trees to block such rough tracks as existed. At the same time every bridge in the path of advance had been skilfully destroyed. In all, the Bloodybacks had to rebuild and considerably enlarge some forty of them; sweating in the stifling, humid green-gloom forest depths, to

[1] Positive evidence is lacking, but it is possible that some of their comrades had earlier fallen victim to the 'clubbed musket' ruse. See above, p. 293.
[2] André, *op. cit.*

hack and haul and thrust a tortured way through the immensity which everywhere confronted them.

Why Burgoyne should have chosen this staggeringly difficult land passage, when, by returning to Ticonderoga, he could have sailed down the Lake to Fort George—whence a road led direct to Fort Edward, less than forty-five miles from Albany—it is difficult to determine unless he felt himself bound by Germain's general directive. His injunction, 'This army must not retreat', would scarcely have been invalidated by a move to *reculer pour mieux sauter*. But flexibility was the last thing Germain's tampering with the original plan had left him. So it was to Fort Edward he forced his way overland at a pace which never exceeded a mile a day; moving thence to Battenkill, five miles from Saratoga.

By now supplies were beginning dangerously to thin out. So, learning that the Americans had large reserves of provisions, ammunition and horses at Bennington, thirty miles south-east of Fort Edward, Burgoyne despatched Colonel Baum, at the head of five hundred German troops, to seize them. Enheartened by assurances of the ready help he would receive from local loyalists, Baum pushed on until he ran into a strong force of hostile militia—led by fiery John Stark—who were speedily amplified by the very individuals who earlier had been posing as loyalists; many of whom had not even bothered to remove from their hats the white paper emblem which bore witness to the oath of allegiance they had earlier sworn to the Crown. Outnumbered and virtually surrounded, Baum fought back with dogged courage. 'Twice he cut his way through the enemy. None of the Dragoons having a shot left, he ordered them to sling their guns over their shoulders, and draw their swords. In this manner he sought to cut his way through the third time.'[1] But all in vain. Swamped by sheer weight of numbers, such of his force as survived were taken captive; a similar fate being visited on the supports, under Colonel Breymann, who had been despatched for Baum's reinforcement. The allied force was the poorer by five hundred men and four field pieces, reducing the effectives to approximately six thousand. As Walpole waspishly commented when the news of Bennington reached England, Burgoyne 'had had bad sport in the woods'.

Nor had better fortune attended on Barry St Leger. For on 18th August a rambling despatch informed Burgoyne that the attempt on Fort Stanwix had proved an utter failure; the Indians still with St

[1] Riedesel, *op. cit.*

Leger's force, deceived by artfully contrived enemy propaganda, having threatened to take their departure *en bloc*.

Indeed, the unpredictable but invariably unruly behaviour of his Redskin auxiliaries constituted not the least vexatious of Burgoyne's many problems. Their drunken orgy after the fall of Ticonderoga had been followed by the wholesale terrorization of the countryside; and their defiant rejection of all restraint had culminated in the barbaric slaughter of the unfortunate Jane McCrae.

Attractive Jenny McCrae was betrothed to a young Provincial Officer serving with Burgoyne; and her prospective husband had offered the alluring but exceedingly ill-chosen reward of an anker of rum to a couple of Indians if they would escort his bride-to-be to the safety of the British camp. Willingly undertaking the service, the two men actually brought their charge to within a short distance of the lines, before a wrangle broke out as to which of the two was entitled to claim the larger share of the recompense. The dispute growing heated, one of the savages, as it appears, with appalling illogicality settled the matter out of hand by despatching the hapless girl with his tomahawk.[1]

American fury at what was misinterpreted as a piece of wanton but fully authorized barbarity, was only matched by 'Gentleman Johnny's' indignant anger at the outrage, and his determination to exact retribution from its perpetrator. It was only when the sinister la Corne Saint-Luc pointed out that the punishment of one Redskin would mean the instant departure of them all, 'massacring whatever defenceless people lay in their path, and carrying terror and destruction among all the peaceful inhabitants of the frontier', that, perforce, Burgoyne was constrained to leave the delinquent's chastening in the hands of the man's own tribe. In the outcome, all but a handful of the savages very shortly afterwards abandoned the expedition.

Having with considerable difficulty garnered thirty days' supplies, Burgoyne resolutely pushed on, reaching Saratoga on 13th September. Resuming his march, on the 18th, he found his way barred by a strong and constantly increasing American force, deployed in a position carefully selected and entrenched for it by the Polish military engineer Tadeusz Kosciuzko.

Having industriously intrigued to secure the appointment, 'Granny'

---

[1] Fiske avers, 'How she came by her cruel death was never known.' Baxter maintains that 'she was shot accidentally by some Americans', possibly in an endeavour to 'rescue' her from the hands of the Redskins and detain her themselves, as a suspected loyalist.

Gates had now superseded Schuyler in the command, to no one's particular satisfaction but his own. His appraisal of Burgoyne's probable intentions, however—as outlined to the American Brigadier, James Clinton—was more than sufficiently shrewd. 'Perhaps Burgoyne's despair', he wrote, 'may dictate to him to risque all on one throw; he is an old gamester, and in his time has seen all chances.'

Good as it was, there was one flaw in the American position—it was commanded by a hill from which the entrenchments could all be raked; and the essence of Burgoyne's plan was that Frazer should make a wide detour to seize this height while Riedesel on the left and Burgoyne himself in the centre kept the enemy fully engaged.

The opening phase of Burgoyne's attack on the American position— five thousand men against a minimum of fourteen thousand—was brisk, completely articulated and resolutely pressed home; the American picket in a clearing at Freeman's Farm, in front of the centre column, being overrun and captured. But Burgoyne was confronted with someone far more considerable than 'Granny' Gates. Without any definite command, Benedict Arnold had contrived to 'borrow' from 'that damned old midwife in buff and blue' some three thousand troops including the skilled marksmen of Daniel Morgan's corps of riflemen; and their intervention proved decisive. 'Several of them placed themselves in high trees, and, as often as they could distinguish a British Officer's uniform, took him off by deliberately aiming at his person.'[1] It was Bunker Hill all over again—the careful, deliberate extermination of the leaders on whom the men in the ranks relied for guidance and example.

The brunt of Arnold's onslaught fell on the British troops of the centre, who were under Burgoyne's immediate command. And throughout the entire day 'he behaved with great personal bravery. He shunned no danger, his presence and conduct animated the troops, for they greatly loved the General. He delivered his orders with precision and coolness and in the heat, danger and fury of the fight maintained the true characteristics of a soldier.'[2]

Had Gates sent his subordinate the reinforcements for which he justly clamoured, the British centre would inevitably have been broken. For Frazer dared not denude the right wing to go to the support of the centre, where the fight put up by the three Bloodyback battalions was

[1] Digby, *op. cit.*
[2] Lamb, *op. cit.*

nothing less than Homeric. 'Few actions have been characterised by more obstinacy in attack and defence; the British troops repeatedly plied their bayonets with their usual success. As the day closed, the Americans retreated on all sides, and left them masters of the field.'[1]

But although the Bloodybacks and their allies bivouacked on the ground they had won, with his force reduced by five hundred casualties Burgoyne had paid too high a price for victory. Yet withdrawal, even had he entertained the idea of it, was now out of the question. Gates was astride his communications, had captured the British flotilla on Lake George, together with three companies of the 53rd, and had brought Ticonderoga under close investment. The best news was that Henry Clinton and a small force of Bloodybacks had set out from New York to try and force their way up the Hudson and make junction with the northern Army somewhere in the region of Albany.

But the days passed without any further news of Henry Clinton, all of whose later messengers—like Burgoyne's—had fallen into enemy hands. By 4th October supplies had become so low that the troops had to be put on short allowance. However desperate, something must be attempted, since the repercussions on Howe of events in the north had to be taken into serious account. As Burgoyne himself expressed it, 'This consideration operated forcibly to determine me to abide events as long as possible, and I reasoned thus: the expedition I commanded was evidently meant at first to be *hazarded*. Circumstances might require that it should be *devoted* [i.e. sacrificed]. A critical juncture of Mr Gates's force with Mr Washington's might possibly decide the fate of the war; the failure of my junction with Sir Henry Clinton, or the loss of my retreat to Canada, could only be a *partial* misfortune.'

On 7th October, therefore, Burgoyne moved out with the Germans in the centre and the British on the flanks, to form a weak line intended to fall on Gates's left. But before the allied force could swing into action the British left was struck by Morgan and at least four thousand followers, with such tremendous impact that Burgoyne and his stubborn Bloodybacks were extremely hard put to it to prevent the front from crumbling. With another American column pressing on Burgoyne's right, Frazer hastened to switch the light infantry and the 24th to form some sort of bulwark to cover the general movement of retreat; he himself falling mortally wounded from the bullet of a marksman perched high in the trees.

[1] Lamb, *op. cit.*

As the thick woods echoed and re-echoed to the sinister 'turkey call' by which Morgan's riflemen signalled to each other, and the fusillade of musketry merged into the barking roar of the cannon, indomitable little Baroness 'Fritzchen' hurried between her three bewildered children and the stricken Frazer, fearing every moment, as she tended him, that her own adored Frederick would be the next to be borne into the flimsy shelter of the house where the women and children and some of the sick and wounded had all been huddled together.

Breymann had been slain outright, Burgoyne's A.D.C., Sir Francis Clarke, had taken a wound which eventually proved mortal, while Acland, shot through both legs, had fallen into enemy hands.

With the British yielding ground step by step, Arnold threw in an attack all along the line. But the onrush was somehow held by Balcarres and the light infantry, and behind this impenetrable wall of defence Burgoyne managed to change position to some heights immediately above the Hudson; although in contracting his zone of resistance he was forced to abandon nearly eight hundred of his sick and wounded.

To all intents and purposes he and the bare 3,500 of his men left fit for duty were surrounded. Even worse, they were virtually starving. There was no rum or spruce beer and the men were gnawing the last crumbs of stale biscuit. For that matter, 'Gentleman Johnny' was in no better case than his men, lacking even a cup of wine to offer the anxious Harriet Acland on the eve of her departure, under a flag of truce, to join her stricken captive husband in the American lines. Obviously the end was near at hand.

On 13th October, following an abortive meeting on the previous day, a final council of war was held, presided over by Burgoyne, and attended by Phillips, Riedesel, Hamilton, and all the surviving Field Officers. Accepting full responsibility for the unhappy plight in which they found themselves, Burgoyne put the question—were they in such a situation that nothing was left to them but capitulation, or would capitulation in such circumstances be considered dishonourable? The passage of a cannon ball over the table at which this delicate point was being discussed may have done something to hasten the conclusion that, as matters stood, capitulation was inevitable and therefore without taint of dishonour.

At ten o'clock on the morning of 14th October the handsome ruddy-faced Kingston proceeded, under a flag of truce, to the American camp as a plenipotentiary charged to define the terms under which the British would be prepared to lay down their arms. Naturally, with Burgoyne's categorical refusal to consider any question of unconditional surrender, there was much argument as to the conditions governing submission. But at length a 'convention' was devised in which the governing clause provided for:

> A free passage to be granted to the Army under Lieut-Gen. Burgoyne to Great Britain upon condition of not serving again in North America during the present conflict; and the Port of Boston is Assigned for the entry of Transports to Receive the Troops whenever General Howe shall order.

Time was to demonstrate how shamefully a civil Administration would fail to carry into execution a solemn commitment made in its name by one of its leading military commanders.

At ten o'clock on the morning of 17th October 'Gentleman Johnny', impeccably garbed in 'a rich royal uniform', rode to the head of the American camp, where Gates, in a 'plain blue frock', awaited him. And thus the two erstwhile Subalterns of the Duke of Bolton's Light Dragoons met again as conqueror and vanquished.

'The fortune of war, General Gates', said Burgoyne, raising his plumed hat, 'has made me your prisoner.' And with unprecedented urbanity Gates replied, 'I shall always be ready to bear testimony that it has not been through any fault of your Excellency'. With the words he returned his captive's proffered sword.

This was worthy of a Horatio Gates all too rarely glimpsed; as was the tact which kept the main body of American troops confined to camp while the Bloodybacks and their German auxiliaries marched, to their own drums and fifes, to pile arms under the commands of their own Officers. No less chivalrous was the courtesy and consideration of the guards who formed the disarmed captives' escort — the tribute of brave men to men of equal courage, who have learned of each other's quality in fair and open fight. In thus honouring the foes who now were at their mercy, they did even greater honour to themselves. —

In England, 'the account of General Burgoyne's treaty with Mr Gates arriving when the two Houses of Parliament were sitting', a correspondent recorded, 'you cannot imagine how furiously, illiberally and indecently the Opposition triumphed on the occasion'.[1] In France, the news was acclaimed with exultant laughter and a darting, feral gleam

[1] *Pennsylvania Ledger*, 7th March, 1778.

in the eye; for surely the time was ripe to exchange the furtive stab in the back for a more open show of aggression.

On 'Change and in the London coffee houses the ungenerous quip was on all men's tongues:

> Burgoyne, alas, unknowing future fates,
> Could force his way through woods but not through Gates.

For at first blush, 'Gentleman Johnny' was condemned out of hand. It was left to the generous, level-headed Carleton to put the whole unhappy episode in its true perspective. 'This unfortunate event', he wrote, 'it is to be hoped, will in future prevent Ministers from pretending to direct operations of war in a country at three thousand miles distance, of which they have so little knowledge as not to be able to distinguish between good, bad, or interested advices, or to give positive orders upon matters which, from their nature, are ever on the change.'[1]

But the general mood of the country was aptly summed up by the London *Evening Post*:

> Gage nothing did, and went to pot;
> Howe lost one town, another got;
> Guy[2] nothing lost and nothing won;
> Dunmore[3] was homeward forced to run;
> Clinton was beat, but got a Garter;[4]
> And bouncing Burgoyne caught a Tartar;
> Thus all we gain for millions spent
> Is to be laugh'd at, and repent.

Brandywine

CORNWALLIS'S COLUMN

3rd Brigade: 15th, 33rd, 44th and 55th Foot: (Major-General Grey).
4th Brigade: 17th, 37th, 46th and 64th Foot: (Major-General Agnew).
Reserves and Light Troops: 2 battalions the Guards, 2 battalions Light

---

[1] Carleton to Burgoyne, 17th November, 1777.
[2] Carleton.
[3] The fugitive Royalist Governor of Virginia.
[4] This is inaccurate. Clinton had been knighted, but he had not been admitted to the Order of the Garter.

Infantry, 2 battalions Grenadiers, 2 squadrons 16th Light Dragoons, 3 battalions Hessians. Mounted and dismounted Hessian chasseurs, four 12-pounders and the battalion guns.

KNYPHAUSEN'S COLUMN
1st Brigade: 4th, 5th, 23rd and 49th Foot: (Major-General Vaughan).
2nd Brigade: 10th, 27th, 28th and 40th Foot: (Major-General Grant).
A Brigade of Hessians.
Frazer's Highlanders (3 battalions).
One squadron, 16th Light Dragoons.
Six 12-pounders, four howitzers, and the battalion guns.

A World in Arms

'There has never been a protracted campaign from which a country has benefited.'

Sun Tzu (400–320 B.C.)

ALTHOUGH SEVERAL YEARS of strife had still to be endured, all that followed Saratoga was post-climactic. As the months went by they witnessed a steady diminution of power which had never been wielded intelligently at those moments of advantage, when its wiser direction might well have brought about the sort of situation out of which a reasonable accommodation could have been arrived at without further bloodshed. After 1777 'peace with honour', reconciliation without lingering bitterness, became a rapidly fading prospect.

That France would openly enter the lists as soon as it seemed reasonably safe for her to commit herself was so starkly apparent that the Cabinet could not ignore it. In the House of Lords the Duke of Richmond realistically advocated the abandonment of hostilities in North America, the better to concentrate on the imminent struggle with the hereditary foe across the Channel. In reply, the gout-ridden, wander-witted Earl of Chatham, swathed in flannel and speaking in a voice that already seemed to come from beyond the grave, at one and the same time demanded the withdrawal of the Army from North America and the continued submission of the Colonists to those Acts of Trade and Navigation they had already repudiated. It was a manifestation of long-faded capacity so painful as to send admirers of the earlier William Pitt shuddering from the Chamber.

For his part, Lord North—after vainly pressing his resignation on the King—strongly urged for an accommodation with the rebellious Colonies which would endow them with what would now be termed dominion status. But, fortified by their knowledge that their treaty with France was on the point of consummation, Congress let it be known that any accommodation must include the cession of Canada, Nova Scotia and Newfoundland, to be added to the North American Colonies in an unfettered federated dominion. 'This is what fifteen years of shilly-shally and the ethics of usury have brought us to', wrote the distinguished surgeon, John Knyveton, in his *Journal*; 'Britain, that stout old ship, drifts while her helmsmen quarrel in the deadly peril of a lee shore.'

The mood of the country in general was reflected in the offer to raise additional regiments forthcoming from the cities of Manchester, Liverpool, Glasgow, Edinburgh, Aberdeen, Birmingham, Warwick and Coventry, as from the Dukes of Argyll, Hamilton and Atholl, and Lords Seaton and Macdonald.

In the meantime all attention was focused upon Howe's efforts to consolidate his grip on Philadelphia. For however inapplicable where this particular conflict was concerned, the belief obstinately persisted that possession of the enemy's capital constituted a stroke from which he was most unlikely to recover.

For that matter, Washington was far from minded to relinquish Philadelphia without a struggle. Having been reinforced by some 2,500 men, at three in the morning of 4th October he launched an assault on the British force concentrated at Germantown, some six miles north of the capital. Washington's plan was to attack 'in different places, to produce the greater confusion, and to prevent the British forces from affording support to each other'.[1]

'When the firing began, Howe rode forward and met the Light Infantry falling back. Thinking that the enemy were not as yet in any strength, he cried out, "For shame Light Infantry! I never saw you retreat before. Form! Form! It is only a scouting party!" Just then the mist rolled aside and disclosed the enemy, who opened fire with several guns.'[2]

But with its demand for co-ordinated movement along four widely separated roads, Washington's plan was far too complicated for his raw

---

[1] Lamb, *op. cit.* Lamb was writing from hearsay, since at the time of the engagement he was still one of the Saratoga captives. He made his escape in the autumn of 1778.

[2] Captain W. H. Wilkin, *Some British Soldiers in America*.

troops and unpractised Staff to carry effectively into execution. A re-markably stubborn stand by the 40th Regiment, posted in the sub-stantial stone-built Chew House, to the north of the township, held up the American onrush; and a heavy mist again settling over the scene of action added further to the confusion—so much so, indeed, that some of Nat Greene's men opened a heavy fire on their comrades in the brigade commanded by Sullivan, believing them to be Hessians. Assailed in rear by what they also mistakenly took to be an enemy force, Sullivan's troops broke up in confusion, which was increased when 'No flint' Grey wheeled up a brigade to envelop Sullivan's right flank. He was also hemmed in on his left. This had the effect of isolating Greene's brigade; and but for the stout rearguard action put up by the hard core of the Continental Line, Washington would have been hard put to it to withdraw his battered forces from the field. Matters had not been bettered by the fact—as duly noted by John André—that a number of the American Officers had gone into action considerably the worse for liquor.

In the two and a half hours' heavy fighting British losses had come to 537, with four Officers and sixty-six other ranks killed, and only fourteen borne away as prisoners. The Hessian wounded numbered twenty-four. American losses totalled 673 killed and wounded, with four hundred captives left in British hands.

The defences blocking the Delaware at Mud Island, with their sup-porting batteries, boom and ponderous underwater *chevaux-de-frise*, were not finally cleared until 15th November; thereafter navigation of the waterway went entirely unimpeded.

With bitter winter weather rapidly hardening, Washington's grossly neglected men trudged off to the camp site selected at barren, unwel-coming Valley Forge. 'Ragged troops, with legs naked and feet com-pletely bare, with shirts hanging in strings above torn breeches', they tramped doggedly through the falling snow, 'the sharp ice ridges slash-ing the feet of the barefoot men so that they left trails of blood.'[1] The honourable members of Congress, of course, were comfortably—and safely—installed in Baltimore.

In Philadelphia, Howe took up his residence in the Penn House, and settled down to enjoy the far from negligible amenities the city could offer him. 'The Philadelphia Tories', the *Pennsylvania Packet* censoriously recorded, 'have opened hearts and homes to the Enemy. Balls, fêtes,

[1] Harry Emerson Wildes, *Valley Forge*.

masquerades, dinners, assemblies and a continuous round of revelry mark their lives'; with the younger Officers finding attractive companionship in a bevy of local *belles* headed by Peggy Chew, Margaret Shippen and Becky Redman. The well-appointed City Tavern hummed with activity; and another newsprint noted that 'Philadelphia now has one hundred and twenty-two new stores, amongst which one is kept by an Englishman, one by an American, and the remaining one hundred and eighteen by *Scotsmen* or Tories from Virginia'. Prices were high, of course—French brandy stood at 19s a quart, West India rum at 15s and gin at 9s; but there was plenty of fine Virginia tobacco and good spruce beer for the man in the ranks, at a price he could easily afford. Thus with versatile John André not only painting the scenery but also playing the leading roles, the Old South Street Theatre echoed to the applause of the most glittering audiences it had ever known. For while awaiting a copy of *The Beaux' Stratagem*, André had opened with Murphy's *No One's Enemy But His Own*;[1] the performance being for the benefit of the widows and orphans of the men of the rank and file who had fallen in battle. And all the while the 'forgotten men' of bleak snow-haunted Valley Forge, half-naked and half-starved through muddle and neglect, in sheer misery drifted away in scores and hundreds, until Washington's losses from desertion came to close upon three thousand. As the Commander-in-Chief himself warned Congress, his army must 'starve, dissolve or disperse to obtain subsistence'.

But if there was little activity on the part of the Americans, other than organizing an occasional raiding party, no greater enterprise was shown by British Headquarters in Philadelphia. Leisured dinners at 'The Indian Queen' and gay supper parties at 'The Bunch of Grapes' chuckled, but without malice, at the cartoon in the current *Westminster Magazine* depicting 'Good-natured Billy' asleep with his leg on the table, a bottle cosily at hand, and in the background a 'transparency' of Burgoyne surrendering at Saratoga.

But Howe's military inactivity was attributable neither to native inertia nor to the crippling weather conditions imposed by a particularly severe Pennsylvania winter. Denied the reinforcements he considered vital, so early as October he had written bluntly to Germain:

From the little attention, my lord, given to my recommendations since the commencement of my command, I am led to hope that I

[1] Founded on Voltaire's *L'Indiscret*.

may be relieved from this very painful service, wherein I have not the good fortune to enjoy the necessary confidence and support of my superiors, but which I conclude will be extended to Sir Henry Clinton, my presumptive successor. By the return of the packet I humbly request that I may have His Majesty's permission to resign.[1]

On 14th April—a little over two months after France's official entry into the war—Howe learned that his resignation had been accepted.

'Good-natured Billy' was far from sorry to pack his bags, placate the prospectively derelict 'Sultana' with a suitable solatium, and arrange for her accommodating husband to continue in his lucrative appointment. But his Officers were determined that he should not take his departure without some expression of the affection and esteem in which they held him. This eventually took the form of a Meschianza—part water pageant and part *fête champêtre*—in which all ranks could participate.

Starting on the Delaware with a procession of decorated boats, it included a mock tournament in the grounds of the Wharton Mansion House, wherein Banastre Tarleton and other Knights of the Burning Mountain contended with the Knights of the Blended Rose for the favours of a select band of Philadelphia's most attractive maidenhood, sumptuously 'dressed in the Asiatic habit'. An elaborate supper and dancing into the small hours of the morning brought this general tribute to the outgoing commander to a close. Of the final moment before 'Good-natured Billy' stepped down into the waiting Admiral's barge, John André subsequently recorded: 'I am just returned from conducting our beloved General to the waterside, and I have seen him receive a more flattering testimony of the love and attachment of his army than all the splendour of pomp of the Meschianza could convey to him. I have seen the most gallant of our Officers, and those whom I least suspected of giving such instances of their affection, shed tears while they bade him farewell.' Soldiers are seldom in error in their judgment of the men set over them in authority.

With Howe's departure the responsibilities of supreme command were taken over, however reluctantly, by Sir Henry Clinton.[2] A man ever at the mercy of second thoughts which were inclined to be in-

[1] Howe to Germain, 28th October, 1777.

[2] Clinton had already sought to resign his command in America, but his request had not been sanctioned.

finitely less robust than his initial impulse, Clinton was best remembered for the neat manner in which he had occupied Rhode Island in the December of 1776; his failure to succour Burgoyne at Saratoga being susceptible to a variety of explanations, all of which could be made to sound convincing enough.

After the French declaration of war Germain's orders to the new Commander-in-Chief were to evacuate Philadelphia and concentrate at New York, as a preliminary to essaying the reoccupation of what were still believed to be the preponderantly loyalist Colonies of Georgia and South Carolina—a return to Germain's obsession with the loyalists and the active support they could be relied upon to render, which offers a perfect example of the wish being father to the thought.

Hard on the heels of this despatch came another couched in very different terms. With the Franco-American alliance a *fait accompli*, all offensive operations throughout the Colonies were to be suspended; Clinton was to reduce his force by eight thousand men, five thousand of whom were to be sent to attack St Lucia, the dominant position in the Windward Islands. The remaining three thousand were to defend British-controlled Florida. Either New York or Rhode Island was to be held as an outpost for the guardianship of Canada.

Germain had directed that the force in Philadelphia should be transferred to New York by water. But with some knowledge of the fatal delays such a sea passage could involve, Clinton resolved to commit his sick and the Philadelphia loyalists now dependent on his protection to Admiral Howe's transports, while taking his Bloodybacks overland to New York—lest Washington take advantage of a tardy passage by sea to arrive in front of the weakly held city ahead of him.

For with winter yielding to an enheartening spring, the American forces had undergone a miraculous reanimation. The commissariat had been placed under conscientious, energetic Nat Greene, and the men at last were properly fed and better clothed. Equally important, where their military training had been concerned, they had come under the instruction of that redoubtable Frederickian veteran Baron von Steuben. Splenetic and exacting, but gifted with infinite patience and understanding, he had taken the men of the rank and file in hand and turned them from an unruly hurly-burly of backwoods fighters into a body of trained soldiers. Hitherto, 'the use of the bayonet had not been understood, they were either left at home or used to toast beefstakes'.[1]

[1] When any such rarities were available!

Von Steuben carefully reoriented that particular outlook in the general process of combining the best qualities of the guerrilla fighter with those of the orthodox trained soldier. Above all, 'he bestowed upon the ragged troops the greatest gift they could have received—the gift of discipline'.[1] He had not long to await the justification of his helpful labours.

The sun could scarcely have been more broiling than on 18th June when Clinton's Bloodybacks crossed the Delaware to march *via* New Brunswick, on the Raritan, to Amboy and Staten Island. News of the movement soon reached Washington's ears, and by afternoon six brigades of American troops were hastening to try and intercept the British force on the Raritan; Washington followed with his main army, which now totalled some 15,000. Hampered by 1,500 military and refugee baggage waggons, occupying twelve miles of the turnpike— on which two bridges had already been cut and many trees felled— Clinton's march-pace was so slow that the American advance-guard, under Charles Lee,[2] had no difficulty in catching up with him at Monmouth Court House; where the Bloodybacks had taken up a sound position on the Heights of Freehold. At this point they were some twenty miles from Sandy Hook. Lee's orders were to assail the flank of the British rearguard and hold it engaged until the American Commander-in-Chief could arrive on the scene with the main body of his troops.

Lee, however, had persistently canvassed the folly of attacking a concentrated body of well-trained, highly disciplined Bloodybacks. 'You don't know British soldiers', he protested, when Lafayette, Wayne and Maxwell clamoured for orders that would send them into action; we cannot stand against them.' Indeed, when a thinly manned but determined charge by the 16th Light Dragoons was stoutly followed up by a few of the Guards and a handful of Highlanders and grenadiers, Lee ordered his men to fall back.

This was too much for 'the Boy',[3] who immediately sent off a message which brought Washington hastening to the spot where Lee's troops, sweating in the oppressive heat, were in a considerable state of

---

[1] Ganoe, *op. cit.* Before von Steuben's arrival the American soldiery lost from five to eight thousand muskets a year. After he took them in hand, the annual loss became negligible.

[2] Recently exchanged for General Prescott.

[3] Cornwallis's somewhat contemptuous sobriquet for Lafayette.

confusion. It was one of the few occasions on which the Commander-in-Chief was provoked into a public expression of angry reproof. Then, as Lee trailed sullenly from the field, Washington, with von Steuben's capable aid, set himself to stabilize a confused and faltering front. But although the task was accomplished with far greater celerity than would have been possible in pre-Steuben days, and the attack resumed with admirable thrust and cohesion, the delay imposed by Lee's temporizing proved altogether fatal. With Simcoe's Queen's Rangers—the 'bloodhounds of the Revolution'—and the British rearguard fighting a stubborn delaying action, darkness brought the encounter to an inconclusive finish. Thereafter, Clinton was enabled to put so considerable a distance between himself and his pursuers that his march to New York was completed without further interference.

The Monmouth Court House engagement was the last major conflict to be fought in the north. The action had cost the Bloodybacks and their auxiliaries 358 Officers and men, sixty of whom had fallen dead from sunstroke owing to the overpowering heat of the day. American losses were almost exactly the same; but Clinton had also to take into calculation the disappearance of some six hundred of his men, three-fourths of them Germans,[1] who had contracted attachments of one sort and another during their sojourn in Philadelphia. It was with considerable pride, therefore, that Simcoe recorded that 'the Queen's Rangers lost no men by desertion'. For his part, Washington marched his troops to their former encampment at White Plains.

On 8th July Comte D'Estaing, with a large fleet from Toulon and four thousand French troops, arrived in Delaware Bay. Admiral Howe having eluded him by a matter of days, the Frenchman put to sea again, heading for New York.

From 1775 to the early months of 1778 Great Britain's heavier sea armament had enjoyed almost unchallenged supremacy at sea. Neither the embryo fleet organized by Washington, nor the navies sponsored by Congress and the individual States, were of the weight and gun-power to embark upon anything more considerable than a contest between vessels in the frigate class.

So far as the British were concerned, the real menace had lain with

---

[1] In all, some 30,000 Germans were sent to America, of whom 12,500 did not return to Europe. Desertion accounted for a far higher percentage of the latter total than did battle casualties or sickness.

the swarm of American privateers who waged an unremitting *guerre d'usure* on vessels plying the three-thousand-mile channel of supply and communication across the Atlantic.

With the outbreak of hostilities no less than two thousand privately owned vessels, manned by seventy thousand hardy fisherfolk and smugglers, had been furnished by Congress with Letters of Marque and Reprisal. An Act of George II[1] had decreed that to qualify for a Letter of Marque a vessel must be of a size to take at least ten guns — 3-pounders or bigger. So by 1775 there were plenty of ocean-going craft quite capable of considerable offensive action; many of whose masters had benefited from their actual experience of privateering during the Seven Years' War.

With a constant stream of maritime traffic making initially for Boston, and subsequently for Rhode Island and New York, there was no lack of opportunity to capture valuable 'prizes'. For with the tremendous amount of mercantile tonnage demanded for the transportation of arms, powder and shot, and considerable stores for the upkeep of the British Army in America it was not always possible for the grain ship, ammunition hulk or troop transport to proceed in convoy, shepherded by a guardian warship. Such was the consequence of the rundown in the Royal Navy under the aegis of the egregious 'Jemmy Twitcher'. And it was a very fortunate 'lone wolf' which contrived to make port on the far side of the Atlantic without encountering a privateer too well armed and too resolutely served to be beaten off by the average merchant craft.

Captain John Manly's feat in seizing the munition brig *Nancy*, off Boston, has already been recorded; an exploit which led to his capture, over the years, of another thirty-four prizes. Marblehead, Salem, Beverly, Gloucester, New London, the Chesapeake and Charleston — each furnished their quota of bold and enterprising privateers, roaming their home waters and even venturing as far as the Caribbean; and the tale of the damage they inflicted is grimly reflected in the Board of Trade returns for the successive years of the struggle. In 1778, for example, a return to Parliament revealed that there were 173 American privateers 'of which authentic account has been received', manned by 14,000 hands and armed with 2,556 guns. Of these, 34 had been taken, leaving 3,217 prisoners in British hands. Conversely, the report recorded that 733 craft had been captured by the Americans, of which 127 had been retaken and 47 released under 'sea parole'. The value of

[1] 32 Geo. II, Stat. I, cap. 25.

the remaining 559 was put at £2,600,000, plus loss of salvage and interest on cargoes.[1]

In consequence of these swingeing losses ship insurance rates were raised from £1 10s a month to £3 5s, while those for cargo increased from 2½% to 5% if with convoy, and 15% and 20% if sailing alone. The Admiralty Board alone expended £1,265,000 for the hire of transports; the Board of Ordnance paying out another £100,000 for the shipment of munitions. So far as private owners were concerned, the risks involved in an Atlantic crossing became so grave that many British consignors preferred to freight their cargoes under a foreign 'flag of convenience'.

The expulsion of American seamen from the Canadian and Newfoundland fishing banks ensured a ready supply of hands who infinitely preferred potentially profitable employment aboard a privateer to serving in the embryo United States Navy; although the latter had far greater appeal than slogging it out with the Continental Line or militia. 'There are at this time', wrote William Whipple, of the Portsmouth (New Hampshire) Military Procurement Committee, to Josiah Bartlett, 'five privateers fitting out here, which I suppose will take 400 men. Besides all this you may depend no public [Naval] ship will ever be manned while there is a privateer fitting out. The reason is plain. Those people who have the most influence with Seamen think it their best interest to discourage the public service, because by that they promote their own interest, *viz*: privateering.'[2] As the outcome of this attitude and of the inalienable preference of the mariner for employment where the greatest profit was likely to accrue, more men were engaged in privateering than served with Washington's Army in every year save 1776.

Inadequate in number as it might be, the Royal Navy did its best to suppress the privateers; a typical encounter being that between Captain Reeves's 28-gun frigate *Surprise* and Captain Manly's *Jason*, of Boston. 'When Captain Reeves hailed and ordered him to strike', the cooper of the *Surprise* subsequently recorded, 'he returned for answer, "Fire away! I have as many guns as you!" He had heavier metal but fewer men than the *Surprise*. He fought us for a long time. I was serving powder as busy as I could, the shot and splinters flying in all directions, when I heard the Irishmen call from one of the guns, "Haloo, Bungs,

---

[1] David Macpherson, *Annals of Commerce*, vol. IV.
[2] Quoted by Donald Carr Chidsey in *The American Privateer*.

where are you?" I looked to their gun and saw the two horns of my study [anvil] across the mouth; the next moment it was through the *Jason's* side. The rogues thus disposed of my study, which I had placed in a secure place as I thought, out of their reach. "Bungs for ever!" they shouted when they saw the dreadful hole it made in the *Jason's* side.'

Shortly after the American vessel struck her Colours; 'and when we boarded the *Jason*', 'Bungs' the Cooper noted, 'we found thirty-one cavalry troopers, who had served under General Burgoyne, acting as Marines on board'.[1]

In European waters a similar *guerre d'usure* was prosecuted by such outstanding naval leaders as Lambert Wickes, in the Bay of Biscay, Gustavus Conyngham in the North Sea and Atlantic, and John Barry and John Paul Jones in British home waters. It was an example of boldly adventurous challenge which was to reach its climax with the epic encounter between Jones's converted East Indiaman, the *Bonhomme Richard*, and the British frigate *Serapis* — one of the most hotly contested engagements in the whole history of maritime warfare.

But prosecution of a *guerre d'usure* cannot in itself ensure naval victory, it can do no more than contribute in a limited degree towards rendering victory possible. Indeed, 'the evidence seems to show that even for its own special ends such a mode of war is inconclusive, worrying but not deadly'.[2]

The entry of France into the conflict put a very different complexion on affairs. The steady reconstruction and strengthening of the French Navy inaugurated by the Duc de Choiseul as First Minister and Minister of Marine had been ably carried forward by M. de Sartine. The outcome was that by the February of 1778 France was in possession of a well built, heavily armed Fighting Marine, headed by sixty-three ships of the line of 64 guns and over, manned by 67,000 well-trained seamen.

The British Navy, on the other hand, had rarely been in such poor case to confront an enemy. Under the neglect and corruption which characterized the Sandwich regime, with eleven of the line away on the North American station, in home waters Admiral Keppel could muster no more than thirty vessels, of which he swore that 'only six ships were fit to meet a seaman's eye'. Even with this inadequate armament great difficulty was experienced in manning the craft. The press was set to

---

[1] W. H. Long (editor), *Naval Yarns.*
[2] Captain A. T. Mahan, *The Influence of Sea Power Upon History.*

work on a scale and with a vigour which left no rookery or tenement unprobed for likely prey. Homeward-bound vessels were boarded in the Downs and their ships' companies remorselessly fleeced of their better elements. To release more men for the Royal Navy an Act[1] was passed permitting merchant craft to sail with foreign seamen forming up to three-fourths of their crews. The East India Company's Court of Directors placed six thousand of their seagoing employees at the Admiralty's disposal, together with their three 74-gun vessels *Bombay Castle*, *Ganges* and *Carnatic*.

But the rundown involved in years of negligence and malfeasance cannot be put right in a matter of months; for if there is one thing less susceptible to improvisation than an Army it is a Fighting Marine. Belated efforts to reconstitute the Royal Navy had not been helped by two relatively successful attempts to fire the dockyard at Portsmouth, the first by Mathurin Duret and the second by Silas Deane's hired emissary James Aitkin, alias 'John the Painter'.

The sorry state into which the Fighting Marine had declined, both as to its command and its combat capacity, was only too painfully demonstrated when Admiral Keppel encountered the French fleet, under D'Orvilliers, off Ushant on 27th July.

Current French battle practice concentrated upon the destruction of the opponents' masts and rigging, with the object of so seriously crippling their adversaries as to render them immobile hulks. The bewildered British response to these novel tactics was further hampered by the lack of co-ordination between Keppel's van and the rear division under his Second-in-Command, Sir Hugh Palliser, who was either unable or unwilling to obey his superior officer's signals.

The outcome of this abortive encounter was not only a disgraceful naval scandal, when the quarrel between two Admirals led to a Court Martial, but freedom for the French squadrons to roam the seas almost at will. With Saratoga, the conflict off Ushant was vitally to affect the whole course of subsequent events.

With D'Estaing's appearance off New York in command of 8 ships of the line and numerous smaller craft, both Howe and Clinton lost no time in organizing every possible means of defence that could be devised;[2] and their energetic measures brought a ready response. Lands-

[1] 16 Geo. III, Stat. I, cap. 20.
[2] Howe had no more than 6 sixty-fours, 3 fifties and six frigates, all under-manned.

men volunteered to serve on shipboard; light infantrymen readily made
good the shortage of Marines. One worthy loyalist, Gideon Duncan,
even offered to turn the small vessel which represented his sole means
of livelihood into a fire-ship, and expressed the hope that he would be
permitted to 'lay the French Admiral's ship a-board', as she swung to
her moorings of the Hook.[1]

But 'for some time after the Count D'Estaing came to anchor the
wind was unfavourable to the execution of his supposed intention; but
on the twenty-second of July it changed to the eastward and the French
fleet was seen getting under way. The long-meditated attack, it was now
supposed, was instantly to be made...But the Count D'Estaing, as soon
as his ships had weighed anchor, instead of attempting to enter the
harbour, made sail to the southward, and was soon out of sight.'[2]

The move to the south was no more than a feint. Putting about, the
Frenchman headed for Rhode Island; where for many months a garrison of some five thousand troops, under Major-General Sir Robert
Pigott, had done little more than tie down an equal number of the
enemy, cantoned on the mainland. Left to himself, Pigott would
scarcely have been able to cope with a strong land-based Franco-
American assault supported by D'Estaing and the fleet under his command. But before hostile operations could be properly developed 'Black
Dick', with a slightly reinforced armada,[3] appeared off Judith Point.

D'Estaing immediately stood out to sea. But the impending fleet
action was frustrated by a violent storm which scattered both armaments in all directions; D'Estaing's flagship, the *Languedoc*, being
totally dismasted. There were two sharp encounters, however, when
the 50-gun *Preston* tackled the 80-gun *Tonnant*, and when the 50-gun
Isis challenged the 74-gun *Cassar*; a leading part in the latter engagement being played by the light company of the 23rd Fusiliers, acting
temporarily as Marines.

In the absence of naval support the Franco-American enterprise
against Pigott and his men made little progress; and with D'Estaing
announcing his intention of putting into Boston for repairs and taking
the French troops with him, operations collapsed. Many of the local
American militia drifted away to their farmsteads, and on 28th August

[1] Beatson, *op. cit.*
[2] Stedman, *op. cit.*
[3] Nine 64s and a 50-gun vessel joined from Halifax and a stray 74 from Admiral Byron's
fleet, which had been widely scattered in its passage across the Atlantic—'Foul-weather
Jack's' usual ill luck with the elements.

Sullivan raised the investment. Pigott followed him up at once, and there was some sharp fighting; and it was only the stout work of the rearguard under Nat Greene which enabled the main body to get safely away. Whereafter, as Captain Mackenzie noted with some satisfaction, 'the Rebels have now to all appearance quitted our Neighbourhood'.

As the outcome of this misadventure considerable ill feeling was generated between the Americans and their allies; there was a dangerous riot between French and Bostonian seamen, and an even fiercer affray in Charlestown; 'a French Major', Mackenzie noted, 'and several others have been killed'.

Clinton, with five thousand troops, arriving at Rhode Island on 1st September, was too late to participate in Sullivan's rebuff. On the return passage to New York, therefore, he contented himself by raiding such privateering havens as Bedford and Martha's Vineyard. Several vessels and many stores were destroyed, many sheep and cattle impounded; activities in which Simcoe's Queen's Rangers, Patrick Ferguson's Rangers, and the men of Banastre Tarleton's Legion were particularly prominent.

In September, a wearied and politically frustrated Lord Howe handed over the naval command to Admiral James Gambier; Vice-Admiral Byron retaining a squadron with which to blockade D'Estaing in Boston. 'Foul-weather Jack's' recently concentrated armament being driven off station by another furious gale, the Frenchman, with his re-fitted fleet, was free to steal out of harbour and head for the West Indies. The same day a force of over five thousand British troops, under Major-General James Grant, also put out for the Caribbean.

Intermixed with French, Spanish, Danish and Dutch possessions in the West Indies, such British island bases as Jamaica, St Vincent, Barbados and Dominica, together with such lesser islets as Tobago, Grenada, Nevis, Antigua, St Kitts and Barbuda, lay at the mercy of America for their supplies of food. This overriding consideration, plus the influence of skilfully contrived propaganda, had done much to weaken the Islanders' support for the British cause, at its best never particularly enthusiastic. The Bahamas were virtually in open rebellion, while 'the favour shown to American privateers by the French at Martinique, even before France took open part in the war, as also by the Danes at St Croix and the Dutch at St Eustatius, all worked for the strengthening of the pro-American party'[1] to be found in all the British

[1] Fortescue, *op. cit.*

possessions. It was undisputable, however, that domination of the Caribbean by the Royal Navy was essential so long as the movement of and communication between the land forces on American soil depended upon the untrammelled passage of vessels of British register.

The principal French base was Martinique; whence powerful forces were speedily detached for the capture of Dominica. Slightly to leeward of Martinique was the French-owned island of St Lucia; and this, in an archipelago in which the trade winds, for three-quarters of the year, blow steadily from south-east to north-west, was all-important. A strong British fleet in possession of St Lucia's excellent harbour of Castries could keep a sharp eye on any enemy armament in Martinique, and if necessary sally forth to engage it with all the advantage of the prevailing wind.

By 10th December General Grant and the troops from New York had joined a fleet under Admiral Samuel Barrington in the Barbados haven of Carlisle Bay. The British were still a hundred miles from their objective, but for all practical purposes were nearer to Castries than was Fort Royal, Martinique, some forty miles to leeward.

By 12th December the expeditious Barrington had started disembark-the Bloodybacks in St Lucia's Cul-de-Sac Bay; and by the next day white flags heralded the surrender of the French garrison distributed over Castries Bay, the height known as Morne Fortuné, and the peninsula of La Vigie, running on the north side of the harbour.

The white flags had scarcely been furled before D'Estaing's fleet out of Martinique hove in sight — a grim spectacle to an Admiral whose ships were outnumbered three to one, as to a General with no more than half the number of the troops at the disposal of the enemy. But neither of them yielded for a moment to despair. Barrington so skilfully disposed of his ships as to render approach to Cul-de-Sac Bay almost impossible; Grant's men were equally well posted on Morne Fortuné and La Vigie. Moreover, while the British boats could easily be prevented from transporting provisions from the Squadron to the Army by day, they could as easily pass through the French cruisers under the cover of night.

Nevertheless the situation of the British could scarcely have been more precarious. For the defeat of the Army would mean that French land batteries would be able to drive Barrington's Squadron into the jaws of D'Estaing's more powerful Fleet; while the Admiral's defeat would automatically bring about the Army's collapse from sheer want of supplies. Moreover, the nature of the terrain had compelled Grant to divide his numerically inferior force; with troops on the heights around Cul-de-Sac Bay, another contingent holding Morne Fortuné to secure the southern shore of Port Castries, and three battalions to hold La Vigie peninsula.

Of the alternatives open to the French commander, he chose to concentrate on a mass attack on Brigadier-General Medows's thirteen hundred Bloodybacks at La Vigie.[1] Veterans of Bunker Hill, Brooklyn, Fort Washington and Brandywine, on this day of agonizing trial they were perhaps the finest troops under arms in the whole of the world.

The Bloodybacks' main position, in rear of the neck of the peninsula, lay on the slopes of a low, scrub-covered hill, with the light companies deployed some way in advance of their comrades. The French columns, advancing from cover to overwhelm or drive in these light companies, found their progress held up and frustrated at every turn. If they sought to extend, they found themselves threatened with a bayonet charge. If they closed up, the nimble light infantrymen rapidly extended and poured in a galling fusillade. When the French columns advanced with solidity and determination, the 'Light Bobs' fell back and disappeared, but only to renew their fire, themselves invisible, from every direction. Their final retirement on their main body was covered by two Officers and three privates, who gallantly sacrificed themselves to ensure their comrades' safe withdrawal.

But now the main enemy swept forward like some ponderous irresistible tidal bore; with French sharpshooters on the flanks taking heavy toll of the Bloodyback ranks drawn up to receive them. Never pausing to fire a shot, the two main columns stolidly ploughed their way up the lower slopes, although frequently changing direction to right or left as though seeking for the easiest way to ascend the hill. Twice one of the columns broke up in disorder and was twice rallied. But at last the whole force drew up and stood at the halt well within close range of their red-coated adversaries. But there was no withering blast of fire such as might have been expected. The British ammunition had almost given out and Medows had passed the word to cease fire. Badly wounded as he was, the General gave his orders calmly and clearly: when the enemy had advanced near enough, the firing line must charge them with the bayonet, then rally upon the main body for a final charge

[1] They consisted of the 5th Foot, and the flank companies of 4th, 15th, 27th, 28th, 40th, 46th and 55th, massed together with those of the 5th in a grenadier and a light battalion.

under the General himself, 'to conquer or fall'. With their weapons dutifully brought down from the 'Present' to the 'Recover', the unflinching mass of Bloodybacks resigned themselves to endure the sharp sleet of the sharpshooters' fire which accompanied their comrades' continued progress up the hill. But as their advance closed in they were brought to a staggering halt by the two last shots from a couple of captured 12-pounders. Instantly realizing that the decisive moment was come, Major George Harris[1] ordered the grenadiers to fire their few remaining rounds into the wilting huddle of Frenchmen, who thereupon faced about and withdrew in considerable disorder, subsequently taking to their boats and returning to their transports.

In three hours of mortal struggle the British had lost 13 killed and 158 wounded; the French 400 killed and no less than 1,200 wounded. After the grim lesson of La Vigie, D'Estaing's subsequent attempts to possess himself of St Lucia were little more than perfunctory; and on 28th December Admiral Byron arrived with his squadron, thus putting an end to the superiority of the French fleet to windward. Barrington was free to put out from Cul-de-Sac Bay, and St Lucia was safe in British hands—a fact whose importance the future was very strikingly to demonstrate.

[1] Subsequently Lord Harris of Seringapatam.

I3

Limping Conflict

'One foot in sea and one on shore,
To one thing constant never.'
William Shakespeare

LORD NORTH's Conciliatory Bills, like the Carlisle peace mission subsequently sent to North America to try and reopen negotiations, were
predictably doomed to repudiation, since they failed to take into
account the Colonists' demand for unqualified independence.

There being no basis upon which hostilities could rationally be
terminated, the conflict continued to pursue its halting course. In ac-
cordance with his instructions, Clinton set about organizing a force,
consisting of two battalions of Frazer's Highlanders, four of Provincial
Infantry,[1] and two of Hessians, totalling about three thousand, under
the command of Lieutenant-Colonel Archibald Campbell, for an expedition for the reclamation of Georgia. For the support of this detachment General Augustine Prevost was given orders to move up to
Georgia from East Florida with such troops as could be spared, and
to take over command once he had effected his junction with
Campbell.

Owing to abominably bad weather, Campbell did not arrive in the
Savannah river until the end of December. Learning that the American
General, Robert Howe, had returned from raiding into Florida, was
encamped at Savannah itself, and was expecting reinforcements,

[1] In all, Clinton had about 4,000 Provincial troops; one corps of which was composed
entirely of Irish deserters from the American Army, under the Colonelcy of Lord Rawdon.
(Clinton to Germain, 23rd October, 1778.)

Campbell promptly got to work, sailing twelve miles upstream to disembark two miles from his objective.

Fired on by an outpost, the Highlanders went in with swinging claymores, while the light infantry worked around Howe's right rear. Once they were in position, Campbell unmasked his four guns and attacked front and rear. Stubbornly fighting back, the Americans found themselves hustled through and beyond Savannah, leaving eighty killed and eleven wounded on the field, to set against British casualties which totalled twenty-six.

Campbell's success brought in a number of loyalists with offers of active help; and the pick of them were promptly formed into militia companies and a squadron of light dragoons.

By 17th January, 1779, Campbell had been joined by General Prevost, who — being short of transport — had experienced such lean times while threading his way through the creeks and broads of East Florida that for days on end his troops had been limited to an unvaried diet of oysters!

With Prevost and Campbell united, the British force under the former's command came to just under four thousand, exclusive of local accretions. The Americans had also been reinforced; but with Prevost's establishment of a line of posts connecting Augusta and the base at Savannah, by the end of February practically the whole of Georgia 'had returned to its allegiance to King George. One tragic incident alone dimmed this brilliant campaign. A body of eighty loyalists marching to join Campbell at Augusta were attacked and captured by the Rebel militia. Seventy were tried by a revolutionary court, and five were hanged. It was but a part of the extreme bitterness which the loyalists and Rebels had shown each other since the war began in the Southern States...In Georgia the loyalists replied to this cruel sentence by reprisals no less bloodthirsty.'[1] Quite clearly what the separatists claimed to be a war of independence was, in fact, a civil war, with all the venom, brutality, barbarous intimidation and equally savage retaliation which such a violent cleavage inevitably entails.

Incessant partisan strife continued to characterize the ensuing months; with Prevost's attempt to secure Charlestown frustrated by an American force under the command of General Benjamin Lincoln. Then with the seasonal heat and increasing sickness curbing

---

[1] Lieutenant-General Sir George MacMunn, *The American War of Independence in Perspective*. Cf. Fortescue, *op. cit.*

activities on both sides, major operations came to a temporary halt.

The successful defence of St Lucia had also put a temporary stop to D'Estaing's activities in the Caribbean. In June, however, a large trading convoy had drawn off the bulk of Byron's fleet to act as escorts; and by the end of the month D'Estaing had emerged to snap up St Vincent and Grenada. With Byron's return the British fleet headed for Grenada, where the Frenchman was immediately, indeed, almost too precipitously, engaged. Since D'Estaing had by far the heavier metal, Byron was roughly handled, the French disabling tactics immobilizing four of the British vessels so that they could contribute nothing further to the fight.[1] As a result D'Estaing was free to return to Grenada's St George's Harbour, while Byron limped off to St Kitts; command of the sea remaining with the French. For such a setback the British capture of French harbours of St Pierre and Miquelon, off the Newfoundland fishing banks, offered small recompense.

With the hurricane season approaching, it was D'Estaing's intention, after a partial refit, to return to France for thorough overhaul. Before he could set out, however, the Americans in South Carolina appealed to him for help. Thither the Frenchman sailed, therefore, arriving at Savannah on the last day of August, at the head of a fleet of twenty-two ships of the line, eleven frigates and a number of transports. The British squadron off the river, taken by surprise, lost two warships and a couple of storeships.

In Savannah Prevost could muster no more than 2,200 effectives, to confront a combined force of 4,500, of whom 3,500 were trained French Infantry. But with the aid of a Negro labour corps the British commander had so powerfully strengthened his defences that although in the assault on the works both a French and an American flag got through to be planted on the parapets, the attack was broken up after suffering some nine hundred casualties, for a loss of fifty-four on the part of the defenders.[2]

Hurricanes wait for no man, so amidst an interchange of mutual recriminations, D'Estaing set his course for Europe, with comparatively little to show for the superiority in numbers and metal he had enjoyed in West Indian waters.

Towards the close of 1778 Clinton had received orders to send a

---

[1] See Byron's despatch, '*Princess Royal* at sea, July 8, 1779'.
[2] French losses totalled 637, American 264.

detachment from the troops in Nova Scotia 'to take post on the River Penobscot, by way of securing a place of reception and a permanent establishment in the Provice of Maine for the King's loyal American subjects who had been driven from their habitations and deprived of their property by the rebels'.[1] Eventually Brigadier-General MacLean and some 650 Bloodybacks arrived on the Penobscot and set about founding a fortified settlement.

The authorities in Boston speedily responded by organizing an expedition for the extirpation of the intrusive Bloodybacks. Under the command of Captain Saltonstall, twenty armed vessels and twenty-four transports, accommodating a substantial body of troops, headed north-east. MacLean's defensive works being no more than half completed, the American landing was first met by a line of picquets, very courage-ously commanded by eighteen-year-old Ensign John Moore. In due course the Bloodybacks withdrew to their tenuous fieldworks, and for a full fortnight endured steady battering from the enemy guns; sallying forth in several sorties which materially retarded the Americans in their work of sapping forward. Then, even more suddenly than they had appeared, the besiegers vanished. A British squadron, under Sir George Collier, had loomed up in the mouth of the river, and after forming line as if for action, the Americans had given way, every vessel seeking its own safety. Two put out to sea but were promptly intercepted. The rest fled upstream. A few were taken, but the majority were driven ashore, where crews and troops took refuge in the forest, foodless and without water. 'Soldiers and sailors soon fell to blaming each other for the disaster; from abuse they came to blows, and from blows to a pitched battle. Fifty or sixty were killed on the spot; a far larger number perished of hunger and fatigue; and only an exhausted remnant found its way back to the settled districts of the province.'[2] Of Saltonstall's squadron every vessel was either captured or destroyed.

On 16th June, 1779, war had formally been declared between Great Britain and Spain; and almost immediately the Bloodybacks in Gib-raltar had found themselves besieged by a numerically superior Franco-Spanish force. Furthermore, a joint fleet was assembled at Brest and 50,000 French troops concentrated in Normandy and Britanny, whose purpose was the immediate invasion of England. So confident were the

[1] Sir Henry Clinton's *Narrative*.
[2] Fortescue, *op. cit.*

allies of success that the Comte de Vergennes was freely named as Viceroy of England, with M. de Cartine nominated as 'Lord Mayor and First Lord of the Admiralty'! Even more sanguine was the Comte de Vaux, Maréchal de France, who from his Headquarters at St Malo solemnly warned his troops that once they were established on English soil they should confine their potations to small beer, since strong beer would be found altogether too heady.

Since a number of Flag Officers had put politics before patriotism by refusing to serve while Sandwich remained at the head of the Admiralty, command of such miserable naval forces as could be mustered to try and repel invasion fell to Admiral Sir Charles Hardy. A veteran of the Seven Years' War, for over eight years his Governorship of Greenwich Hospital had denied him any form of sea service. Moreover, he was old for his sixty-three years and indeed not far from senility. At the head of thirty-five sail of the line and a few supporting craft, Hardy hovered between Plymouth and Tor Bay, while an enemy armada of sixty-six sail of the line and innumerable smaller rates lorded it in the western approaches of the Channel. Throughout July, August and September, however, there was constant stormy weather, with seas that ruled out any possibility of committing the four hundred invasion barges to a Channel crossing. Aboard the enemy vessels there was an increasing shortage of provisions, while 'ship's fever' and other ailments were so epidemic that, with a sick list of eight thousand d'Orvilliers ultimately abandoned all plans for invasion. In Paris Sartine hastily explained that 'greater aid could be afforded the Americans by the transfer of naval activity to the Caribbean'; where Mobile and Pensacola, on the Florida coast, were shortly to be wrenched from British possession. At no moment since the Dutch penetration of the Medway in the June of 1667 had England's peril been so great — or the people's appreciation of the threat so scant.

For Clinton in New York the early months of the year had brought such a spate of contradictory orders and peremptory suggestions that the British Commander-in-Chief had been constrained to write Germain, 'For God's sake, my lord, if you wish me to do anything, leave me to myself, and let me adapt my efforts to the hourly change of circumstances. If not, tie me down and take the risk of my want of success.'

Fundamentally, Clinton's aim was to bring Washington to the choice of abandoning the line of the Hudson or of fighting a decisive battle on

11*

disadvantageous terms. But for this he needed substantial reinforcement, and although Germain was expansive enough on paper about additional troops, the actual men were not forthcoming. Clinton therefore had to content himself with such gadfly raids as those on Verplanck's and Stony Point[1] commanding the main route across the Hudson below the Highlands—to which the best riposte Washington could engineer was to occupy West Point in force.

For the American Commander-in-Chief was in little better case to embark upon major operations than was Clinton. In a military sense, such men of the Continental Line as were still with him had never been in better shape—von Steuben had seen to that. But his numbers were pitifully few; and it was idle for Congress to offer bounties to reinforce the Continental Line when the different States could—and would—always outbid them to enlist levies for their own regional security. In any case the purchasing power of the scrip authorized by Congress had depreciated so abnormally that when men referred contemptuously to something as being virtually of no value they described it as not being 'worth a Continental'. With clothing and equipment still in short supply and pay—such as it was—months in arrear, the mutinous mood of the troops was such that Washington had no option but to petition Congress for permission to introduce the lash as the punishment for certain of the more heinous military crimes. Hereafter, there were to be bloody backs on both sides of the fence![2]

With the withdrawal of D'Estaing's fleet after its repulse before Savannah, Clinton was free to transport troops by sea in whatever direction he pleased. A few reinforcements had reached him, 'although they brought with them a malignant jail fever which soon spread itself through the rest of the Army and sent about six thousand of the best troops to hospital.'[3] Ultimately, however, Clinton found himself in a position to organize an expedition for the conquest of Carolina. Georgia was no longer in a position to send or receive goods or remittances to France or the West Indies; if Carolina could be reduced to a similar state of mercantile impotence the iron law of economics would supplement military victory to bring about submission.

So Clinton, having evacuated the Rhode Island garrison to bring his

---

[1] Stony Point was subsequently retaken in a model night attack led by 'Mad Anthony' Wayne. It was finally abandoned by both sides.

[2] With the American forces, however, the maximum award was 500 lashes.

[3] Clinton, *op. cit.*

force up to a total of 7,600, headed south; 'although he had a healthy distrust of plans which depended for their success on the co-operation of the inhabitants'.[1] The passage was so stormy that it was 11th February, 1780, before the British armada made the mouth of the Edisto, to push across the chain of islands to Charleston. Much of Clinton's artillery had gone to the bottom in a storm, and nearly all of his gun-teams and cavalry horses had perished at sea. But he lost no time in establishing his base on St John's Island and in throwing a line of works across Charleston Neck, between the Ashley and Cooper rivers, which enclosed the city on the west and east. With blustering Admiral Marriot Arbuthnot forcing his way past the Fort Moultrie batteries, for the loss of twenty-seven seamen, killed and wounded, Charleston – with its garrison of seven thousand Continental Line and militia – was closely invested.

A successful foray to the American *entrepôt* at Biggin's Bridge, conducted by Tarleton and Ferguson at the head of their respective Legions, completely severed Charleston's communications with the North. On 26th April Lord Rawdon arrived from New York with a reinforcement of 2,500 men, who were deployed so as to block any Rebel aid originating in the area to the east of the Cooper; while Fort Moultrie fell to the combined efforts of the Fleet's guns and a landing party of seamen and Marines. Two summonses to surrender had been rejected when, on 6th May, the Bloodybacks opened their third parallel [trench] within two hundred yards of the enemy abattis. On the 8th the British drained the canal in front of the fortifications, 'and the picquets, crossing the ditch by sap, advanced within twenty-five yards of the American works'.[2] Four days later General Benjamin Lincoln capitulated unconditionally. Having twice previously rejected a summons, he was denied the customary 'honours of war', his troops being ordered to march out with Colours cased and with their band playing an *American* march-tune. American losses had come to 92 killed and 146 wounded. So for casualties amounting to 76 killed and 179 wounded the Bloodybacks had brought about the surrender of 5,500 Officers and men and over 1,000 sailors; their spoil of war including 17 Colours, 391 guns, 5,000 muskets and large quantities of stores and ammunition. Since this brilliant success occurred on the very scene of his earlier

[1] Wilkin, *op. cit.*

[2] Lamb, *op. cit.* After his escape from captivity Serjeant Lamb had been posted to his old formation, the 23rd Foot.

failure, Clinton found it particularly gratifying. He was yet to learn that in the larger sense its influence upon events was purely transitory.

For the danger of seeking to prosecute the war in two widely separated regions of America was daily becoming more apparent. Moreover, at any moment the return of the French fleet might be expected, with the dire threat to communications, as to further enterprises, which this entailed. So Clinton hastened back to New York with four thousand men, leaving Cornwallis — newly returned from England — to complete the conquest of the Carolinas; a dispersion rather than a concentration of force more typical of the politician-amateur strategist than of the trained and experienced soldier.

Left on his own, 'Old Corncob' — the troops' invariable name for Cornwallis — found himself in the invidious position of a leader commanding a small Regular force dependent upon extremely vulnerable lines of communication and supply, in an extensive area swarming with extremely active and wily guerrillas. With such formal engagements as his encounter with 'Granny' Gates at Camden, on 16th August, Cornwallis could be relied upon to make use of his Bloodybacks to very best advantage. Gates was struck hard and hustled into precipitate retreat; while a little later the impetuous Tarleton brought off a neat surprise attack on the bivouac sheltering Colonel Thomas Sumter and his followers, of whom a hundred and fifty were killed or wounded and over two hundred taken captive. But the guerrillas were not so easily dealt with; while the scattering of the British and their loyalist supporters in a number of small, widely separated posts was an open invitation to their opponents to mop them up in detail. One of the first victims of this fatal policy of dispersion was Patrick Ferguson, whose death at King's Mountain, at the head of a battered remnant of his Rangers and Militia, offered little encouragement for loyalists actively to intervene in support of the British cause.

In the North a squadron transporting six thousand French troops put in to Rhode Island, where the whole force was speedily blockaded by Admiral Marriot Arbuthnot. With Washington and Clinton equally watchful for any movement on the part of his opponent, events were given a dramatic but ugly turn by Benedict Arnold's unsuccessful attempt to 'sell out' West Point to the British; the traitor's flight to Clinton's protection; the arrest of the gallant but unfortunate André in civilian dress behind the American lines; his trial and condemnation as a spy; and the inevitable death sentence which no one deplored more sincerely than the members of the Court Martial whose inescapable duty it had been to impose it.

In the West Indies the position was one of virtual stalemate. A French attack on St Lucia was resolutely beaten off, despite the sickly state of the Bloodybacks garrisoning the island. An inconclusive action between de Guichen and Admiral Rodney was followed by an abortive attempt to overpower the Spanish defences on the Nicaraguan isthmus — a failure entirely attributable to the insufficiency of the British troops and warships committed to the task.

A predatory force, under Major-General Leslie, was then sent to the Chesapeake with the object of gaining touch with Cornwallis and severing enemy communications between Virginia and Carolina. At the last moment Cornwallis, confronted with the disturbing realization that the tranquillity in South Carolina on which he had relied was entirely illusory, begged that Leslie might be sent to Cape Fear, where his co-operation might really prove of value.

Naval resources in the Caribbean were further reduced by the effects of a violent hurricane which in early October struck Jamaica and Barbados in two successive blasts of unprecedented fury. Not only were buildings and harbour facilities razed to the ground,[1] but twelve warships were lost and twenty-three others were damaged in greater or lesser degree. Enemy shipping also suffered, if not so direfully; while in a second tornado St Lucia, Lucia, Dominica, Grenada and St Vincent also underwent considerable destruction.

Later in the same month Great Britain's difficulties were increased by the Northern Powers' declaration of a state of Armed Neutrality;[2] a hostile demonstration which, among other things, deprived Great Britain of her principal source of ship's timber and masting. Since Holland was not only known to have been rendering covert assistance to the revolted Colonies, but to be on the brink of concluding a treaty with them, war was declared on 20th of December. Almost immediately they were given ample cause to rue their hostility, for Rodney's capture of the Dutch outpost of St Eustatius secured the most richly bulging storehouse and source of enemy supplies in the whole of the West Indies. Six men of war and a hundred and fifty merchantmen were seized in the bay, and thirty more, with an armed escort, were pursued

[1] The Governor's residence at Bridgetown, Barbados, with walls over three feet thick, was tumbled into complete ruin.

[2] The coalition was made up of Russia, Sweden and Denmark.

and taken outside; while the value of the war booty gathered in came to £4,000,000 sterling.[1]

Shortly after the Dutch islands of Demarara and Essequibo were captured by a squadron of British privateers. But Admiral Sir Samuel Hood was unable to prevent de Grasse from sailing into Martinique to add the four warships sheltering there to the twenty-one warcraft he had brought with him from Brest. A French attempt to capture St Lucia, however, ended in failure; although Tobago was taken after a stout resistance, Rodney appearing on the scene too late to avert the island's surrender. Inferior strength at sea in the Caribbean, and the demands of Clinton for vessels to maintain his communications with the South and to protect New York, had strained the Royal Navy's limited resources far beyond their capacity. The wonder is that they had done as well as they had.

On the mainland Washington had despatched a force under 'the Boy' to head off Benedict Arnold, whom Clinton had entrusted with the command of yet another diversionary operation on the Chesapeake; although Simcoe was also sent along to keep a wary eye upon a man whose demonstrable facility for turning his coat was such as scarcely to inspire confidence. In the event, Arnold raided as far up-country as Richmond, wreaking considerable damage before retiring to Portsmouth (Virginia); where he was joined by another 'force of detachment' under Major-General 'Minden' Phillips.

Washington was bitterly disappointed that Lafayette had failed to corner the arch-traitor, Arnold. But it had been impossible to assign the task to Nat Greene – by far the Commander-in-Chief's most reliable subordinate – since his services were urgently required in the Carolinas; where a rebuff inflicted on Tarleton by Sumter had done much to revivify enthusiasm for the cause of independence.

Temporarily based at Winnsborough, a township some twenty-eight miles north-west of Camden, Cornwallis was convinced that if anything like permanent tranquillity were to be established in the South, it was essential that he should exchange a purely defensive posture in the coastal areas for an aggressive move to clean up the interior – particularly in North Carolina – even if this involved denuding the New York garrison of yet more troops to act as reinforcements.

---

[1] To Rodney's chagrin, much of this valuable booty was recaptured by the French while it was in transit to England.

Detaching small forces to either flank to cope with such partisan leaders as might seek to harry and hinder his advance, 'Old Corncob' set out to try and force a general action on Nat Greene, which he hoped would prove decisive. By a very able and teasing withdrawal, Greene succeeded in luring his adversary as far inland as the Roanoke. By this time the Bloodybacks were pretty well worn fine. In six weeks they had marched two hundred and fifty miles; they were short of supplies, and dangerously remote from their nearest reserve of stores. Moreover they harboured the depressing knowledge that their left flanking force under Tarleton had been badly defeated at Cowpens.

But there was no sign of demoralization among them when, on 15th March, Nat Greene at last turned to offer battle at Guildford Court House. With 1,715 men of the Continental Line and 2,600 militia,[1] Greene enjoyed a clear numerical superiority over his opponent, whose effectives came to under 2,000,[2] less 350 men left to guard the baggage and dwindling supplies.

Marching up the Guildford Road, the half-starving Bloodybacks found their opponents established in an excellent position just below the Court House. They immediately deployed; Cornwallis having determined to try and turn the American left, where the terrain was a little less enclosed by timber. Amidst a punishing sleet of bullets the two wings steadily advanced across the clearing on either side of the road, to go in with bayonet. But although the American centre gave way before the menace of the cold steel, heavy fire continued to batter at the Bloodybacks from both flanks. With the supporting British battalions wheeling outwards to deal with the fusillade beating in obliquely from the woodlands, the enemy sharpshooters were hunted from tree to tree, and the whole line pressed forward. Halted and driven back by Greene's experienced and courageous 1st Marylanders, the Bloodybacks were speedily rallied and once again went in to the attack. But the Guards were badly broken up by the Marylanders and by a sudden onslaught on the part of Colonel William Washington's small corps of cavalry.

For a time the action flagged; but weary and famished as they were, the redcoats were still full of fight. To the thud of drums and the

---

[1] William Johnson, *Sketches of Nathanael Greene.*

[2] Fortescue, *op. cit.* Cornwallis's force was made up of two Guards battalions, Frazer's Highlanders, the 23rd and 33rd Foot, Bose's Hessian Regiment, some Jägers, grenadiers and light infantry, together with Tarleton's cavalry.

squealing fife, the thin red line again strode resolutely forward. As Tarleton's cavalrymen swept away the militia's resistance on the right, the Bloodybacks' bayonets again came down to the charge. Greene's men loosed a searing volley, but although it took heavy toll of the advancing ranks, it failed to halt them. Then as Tarleton and the Hessians came round on the flank, Greene, seeing that the day was lost, gave the signal to retreat.

'Never perhaps has the prowess of the British soldier been seen to greater advantage than in this obstinate and bloody conflict.' Short of food, preposterously under strength,[1] the Bloodybacks had driven hard-fighting adversaries of twice their number from a position chosen and advantaged with all the enemy commander's wonted sagacity and skill.

But the Americans had exacted a very heavy price for victory — 28 Officers killed and wounded, 93 rank and file killed and 439 wounded.[2] And a minuscule force such as Cornwallis commanded on 15th March cannot win such costly victories and continue usefully to survive in the field. 'Old Corncob' had been gulled. Greene had drawn him far from his base of supplies, harrying him all the way, and finally exacted an appalling toll for a Pyrrhic victory which led nowhere — except to more privation and continued harassment. Cornwallis might be winning the battles, but it was Greene who was gaining the campaign.

After two days' rest for his exhausted troops, Cornwallis — leaving seventy of his critically wounded to the mercy of the enemy — limped back the hundred and seventy-five miles to Wilmington (North Carolina), the nearest base at which he could be supplied by sea. It was a move which, as Clinton clearly perceived, 'exposed the two valuable Colonies behind him to be overrun and conquered by that very army which he boasts to have completely routed only a week or two before'.[3]

At Wilmington Cornwallis suddenly took it into his head to set off along the coast to link up with the British detachment sent by Clinton to the Chesapeake.

This was Greene's opportunity to set to work to mop up the eight thousand Bloodybacks still left in the South, but scattered between Charleston, Savannah and a number of small posts. Held off by Lord

[1] For example the two battalions of Guards, including Brigadier and Staff, together with the detached grenadier and light companies, came to no more than 481 all told.

[2] Greene lost 79 killed and 185 wounded, but among the 'missing' were over a thousand North Carolina militia.

[3] Clinton, *op. cit.*

Rawdon at Camden and by his successor at Eutaw, it was none the less clear that the British grip on Georgia and the Carolinas was as progressively, as inevitably, being loosened.

It was still Clinton's hope, however, that, while Cornwallis continued to hold Greene in check, a movement by Arnold and Phillips could be developed which would cut off American supplies to the South and perhaps — in concert with the New York troops — carry operations successfully into Pennsylvania; a pincer movement which Washington would find it hard to parry. Alternatively, an attempt might be made to assail and defeat the French fleet at Newport and such of their troops as were stationed on Rhode Island. All thought of such designs was abruptly terminated, however, with the unexpected and unwelcome news that Cornwallis was marching up to Virginia to take over command from Phillips. This intelligence was followed, on 9th June, by news that Phillips had died, and that 'Old Corncob', with a mere 5,300 troops, was individually seeking to consolidate the British position in the South by attempting the conquest of Washington's own State of Virginia — where active loyalist support was at a minimum.

Anticipating a strong Franco-American assault on New York, and in great uneasiness about the Royal Navy's power to dominate local waters, Clinton ultimately sent his subordinate orders to 'take up a defensive station in any healthy position he preferred'.[1]

Having soundly trounced Lafayette on the James river, Cornwallis moved down to Yorktown, the 'tobacco township' on the York river, parallel to and east of the James, on the tip of a peninsula where he could furnish protection for the shipping on which he would have to rely for supplies and reinforcements. A small force, including Tarleton's and Simcoe's respective formations, was thrown into Gloucester, on the other side of the waterway. In this isolated position Cornwallis settled down to await the additional battalions which Clinton had been hustled into promising for his subordinate's support.

It was at this juncture that Washington learned of Admiral de Grasse's safe arrival from the West Indies and his intention to emerge from his James river anchorage, elude the British squadron patrolling between New York and the Caribbean and land a contingent of 3,200 troops at the head of the Chesapeake. Immediately the American leader and his French colleague, the Comte de Rochambeau, led their combined forces south; the continued investment of New York being

[1] Cornwallis, *Correspondence.*

entrusted to the somewhat pedestrian but reliable Major-General William Heath.

Belated news of de Grasse's movements brought Rear-Admiral Thomas Graves hurrying to the Chesapeake. Here, on 5th September, the British squadron caught their enemies emerging, in somewhat straggling formation, from the shelter of Cape Henry into the open waters of the Bay.[1] 'Graves was in a position almost beyond the wildest dreams of a sea commander',[2] but the Rear-Admiral's rigid observance of outmoded, over-formalized Fighting Instructions and a hopeless muddle over signals threw away all chance of victory. By the day's end the British had lost command in local waters; and with Graves's withdrawal to New York to refit, the French were free to block the York river and cut off Cornwallis from all immediate hope of support.

By 14th September Washington and Rochambeau had joined Lafayette at the head of 9,000 American and 7,000 French troops, with a formidable train of artillery; and the combined force lost no time in moving upon Yorktown. To hold this little township of sixty homesteads Cornwallis could muster 7,500 Bloodybacks, merchant seamen and Royal Navy hands from the 44-gun *Charon*, the *Guadeloupe*, and three transports, blocked in the York river—less the 500 troops detached to Gloucester.[3] The few 18-pounders available were supplemented by a fair number of coehorns, a species of mortar of small calibre and limited range.

Covered both east and west by swamplands, Yorktown had been furnished with three redoubts, with small additional earthworks covering the marshy approaches. The town itself was protected by a stockade and hastily improvised earthworks, enclosing an area far too restricted for safety; while supplies were barely sufficient to last out three weeks, and were already deteriorating in quality.

By 28th September the Franco-American forces were moving into position—the French contingent facing the British right—to form a *demilune* whose extremities were bounded by the York river, both to the east and west. Few besiegers can have had their objective better centred; and the task of overcoming resistance was put vigorously in hand.

[1] Graves's Despatch, *London at Sea*, September 14th 1781.

[2] James, *op. cit.*

[3] In addition to the Guards contingent, the garrison included elements of the 7th, 23rd, 33rd, 60th, 63rd, 64th and 71st Foot, a handful of Gunners, Bose's Hessians and certain other German auxiliaries, and a few Loyalist Volunteers.

Dawn light on 1st October revealed that the British had abandoned their outer line of defence, where the earthworks linking the three redoubts, having been little more than traced, were quite untenable.[1] Yet that night Cornwallis wrote assuring Clinton that, providing relief were not too long delayed, 'York and Gloucester will both be in possession of His Majesty's troops'.

By 6th October the besiegers had opened their first parallel, a mere five hundred yards from Yorktown's inner line of works; and while Tarleton and his Legion skirmished bloodily with Lauzun's Hussars in the countryside beyond Gloucester, the weight and intensity of the cannonade directed at Yorktown's frail defences steadily mounted. On the York river red-hot shot severely hulled the *Charon* and the three transports before they could slip their cables, only the *Guadeloupe* escaping to find shelter behind a bluff.

Opening an inner parallel on 11th October, the besiegers soon discovered that it was enfiladed by the two redoubts on the left face of the British defences, and it was resolved to carry them forthwith. Delay could not be tolerated since de Grasse was under orders to return to the West Indies and could not indefinitely maintain the blockade which barred the way to any seaborne sources of relief for Yorktown's defenders.

On 14th October, therefore, two assault parties, one American and one French, stole out under cover of darkness, intent on storming the redoubts. With Alexander Hamilton at their head, the American detachment tore their way through the hampering abattis and scrambled up into the work. It was a hand-to-hand struggle, fought out with clubbed musket and the cold steel, with the unsupported handful of Bloody-backs outnumbered and overwhelmed until the few left unwounded sullenly threw down their arms. If the French took longer over their share of the task, it was because they had waited for their pioneers to clear the obstacles holding up their advance. With the redoubts in the allies' hands, the guns mounted in them were swung about to add their fire to the general cannonade of the crumbling British defences.

The rain of missiles was maintained so furiously that two nights later a sortie was launched from the British lines on the American artillery positions. Led by the two Commanding Officers of the Guards — Lake

---

[1] French maps of defences they have ultimately overcome are apt to delineate them as far more formidable than they were in fact. The author's aerial survey of the terrain revealed that this was certainly the case with their Yorktown maps.

and Abercrombie — three hundred and fifty men went briskly into an attack which momentarily carried all before it. The two redoubts were temporarily won back; eleven guns were spiked, and close on a hundred of the enemy killed or wounded. But the advantage gained could not be held. Allied reinforcements were hurried to the scene of action, and in remarkably short order the raiding party was thrown out of the works it had briefly repossessed. Roll-call disclosed a heavy list of casualties; and since nothing more effective than bayonets had been employed to spike the enemy guns, they were soon repaired and again in action.

Despite another assurance that relief was on the way — received on 10th October — there could be no dispute that the situation of the besieged was deteriorating rapidly. Battle casualties were approaching five hundred, with dysentery and 'marsh fever' claiming their many victims, the sick numbered close on two thousand; food was running short; the defence works were so battered as to offer the minimum of protection. Only one 8-inch and a little over a hundred coehorn shells remained in hand. An attempt to pass over to Gloucester and fight a way through to the escape route up the peninsula was frustrated by a violent storm of wind and rain, which drove away many of the troop-laden boats helplessly downstream — to be picked up by de Grasse at the rivermouth.

On the morning of 17th October, with the crescendo of enemy gun-fire steadily mounting, a scarlet-clad drummer was seen to clamber up the hornwork in the centre of the tumbled British defences, resignedly beating the *chamade*.[1]

As the guns fell silent an English Officer was brought into the Allied lines bearing a formal request for 'a cessation of hostilities,...to settle terms for the surrender of the posts of York and Gloucester'. With the certain knowledge that Clinton was straining every nerve to come to the beleaguered garrison's relief, the Commander's unlooked-for submission scarcely reflected the Bloodybacks' readiness to hold out to the last round.

There was considerable exchange of correspondence before the terms of capitulation were finally agreed. For on one point Washington had proved obdurate. Since at Charleston General Lincoln had been denied the customary 'honours of war', the British in Yorktown should suffer

---

[1] After a careful reconnaissance of the terrain, the author came to the settled conclusion that despite his difficulties, given the will, Cornwallis could have prolonged his defence by several days.

a similar degree of abasement — marching out to lay down their arms with their Colours furled and cased and with their band playing an *English* air.[1]

Cornwallis was scarcely in the mood to bargain for less humiliating terms. The best he could do was to obtain clearance for the sloop *Bonetta* to carry tidings of the surrender to New York. With this, he crammed the vessel with loyalists whose fate, had they been allowed to fall into enemy hands, would almost certainly have been the hangman's rope.

Then, a little before noon on 19th October, with the Franco-American forces drawn up in double rank along the York–Hampton turnpike, the Bloodybacks strode forth from battered Yorktown to make surrender. With their precious Colours duly cased, grim-faced and tight-lipped, but spick and span in newly issued uniforms, they marched out to the ironically apposite English air of 'The World Turned Upside Down'.

Pleading a convenient indisposition, Cornwallis was absent from the final ceremony of surrender, being represented by his Second-in-Command. So it was Brigadier-General O'Hara who formally rendered up his sword, not to Washington or Rochambeau, but to the eager hand of Benjamin Lincoln.[2] For him, at least, the wheel had swung full circle.

On that same day Clinton, escorted by a strong naval armament, sailed to his subordinate's relief, reaching the Chesapeake just five days too late.

---

[1] Actually, there was no analogy between the Charleston and Yorktown surrenders, since at Charleston General Lincoln had twice been summoned before agreeing — on the third occasion — to submit; grounds enough, according to current military practice, to warrant the terms imposed on him.

[2] He had been exchanged for General Phillips in the previous November.

14

For Whom the Bell Tolls

'Peace is come and wars are over,
Welcome you and welcome all,
Where the charger crops the clover
And his bridle hangs in stall.
Rest you, charger, rust your bridle;
Kings and Caesars keep your pay;
Soldier sit you down and idle
At the inn of night for aye.'
A. E. Housman

THE WEARIED CONFLICT did not end with Yorktown; but the writing clearly was on the wall. With long-enduring strife in India to support as well as the campaigns in Europe, North America and the West Indies, Great Britain's inadequate and ill-organized resources – particularly those of an under-nourished Royal Navy – were quite unable to cope with the demands made upon them, even had her commanders been spared the handicap of the uninformed and frustrating political direction by which their activities were controlled. North, amiable, bumbling, 'with the look of a blind trumpeter'; Germain, with neither skill nor understanding, and lacking even that tradition of statesmanship which prevents men without either from doing irreparable harm; Sandwich, so corrupt that plain honesty of purpose was beyond the range of his comprehension – these were the men by whom the Bloodyback was thrust blindly to and fro across the board in a deadly game wherein the pawns could look for no more than sacrifice.

In effect, Yorktown was but the herald of further disaster. For de Grasse, having left the Chesapeake on 5th November, was forced by unfavourable winds to abandon a projected attempt to capture Barbados, and turned his attention to the lesser task of snapping up St Kitts. But for the treachery of the planter oligarchy, Admiral Hood and the garrison commander, Brigadier-General Simon Frazer, would almost certainly have been able to hold their own. As it was, the island's

342

fall followed closely on the recapture of St Eustatius and St Martin by another French expedition which set out from Martinique. Nevis and Montserrat being entirely without defences, fell immediately, while Demerara and Essiquibo were recovered with such little effort that de Grasse started to work out ambitious plans for the subjugation of Jamaica.

In European waters Rear-Admiral Richard Kempenfelt's successful raid on a convoy shepherded by de Guichen was more than offset by the loss of Minorca; although Gibraltar continued to defy every attempt to bring it to submission.

At this juncture Admiral Rodney, arriving from Europe with twelve ships of the line, made contact with Hood to the eastward of Antigua. De Grasse promptly took shelter in Port Royal, while Rodney put into Gros Islet Bay, St Lucia; the Bloodybacks' tenacious retention of which was now to reap a handsome dividend. For the French fleet at Martinique could make no move without it coming to the immediate attention of the watch-dog British frigates based on Castries. Day after day Rodney clambered up the rocks of Pigeon Island, peering eagerly for the signal which would notify that de Grasse had put to sea.

It came at last on the 8th of April. Setting out to attempt the conquest of Jamaica, the French fleet and troop transports were eventually intercepted by Rodney in the Saintes Passage between Dominica and Guadeloupe.

After certain opening exchanges from which Hood's van — separated by gusty winds from the balance of the fleet — managed to extricate itself from a situation of no little peril, nightfall brought activities to a temporary halt. Next day, as the rival fleets were sailing past each other in orthodox line ahead, exchanging thunderous broadsides, a flaw in the capricious wind created two gaps in de Grasse's formation, through which Rodney's centre and Hood's rear divisions were free to pass — unorthodox as such a procedure might be in terms of contemporary Fighting Instructions.

With the enemy's line of battle thus fortuitously broken just abaft the centre division and the van, Rodney promptly seized his opportunity and steered his own 90-gun *Formidable* through the foremost gap, passing within pistol shot of the *Glorieux*, which was raked by every gun that could be brought to bear. Hood, now bringing up the English rear, eagerly followed his leader's example, slicing through the second fissure just abaft the Frenchman's van. In that moment the enemy fleet ceased to be a line of battle, but dissolved into three dislocated fractions, to be minced to pieces by the pounding British guns. In the general *mêlée* which ensued, Gallic morale speedily evaporated under a hammering such as the French Navy had not experienced since Hawke's victory at Quiberon Bay in the November of 1759. De Grasse, in his splendid 104-gun *Ville de Paris*,[1] was forced into surrender, 'and of the remainder of the French ships, those that were not sunk or captured fled, without semblance of anything but flight, in disintegrated consternation'.[2]

Small wonder the fourteen-year-old 'Captain's servant', Joseph Sidney Yorke, could write exultantly to his uncle, Lord Hardwicke:

> We have stopped all the Proceedings of the French against Jamaica. We have taken, burnt and Sunk 6 Sail of the Line. The *Ville de Paris* of 110 Gune (*sic*) struck at [to] Us, and Sr Charles Douglas went on Board of her and said that the *Formidable* was a Bomb Boat [Bomb Ketch] to her. De Grasse is a Prisoner on Board this Ship and he is all most a head taller than Brother Charles...I suppose the French did not lose Less than 6000 Men Prisoners, and I sincerely believe that had it been day Light 4 hours Longer, We must have destroyed them all, but as it is they are dispersed all over the west Indies. Two Admls are taken and I don't know who will command them. I hear there is 80,000 Dollars on board the *Ville de Paris*, which I believe is truth.[3]

British victory in the battle of the Saintes not only wrested Naval superiority from the French, but also 'marked the beginning of that fierce and headlong yet well-calculated style of sea-fighting which led to Trafalgar, and made England undisputed mistress of the sea'.[4]

A little later a motley contingent of Rangers, logwood cutters, Indians, and a few Bloodybacks attacked and took captive the entire Spanish force on the Black river, thus regaining for England all her possessions in the Gulf of Honduras.

Yet, ironically enough, even as the vital contest of the Saintes was being fought out, a missive was on its way terminating Rodney's command and recalling him to England. For North's Government had

---

[1] The *Ville de Paris* was the finest ship afloat. She had been presented to Louis XV by the City of Paris, and was said to have cost, for those days, the tremendous sum of £156,000.

[2] Callender, *op. cit.*

[3] B.M. Add. MSS. 35395, f. 132.

[4] David Hannay, *Rodney* (*English Men of Action*).

fallen, to be replaced by an Administration led by Rockingham, Shelburne and Charles James Fox—a Whig cabal to which an inherent
Tory such as Rodney was plain anathema. Such is the purblind rancour
of political prejudice that the fact that he was also one of Great Britain's
outstanding sea-fighters was not even taken into consideration.

It is to be admitted that, in a gubernatorial sense, Rockingham in-
herited something of an Augean stable. In Europe, Great Britain was
fighting a venomously hostile coalition of such combined strength that
it demanded all her effort to hold her adversaries at bay. With falling
trade, a National Debt in excess of £249,000,000, dwindling material
resources, and an acute shortage of man-power for her fighting forces,
interest in the wilting struggle in North America was bound to take
second place to her preoccupation with events nearer home.

In the Southern American Provinces the British grip extended to
little beyond Savannah and Charleston, and the coastal strip by which
they were linked. In New York Clinton was in no better case to animate
operations against Washington and his French ally than they were to
embark upon the close investment of the city; under strength as the
American forces were, and still shaken by the recent mutiny of six
regiments of the Pennsylvania Line. 'Washington is on the North river
in our vicinity and cutting all sorts of capers which no one bothers
about', wrote an Officer of the New York garrison to friends in Germany. 'Our Rebels feel more and more the iron rod of Congress; many
sigh under it, and wish for the old government, but they dare not
venture to betray their sentiments. The circumstance that our troops
have had to abandon places after most of the inhabitants had come out
openly for the King, has rendered many unhappy and the rest shy...'

In this shrewd comment the writer put his finger on the fundamental
flaw in Germain's belief that the Thirteen Colonies could best be preserved to the Crown by the efforts of the loyalist element amongst their
population. In many isolated instances the loyalists had fought in the
British cause with outstanding courage and tenacity. But their poten-
tialities had never been fully realized. They had been recruited *ad hoc*,
as extraneous additions to the Regular Army,[1] without a proper command structure, and lacking that enheartening sense of integration
which only comes to those who join an armed force long established
and firmly rooted. Moreover, as another acute observer had earlier
noted:

[1] A certain number had enlisted direct into British Regular formations.

We seem through this war to have adhered to the injudicious plan of dividing our Army into numerous detachments, to carry on operations in several Colonies at once, by which means we are not formidable in any one place, and actually raise more troops for the Enemy than they could possibly draw together in one, or even two Armies. We have been induced to act thus by the vain and ill-grounded hope of finding numerous bodies of Loyalists to join and co-operate with us, but we should have learned by experience how little assistance is to be expected from them; indeed, we cannot with reason expect those that are Loyal will declare their sentiments until they find us so strong in any one place as to protect them *after* having joined. Our taking post at various places, inviting the Loyalists to join us, and then evacuating those posts and abandoning the People to the fury of their bittered Enemies has deterred them from declaring themselves until affairs take a decisive turn in our favour; and we shall then find the People eager to declare their loyalty; while this remains doubtful we should not expect it.[1]

Above all other considerations the reclamation of the Thirteen Colonies was not, fundamentally, a task to be entrusted to such an Army as could be raised, transported and maintained three thousand miles across the Atlantic under contemporary conditions. Given an adequate Royal Navy, the best contribution the Army could have made to the common task would have been to secure the line of the Hudson, thus severing the Southern Provinces from Massachusetts, the heart of the rebellion. Thereafter, the efficient blockade of the ports through which flowed the foreign trade upon which the Colonists were so vitally dependent might have forced Congress to the conference table. As it was, 'in the vast spaces of North America the Army's motion was like the passage of a ship through the sea whose track is soon lost'.[2] It was the failure to remedy the rundown of the Royal Navy in the period immediately following the 1763 Peace of Paris which foredoomed Great Britain's attempt to reclaim her rebellious North American dependencies to failure. 'It was the Navy which dowered England with the Dominion across the seas, and it was the failure of England to maintain her fleet which robbed her of the means of retaining that Dominion.'[3]

---

[1] Mackenzie, *op. cit.*   [2] Vice-Admiral Samuel Graves.   [3] Callender, *op. cit.*

It was obvious from the outset that the Rockingham Administration was eager to arrive at some sort of accommodation which would bring hostilities to an end. But with *pourparlers* bedevilled by the envious competition to overreach each other and secure control of them which arose between Fox and Shelburne, negotiations proceeded at a laggard pace; although Great Britain's hand had been strengthened by Rodney's victory of the Saintes and General Eliott's indomitable defence of Gibraltar.

With what amounted to an undeclared suspension of active operations, New York — first under Clinton and then under Carleton, who now succeeded him — settled down as best it could to its role of garrison town and refugee for those steadfast loyalists whose undisguised attachment to the throne had exiled them from the respective communities in which they had heretofore been welcome and respected members. Their influx, plus the effects of the great fire and a second conflagration which had occurred in 1778, added acutely to the housing problem; while the confiscation of all their property, other than such few possessions as they could carry away with them, gave rise to another grievous problem, to deal with which there appeared to be no immediate solution. It was only by the Bloodybacks' unofficial gifts in addition to the daily dole of fuel and rations that some of the more indigent among these pathetic refugees contrived to keep the wolf at bay.

A prolonged drought, which dried up most of the wells, added to the city's hardships, until the Bloodybacks were set to work digging for water, a move which alleviated the worst distress. With evacuation a growing probability, shipping from England declined in volume, with consequent shortages to add further to the inhabitants' discomfort; although there was a certain amount of surreptitious trade between separatists urgently in need of English manufactures and loyalists still in possession of a modicum of them, and ready to exchange them for cash or produce, even at some sacrifice. Supplies were uncertain and fluctuated in volume; and when flour was hard to come by bakers were required to put their initials on their loaves so that those guilty of overcharging or selling short weight could be identified and punished.

In the way of day-to-day amenities, there was still an occasional production to be seen at the Theatre Royal — the former John Street Theatre — while concerts were still given *al fresco* on the promenade opposite the ruined Trinity Church. Fox-hunting gave the Officers some amusement, and racing on 'Ascot Heath', five miles east of the ferry landing on Long Island, excited the interest of all ranks of the Bloody-backs, who also turned out in large numbers for cricket, hurling matches, and the Irish game of 'Common'. For those with a taste for aquatics, bathing facilities 'upon the plan of those used at Margate' remained available on the North river. Cock-fighting had its devotees amongst all ranks, from the highest to the lowest; and if the City Tavern, the Queen's Head and Fraunce's Tavern did a thriving business with the 'nobs', so did the sordid dram-shops clustered about that insalubrious 'Canvas Town' which had come into being in that part of the city which had suffered the worst devastation at the time of the great fire. There—as heretofore—the less discriminating Bloodyback swilled his New England rum[1] and 'white' whiskey, and partook of such dubious fleshly delights as could be bargained for with the local drabs; rewarding them either with depreciated American scrip, Spanish dollars or pictreens. Tap-to was still beaten at 8 p.m.; but this little affected the brisk trade plied by the illicit boozing-kens in 'Canvas Town', the docks area and Cruger's wharf.

With news that the preliminary articles of peace had been signed with France and Spain on 20th January, tension relaxed still further; although for the refugee loyalists the outlook could scarcely have been more discouraging. From a civil population which in 1781 had amounted to 26,000, New York's total had swollen in 1783 to over 33,000; the majority of whom had lost home, wealth, and worldly goods, and faced a future which could scarcely have been more dubious. For some four hundred and sixty of the hardest hit, Nova Scotia land grants, stores, clothing, medicines and farming implements, arms and ammunition, were provided through the personal generosity of King George. Others set out for Canada. For denuded as they might be of their North West Territory,[2] in the United States' favour, under the terms of the treaty on the brink of consummation in Paris, the Canadians still had a welcome for those of their own kith and kin who had been driven into exile. And, in general, America's loss was Canada's gain.[3]

As intelligence reached New York that the final articles of the treaty of peace had been agreed on 8th April, the military authorities began to

---

[1] Jamaica rum commanded 3s 6d a gallon, but New England rum sold for 1s 9d a gallon.

[2] Now the States of Michigan, Ohio, Illinois, Indiana and Wisconsin.

[3] By July 1783 it was calculated that 1,859 loyalists had reached New Brunswick, 5,339 had opted for Canada, and 8,000 for Nova Scotia. Another 1,000 sailed for the Bahamas.

concentrate outlying detachments preparatory to evacuating the units to England. From a garrison of 9,600 in 1781, the total of Bloodybacks and German auxiliaries, plus exchanged prisoners of war, rose to 17,200. A trickle of deserters – principally amongst the Germans – stole away to join the not inconsiderable number of those who had earlier abandoned the ranks. But for the most part the Bloodyback was well content to turn his back on a land wherein his prowess and devotion to duty had brought him victory after victory – Long Island, White Plains, Fort Washington, Brandywine, Germantown, Savannah, Charleston – which in the long run had availed the cause he fought for not a whit. It was not the regimental Officer or the man in the ranks who had faltered when, through muddle, incompetence and arrogant interference on the part of a London office, they had found themselves confronted at Saratoga with an army of equal valour and tenacity, and more than twice their number. It was not the rank and file of the Bloodybacks who had lost their nerve at Yorktown, or had willingly thrown down their arms at Stony Point. Theirs not to reason why. They had done their duty, and more; and it was with no sense of shame or self-reproach that they filed aboard the waiting transports, warmed by all the homeless wanderer's eager thoughts of homeland.

The 25th of November saw the last British formation withdrawn from the Battery and marching to embark, with a hostile, muttering crowd of the city's new 'patriot' population thronging the sidewalks as the orderly files trudged solidly to the quayside.

But the final boatload of Bloodybacks did not put out from Staten Island till the early days of December. As the whaleboat cleared the shore the rowers, resting for a moment on their oars, turned their heads to look back on the flagstaff, from which their last act had been to lower the Union Flag and cut the halliards. Swarming about the naked staff, it was the crowd's obvious resolve to raise the Stars and Stripes without a moment's delay. But the halliards were in strings, and when one active fellow sought to clamber up the pole, he slid helplessly to the ground – for just prior to their departure the Bloodybacks had thoroughly greased the staff from head to foot. It was not indeed until cleets had been hammered in all the way up the pole that it could be scaled, and 'Old Glory' nailed firmly in position – while the Bloodybacks once more bent to their oars and went chuckling on their way.

Crude, maybe, and a trifle childish. But the Bloodyback had always nurtured a somewhat wry but resilient sense of humour. And time and time again it has helped to sustain him through the unnumbered perils and privations he has been called upon to endure; it has stabilized him in the first flush of conquest; he has never surrendered it even in the rare hour of his defeat. Possibly that is why, in three hundred years of service, his rendering of account has shown such a remarkably substantial balance on the side of victory.

'The Bloodybacks'!

' "They shall be mine", said the Lord of Hosts, "in that day when I make up my jewels." '

Appendix A

The Navigation Acts

THE FIRST Navigation Act was introduced by Richard II in 1381[1] for the purpose of ensuring that native wool and wool-fells should be transported from the homeland to the staple at Calais exclusively in English vessels manned by predominantly English crews, under an English *rector* or shipmaster. An unequivocal measure of 'protection', it was designed to secure a native monopoly in the wool-carrying trade, in which alien shipowners had hitherto participated. In practice, however, it was found that there were not enough English bottoms, or crews to man them, to deal with all the freight in transit; so permission had to be given to employ foreign craft where no native vessels were available.

This legislation was considerably tightened by Henry V, Henry VII, and by his successor, but was temporarily suspended by the Regency Council governing the country during the minority of the ailing Edward VI.

In 1650 the Parliamentary party extended the existent Navigation Act to prohibit all trade with those overseas dependencies still faithful to the Stuart cause. This interdict was followed by another enactment, of October 1651, as stringent as any of its predecessors. This Cromwellian measure forbade the importation of goods into England except in English ships, manned by native crews, or in the vessels of the nation

[1] 2 Rich II, Stat. V, cap. 3.

351

which produced the commodities. The legislation was specifically aimed at the Dutch carrying-trade; and as the outcome of the first Anglo-Dutch war (1652–1654) the Hollanders had no option but resentfully to accept it.

Reaffirmed and even stiffened under the Restoration,[1] the legislation ordained that bond should be entered into to ensure that certain 'enumerated commodities', such as sugar, tobacco, indigo, ginger, fustic, brazil and other dyeing woods—but not grain, hides, lumber or fish—should not be exported from any of the Plantations *save to another Colony or the homeland.* In effect, while the Ordinance of 1651 had been enacted in the interests of English shipping, the Acts of 1660 and 1662 extended their protection to the English manufacturers. Indubitably, the trade of the Plantations suffered temporary restriction. But England's straitened economic condition in the earlier years of the Restoration clearly demanded the adoption of the principle that the commercial well-being of the mother country and her satellites must not be thwarted by the particular interests of any individual Colony; the whole must be accepted as being greater than the part. Such temporary hardship as the pursuit of this policy might involve would be as nothing compared with the ultimate benefit the Colonies stood to derive from it, if and when the King's concept of a closely integrated 'marine empire' should have been carried successfully to a conclusion. In the interim the mother country, as the hub of national activity and the centre of authority, looked to the Colonies to help sustain her, as rural parishes help support the market town in their midst. Moreover, as Adam Smith was careful to emphasize in his *Wealth of Nations*, 'as defence is of much more importance than opulence, the Act of Navigation is, perhaps, the wisest of all the commercial regulations of England'. The outcome has been summed up by Sir Charles Petrie in his comment, 'England has rarely been so prosperous as under Charles II.'

At times, owing to the difficulty of shipping exclusively English-born crews, the Acts had to be modified—as in 1779, for example—to permit the 'dilution' of a ship's company by the temporary engagement of foreign hands.

The Navigation Acts were finally repealed in 1826, and a new set of regulations established of a generally less restrictive character.

---

[1] 12 Car. II, Stat. I, cap. 18, 32, and 13 & 14 Car. II, Stat. I, cap. 11, clause 6.

Appendix B

Navy Victualling

THERE WAS one thing upon which Samuel Pepys harboured no mis-conceptions. 'Englishmen', he wrote, 'and more especially seamen, love their bellies above everything else, and therefore it must always be remembered in the management of the victualling of the Navy that to make any abatement of them in the quantity or agreeableness of their victuals is to discourage and provoke them in their tenderest point, and will sooner render them disgusted with the King's service than any other one hardship that can be put upon them.'

In this belief Pepys drew up the following scale of dietary, and – to do him justice – strove his utmost to ensure that the hands serving in H.M. ships should receive it 'without abatement'. If he did not always succeed in his aim, the fault was certainly not his.

'One pound averdupois of good, clean, sweet, well-bolted with a horse-cloth, well baked and well conditioned biscuit; one gallon, wine measure, of beer; two pounds averdupois of beef killed and made up with salt in England[1] of a well-fed ox, for Sundays, Mondays, Tuesdays and Thursdays, or instead of beef, for two of these days one pound averdupois of bacon or salted English pork, of a well-fed hog, and a pint of pease (Winchester measure) therewith; and for Wednesdays, Fridays and Saturdays, every man, besides the aforesaid allowance of

---

[1] There was a strong prejudice in the Royal Navy against Irish beef, which John Hollond averred in his *Discourses of the Navy* (1638–1659) 'greatly discouraged the seaman'.

bread and beer, to have by the day the eighth part of a full-size North Sea cod of 24 inches long, or the sixth part of a haberdine[1] 22 inches long, or a quarter part of the same if but 16 inches long; or a pound averdupois of a well-savoured Poor John,[2] together with two ounces of butter, and four ounces of Suffolk cheese,[3] or two-thirds of that weight of Cheshire.'

The great drawback to this diet — as of practically all the many varieties of subsistence furnished for consumption by the 17th and 18th century seaman — was that it was entirely lacking in any anti-scorbutic element. Thus despite the admirable investigatory and experimental work regarding the problem of scurvy, its cure and prevention, carried out by James Lind, Sir Gilbert Blane and Thomas Trotter, it remained the seafarer's abiding scourge until steam propulsion arrived to shorten the time spent on passage, and a system of refrigeration was adopted on shipboard which served to keep vegetables and fruit reasonably fresh for the duration of the voyage.

[1] Salted or sun-dried cod.
[2] Salted or dried hake.
[3] Suffolk cheese had a bad name with the Army, and on one occasion its issue nearly provoked a mutiny. But the Royal Navy accepted it without demur.

Appendix C

Regimental List

Original Number		Subsequent Title
1st	Foot	R. Scots
2nd	,,	R. W. Surrey R.
3rd	,,	E. Kent R.
4th	,,	R. Lanc. R.
5th	,,	Northd. Fus.
6th	,,	R. War. R.
7th	,,	R. Fus.
8th	,,	L'pool R.
9th	,,	Norf. R.
10th	,,	Linc. R.
11th	,,	Devon R.
12th	,,	Suff. R.
13th	,,	Som. L. I.
14th	,,	W. Yorks. R.
15th	,,	E. Yorks. R.
16th	,,	Bedf. Reg.
17th	,,	Leics. R.
18th	,,	R. Ir. Regt.
19th	,,	York R.
20th	Foot	Lanc. Fus.
21st	,,	R. Sc. Fus.
22nd	,,	Ches. R.
23rd	,,	R. W. Fus.
24th	,,	S. Wales Bord.
25th	,,	K.O.S.B.
26th	,,	1st Bn. Sco. Rif.
27th	,,	1st Bn. R. Innis Fus.
28th	,,	1st Bn. Glouc. R.
29th	,,	1st Bn. Worc. R.
30th	,,	1st Bn. E. Lanc. R.
31st	,,	1st Bn. E. Surr. R.
32nd	,,	1st Bn. D. of Corn. L.I.
33rd	,,	1st Bn. W. Rid. R.
34th	,,	1st Bn. Bord. R.
35th	,,	1st Bn. R. Suss. R.
36th	,,	2nd Bn. Worc. R.
37th	,,	1st Bn. Hants. R.
38th	,,	1st Bn. S. Staff. R.
39th	,,	1st Bn. Dorset R.
40th	,,	1st Bn. S. Lanc. R.

41st Foot	1st Bn. Welsh R.
42nd ,,	1st Bn. R. Highrs.
43rd ,,	1st Bn. Oxf. & Bucks L. I.
44th ,,	1st Bn. Essex R.
45th ,,	1st Bn. Notts & Derby R.
46th ,,	2nd Bn. D. of Corn. L. I.
47th ,,	1st Bn. N. Lanc. R.
48th ,,	1st Bn. North'n R.
49th ,,	1st Bn. R. Berks R.
50th ,,	1st Bn. R. W. Kent R.
51st ,,	1st Bn. Yorks. L. I.
52nd ,,	2nd Bn. Oxf. & Bucks L. I.
53rd ,,	1st Bn. Shrops. L. I.
54th ,,	2nd Bn. Dorset R.
55th ,,	2nd Bn. Bord. R.
56th ,,	2nd Bn. Essex R.
57th ,,	1st Bn. Midd'x R.
58th ,,	2nd Bn. North'n R.
59th ,,	2nd Bn. E. Lanc. R.
60th ,,	K.R.R.C.
61st ,,	2nd Bn. Glouc. R.
62nd ,,	1st Bn. Wilts R.
63rd ,,	1st Bn. Manch. R.
64th ,,	1st Bn. N. Staff. R.
65th ,,	Y. & L.R.
66th ,,	2nd Bn. R. Berks. R.
67th ,,	2nd Bn. Hants R.
68th ,,	1st Bn. Durh. L. I.
69th ,,	2nd Bn. Welsh R.
70th ,,	2nd Bn. E. Surrey R.
71st ,,	1st Bn. High. L. I.
72nd ,,	1st Bn. Sea. Highrs.
73rd ,,	2nd Bn. R. Highrs.
74th ,,	2nd Bn. High. L. I.
75th Foot	1st Bn. Gord. Highrs.
76th ,,	2nd Bn. W. Rid. R.
77th ,,	2nd Bn. Midd'x R.
78th ,,	2nd Bn. Sea. Highrs.
79th ,,	1st Bn. Cam. Highrs.
80th ,,	2nd Bn. S. Staff. R.
81st ,,	2nd Bn. N. Lanc. R.
82nd ,,	2nd Bn. S. Lanc. R.
83rd ,,	1st Bn. R. Ir. Rif.
84th ,,	2nd Bn. Y. & L. R.
85th ,,	2nd Bn. Shrops. L. I.
86th ,,	2nd Bn. R. Ir. Rif.
87th ,,	1st Bn. R. Ir. Fus.
88th ,,	1st Bn. Conn. Rang.
89th ,,	2nd Bn. R. Ir. Fus.
90th ,,	2nd Bn. Sco. Rif.
91st ,,	1st Bn. A. & S. Highrs.
92nd ,,	2nd Bn. Gord. Highrs.
93rd ,,	2nd Bn. A. & S. Highrs.
94th ,,	2nd Bn. Conn. Rang.
95th ,,	2nd Bn. Notts. & Derby R.
96th ,,	2nd Bn. Manch. R.
97th ,,	2nd Bn. R. W. Kent R.
98th ,,	2nd Bn. N. Staff. R.
99th ,,	2nd Bn. Wilts. R.
100th ,,	1st Bn. Leins. R.
101st ,,	1st Bn. R. Muns. Fus.
102nd ,,	1st Bn. R. Dub. Fus.
103rd ,,	2nd Bn. R. Dub. Fus.
104th ,,	2nd Bn. R. Muns. Fus.
105th ,,	2nd Bn. Yorks. L. I.
106th ,,	2nd Bn. Durh. L. I.
107th ,,	2nd Bn. R. Suss. R.
108th ,,	2nd Bn. R. Innis. Fus.
109th ,,	2nd Bn. Leins. R.
Rifle Brig.	Rif. Brig.

Bibliography

MSS SOURCES

P.R.O.

C.O. 5/92–105. Military Correspondence, 1775–1782.
C.O. 5/116. Memorials to Lord George Germain.
C.O. 5/7. Précis of Orders for Raising Provincials.
C.O. 5/155–56. Promiscuous and Private Letters, 1777–1778.
W.O. 1/10. Correspondence of Generals Howe and Clinton with Secretary at War.
W.O. Secretary's Common Letter Book.
W.O. Miscellaneous Orders (Guards and Garrisons).
W.O. Warrant Books.

HISTORICAL MSS COMMISSION

Abergavenny MS.
Dartmouth MS.

Sackville MS.
Sloane MS.

HARLEIAN MSS

Journal of the English Army in the West Indies.
Private Papers of the 4th Earl of Sandwich.
The Bouquet Papers.
The Cornwallis Papers.
The Parliamentary Register, edited by John Almon and John Debrett.
Journals of the House of Commons.

PERIODICALS AND NEWSPAPERS

The Connoisseur.
The Examiner.
The Gentleman's Magazine.
The Gentleman and Ladies' Museum.
The London Chronicle.
The London Gazette.
The London Evening Post.
The Remembrancer.
Scots' Magazine.
The Westminster Magazine.
The Naval and Military Sketch Book.
The Naval and Military Magazine.
New York Journal.
Boston Evening Post.

PAMPHLETS

The Radstock Pamphlets.
Regimental Histories.

PRINTED WORKS

Adams, C. F.: *Studies, Military and Diplomatic.* 1911.
Adams, James Truslow: *The Epic of America.*
Alden, C.S. and Westcott, A.: *The United States Navy.* 1946.
Amherst, Jeffery: *The Journals* (edited by J. Clarence Webster). 1930.
Anburey, Thomas: *Travels Through the Interior Parts of America.* 1789.
Anderson, Troyer S.: *The Command of the Howe Brothers during the American Revolution.* 1936.
Andrews, Charles MacLean: *Narratives of the Insurrection, 1675–1690.* 1915.
Andrews, John: *History of the Late War.* 1786.
Anon: *A Private Soldier of the Regiment of Foot, late Sir Peter Halkett's* n.d.
Atkinson, C. T.: *British Forces in North America, 1774–1781.* 1941.

Barck, Oscar T.: *New York City during the War of Independence.* 1931.
Bass, W.: *The Green Dragoon.* 1957.
Batchelder, S. F.: *Burgoyne and his Officers in Cambridge.* 1926.
Beatson, Robert: *Naval and Military Chronicles.* (6 Vols.) 1804.
Bedoyere, Michael de la: *George Washington.* 1935.
Belcher, Henry: *The First American Civil War.* (2 Vols.) 1911.
Billias, George Athan: *General John Glover.* 1960.
Bird, Harrison: *March to Saratoga.* 1963.
Bolton, C. K. (Editor): *The Letters of Hugh, Earl Percy.* 1902.
Bouchier, Jonathan (Editor): *Reminiscences of an American Loyalist.* 1925.
Bradley, A. C.: *The Fight with France for North America.* 1908.
Broughton Delves: *Officer and Gentleman.* 1944.
Burgoyne, Lieutenant-General John: *Orderly Book.* 1860.
Burnet, Gilbert: *History of My Own Times.* 1906.
Byfield, Nathaniel: *Account of the Late Revolution.* (1689).

C(alef) J(ohn): *The Siege of Penobscot by the Rebels.* 1781.
Callahan, North: *Royal Raiders.* 1962.
Callender, Sir Geoffrey: *The Naval Side of English History.* 1924.
Cameron, Duncan: *The Life and Adventures and Surprising Deliverance of.* 1756.
Carlyle, Thomas: *Cromwell.* 1908.
Chamberlayne, Edward: *Anglia Notitia.* 1704.

Clinton, General Sir Henry: *Narrative.* 1953.

Clode, Charles M.: *The Military Forces of the Crown.* (2 Vols.) 1869.

Corbett, Sir Julian: *England in the Seven Years' War.* 1907.

Cornwallis, Earl: *The Cornwallis Papers.* 1859.

Cresswell, N.: *Journal, 1774–1777.* 1925.

Cuneo, John R.: *Robert Rogers of the Rangers.* 1959.

Curtis, Edward E.: *Organisation of the British Army in the American Revolution.* 1926.

Dana, Elizabeth E.: *The British in Boston.* 1924.

Davidson, R. L. D.: *War Comes to Quaker Pennsylvania.* 1957.

Dickerson, Oliver M.: *Boston Under Military Rule.* 1936.

Digby, Lieutenant W.: *Journal.* (Edited J. P. Baxter.) 1887.

Donkin, R.: *Military Collections & Remarks.* 1777.

Doren, Carl van: *Secret History of the American Revolution.* 1941.

Dorson, Richard M.: *American Rebels.*

Doughty, A. and Parmalee, G. W.: *The Siege of Quebec.* 1901.

Doyle, Joseph B.; *Frederick William von Steuben.* 1913.

Drake, S. A.: *Burgoyne's Invasion of 1777.* 1889.

Drake, Samuel G.: *Tragedies in the Wilderness.* 1841.

Dupuy, Colonel R. Ernest.: *A Compact History of the United States Army.* 1956.

Einstein, Lewis D.: *Divided Loyalties.* 1933.

Eelking, M. von.: *German Allied Troops in North America.* 1893.

Evelyn, John: *Diary.* 1906.

Ferguson, Patrick: *The Narrative.* P.R.O.

ffoulkes, Charles: *Arms and Armament.* 1945.

Field, Colonel Cyril: *Old Times Under Arms.* 1939

Field, Colonel Cyril: *Old Times Afloat.* 1932.

Firth, C. H.: *Cromwell's Army.* 1902.

Fiske, John: *The American Revolution.* (2 Vols.) 1895.

Fitzmaurice, Lord Edmond: *The Life of William, Earl of Shelburne.* 1875–1876.

Fletcher, H. L. Aubrey: *A History of the Foot Guards.* 1927.

Flexner, James T.: *The Traitor and the Spy.* 1953.

Fonblanque, E. B. de: *Political and Military Episodes.* 1876.

Force, Peter (Editor): *American Archives.*

Ford, Worthington E. (Editor): *The Writings of George Washington.* 1889–1892.

Fortescue, Hon. Sir John: *History of the British Army.* (Vols I to III.) 1900–1930.

Fortescue, Hon. Sir John: *Following the Drum.* 1931.

Fortescue, Hon, Sir John: *The British Soldier and the Empire.* A.T.S.

Fortescue, Hon. Sir John: *Expedition to the West Indies.* 1893.

French, Allen: *The First Year of the American Revolution.* 1934.

French, Allen (Editor): *A British Fusilier in Revolutionary Boston.* 1926.

Ganoe, Major William A.: *History of the United States Army.* 1932.

Gardner, James: *Above and Under Hatches.* 1836.

Gilbey, Thomas: *Britain at Arms.* 1958.

Gordon, Hampden: *The War Office.* 1935.

Graham, G. S. (Editor): *The Walker Expedition to Quebec.* (Navy Records Society.)

Graydon, Alexander: *Memoirs of His Own Times.*

Grose, Francis: *Advice to British Officers.* 1782.

Grose, Francis: *Military Antiquities.* (2 Vols.) 1786.

Guedalla, Philip: *Independence Day.* 1926.

Hadden, J. M.: *Braddock's Expedition.* 1884.

Hadden, J. M.: *Washington's Expeditions* (1753–1754). 1885.

Hadden, J. M.: *Journal in Canada and on Burgoyne's Campaign.* 1884.

Halkett, J.: *Orderly Book.* (In MS.)

Hamilton, Charles (Editor): *Braddock's Defeat.* 1959.

Hamilton, Edward P.: *The French and Indian Wars.* 1962.

Hamilton, F. W.: *The Origin and History of the First or Grenadier Guards.* 1874.

Hannay, David: *Rodney (English Men of Action).* 1910.

Hargreaves, Reginald: *The Narrow Seas.* 1959.

Hartmann, Cyril H.: *The Angry Admiral.* 1953.

Hatch, L. C.: *Administration of the American Revolutionary Army.* 1904.

Hawkins, William (Editor): *Statutes at Large.* (6 Vols.) 1735.

Hay, Ian: *The King's Service.* 1938.

Heath, Major-General William: *Memoirs of the American War.* 1904.

Henry, Alexander: *Travels and Adventures in Canada.* 1809.

Hough, Franklin B.: *The Siege of Savannah.* 1866.

Howe, General Sir William: *Orderly Book.* 1890.

Hudleston, F. J.: *Gentleman Johnny Burgoyne.* 1928.
Hutchinson, T.: *Diary and Letters.* 1883.

Inglis, Colonel C. J.: *The Queen's Rangers in the Revolutionary War.* 1956.

Jackson, H. M.: *The Queen's Rangers.* 1935.
James, Charles: *The Military Companion.* 1803.
James, Captain W. M.: *The British Navy in Adversity.* 1926.
Johnson, William: *Sketches of Nathanael Greene.* ND.
Jones, E. Alfred: *The Loyalists of Massachusetts.* 1930.
Jones, Thomas: *History of New York During the Revolutionary War.* (2 Vols.) 1879.

Kellog, Louise Phelps: *The British Regime in Wisconsin and the North-West.* 1935.
Ketcham, Richard M.: *The Battle of Bunker Hill.* 1963.
Knott, Louis: *Robert Dinwiddie,*
Knox, Captain John: *An Historical Journal of the Campaign in North America.* 1769.
Knox, Dr William: *Summary of the British Settlements in North America.* 1752.
Knyveton, John: *The Journal.* 1946.

Lamb, Serjeant R.: *Journal of Occurrences in North America.* 1809.
Leach, D. E.: *Flintlock and Tomahawk.* 1958.
Leach, D. E.: *The Northern Colonial Frontier.* 1966.
Leake, Stephen Martin: *Life of Sir Martin Leake.* 1918–1919.
Lee, Henry: *Memoirs of the War in the Southern Department of the United States.* 1827.
Lewis, Michael: *The Navy of Britain.* 1948.
Lewis, Michael: *The History of the British Navy.* 1957.
Lewis, Michael: *England's Sea Officers.* 1948.
Lillington, Thomas: *The Narrative.* ND.
Listen, Ensign Jeremy: *Concord Fight.* 1931.
Lloyd, Christopher: *The Nation and the Navy.* 1954.
Lloyd, Christopher: *The Capture of Quebec.* 1959.
Long, J. C.: *Lord Jeffrey Amherst.* 1933.
Lossing, B. J.: *Field Book of the Revolution.* (2 Vols.) 1850.
Lowell, B. J.: *The Hessians in the Revolutionary War.* (2 Vols.) 1851–1852.

Lushington, S. R.: *The Life and Services of General Lord Harris.* 1840.

Macdonald, Captain Alexander: *Letter Book.* 1882.
Mackesy, Piers: *The War for America.* 1964.
Mackenzie, Frederick: *Diary.* (2 Vols.) 1930.
MacMunn, Lieutant-General Sir George: *The American War of Independence in Perspective.* 1939.
Macpherson, David: *Annals of Commerce.* (2 Vols.) 1806.
Mahan, Captain A. T.: *The Influence of Sea Power upon History.* 1889.
Mahan, Captain A. T.: *Types of Naval Officers.* 1902.
McCardell, Lee: *Ill-Starred General.* 1958.
McGuffie, T. H.: *Rank and File.* 1964.
Marshall, John: *The Life of George Washington.* 1804–1807.
Moore, F.: *Diary of the American Revolution.* (2 Vols.) 1859–1860.
Moorhouse, E. Hallam (Editor): *Letters of the English Seamen.* 1910.

Newsome, A. R. (Editor): *A British Orderly Book.* 1928.
Nickerson, Hoffman: *The Turning Point of the Revolution.* 1928.

O'Conor, Norreys J.: *A Servant of the Crown.* 1938.
Oldmixon, John: *The British Empire in America.* 1708.
Orme, Robert: *Journal.* 1755.

Pares, Richard: *War and Trade in the West Indies.* 1936.
Pargellis, Stanley: *Lord Loudon in North America.* 1933.
Pargellis, Stanley: *Military Affairs in North America, 1748–1965.* 1936.
Parkman, Francis: *Half a Century of Conflict.* (2 Vols.) 1908.
Parkman, Francis: *Montcalm and Wolfe.* (2 Vols.) 1917.
Parkman, Francis: *The Conspiracy of Pontiac.* 1894.
Pausch, Captain: *Journal.* 1886.
Peckham, Howard H.: *The War for Independence.* 1958.
Peckham, Howard H.: *Pontiac and the Indian Uprising.* 1947.
Pepys, Samuel: *Diary.*
Percy, Hugh, Earl: *Letters.* 1902.
Pettengill, Ray W.: *Letters of German Troops.*
Poley, A. R.: *The Imperial Commonwealth.* 1921.
Prince, Samuel: *Letters.* (1689.)
Proctor, Alfred: *Drums in the Forest.*

Read, D. B.: *The Life and Times of General John Graves Simcoe*. 1890.

Reeves, Richard: *Correspondence*.

Richards, Frederick B.: *The Black Watch at Ticonderoga*. n.d.

Richmond, Admiral Sir Herbert: *History of the Navy in the War of 1739–1748*. 1920.

Roberts, Oliver A.: *History of the Ancient and Honourable Artillery Company of Massachusetts*. (2 Vols.) 1898.

Roberts, W. Adolphe: *The French in the West Indies*. 1942.

Robinson, Eric (Editor): *Letters of a Scots Officer from America 1773–1780*. 1951.

Rogers, Robert: *Journals*. 1765.

Roskill, Captain S. W.: *The Strategy of Sea Power*. 1962.

Ross, Charles (Editor): *Correspondence of Charles, First Marquis Cornwallis*. 1859.

Sabine, Lorenzo: *Biographical Sketches of Loyalists in the American Revolution*. 1864.

Sandwich, John Montagu, 4th Earl of: *The Private Papers*. 1932–1938.

Sargent, Winthrop: *History of an Expedition to Fort Duquesne*. 1865.

Sargent, Winthrop: *The Life and Career of John André*. 1861.

Scouller, R. E.: *The Armies of Queen Anne*. 1966.

Seymour, William W.: *On Active Service*. 1939.

Sheppard, F. W.: *Red Coat*. 1952.

Shipp, John: *The Military Bijou*. (2 Vols.) 1831.

Shy, John W.: *Toward Lexington*. 1965.

Shy, John W.: *A New Look at Colonial Militia*. 1965.

Simcoe, John Graves: *Military Journal*. 1844.

Smelser, M.: *The Campaign for the Sugar Islands, 1759*. 1955.

Smith, D. Bonner: *The Barrington Papers*.

Smith, Paul H.: *Loyalists and Redcoats*. 1964.

Sparks, Jared (Editor): *George Washington's Writings*.

Stacey, C. P.: *Quebec 1759*. 1959.

Stedman, C.: *History of the Origin, Progress and Termination of the American War*. (2 Vols.) 1794.

Tanner, J. R.: *Samuel Pepys and the Navy*. 1919.

Tarleton, Lieutenant-Colonel Banastre: *A History of the Campaign of 1780–1781*. 1788.

Tarleton, Banastre: *Memoirs*. 1787.

Tebbel, John: *George Washington's America.* 1954.
Tourtellot, Arthur B.: *William Diamond's Drum.* 1960.
Turner, Jackson: *The Frontier in American History.* 1921.

Wallace, Willard M.: *Appeal to Arms.* 1951.
Watteville, H. de: *The British Soldier.* 1954.
Webster, J. C. (Editor): *The Journal of Jeffrey Amherst.* 1930.
Wertenbaker, Thomas J.: *Torchbearer of the Revolution.* 1965.
Whistler, Henry: *Journal of the West Indies Expedition.* (Sloane MS.)
Willcox, William B.: *The British Road to Yorktown.* 1946.
Willcox, William B. (Editor): *The American Rebellion.* 1954.
Willcox, William B.: *Portrait of a General. Sir Henry Clinton.* 1964.
Willcox, William B.: *British Strategy in America.* 1947.
Wildes, Harry E.: *Valley Forge.* 1938.
Wilkin, Captain W. H.: *Some British Soldiers in America.* 1914.
Wilkinson, James: *Memoirs of My Own Times.* (3 Vols.) 1816.
Willson, Beckles: *The Life and Letters of James Wolfe.* 1909.
Wilstach, Paul: *Patriots Off Their Pedestals.* 1927.
W.L.S.: *Letters of Brunswick and Hessian Officers during the American Revolution.* 1891.
Wortley, Hon. Mrs E. S. (Editor): *A Prime Minister and His Son.* 1925.
Wraxall, Sir N. W.: *Historical Memoirs of My Own Times.* 1904.

Van Tyne, Claude Halstead: *The Loyalists in the American Revolution.* 1905.
Venables, General Robert: *The Narrative.* (Edited C. H. Firth.) 1900.

Selective Index